## Date Due

| BC 2 Feb 84 | | | |
|---|---|---|---|
| BRL Oct 85 | | | |
| BRF Jan90 | | | |
| CE Apr90 | | | |
| | | | |
| | | | |
| | | | |
| | | | |
| | | | |
| | | | |
| | | | |
| | | | |
| | | | |
| | | | |

# UNFINISHED BUSINESS

*Also by W. Gunther Plaut*

## NON-FICTION

Mount Zion—The First Hundred Years *(1956)*

The Jews in Minnesota *(1959)*

The Book of Proverbs—A Commentary *(1961)*

Judaism and the Scientific Spirit *(1962)*

The Rise of Reform Judaism *(1963)*

The Growth of Reform Judaism *(1965)*

The Case for the Chosen People *(1965)*

Your Neighbour is a Jew *(1967)*

Page Two *(1971)*

Genesis—A Commentary *(1974)*

Time to Think *(1977)*

Numbers—A Commentary *(1979)*

The Torah—A Modern Commentary *(1981)*

## FICTION

Hanging Threads *(1978)*
(published in the United States under the
title The Man in the Blue Vest and Other Stories)

# W. Gunther Plaut

# UNFINISHED BUSINESS

## An Autobiography

LESTER
&ORPEN
DENNYS
*PUBLISHERS*

*Canadian Cataloguing in Publication Data*
Plaut, W. Gunther, 1912-
Unfinished business

Includes index.
ISBN 0-919630-41-3

1. Plaut, W. Gunther, 1912-    2. Rabbis – Canada – Biography.   3. Rabbis – United States – Biography.
I. Title.

BM755.P62A38     296.6 ′1 ′0924     C81-094431-6

*Production by Paula Chabanais/P.C. Productions*
*Design by C. Wilson/Sunkisst Graphics*

Every reasonable effort has been made to trace ownership of copyright materials. Information will be welcomed which will enable the publisher to rectify any reference or credit in future printings.

The day is short and the task is great . . .
and the Master of the house is pressing.
You are not required to complete the work,
but neither are you free to abstain from it.

Ethics of the Fathers 2:20-21

*For my parents who made these memoirs possible;*
*for Elizabeth to whom they primarily belong;*
*for Walter and Billy who did not live to read them;*
*and for my children and grandchildren*
*who make the future bearable.*

# CONTENTS

# Prologue

WHEN I WAS TWENTY YEARS OLD
the world in which I had grown up suddenly came to an end: the
Nazis came to power. Their torchlight parade on January 30,
1933, is an event that every once in a while flashes with white
heat on my memory. It was a day that changed my life—and this
book is a reflection of its consequences.

Less traumatic though not less insistent is another encounter—
this one highly personal—which I have probably recalled more
often than anything else that has ever come across my horizon. It
was a blunt statement by my cousin Leo, whom I feared
somewhat, despised a bit, and yet admired at the same time. I
forget what the occasion was, but his words are etched with
brutal precision in my mind.

"Günter," he said, "you are very lucky and have been en-
dowed with many things. You've got everything going for you except that you are intolerably arrogant, you think you know it all,
and you are so impressed with yourself that it makes me sick. If
you'll remember even part of what I've told you, it'll do you more
good than all the crap they're handing out to you at the university."

I've remembered all of it verbatim. At the time I hated Leo for
saying it, especially because I knew he was right. Later I often
had occasion to remember it, though not often enough, I am
afraid. Now, more than a generation after Leo was taken to
Theresienstadt and then murdered at Auschwitz, I want to begin
my reminiscences with a tribute to a teacher who never tried to
be one, who was simply frank, and wholly admirable in his frankness. He did a lot for me. With that one remark he cut across the
great, woolly, egocentric cocoon in which I was enveloped, and
exposed me to the world as I was. I've used his scalpel often, and

always when I use it I remember him in gratitude.

Perhaps this is an odd way to start an autobiography. For me it is a means of making sure that the constant I, I, I—unavoidable in this type of writing—does not overwhelm the events of which I want to tell. I start with Leo because I will need a lot of balance. And truth, as much of it as I can put down on paper.

There will be limits to that. It is hard to say everything you think about the living, and sometimes even about the dead. There are some experiences you refuse to dredge up; others you bring to light and then decide to bury again. I aim at a book neither of confessions nor primarily of personal and social criticism. I just want to relate what one man has seen in his life, on various continents and at different times, from the days of the First World War and the German revolution to the rise of Hitler and his assumption of power. I want to describe the life of a man who started in law and then went into the rabbinate; who dabbled in politics and literature; who went from Nazi Germany to a new world beyond the ocean; who experienced war first-hand and was present at the liberation of a concentration camp; who loved his people and battled ceaselessly for and sometimes with them; who saw the starving children in Biafra and the well-fed in the halls of power; who was privileged to be present at many of the crucial landmarks of this century. A lot of people will march through these pages, many of them the great of our times, others less well known, who have influenced me or whose paths have crossed mine. I have been lucky, luckier than most. What I have tried to do I have tried with abandon; therefore, when I have failed, I have failed spectacularly.

Everyone about to undertake a difficult and often tedious enterprise asks himself, *Cui bono?* "Who will benefit by it?" In this case the greatest gain, of course, is to him who writes and thereby purges his soul. But I hope that others may be entertained by the variety of experiences, instructed by some of the observations, may obtain a new perspective of events and persons, and perchance find something of themselves in one man's struggle to come to terms with life.

Do not expect philosophical disquisitions or erudite observations; they belong to another form of writing. This book is my looking-glass. The reflections I see are sometimes bright and sometimes covered by the dark mist of years gone by. In telling the story I hope that my cousin Leo will, from time to time, look over my shoulder and not be too displeased with what he sees.

# Chapter 1

---

# INNOCENCE

MY FIRST MEMORY IS OF FLAGS waving, people shouting. Father told me later that this must have been the victory celebration after the Germans routed the Russians at Tannenberg. Perhaps, though at the age of two one is a little young to remember events of this kind. Psychologists claim of course that we never forget anything—the only problem we have is to bring the stored-up information to the surface. In any case, flags and hysterical masses shouting into the wind were to be part of my childhood years, that much I do remember clearly.

We moved to Berlin in 1914 from Münster, the capital of Westphalia, where I was born. Father had headed a Jewish teachers' seminary located in that heavily Catholic university town; he had made his way from a backward village in Hessen to a teacher's position in Silesia and from there to Münster to serve in the seminary as Rector, resident head teacher and supervisor of students and their activities. An apartment on the second floor went with the position, and there, in November 1912, I was born to Jonas and Selma Gumprich Plaut.

The building, Am Kanonengraben No. 4, survived the destruction of the Nazis and of the Second World War. In 1972, when I visited there, the secretary of the minuscule Jewish community was housed in our old apartment, for the building was still owned by the community. However, nothing will tell the casual visitor of the hustle and bustle of former years, the adolescent dreams and anxieties, the chants, the prayers, the melodies which filled its walls. I have often wondered where fate took those young students who received their training from my father

1

and from his predecessor, Dr. Max Spanier. Dr. Spanier was a biblical scholar and friend of the family; it was he who eventually brought my father to Berlin, to join him as second in command of a Jewish girls' school. He was a small man with a goatee, kindly eyes and a ready smile. When many years later I emigrated to the United States he gave me a small Oxford dictionary to make my transition to the New World easier. It was the *vade mecum* of my early years in America and it still stands in an honoured place in my home. Many are the times when I remember Dr. Spanier and his wife; they committed suicide in the late thirties when the police came to drag them to a concentration camp.

Pictures of Father in those early years show him as a slender man of medium height, nattily attired, black hair combed back straight, and sporting a tiny trimmed mustache. He had the air of a successful businessman and had in fact the capacity to be one. But he was, above all, an intellectual and a magnificent teacher. Every once in a while I used to come across people who asked me whether Jonas Plaut was a relative of mine, because in Berlin, back in the days of the First World War, they had had a teacher they would never forget. Father was a purveyor of ideas, and he stimulated the mind. He had a healthy dose of skepticism with the occasional tinge of cynicism, a marvellous sense of humour which he crowned with hearty laughter. I still recall his merry outbursts, especially on the cherished occasions when his second cousin, Joseph Plaut, Germany's best known soliloquist, came to visit.*

Father loved books. I would come to appreciate how fortunate I was to grow up in a home with a splendid library. While the German classics were of course present, the collection was heavily weighted towards history and biography. It was an environment in which my Bar Mitzvah gifts were expected to be books, not fountain pens or watches. Indeed I received a large number of volumes for my *rite de passage*, and carried some of them with me to the New World.

Shortly after his arrival in Münster, about 1910, Father met a young lady who was taking her sister to the elementary school affiliated with the seminary. Selma Gumprich came from a large family and a well-to-do home. The Gumprich house no longer stands; it was bombed out in the Second World War. It was in the

---

* Joseph survived the war in South Africa, then resumed his successful stage career in Germany when he was in his late seventies. His records remain a delight.

finest part of town, adjoining the big estate of a local nobleman, and close to the centre of the city—today the Münster Opera is but a block away.

The house was set back from the street and had three large storeys with some twenty rooms, plus a basement in which horses, landaus, dogcarts and the automobile were kept. In the rear were the servants' quarters, a buttery, and sheds for cows and chickens. The little local river, the Aa, flowed behind the building, through a beautiful garden big enough to graze horses and grow fruits and vegetables. It all seemed splendid and grandiose to me; even the little Aa, which was hardly more than a rivulet, could turn into quite a treacherous torrent when the rains came. My grandmother Julie, a smallish elegant woman who ruled over her large household with quiet persistence, never failed to warn me against the dangers of the Aa. The major result, I think, was that I developed a considerable fear of water, and though in later years I learned to swim I never became fond of it.

Grandpa Salomon—"Opa" to us—was a big man with a booming voice which frightened children and grandchildren alike, and probably terrorized his customers as well. At age thirteen his father, who lived in a small Rhenish town, had (so the family story went) told him, "Salomon, the other children will need money to get on in the world; you won't need any, for you have your brains." So at thirteen he left home, worked at various jobs and eventually entered the cattle trade. He was successful and came to own a number of farms, a fair-sized herd of animals and a mansion at Neubrückenstrasse 18. In 1911, just before my parents were married, the establishment burned down, which robbed my mother of her trousseau but enabled Grandpa to re-establish his presence in the town with a more magnificent structure, the one that I was to know.

Whenever I visited I was put in a room on the top floor which looked out over the front yard towards the church. Even as the Aa behind the house was to hold terror for me, so did the church in front. From its spire hung three cages, telling left-overs of the Anabaptist revolution of the sixteenth century. In these cages the tortured bodies of three leaders of that period, who had briefly controlled Münster and turned it into a communist enclave, had been exhibited as a warning to the multitude. Their skeletons were said to have remained suspended above the city for many decades. From my window I used to look at the cages and imagine the three men sitting there screaming and eventually fading away while the crowds stood below and jeered at them. After a while I identified these crowds with the religious processionals that wended their way through the city and always passed our house; Münster was a thoroughly Catholic city, and religious ceremonies were public celebrations. It was a picturesque town with gabled buildings and colonnades, with scores of churches and historic sites—all of them destroyed in the Second World War but later rebuilt according to pre-war pictures.

The Jews were, as everywhere else in Germany, quite unintegrated, allowed to make a living and not much else. Economically they did quite well, and had been able to build a splendid synagogue where Grandpa, a member of the board, took me regularly. He was Orthodox, but I never heard him object to the unconventional organ in the synagogue. I still remember sneaking away from our seat and watching the organist, a gentile, pump the instrument with his feet. When I offered to help him he shooed me away with evident horror. "What," he exclaimed, "a Jewish boy should do this on the Sabbath? Begone!"

Grandpa was demonstrative about his religious habits. He donned his *tefillin* (phylacteries) regularly in the morning and went to the front office where his customers, most of them gentiles, were gathering. There he would pace up and down saying his prayers, his phylacteries in place, and his customers would wait quietly until he was finished. I would sit in the corner and watch the proceedings. The moment he reached his last Amen, and even before he had removed his *tefillin*, he would boom a good morning at those assembled; seconds later he would be deeply embroiled in business. I often wondered how he could keep his mind on his prayers when the affairs of the world were so visibly pressing.

Grandpa's birthdays were always grand occasions when the whole family, a fair number of us by that time, assembled in the large dining room. I remember one such day with special clarity. It was 1917 and I was not quite five years old. A flowered wreath bearing the number "65" was placed over Grandpa's high chair at the head of the table and I, being one of the youngest present, was struck with awe and admiration over the wonder of it all. In later years I often constructed an imaginary scenario around that day. Suppose that at that moment of his glory, the big man, surveying his descendants and the relative splendour of his realm, had been stricken and had died on the spot. "What a pity," everyone would have said, "to be taken now when he has so much to live for." But had he? In the years that followed, tragedy destroyed his family. Two sons, Max and Walter, both officers in the German army, met death at the front. Grandpa's wealth was largely dissipated by endless law suits and rising inflation. My grandmother died. Hitler came to power and two of Grandpa's children were caught by the extermination machine; the survivors scattered all over the globe, while he, too old by then to go anywhere, eventually died in Kaiserswerth, near Düsseldorf, where one of his sons lived, to be buried not where the family had been laid to rest, but alone in a strange cemetery. A stone placed there in recent years bears his name. We do not know where his grave actually is.

I have since returned to Münster and lectured at the new university. The place where the house once stood is occupied by new buildings. The Aa seems greatly reduced in size and no longer frightening. The city tries desperately to look as it once did, but the new gables have an artificial air. A rebuilt synagogue serves a nearly extinct community in a pleasant city where I am now a thorough stranger. Yet stranger still, to me: the university grounds were once Grandpa's farm land. This was our land—yet, like everything else in Germany, never ours at all.

Though Münster holds many memories for me, it is not the only place to which I trace my roots. Mother and I were born there, but before that the family came from other Westphalian towns, and before that from Trier (Treves), or so family tradition had it. But in the little village of Willingshausen in the backwoods of Hessen where Father's family had its origins, the roots are deep and can still be traced. There the tombstones mark deaths and births of my ancestors going back to the middle of the eighteenth century. There, nothing has changed. When we visited in the 1960s, the women's Sunday dress was still what it had been generations before, and if there was a change in mentality, ordinary conversation did not reveal it. Willingshausen had five hundred inhabitants in the old days, now it has seven hundred; and the village of Merzhausen, a few kilometres away, is about the same size. A little river, the Schwalm, flows through the softly undulating hills and rich fields, isolated by elevations of moderate height and traditions as high as mountains. These are the hinterlands of Germany, its "Kentucky hills", where ancient dress and habits express the unaltered outlook of the people. Their views have been narrowed by centuries of exclusive preoccupation with themselves and demand little knowledge of the world. The streets are hardly more than cobblestone alleys, the houses as gnarled as their inhabitants. No one has ever been rich here except the baron to whom all this once belonged. In fact, most were poor, and the few Jewish families were near the bottom of the economic scale, eking out their meagre livelihood by trading cattle (which, because Jews engaged in it, became a despised occupation) and raising vegetables in tiny patches behind their homes.

Though poor, each family did have a home. Ours was built in 1783 (and I found it still standing in the sixties). The rooms were small and dark, the steep narrow staircase challenging the climber to a feat of aerial acrobatics. In this house my father was born and his father and grandfather before him. Father never lost his affection for the place, but it was nostalgia more than anything else—in practice he tried to get as far away from it as he could. Still, long after he had experienced the vagaries and pretences of the big city, he would say to me, "The only person in our family who is still a human being with his two feet on the ground is my brother Levi."

Levi was the eldest of the seven Plaut children and as the eldest he inherited the house while the others left for neighbouring villages and towns or the big city. Father's intuition about his oldest brother and his earthy strength was borne out during the war. Captured by the Nazis and sent to a concentration camp, Levi, then in his seventies, somehow survived, as did his wife. The two were discovered in Theresienstadt (Terezin) and later returned for a "triumphal" visit to Willingshausen—but thereby hangs a tale, and I will return to it later.

My paternal grandfather, Moses Plaut, died in 1891 when my father was eleven. Grandma Bertha was a sturdy woman from the Goldschmidt clan, who were amongst the earliest Jewish settlers in Hessen. I never came to know her too well, for I visited only rarely. Perhaps my parents felt that for a growing boy there were not enough attractions in the backwaters of Germany, and so I was exposed to the village family for only a few days at a time. A pity, for I would like to have known Grandma better. The Plauts and Goldschmidts were a fascinating and, as I would learn later, thoroughly intelligent lot.

Much of what I know about the family comes from my wife who for many years has made genealogy her special field of research. She knows more about the Plaut clans than any of us who were born to this dubious purple. These facts are clear: long before most of the Jews took family names (which in Germany happened mainly during the early part of the nineteenth century) there were several dozen families who for hundreds of years had carried their particular cognomens: among them the Wallachs, Guggenheims, and Katzenellenbogens. The Plauts also belonged to this select group. Their tribe centred for some centuries in Hessen, but the earliest members of the family traced so far were scholars in Spain and Italy in the twelfth century.

The origin of the name Plaut is not clear, but I believe that the simplest explanation is that it came from the Latin *plautus*, which described a flat sword and flatness in general. There was, of course, an ancient Roman writer of comedies by this name— with him, however, we claim no relationship. In European folk tradition Jews were said to be flat-footed (this amongst their other laudable characteristics); I still remember the antisemitic cartoons of my youth which always showed us waddling rather than walking. Perhaps somewhere the epithet of the flat-footed Jew was attached to one of my ancestors, though in the thousand or so years since we acquired the opprobrium we have defied physiology and grown quite normal feet.

The family wandered from southern Europe to the north and settled in Germany. Few of them went east—we know of only one Plaut family in eighteenth-century Poland. In later times, though, they spread through every conceivable part of the world. Even the Moscow telephone book (if you are lucky enough to be able to get one) is said to list a family of that name. North America is full of them. You will find them in São Paolo and Hod Hasharon, in Paris and in London, in Germany and in the Transvaal. Much of this is due to the migrations of the nineteenth century and the rest was accomplished by the dispersion in the Hitler years. Regional influences caused changes in the name. My grandfather Moses has Blaud inscribed on his tombstone in Merzhausen* because that was the way it sounded to the local stonemason. In France they are sometimes called Bolad and elsewhere they are listed as Blout.

If the gentile inhabitants of Willingshausen and Merzhausen were isolated from the world, the Jews lived in an additional intellectual ghetto of their own. They did not attend the public schools; instead the ten families, who had a small synagogue

---

* Where the Jewish cemetery for the twin villages is located.

room in Merzhausen, engaged a Jewish teacher for their
children. He taught them civics and German and, of course,
Jewish subjects. It was a simple elementary school, but Father's
grounding in literature, German as well as Hebrew, was
remarkable.

His schooling shared one feature with the most sophisticated
city school: it gave a place of honour to the art of memorization.
My father spoke in sentences that carried images from biblical
and Jewish sources; quotations from Latin and Hebrew, from
Goethe and Isaiah, flavoured his conversation and gave it a
quality that our flat and colourless speech has totally lost. This
was no put-on to impress anyone. All our friends did the same. It
was an ambience of communication that was infinitely richer
than anything we find today. When I was young I imagined that
Father knew the entire first part of *Faust* by heart. He probably
did not, but he quoted it often enough and at sufficient length
that when I first came to read it, the words sounded very
familiar.

Father often told me how he liberated himself from the con-
fines of Willingshausen. He and his older brother, Raphael, first
made their way to Marburg where they enhanced their formal
education sufficiently to entitle them to a teacher's certificate.
Both brothers then obtained positions in Silesia, my father in
Rybnik, Raphael in Sorau. Raphael, who remained ultra-
Orthodox in conviction and habit, later went to Hamburg where
he became the director of the old Am Papendamm orphanage.

Father went to Münster. When he arrived there he was a
handsome young man who loved to eat (and eat the best, which I
am sure he could not as yet afford) and dress to perfection (in
later years he had his shirts hand-tailored). Religiously he was
then still a conformist, although as time passed he became a
liberal. This good-looking new young teacher carried off a young
lady who by all odds was a great catch: a woman of breath-
taking beauty who had been sent to a French finishing school in
Nancy, who played the piano, sang, and was the proper child of a
traditional Jewish family.

Their marriage followed the prescribed pattern of the times in
that my mother passed from the lordship of her father to that of
her husband. In this respect Father was fully part of the traditions of his age: women, like children, were to be seen and not
heard; politics was not discussed in their presence; literature
was available to them but not a necessary adjunct of their lives;

serious discussions were held with men, not with women. The subjugation of women and the shackling of their spirits was part of the culture in which they lived. It took my mother many years to liberate herself, for she had a bright and unusually agile mind. It was not until she was eighty-nine years of age that she finally decided to go to university, and take courses in French literature and mediaeval history.

## Memories of the First War

We moved to Berlin just as the First World War was about to break out. Father had accepted Spanier's invitation and he became Rector at the Jewish Girls' School on Kaiserstrasse.

Our first apartment was at Neue Kantstrasse 25, in Charlottenburg, and very middle class, very *bürgerlich*. The furniture we had was typically German, which is to say heavy, even massive. I wonder whether this was an expression of the German psyche which pretended that one's surroundings were solid when in fact they were not. A little while later we moved into a ground-floor apartment around the corner at Trendelenburgstrasse No. 1, where the rooms were larger. Soon people began wearing uniforms, and then Father too came home decked out in bright shining buttons and side arms which I was instructed never to touch. As it turned out, his nearsightedness deprived the Germans of his frontline contributions—though, in truth, these would have been negligible. He did not incline towards the physical, and the sight of blood made him sick. He was an aesthete, and the war was not for him. Nor were the Kaiser and the imperial system his cup of tea; Father was a republican, the paper he read was the *Vossische Zeitung*, which some years after the end of the war carried Remarque's *All Quiet on the Western Front* before it was published in book form. Politics was Father's *milieu*, and he and his friends were forever discussing the power struggles in which the average little man was a hapless pawn. No wonder Hans Fallada's *Kleiner Mann, was nun?* (*Little man, what now?*) became a favourite book of his.

Father was assigned to the War Ministry and thus lived at home while the flower of German youth was dragged off to the war. He had beautiful handwriting and the Government employed him, in addition to other duties, to write legible death lists in the War Ministry. There were lots of names to write as the years went on, amongst them two brothers of my mother. When I look at Kollwitz' lithograph "The Mothers"—that haunting image of women staring blankly at the wall where the dreaded lists were posted daily, the resignation in their faces infused with the knowledge that the Angel of Death will have his way—I always see my father behind them, writing away, name after name. How often, I wonder, did he come across someone he knew? Four years of writing out the results of carnage is a long time. When the war was over Father was an even more passionate hater of war. He blamed the Kaiser and the German aristocracy for their insane ambitions, and he was glad when the revolution came.

The war years changed the face of the neighbourhood. The men were absent, the streets were empty and became our uncontested playground. During the summer we wore no shoes, for leather was hard to come by. Food became a topic of conversation at home and amongst my playmates. The Allied blockade was exacting its toll; the winter of 1917 reduced the Germans to a diet of potatoes and herring and whatever they could grow in the back yard. We had a small garden patch where Mother tried to coax unwilling vegetables from the ground. We even had some tomato stalks, a novelty in those days. I received one of the few beatings I can remember when I was careless with the tomatoes and knocked them off before they had ripened. The result was that for many years I wouldn't touch tomatoes. I eat them now, but not with real relish, for I still see our garden in Berlin and recall my early misdeed and its painful consequences.

From time to time Mother would go to Hessen to get some meat for the family. The farmers never suffered hunger and our relatives kept us supplied when the need arose. Mother used to tell us how she hid the results of her foraging in her bloomers. It was a dangerous business to hoard food without a permit, but she was lucky, perhaps because she was so good-looking.

She also took in some boarders. One was her youngest brother Fritz, who had a crippled arm and an inferiority complex. He was a left-hander like myself and taught me how to throw a ball, which was an accomplishment not highly rated in his family— they thought rather little of him.

Being left-handed meant sharing certain disabilities. In those days the true nature of this characteristic was not recognized. One was supposed to be right-handed and do everything "right".

A stubborn left-hander was considered a recalcitrant student who had to be forced into the acceptable scheme of things. In consequence, many of us became stutterers, and for some years I had a bit of difficulty getting my words out, though not enough to arouse the anxiety of my family. Fritz, of course, had no trouble in this regard; because he did not have the full use of his right hand, he escaped the ignominy of the "sinister" fraternity.

Fritz was never lucky. After an indifferent career in banking he fled in the 1930s to South America, but he was not successful there. From time to time Mother used to send him money. Eventually, after Hitler's fall, he returned to Germany and died there. We never talked much about him, but the time he spent with us is etched quite clearly in my memory—and my memories are all good. Despite his mangled arm he developed in me a love for sports which I have never lost. Athletics became and has remained an important aspect of my existence: when I am active I feel well and mentally creative, and when I am condemned to sit still for days or weeks on end, my mind too becomes sluggish.

At some time towards the end of the war my parents made a capital error: they presented me with a birthday gift of a cuirassier helmet, buckle and sword. I sharpened the latter assiduously at the curb stone, and with my martial elegance and equipment I achieved a senior role among my contemporaries, for not surprisingly we played war games and conquered "territories". We were after all German boys; the world was against us and we were going to show them. I think I was five years old at the time and our side had "conquered" some territory in the neighbourhood sandlot.

"I hereby take possession of this territory," I proclaimed loudly, the strong and brave leader of a fearless gang of shoeless children, and with a grand and telling gesture I plunged my sharpened sword into the ground—even children knew the symbols which accompanied the territorial impulse. The trouble was that I stuck the sword through my left foot, which laid me up with a nasty infection for some weeks and for the time being ended my military career.

After my foot healed my energies were directed towards a sports club which had its facilities not far from where we lived. There I would go whenever I could, and watch teenagers (men to me) run endlessly around the cinder track or heave the discus and javelin. I must have appeared often enough to be noticed, for one kindly member gave me an over-sized sport-shirt with the club symbol emblazoned on it, a black c in a circle, which I displayed proudly at home without, I am afraid, eliciting the slightest interest. The sports club was also the place where, after the war, I first saw the idol of my early years, Paavo Nurmi, the great Finnish runner whose style I imitated. On my short legs I would run around the track pretending to be Nurmi, consulting an imaginary stop-watch in my hand to see what new record I had just broken. In Finland they have erected monuments to the famous athlete. They do not know that he also has one standing tall and firm in my mind.

While Father was writing his lists at the ministry, Mother kept house, cared for the boarder and taught her only son the elements of reading and writing. She must have done a good job of it, because I emerged from her classes with presentable hand-writing and a love of reading. She also taught me French, which she knew well from her days in Nancy. Her accent was impeccable and she made it attractive for me to learn the language.

War years ... I remember my uncles Max and Walter, especially the latter who was the apple of my mother's eye. Both brothers died at Verdun, first Max and then, shortly before the war ended, Walter as well. For the first time I began to understand what sorrow meant. The tears in our house were copious; the fact that so many other households had similar reasons for grief was no help.

Everything was coming apart. The whole social structure was crumbling as Germany teetered on the brink of defeat and revolution. I was six years old when the war ended. The following year my brother was born, and was named Walter. When my grandmother came to visit I suggested that as a sign of joy she should turn a somersault at the entrance to our apartment. She politely and firmly refused, which was a big disappointment to me but a source of never-ending merriment to her as she told and retold the story of my wheedling. For a six-year-old who had never gone to school and who spent a good deal of his life on the street, those were exciting days. Revolution has a habit of spilling over into daily life; while there was no shooting in our neighbourhood, there was many a fracas, and guns were worn by men both in and out of uniform.

It was finally time for me to go to school, but everything was so badly disrupted that my parents decided to keep me at home for a while longer. Only when I visited Münster was I sent as a visiting student to the teachers' seminary, and not until I was eight years old was I at last delivered to the public school system of Germany. The republic had just adopted a constitution; the Kapp putsch, first of the right-wing rebellions, was being planned; Bavarian Prime Minister Matthias Erzberger was murdered. Fritz Ebert was President; an Austrian corporal released from his fighting unit was joining the newly-founded National Socialist Democratic Party; and I became a fourth-grade student in public school.

## School Days in the Weimar Republic

School proved to be a challenge. I had a teacher of German grammar by the name of Wiedemann who drummed it into our brains that language needed to be given full respect, and that he would treat anyone abusing it as if he had stolen something from the National Treasury. He meant it and his punishments, crisp slappings with a giant ruler, instilled in us a sense of anxiety and awe. But Wiedemann rarely had to use his physical powers, for he was a splendid teacher who could well have done without his threats. "If you understand German grammar properly," he said, "you will have no difficulty in Latin or Greek or English or French." He proved to be right, at least as far as I was concerned.

I was the youngest in the class and though—or because—my schooling had been private so far, I moved up quickly in the class standings. Four times a year the faculty would issue an official list of ratings, and four times a year the seating plan of the class would be adjusted accordingly. The number one student sat on the right rear bench, the number two student next to him and the poorer students were assigned the front row where the teachers' eyes and rulers could quickly reach them. I had no difficulty with the work, and soon I was number two. I was physically smaller than the others, but being in a class of older students was no problem for me then; later it proved to be disastrous and spoiled my schooling for some years.

When I was nine years old I received my first serious political instruction. On coming home in the afternoon I noticed that the streets were unusually crowded. Excited people were gathered around a news-stand. I joined them, as children do. It was a bad piece of news they were reading, as even I could appreciate:

Walther Rathenau, Germany's Foreign Minister and a Jew, had
been assassinated. I ran home to tell Father, who was already at
lunch.

"You're late," he said, "what held you up?"

"Rathenau is dead," I blurted out. "They killed him."

My father dropped his knife and fork and jumped up from the
table.

"My God!" he cried. "Are you sure?"

I told him about the crowd at the news-stand—this was before
the days of radio—and he shook his head.

"Günter," he said, "if this is true, and I'm afraid it is,
remember this day. It bodes ill for Germany and worse for the
Jews. Our honeymoon with equality and freedom was very short.
A divorce is coming, and it will be bitter and bloody, and we'll get
the short end of it. Mark my words."

What he said frightened me greatly, though I did not fully
understand it. Unfortunately Father's judgement, in this as in so
much else, proved all too accurate as the years went by. Would
that he had taken the proper actions after his analysis! Alas, he
was primarily a theoretician, not a doer.

In a sense, the murder of Rathenau marked a watershed in my
life. I had known that I was a Jew and that being Jewish meant
that one had special status. I'd been told that for years, as far
back as I could remember. But now it had all somehow come
closer. My father, usually a placid man, was agitated beyond
words and deeply troubled. Thereafter, even I could discern a
slightly altered pattern to his thought. In a way it meant that, for
me, childhood was over. I was growing up.

That year another fundamental change took place in my life.
Father gave up his post as a teacher in the Jewish Girls' School
and accepted the directorship of Germany's most respected
Jewish orphanage, which had been founded by Baruch Auerbach
in 1833 and was famous for its progressive policies. Auerbach
had approached his responsibilities with a simple idea: the fact
that his wards were orphans meant that they should be treated
with an extra amount of attention and love, and that they should
be given, if at all possible, the same opportunities as children
reared by their own families. This concept attracted to "Auerbach" (as the institution came to be known) a number of outstanding sponsors. In the course of time the privately funded institution was able to create a physical, mental and emotional environment which won it the admiration of the community. When

boys or girls showed promise they were given the chance to go to high school and then university, and for this purpose, if necessary, remain as assistant teachers at Auerbach.*

Our move to Auerbach meant that our apartment was now part of an institution. My parents were no longer private citizens at home; they were always available to anyone who needed them. They rose at an early hour, and the seven o'clock bell which announced breakfast for the 120 boys and girls became my time signal as well. Where before I had sought companionship amongst my school friends, now there was no need to go outside, there were always boys to be with. Yet I failed to develop ties of truly deep friendship with any of them. Part of the reason was the position which my brother and I held amongst the others—one of apartness and privilege.

However, most of the things important to a boy were now right at hand. After we had returned from public school and done our homework we played soccer, we raced on bikes around the large courtyard, and endlessly we played chess. We had a drama group and published an institutional newspaper. In the boys' and girls' wings the counsellors were young men and women of good education who could hope to be an example to those entrusted to their charge.**

Auerbach lay at the northern end of the city, at Schönhauser Allee 162, not far from the small cemetery where some of Berlin's great Jews lie buried. The north end of town was lower middle class to proletarian, which became evident at once when I was enrolled in the nearest public high school: the level of student interest was markedly lower than it had been in Berlin's west end. Within a few short months I became the number one student in the class, a position which I never relinquished during the years I spent there. Not until I arrived at law school in 1930 did I find out that my putative excellence in high school was in part due to the fact that most of the students around me did not expect to go to university, and were more interested in getting a job than in higher education.

* Among the alumni of Auerbach are Klaus Goldschlag, Canada's ambassador to Bonn, and Hollywood photographer Bruno Bernard.

** In 1980, I received a visit from Alex Turney who as Alex Teitelbaum had been at Auerbach from 1925 to 1935. He rendered a moving testimony of Mother ("she became my second mother") and Father ("a soft-hearted intellectual") and of the institution itself: "We were made self-reliant, were encouraged to achieve our highest potential and to do so with disciplined effort. When we left school on an afternoon we went home like everyone else. Auerbach was home to us, in every way." Alex was my brother Walter's age and his closest friend.

Classes were held six days a week. They started at eight o'clock and adjourned at two-thirty, after which there might be extra-curricular activities such as track and field. On Saturdays school ended at one o'clock. One of my Jewish classmates was Orthodox, and though he attended classes on the Sabbath he steadfastly refused to write, which won him my admiration and the cordial dislike of some teachers who had to give him extra time to make up tests that had been scheduled for Saturdays.

I was now more keenly aware of my Jewishness. At Auerbach we held a daily prayer service in a small *Gebetsaal*. In the 250-seat synagogue on the third floor directly above our apartment was housed a Liberal congregation of which my father was one of the co-founders and guiding spirits.

Because of my protected environment, antisemitism—which was then growing alarmingly in Germany—did not affect me overly much. Technically, denominational differences played a role at public school only when Holy Days came around or when we went to the state-sponsored classes in Religion. For years a certain Herr Schimmelmann came to our school to teach the Jewish students. He was an object of ridicule, if not contempt, for he was totally incapable of conveying anything of our heritage to us. The only reason we abided him at all was the leniency with which he graded us—for grades did count, even in Religion. All of us received a 1, the scale being 1 for excellent, 2 for good, 3 for average but passing, 4 for failure and 5 for utter failure. Any 1 helped one's average.

In those earlier years my greatest problem in school did not arise from the growth of political antisemitism—that came later. It arose from the fact that, in a class including many older students (repeating grades because of previous failures), I was the youngest. In this all-male school, sex was a major subject for discussion in the halls and even in class. My classmates had gone through puberty and some of them, judging by the accounts of their exploits, had had sexual experiences with boys as well as with girls. It quickly became evident to students and teachers alike that I was an innocent, uninstructed child who did not have the vaguest idea what the fuss was all about.

There was no way of asking my parents. As a boy I would not have considered speaking to my mother about it, and my father would have been terribly embarrassed. He who spoke so eloquently on every other subject would not have known what to say. I went to dictionaries and encyclopaedias but they were of no help. I did not even know how boys differed anatomically from girls. All I knew was that my ignorance was becoming more and more painful at school. Students and even some teachers would amuse each other with *double entendres*—and I would have no idea why everyone was snickering deliciously. Not only that, but I was also one of the smallest students, and was battered by the others almost at will. There was at least one year in this dismal period when I hated the idea of going to school altogether, when I frequently pleaded illness so I might stay away.

I knew instinctively that standing number one in the class was no asset as long as I was unable to compete physically with the others. Sometime around the age of fourteen I made up my mind that I would develop my natural interest in athletics as far as possible. If I could be number one in track and field as well as in class, perhaps I might be more acceptable. Every day, as soon as I came home from school, I practised running 1,500 metres in the Auerbach courtyard. Indeed at the next school meet I won the event, much to everyone's surprise.

That was only the first of two athletic contests in which I succeeded in being a "sleeper". My cousin Leo had given me a tennis racket, and though I had never been to any match, and had no courts within easy reach—there being only a few public courts in Berlin in those days—I borrowed a book from the library which told me all about the rules, the strokes, and the tactics. Day after day I practised hitting some old balls, worn right down to the rubber, against a wall in the courtyard. I went to see the great Bill Tilden play on one of his exhibition tours, and after watching him in full flight I placed him on the pedestal next to Paavo Nurmi in my private pantheon. Finally I entered the North Berlin High School tournament. I had never played against anyone, I had never even been on a tennis court, but I gained second prize in this sectional tournament. I don't remember what happened about the sexual taunts; I do know that school was bearable again. A painful period of growing up was behind me.

My early memories of being distinctly and differentially Jewish relate to my experiences in high school. I suppose that Sabbath and Holy Day observance were so much a part of us that they blended totally into the context of our lives. Everyone I knew attended Jewish classes in public school and everyone I knew was Bar Mitzvah. I sat with Grandpa in the synagogue when I visited Münster; I sat with my father every Friday evening when we went upstairs to attend the service. It would never have occurred to me to say that I had something else to do or that I did not feel like going. Attending Friday evenings and later, when I had finished with high school, Saturday mornings, was as normal as breathing. When I came home from school on Friday afternoons my blue serge suit would be laid out on my bed. Shabbes was coming.* Father's *Zylinder* (top hat) would be set out for him and was worn with pride. In some communities wearing the silk hat denoted that one was a member of the synagogue or community board, but I think in Berlin this distinction did not apply or was not strictly observed. On a Shabbes morning many people in our neighbourhood could be seen wending their way to the synagogue in somewhat incongruous attire, for the hat was not necessarily accompanied by a formal suit—it might be worn with a grey or brown outfit. This was just one more paradox of Jewish life in Germany: all week Jews tried to blend inconspicuously into the life of the community, but on Saturdays their mode of dress proclaimed publicly, "I am a Jew."

I was Bar Mitzvah like everyone else and prepared myself by paying an occasional visit to the rabbi of the upstairs synagogue, Dr. Martin Salomonski, a kindly gentleman given to flowery sermons and writing novels which my father—no mean literary critic—found cloying and maudlin. I have one outstanding memory of the man: I still see him mounting the *beema*** at the beginning of services, going to the ark, facing it silently for a few moments and then bowing to it before going to his seat. This gesture of public reverence impressed itself deeply on my mind.

The Bar Mitzvah ceremony itself—a traumatic rite for any youngster—left me only two memories: one, naturally, of the many books I received; the other of my reading the Haftarah.† I had complained to Father—not too seriously, of course, but complained nonetheless—that my portion (the beginning of First Kings) was unduly long.‡ Why was I born to be punished in such a fashion? He shrugged his shoulders in his usual fashion and said, "I have it from high authority that the Heavenly Court will consider your complaint at its next session."

---

* This was the way the seventh day was referred to, before the Israeli pronunciation "Shabbat" took hold.
** The elevated platform.
† The prophetic selection assigned to the Sabbath.
‡ The text held its secrets, as well. It tells of King David's old age, when he could never get warm. His courtiers provided him with a young virgin to make him warm, but to no avail—"the King was not intimate with her." I studied the text without comprehending it, and no one was prepared to enlighten me.

When the ordeal was finally over I went to sit with my father.

"You know, it wasn't really as long as all that," I ventured, whereupon he, placing his glasses on the top of his head—an inevitable sign that something of great importance was about to come—replied, "Of course it didn't appear long, because you left half of it out."

I'm not sure that I did, but I must have skipped something; at any rate, I did not pass with flying colours. I often told the story to an aspiring youngster coming to me prior to his Bar Mitzvah, trembling from head to toe wishing the trial were already ended. I told him that he should not worry about making mistakes; that the only punishment that could possibly be meted out was that he be condemned to become a rabbi.

I did not chant my portion because I was deemed to be unmusical, something Father would proudly assert since he himself had long been classified in such a manner. Mother, on the other hand, played the piano and sang very well (in fact, she was part of a temple's volunteer choir well into her eighties), so I obviously took after Father. My piano lessons had been a catastrophe; I had bowed unwillingly to the middle-class standard which required that every boy and girl be exposed to some musical instruction. It was like cod liver oil: it was simply declared to be good for you. Good or not, I escaped eventually only to find out decades later that I had a good ear for music and, had I been trained properly, might have sung passably. Father would have shaken his head if he had known that in later years his son would attend concerts, and even become a director of the Toronto Symphony.

The cantor in our synagogue was a smallish man by the name of Jakubowski. His voice was quite good, but he disappointed me grievously when, one Yom Kippur, I found him in the washroom breaking his fast with a furtive glass of water. After that he never seemed to me to sing as well as before. The synagogue had a mixed choir and an involving service—so involving, in fact, that my brother Walter and I occasionally "played synagogue", for we knew enough of the service and its music by heart. Our home was kosher but my parents' attitude was by now Liberal. The question of my writing in school on the Sabbath was never raised, nor was I ever urged to put on phylacteries or even say my morning prayers. I said them regularly nonetheless, but in abbreviated form, and I prolonged them only when I lay in bed at night before I went to sleep.

My first religious experience came to me one night in an over-powering fashion. I was standing at the window looking out into the starry night when suddenly I began to ask myself, what is behind the last star? I began to tremble with an unnamed anxiety, realizing that I was face to face with the presence of a question that had no answer, a sense of the infinite so compelling that I could hardly bear it. Even now, when I look up at night and the firmament sparkles in all its splendour, something of that awe remains and the question surfaces, not quite as insistently but real nonetheless. I should add at once that this in no wise presaged my later entrance into the rabbinate. In those days, and for many years to come, that was furthest from my mind. Not that I knew what I wanted to be; it was a problem which I did not as yet have to face.

I seldom played with my brother. He was seven years younger, and for a teenager a brother so much junior is no companion and is sometimes just a nuisance. Walter proved to be a fair but not first-rate student, and it was a capital mistake for him to be enrolled in the school where I had done so splendidly. In this regard I was always a burden to him and the error was compounded by making me his sometime tutor. I had no training for it and I was impatient; it was a poor start for a complex relationship. In addition, I was perceived by him (though not by me) to be my parents' favourite, the first-born, who showed some promise intellectually and for whom they both had their own individual dreams. I was unaware of it at the time, but in retrospect it was clearly a scenario bound for potential conflict.

When I was not busy with my companions at Auerbach I was in my parents' library. One section dealt with Jewish history and Father encouraged me at an early age to explore this forest of adventure and to read as much as I could. I did, and at one point even set myself to reading the multi-volume encyclopaedia from A to Z. I did not get very far; still, it did stimulate my appetite for the sciences.

While being Jewish was an easy and normal way of life at home, it became a growing problem in public school. I spent eight long years in an environment of increasing unrest and violence. Inflation was beginning to ravage the country to a degree unparalleled in history. The postage stamp which yesterday had cost a few pfennigs would cost a hundred marks shortly after, and then the price went to a thousand, a million and more. Goods had astronomical labels attached to them and it all was quite meaningless. It came to this: money had no value and nothing was the same from one day to another. My father had a birthday coming and I had a few pfennigs saved up for it. I had admired a picture frame in a window on my way to school. When I finally entered the store a few days before his birthday, and wanted to purchase the frame for the price I had seen advertised some weeks before, the man looked at me with pity. My seventy-five cents would not buy the dust under the counter, he said. The frame was now worth five million marks, "but only today," he said, "tomorrow it will double or treble." It was one birthday on which Father received a story rather than a gift.

We had to pay our tuition to the school once a week and then every day. One day I forgot to hand over the money. To say that I incurred the displeasure of my father, who had to shell out a multiple of the original amount, is to put it mildly.

In the mid-twenties, after Hitler's release from Landsberg prison and the publication of *Mein Kampf*, Nazism started to make great strides. There were some easy converts in our class, chief amongst them a student who usually sat directly in front of me. His name was Schultz. When the long intermission came at 10:20 a.m. and the teacher left the room, he would face me and hit me squarely across the mouth. This was accompanied by a ritual exclamation, "You shitty Jew, that's yours for the day."

I was very much smaller than he and after a while I became so accustomed to his assault that even the dread of the intermission bell faded away. His hitting me and his expletive became part of the scene, just as antisemitism had become an aspect of the cultural *milieu* of the country. One day Schultz was sick. The bell rang and automatically I stood up to receive his blow. Somehow, in a masochistic way, I missed it. But he was back the next day.

There was another Schultz in my life, a teacher of mathematics in one of the lower grades. He was feared for his quick temper and physical attacks on his students. I had been away from school because of illness or Holy Days—at any rate, I had missed the opening discussion of fundamental geometry. Schultz stood in the aisle and pointed to the blackboard.

"Plaut, describe what you see."

I stood up—we always had to stand when answering—and, unaware that great teachings had been handed down during my few days' absence, reported, "Over there is a right angle and next to it a left angle."

"What!" he screamed, and before I had time to duck, the back of his hand slapped me across the mouth and scratched one eye.

"A left angle, indeed! You'll stay after school."

The worst part was not that I had given a wrong though perfectly logical answer but that I had forgotten that Schultz was left-handed. I had watched his other hand and was unprepared for the sudden slap. There were so many things one had to keep in mind in those days.

The greatest disappointment of my school days was my neighbour Fritz Jewan, a bright, tall, stout fellow who was always number two in the class and who therefore sat next to me for over six years. We were on good terms, so I thought; but one day, it must have been in 1928, he came to class wearing a swastika in his lapel. I never spoke to him again. For two full years we sat next to each other day after day, six days a week, but we were strangers from then on until we graduated and parted forever. Worse, by his fiat we had become enemies. For he now started to taunt me, which was easy because I was small and he was big. One day he drove me beyond my level of endurance. This level was rather high, since I had for so many years been the butt of ridicule from teachers and the victim of physical aggression from students. But Jewan got to me that morning during intermission. I then did something I had never done before: I swung at him and with one blow flattened him, and his head hit the stone floor with a dull crack. He lay unconscious for several minutes, and for a moment of anxiety mixed with joyful satisfaction I thought that I might have killed him. No such luck; he came to. But he never repeated his taunts. I took a look at myself and discovered to my amazement that I had grown as tall as the others and, being a better athlete than most, was in far better physical shape than they. Subsequently I took a few classes in jiu-jitsu, which was taught at Auerbach, and was never bothered again by any of my fellow students. That bout with Jewan convinced me of something else: that antisemites thrive on Jewish weakness and fear, that their physical prowess is limited by cowardice and evaporates in the face of strength and guts. I learned it then and never forgot the lesson.

Eventually I lost track of all my classmates save four of my Jewish friends. Poldi Kuh went to England (where he died); Arno Lachmann settled in Texas; Bruno Sommerfeld (an Auerbacher who became first a Doctor of Laws and then, as Bruno Bernard, a famous photographer) moved to California; and Harry Lewinsky practises as a surgeon in Israel. I sometimes wonder what happened to the others, how many of them died in the war, how many survived and where they are today. I wonder how many would remember me if they read these lines.

Together with Bruno I joined the Society for French–German Understanding. The members were mostly adults. They met to speak French and to participate in recitations as well as in discussions which frequently went over my head. In these circles I first learned about Freud and was moved to read *Totem and Taboo*. It was a new world which, lacking any guidance, I could not quite comprehend. Because of our membership in this Society, Bruno and I were amongst fifty German students chosen in the summer of 1928 for an exchange program with France— which was, in those post-war years, a quasi-revolutionary adventure which attracted much public attention.

We were put up in an old school at Boulogne-sur-Mer together with fifty French students. Unfortunately the boy assigned as my companion must have been the youngest of the lot. He was socially even less mature than I, if that was possible, and was a child intellectually as well. But in every other respect the trip was a huge success. I saw a new world through the eyes of competent guides and teachers, and after six weeks it all ended with a reception by the famed Aristide Briand, France's counterpart to Gustav Stresemann and its Minister of Foreign Affairs. For our stay in Paris we were housed in another school that had been erected many centuries before. Its dark rooms and dank halls bespoke its age, and the neighbourhood too left much to be desired. We were not far from Place Pigalle, and no one had warned us about the prostitutes prowling the streets. I, of course, had not yet fully emerged from my cocoon of innocence and was therefore especially vulnerable. One evening, as I stood looking at a shop window, a young woman hardly older than I stood next to me. Before I knew what was happening she had taken my hand, exposed her breast and made me touch it.

"You like it?" she invited me.

I fled in terror. I was quite unaware that similar attractions could be had in Berlin not far from where we lived. Thus ended my educational excursion into France.

## Student Days

It is hard at any time to analyse one's own personality; it is a little easier if one looks back at the more distant past.

When I graduated from public high school I was seventeen and a half years old, mentally alert and socially inept. I had lots of acquaintances and many companions, but no truly close friends; though Bruno and I spent much time together, our relationship did not go beyond a certain point. I did not know a single girl in any personal sense. I had never had a date nor can I remember any party at which girls were present. Public schools were all-male. While we had celebrations at Auerbach, girls did not figure in them, at least not for me.

There had been some possibilities of making deeper attachments of another kind. When I was eight years old I joined Kadimah, a Zionist youth group which was a successor of the original Blau-Weiss.* It is hard nowadays to recover the meaning and feeling of youth movements during that era. They were not centred around a Y or a camp. They were close associations often led by young adults and founded on some identifiable doctrine or mystical philosophy, and they featured endless discussions and Sunday hikes. Hiking was the physical expression of all youth movements and I did plenty of it during my high-school years. On summer trips hiking meant carrying your rucksack, living with your fellows, staying in a youth hostel at night and, around the campfire after the cook-out, debating everything from the meaning of Jewish life to the relationship of Jew and German. My parents were not Zionists and did not encourage my belonging to Kadimah, although at no time did they oppose it. After a while I drifted away, but not before I had absorbed something of the Zionist ideal and understood the essential contradiction between Jewishness and Germanness. My father never discussed this matter with me, which was a pity. I don't believe it was much of an issue with him at that time; after all, the family had been in the country for many hundreds of years. Palestine was for others, not for them. The streak of realism and cynicism which underlay so many of his convictions must have spoken to him with another voice as well, but he chose not to listen, and so there was nothing to talk about with his son.

I finished high school in 1930, the end of what had been the "roaring twenties" not only in America but in Germany as well. During that decade Berlin was a fantastic city in which to grow up, and though I was too young to take it all in I was old enough to

---

* "Blue-White", the first Zionist youth movement in Germany, founded in 1913.

be the beneficiary of some of its unique splendour. In 1978 the French pianist, Claudio Arrau, described the Berlin of the 1920s as a city of culture and excitement the likes of which had never been duplicated. It had four full-fledged opera houses and companies at the same time, with the all-time greats Leo Blech, Otto Klemperer, Wilhelm Furtwängler and Bruno Walter directing them. The theatre was dominated by directors Max Reinhardt and Erwin Piscator. The literary scene featured dramatists like Gerhart Hauptmann and Ernst Toller, poets and novelists like Rainer Maria Rilke, Thomas Mann, Jakob Wassermann, Stefan and Arnold Zweig and Franz Werfel. Journalism was at its height; splendid magazines like *Die Weltbühne* and a host of daily papers kept the political juices flowing. There were magnificent art museums and a university of unequalled reputation. Berlin was the scientific capital of the world, where Albert Einstein and Max Planck held sway; where we watched Elizabeth Bergner, Fritz Kortner and Max Pallenberg on the stage; where cabaret was flourishing and the air was rife with excitement. It was a land in which inflation and deflation, violence and reason lived side by side in a marriage that didn't work. We had a republic which allowed even those who vowed to destroy it their unlimited rights. Berlin, capital of the republic, was a great city in the twenties, and its ambience rubbed off on the young man who was now ready to enter university.

For my father, Erich Maria Remarque became a paradigm of the times. They both hated war, and found the times out of joint. "His family name was originally Kramer, which is Remark spelled backwards," Father told me. "But then everything is backwards in this country of ours."

It was. Hitler's legions were growing and violence in the streets became normal. The day of the high-school orals (matriculation was based on comprehensive examinations) came and went, and Mother was happy to learn that I had passed standing number one. Father never mentioned that fact. I think he simply expected it.

In Germany there was no college education in the North American sense. After matriculation (called *Abitur*) one went directly into professional school. But what would it be for me? I had no particular proclivity. I was good in a number of subjects and with a little encouragement might have gone into mathematics or possibly architecture, but those were not subjects with which my family was familiar. There was a time when

Father thought I might succeed him at his post at Auerbach
some years hence. Meanwhile, he suggested, why not go into law
which was a door to many possibilities? One could become a civil
servant, a diplomat, a judge or, of course, a lawyer. My cousin
Leo offered to take me into his firm.

"I'd make more money if I had a good lawyer associated with
me," he said self-deprecatingly.

He was always in financial straits and on many occasions my
father had to lend Leo money so that he could pay his bills. Occasionally he paid something back, though never the whole amount.
Father made light of it.

"I'll get it back from him in cards," he said.

For he and Leo and another lawyer, named Arndt, used to play
once or twice a week at our apartment. They played *Skat* and
Father always won. He had an uncanny sense for cards and
would have made a splendid chess player. He had a vision of the
game as a whole. After a card or two had been played he knew
precisely what everyone was holding and did not need statistics
to tell him what the relative chances of a certain play might be.

He had the same holistic sense in other matters as well. I
remember doing my algebra one day and trying to solve some
problem by means of x, y, and z. He stopped briefly at my working desk and asked what the problem was. I told him.

"Why," he said, "is this what they make you do at home? Can't
they give you something more difficult?"

I remembered that in his schooling Father had never been exposed to the wonders of algebra. I countered with a superior
smile.

"So, what is the answer?"

He told me. Half an hour later I came up with an answer
myself. He had been right.

"But how did you know?"

He said, in his typical way, "It was obvious."

To him it was. He saw the problem as a whole and not in the
fragmented way of a student of algebra. That was the way he
looked at life and as I grew into my university years he had occasion to teach me further. The first lesson came after my
matriculation and even before the semester had begun.

"I think," he said, "you ought to earn a little money." That
seemed a good idea, although I was not quite sure what I would
spend it on. I had never handled money in any meaningful sense,
and here I was, a grown-up little boy of seventeen entering law

school, without experience in life's two most important areas (so one heard it said): sex and money.

"I think you would do very well as a tutor," my father confronted me one day, and when I agreed he continued.

"In fact, I've found a family that needs a young man like you. It's the Warburg–Hahn clan; they live out in Wannsee [a fashionable western suburb]. Their son has had polio and needs to be tutored at home. Do you think you could do that twice a week?"

I did not see why I shouldn't be able to.

"I've made a date for you this Thursday," he went on, "and if you like what you see and they like you, you can make your own arrangements thereafter."

I ventured to ask whether pay had been mentioned.

"No," he said, "that's up to you and them."

"But how would I know what to ask?"

"Well," said Father, "what do you think you are worth?"

I speculated, with less than my usual natural conceit.

"I have no experience, and I'm young. Maybe fifty pfennigs an hour."

"Really!" said Father. "Let me tell you something, Günter. If you ask for fifty pfennigs, they'll show you in by the service entrance next time you come. But if you ask them for a good stiff fee they'll receive you at the front door and ask you for lunch."

"And what would a good stiff fee be?"

"That's up to you. You're a young man on your own now, so you have to make some decisions for yourself." He left me with that to ponder.

On Thursday I took the train to the suburbs and there, on a magnificent estate, met the young, paralysed scion of the family, the heir of two great industrial traditions, the Warburg banking empire and the Hahn industrial holdings in the Rhineland. The boy was pleasant and affectionate and we struck it up at once. His mother sat with us, a distinguished lady who was well known in the upper circles of Berlin society, as I was to learn later. Everything went smoothly, but money was never mentioned. I arranged the hours when the instruction would take place and Mrs. Hahn accompanied me to the front door. Just as I was about to leave she said, "Oh, incidentally, we did not arrange for a fee. How much would you charge?"

Before my reason could get hold of my tongue I blurted out "Ten marks," which was an exorbitant overcharge, to put it mildly. If anyone made that much per hour, I did not know him.

Mrs. Hahn was unruffled. "That will be fine," she said, and warmly shook my hand.

When I returned the next week for my first lesson the butler was at the door.

"Mrs. Hahn is wondering whether you would have lunch with the family," he said, and bowed.

Law school opened up a new world for me. For the first time I was part of a co-educational system. I had no idea how to talk to attractive women, and they all seemed attractive to me. I joined the Social Democratic Students' Union, but after attending a few meetings found their program weak; my first foray into politics was short-lived. There was little opportunity for personal contact at school. Students showed up for class—if they came at all—and sat and scribbled their notes, and then professor and students left for their various destinations.

The German law school had its own special rules which distinguished it remarkably from the educational system of high schools. One needed to register for a certain number of prescribed courses during the three-year period, which was the minimum span before one could take examinations; but, except for seminars, class attendance was not compulsory. You had your registry book signed on the first and last day, and what you did in between was your own business. This had one palpable advantage: there was no need to sit through boring classes. We selected the man (there were no women teachers on the faculty) who had something to say. The two extremes are best illustrated by two professors. One was Professor Stutz, who taught church law, a short stocky man with a clipped beard who was reputed to be the most boring of them all. I selected his class, if one could so call it, to do some homework for my seminars. One day I was well ensconced when the professor came in, mounted the rostrum and began, "Gentlemen!"—whereupon he looked up and saw that I was the only student present in the room. Without blinking an eye he corrected himself and said, "Sir!" and proceeded with his forty-five minute lecture while I attended to my work. It was a perfect symbiosis.

In sharp contrast were the classes of Martin Wolff who taught contracts and other aspects of civil law. Wolff was very small and had an unpleasant, grating voice—but he had a mind that was razor sharp, and his textbook on the civil code was standard in every German university. He lectured in the "Grosse Aula", the largest auditorium, and must have attracted some fifteen hundred listeners who hung on every word that fell from the mouth of the sage. There was, of course, no opportunity for questions. The little man on the high podium spoke in his fearfully pitched voice unaided by any microphone, and the pens scratching away in the notebooks were his echo. Only a portion of those in attendance were actually registered in his course; no matter, what he had to say was too good to be missed. That was true even for the large number of students with swastikas on their lapels, whose contempt for Jews did not keep them away from the classes of the Jewish professor. Wolff turned out to be not only a splendid jurist but also an astute observer of the political scene; he left the country in time to seek refuge elsewhere.

Despite my early success on the tennis courts I did not pursue the sport, but instead turned with increasing seriousness to soccer. I was soon accepted on the junior team of a major-league club which had its playing field in one of the workers' sections of the city. I was the only Jew on my team and the only one who was at university. The rest were sons of labourers, decent enough to accept the oddball in their midst. In all the time I played soccer during the next three years I never heard an untoward remark or had an unpleasant experience, with these young men or with the seniors whom I would soon join—and this in a society that was shot through with hatred of Jews, a society in which antisemitism became in many circles a part of one's political baggage.

I had the same experience in the workers' chess club which I joined in our neighbourhood. There I met mostly simple, older men and they too accepted me with a warmth that stood in sharp contrast to what I had experienced in high school and was now seeing at the university. Some years later, after the Nazis came to power and Jews were barred from all gentile sporting events, a delegation from the chess club came to our apartment. "Even though they have passed the regulation, we want you to know that you're still welcome in our midst," they said.

I never forgot this act of kindness and courage.

With law school consuming little time, with no girl friends to take on dates and soccer strictly a weekend pastime, I was more and more frequently attracted to the chess room at the university. It was there that I met the man who would become my first real friend, and much in both our lives was changed by our meeting.

Heinz Frank came, on his paternal side, from an old German family. His father had a minor civil-service job and the family lived in modest circumstances in the workers' quarter in Neukölln. Heinz had a high forehead and inclined to portliness. He had a large nose and narrowly set, strong eyes, and a marvellous sense of humour punctuated by infectious laughter which was much like my father's—no wonder that in later years the two became close friends. Heinz was the greatest intellect I ever met. His retentive faculties were stupendous, and though I myself had a good memory, it was nothing compared to his. He remembered everything. After reading a page once or twice he could recite it by heart. His faculty for acquiring new languages was equally astonishing. One day we discussed Cervantes, and since he had just reread *Don Quixote* he wondered how faithfully the translation rendered the original early Spanish. He knew no Spanish, let alone mediaeval Spanish, but after several weeks he announced that he had just finished reading Cervantes in the original—in that short time he had acquired the knowledge and vocabulary of a tongue which was utterly strange to him. The same thing happened later on when he decided to woo Sabina, his future wife, a cousin who lived in Warsaw: he learned Polish, then went, saw and conquered.

His memory for quotations was endless and he had a special love for trilingual puns—usually in German, French and Latin. Amongst the many regrets I have is that he is no longer alive as I write these memoirs. Not only would he keep me straight in my recollections but he would remember events I have long forgotten.

We met in the chess room, and our friendship was immediately a *fait accompli*. We played throughout the whole day and the next and the next, and thereafter we took to playing at his home (where his mother never failed to serve little sardine sandwiches) or mine. We played inside or, when the weather was nice, on the balcony. Often we played five days a week, and for a while neither of us paid any attention to law school or anything else. We were evenly matched. I was the more aggressive, daring player, he was the masterful defender. We often compared our styles: I was the Emanuel Lasker, he was the incomparable and in the end more successful José Capablanca. We were not top class but quite good; Heinz would later become a well-known player in Canada. The chess board became for us the place where we exchanged ideas about the world, and laughed—

laughed especially. We hatched marvellous schemes together and lived in part in a home-made world of fiction.

One day—I think we were then in our second year at law school—we dared each other to join in a commercial venture. The proposition was simple. There were many students in law school who never attended a single class, but instead indulged in duelling and drinking. What if we established a private law school which would help these "intellectuals" grasp at least the beginnings of their future profession? To be sure, Heinz and I had passed only a few semesters and could therefore hardly be classed as experts in the field. But as Heinz always said, "It all depends on with whom you are compared," and compared to our future students we were professors of extraordinary standing. These private schools were a familiar aspect of the law scene: all students, even those who attended university faithfully, would go to a *Repetitor* who would prepare them for the comprehensive law exams. Depending on how well one was prepared, such a period of private tutoring might last anywhere from six months to a year or even more. But there were some who preferred to do a little catch-up work from time to time.

*Gesagt, getan.* By word of mouth we let it be known that we would tutor students in the fundamentals of legal theory. Heinz assembled the material and organized the course; I obtained the students. We taught for two hours one afternoon a week and for a while had no fewer than twenty students, some of whom had been registered at law school for years on end. We were now their professors and as I think back on it I like to reassure myself that at least we did not cheat them. We took very little money and probably taught them something. One thing is certain: no one acquired his legal education from stranger teachers than us.

Going to a university away from home was in those days—it was now 1931—not the usual thing to do. However, my parents believed that I had to have at least one fling at independent living, and arrangements were made to send me to Heidelberg for one semester. I was quartered at the home of a widow named Müller; her husband had written a textbook of Bible stories which had been a favourite of my childhood years. My room had the usual furnishings: an over-stuffed bed, a chair, a table and a stove. Since I was there during the warmer months of the year, the stove served as my storage bin for food. An icebox would have been deemed an unnecessary luxury.

Heidelberg was a restless town and its university was the focal point of continuing disturbances. Here too I joined the Social Democratic Students' Union and this time I was given my first assignment: to distribute leaflets at a street corner. I was too naive to know what I was in for. It turned out that these assignments made a man of me, at least in one sense: I had to swallow my cowardice and stand up to others regardless of consequences. Some of my friends carried knives. I never did, but we brawled often. On one occasion I was confronted by a gang of Nazis. All of them wore the little caps of the duelling fraternities and sported the facial scars which were the accepted insignia of fencing heroics. They surrounded me, knocked the leaflets out of my hand and started to push me around. I did the only thing I could do under the circumstances: I tried to face them down.

"Come on, you cowards," I said. "Six against one! Is this what they teach you in your fraternities? How about one at a time?"

They looked at me, spat on the ground and walked away. I felt I had won that battle and was quite proud of myself. On other occasions I was less lucky.

I applied to the Varsity soccer team and with my past record was readily accepted. We played other universities in southern Germany as well as some in France. From the French expedition I carried home my most enduring memory of those days: for the first time I kissed a girl.

We were playing in Strasbourg, and after the game our hosts gave a party which included girls. The one assigned to me walked with me after supper, and while I tried in my embarrassment to make idle conversation, she abandoned all preliminaries and kissed me squarely on the mouth. This turned out to be the end of the encounter—I never knew whether it was meant to go further or not—but my anxiety had already reached a peak. I was positive that this contact with what was evidently a fast and loose girl would give me venereal disease, and for weeks thereafter I examined myself before the mirror. I had come from very protected surroundings.

Shortly after that I met Ulla, a Swedish student, who became a good friend and who taught me how to be at ease in female company. I corresponded with her for some time after I returned to Berlin and earned the severe displeasure of my parents when they discovered my ever-so-slight infatuation. Ulla was not Jewish and came from no family my parents had ever heard of.

My various interests and extracurricular involvements in

Heidelberg caused me to neglect my school-work rather badly and I failed one course—the first and only failure in all my school experience. I was shaken beyond words, which was a good thing, for I resolved to take my studies more seriously thereafter. But my resolution was short-lived; on my return to Berlin I found that the Nazis were getting more vocal, the street brawls more frequent. I was caught in the turmoil. The students who joined the Social Democratic Union were decent, idealistic chaps but they were clearly on the defensive. They lacked the perfervid devotion of the Communists on the one side and the Nazis on the other. Father neither approved nor disapproved of my activities. I believe he never fully understood the physical and often dangerous aspect of my involvement. He was a supporter of the Democratic State's Party which had been strong in the early days of the Republic but was losing ground steadily. The *bon mot* of the time was an adequate reflection of its diminishing membership.

"What do you think the Democratic State's Party will do?"

"Nothing."

"How do you know?"

"Because I know both gentlemen."

We continued to read the *Vossische Zeitung*, which employed splendid literary talent. It was Germany's oldest newspaper, having been founded in 1701. When the Nazis came to power it suffered the fate of all opposition papers and had a quick and inglorious end.

Of course, I took up my friendship with Heinz. We studied together, played chess, and participated in a variety of tournaments. I found out that I had a knack for problem-solving and to my surprise won the first chess tournament I entered. (The book I received as a prize is still in my library. It deals, in a rather abstruse way—in both German and English—with the theory of chess problems, and to this day I have never solved the mysteries of its language.) My unlooked-for success encouraged me to occupy myself with the composition of chess problems, and on many a long journey, and later during army days, I whiled away lonely hours with composition and problem-solving.

My studies started to lag again when soccer and then tennis began to claim me more seriously. I went back to my old soccer club and made the senior team, which played in the major leagues. I was in the company of men from whom I differed in every respect except our love for the game. All of them were workers, employed or unemployed. They taught me much, including the dubious habit of drinking more beer than was good for me.

My brother Walter usually accompanied me to the games. Up to this point the spread of our ages had been too great to permit any close relationship, but now I was helping him with preparations for his Bar Mitzvah and sharing with him some outside activities, which meant that at least we were spending a little time together.

At the beginning of 1932 I saw a notice posted on the bulletin board of the university. It informed students that a scholarship would be available for the law school at Stanford University in the United States. I thought that a change of this kind would be a great experience. I applied, passed the physical examination, and did reasonably well on an English literacy test. A young man who had come back from such a stay at an American university told us strange tales about that far-away country. One thing especially I remember: "When you go on a date," he said "you pay for the girl—not like here in Germany where everything is Dutch treat; also, before you pick her up in your car you send a corsage."

A car ... corsage ... pick her up—it all sounded like a wonderland which I had to see. To my surprise, the indications were that I would be accepted and I was asked to clear the matter with the Dean of my own law school. Here my reception was less favourable.

"Herr Plaut," said the Dean, "you are making a fundamental mistake. American law has nothing in common with German law and your year at Stanford will be a total waste as far as your ongoing studies here are concerned. You will not be able to apply any of the credits in our law school and in addition you will forget much of what you have learned here. Why don't you finish law school here, take your exams and then go?"

I took his advice and turned down the scholarship. Had I been more alert to the signs of Germany's gathering storm I would have disregarded his advice. I have often wondered what course my life would have taken had I accepted and found myself in the United States at the time when Hitler came to power. I might never have returned; I might instead have finished law school in California. And I would certainly never have entered the rabbinate.

Why could I not see the danger? We had lived in the midst of turmoil for so long that we accepted it as a normal condition. We had grown up in the midst of vicious antisemitism which had become endemic to the German social climate, and it too had become normal to us.

## The Evil Ones

The Nazis were threatening, the Communists were strong, Social Democracy was tottering, but we all assumed that basically Germans had good sense and that matters would turn out all right. After all, Jews had been identified with Germany for close to two thousand years; for better or for worse it was our home.

Later notions notwithstanding, we did not feel that we were "one hundred per cent Germans". Quite the contrary: we knew we were Jews and we made no bones about it. I, like thousands of others my age, tried to live in two worlds at once. I was, so to speak, a Jew at home and a German in the streets. I continued to go regularly to the synagogue; I read Jewish books and Jewish periodicals and even acted as a lay preacher at congregations of young people. But otherwise my life was that of a German student who had a flair for athletics and some involvement in politics. My lack of vision was shared by the majority of my contemporaries.* In hindsight it is easy to say that we should have known what was coming. But there was no way we could have known, for there was no precedent for Hitler.

I saw him on one or two occasions, at mass rallies to which I was detailed by my Student Union. I heard Joseph Goebbels, who was a rabble-rouser though not the kind of spellbinder the Führer was. When I stood in the crowd in Berlin's central park, the Lustgarten, I had a gut feeling that insanity might after all overcome all of us, but when I returned home—to the warm, comfortable, middle-class environment to which I was used—my fears disappeared and everything seemed normal. I finished law school just as Hitler came to power. On January 30, 1933, President Paul von Hindenburg asked the former corporal to head a new government. That night the city exploded with the raucous

---

* My records show, however, that I was somewhat uneasy about the turmoil in Germany. A lay sermon I gave on Rosh Hashanah in 1931 was shot through with pessimism, although it ended on an optimistic note: "The day will come when even the longest winter night will have its end and then will shine the sun of happiness and peace." I was just turning nineteen.

voices of storm troopers carrying torches through the darkened
streets.

"When Jewish blood spurts from our knives, things will go
twice as well," they chanted.

That night I was afraid and wondered why I had not gone far
away, to America.

That too passed, and I had to begin my exams. Hitler was ar-
ranging the March elections which brought him undisputed
power. The anti-Jewish decrees had not as yet been promulgated.
I was accepted as a candidate-in-law and entered the dreary
period of examination which lasted close to six months. It began
with a problem theme which we were mailed by registered post
and which we had to work up in six weeks. If the paper was accepted one was called for written and, in the end, for oral examinations.

Then came April first and the boycott of Jewish stores. The
first public laws restricting our activities came into effect. I was
twenty years old. I gave up all my gentile contacts and shut
myself away in the law library of the university. During the first
half-year of Hitler's rule I confined my thinking to the isolation of
my study cubicle. It was an escape, convenient and effective.
When I emerged, with my exams well in hand, I found that our
universe had drastically changed.

By Nazi decree my law career was now ended; Jews would no
longer be admitted to the internship necessary for admission to
the Bar. At twenty years of age, after a breezy and thoughtless
flirtation with law, I was a young man without a profession—
simply because I was a Jew. The Nazis separated me permanently from a world that for a while had appeared to accept me
for *what* I was rather than *who* I was. My athletic contacts were
severed and, except for my chess-playing worker friends, all
relationships with gentiles were at an end.

In retrospect it all seems like a dream. Why, now that the
Nazis were in power, did I not make immediate arrangements for
emigration?* I have no answer to the question except to admit
that I was emotionally half asleep, lulled into a sense of false
security by the gradualness of much of the Nazis' official anti-

* In those days the Nazis did not prevent us from leaving; on the contrary, they encouraged us to quit the country, although we could take no money with us. This free
emigration gave rise to the *canard* that Nazis and Zionists worked hand in glove.
Nothing, of course, was further from the truth; but in the early days the Nazis put no
obstacles in the way of Zionist efforts to get young German Jews to go to Palestine.

semitic program. Our ghetto was social and intellectual, not physical. We simply shifted our focus away from the Germany in which we had lived to an exclusively Jewish ambience: in theatre, in music, and in sports.

I was already a member of two major Jewish athletic organizations and now gave them the full attention which I had lavished on similar efforts elsewhere. I played soccer with Hakoah's first team, which met other Jewish formations from different cities and even from Vienna; and I played tennis at Bar Kochba, which had a set of good courts in the west end of the city. Instead of competing with Germans, we now played against Jews, but otherwise the tournaments were like any others: the enthusiasm, the desire to win, were no different. Just before I began my written tests I won the German-Jewish championship in tennis singles and, if memory serves me right, with my regular partner, Nathan Lieber, in doubles as well. We entered tournaments in various German cities as if the Nazis didn't exist. We were quartered with the finest Jewish families and had a wonderful time. It was a new make-believe world, we were half dead but thought we were alive, we believed that it would all blow over in time. Father often said, "The Germans are too cultured a people, their instincts are too good to let this madman stay in power for long." After all, our family had muddled through the last four hundred years in this country and we would do the same this time around.

The only thing I can say in explanation of my obtuseness is this—and admittedly it is very little: during those early years the Nazis themselves did not have any idea how far their anti-semitism would take them in the end. At that moment their textbook plans called for the disaffiliation of Jews from German economic life and the encouragement of their emigration. The fact that we were now effectively reduced to second-class citizens did not then hurt as much as one might think. The reason was simple: we had in truth never been first-class citizens and we knew it. The difference at that point was one of degree. A policy which previously had been practised clandestinely had now achieved official blessing.

But withal, I was a man without a job. What could I do? We briefly considered that I might continue my studies in England, but British law was utterly different and I would have had to begin all over again. Our family council agreed that a temporary holding action was called for, and I was encouraged to see whether I could obtain a doctorate in law from some German university. This would be useful even though I would not be allowed to article, and Jews were not yet barred by law from obtaining it. Berlin was considered out of the question, as its demands were too steep. The degree there was *Doctor iuris utriusque*, doctor of both German civil and Roman (church) law, and one had to know Latin as well as canon law and fulfil requirements which I did not feel I could handle. So I set off for Heidelberg where I was rejected by Professor Lewy (to whom as a Jewish professor I had turned for help) because I had once failed his course. I went to Erlangen where a doctorate was proverbially easy to obtain. But when they asked me whether I was an Aryan and the answer was no, I was summarily refused.

Crestfallen, I came back to Berlin and on a dare went back to the university. I had always enjoyed Professor Hans Lewald's classes in international law and I approached him (he was reputed to be partially Jewish) in the hope that I might be allowed to enter the program. He chose to overlook my lack of solid grounding in the discipline which was his specialty, and to my surprise accepted me without much fuss as a doctoral student. It was the only time during the Nazi period when I was treated better *because* I was a Jew. Professor Wolff agreed to be my co-sponsor, and with these two great names to protect me I plunged into a new round of studies. Jewish and half-Jewish professors were then still teaching; they were not dismissed until several years later.

The thesis which the professors approved was bound to shake the legal world: "The Nullity of Marriage in German and Swiss International Law." It dealt with the status of marriages that had been contracted by citizens of different countries. I took some extra courses, I studied Latin, I read day and night and after half a year I had produced a thesis. Lewald read it at once and after a few days returned it to me.

"Herr Plaut, you are proposing an unusual theory of law. I don't believe a court would accept it, but I will, because you show considerable—though I believe mistaken—ingenuity."

Wolff was not so kind; he rejected the thesis. I was crushed. Without Wolff's approval the whole effort had been for nought. I requested a private interview which was granted.

It must be understood that in the 1930s a student talking to his professor, except in a petitional sense, was a rarity. To argue with a professor was simply out of the question, and to argue with Martin Wolff would be to defy the best legal mind in Germany. But I was desperate and actually challenged the great man's opinion. I defended my thesis with vim and more than a pinch of nerve. In retrospect I rather think it was the first time that Wolff had ever been spoken to in this fashion by a mere student, who by definition belonged to the lower orders of mankind. He sat hunched up in a huge chair in his study and said to me: "Herr Plaut, I don't buy a single word of what you say and I stand by my previous judgement. Your argument is worthless. But your persistence and nerve are admirable—I will close both my eyes and let your thesis pass."

I felt like kissing him, but there were limits even to my *chutzpah*.

I do not remember how I got past my written exams, especially in church law which required the handling of Latin sources. I must have guessed with remarkable success. In any case I finished and by July of 1934, some seven months after I had begun my program, I had achieved the unlikely: at the university where no one in his right mind would take his legal doctorate, I had come to the oral examinations. My thesis was printed (at my parents' expense, of course) and, following old-fashioned custom, my oral theses were posted on the bulletin board of the law school. My friends Heinz Frank and Bruno Sommerfeld agreed to be my disputants and were well rehearsed in advance. This part of the proceedings was pure formality, a left-over from mediaeval practice.

On July 24 I was called in for the examinations. Members of the faculty attired in purple robes sat forbiddingly on a high rostrum and the little candidate stood trembling below. The disputation proceeded as we had rehearsed and the orals themselves went by without a major incident. I was afraid of one of the professors, a declared member of the Nazi Party, but for some reason he never asked a single question. Perhaps he did not deign to address the little Jew before him. The august professors then retired and returned shortly thereafter, and Chancellor Ernst Heymann made the formal announcement. I had passed. The bedell handed me the doctoral book for signature. I noticed that I was number 588, in a school that was then 124 years old.

My parents were not present that day, they were on holidays taking the baths at Bad Kissingen. I informed them and received a postal card in return, addressed to "Herr Doktor Günter Plaut". It was my first piece of mail bearing the cherished title. I have it yet.

# New Visions

I now had a doctorate in addition to my law degree, but my situation had worsened. Precious months had gone by and I was right where I had been before: a young man with no prospect of making a living and no discernible future.

When my parents returned to Berlin we discussed the situation endlessly. One day Father took me into his office and made me a proposition which was to change my life permanently.

"You know," he said, "I still believe that the Nazi idiocy will soon come to an end. I still believe that we have a future in this country. So the thing to do is to wait it out and do so in the most intelligent and constructive fashion. Some day you'll be back in law and then you'll pursue a career as a judge or a lawyer or a diplomat." (Poor dreamer! He was serious and I was not clever enough to disagree with him.)

"So, Dad?"

"While you are waiting, why don't you increase your knowledge of Judaism? After all, we are persecuted because we are Jews, so why not find out what it really means to be a Jew? I mean in depth, not just going to services and celebrating the Holy Days and associating with Jews. Why don't you go to the Hochschule?"

He was referring to the rabbinical seminary of which Rabbi Leo Baeck was president.

"But Dad," I said, "I don't have the Hebrew knowledge to go there. I know prayer-book Hebrew by rote only: I can't translate much, I've no vocabulary and I know absolutely no grammar. How could I possibly take a course at the Hochschule?"

"I've thought of that," he said. "The thing to do is get you a tutor who will prepare you so you can enter in the fall. In fact," he added with a dry smile, "I have contacted a young man who needs the money, a student at the university who comes from Warsaw and is reputed to be a fine Hebraist."

As usual my father had not only made a proposition, he had already, in anticipation of my agreement, taken the necessary steps to implement it.

"He will come tomorrow. I hope you like him. And if you agree this should be the course of action for the next few months, let us see how it goes. Any learning you acquire at the Hochschule will be a permanent benefit."

What was I to say? Under the circumstances it all seemed very reasonable and the idea that I should study Hebrew and take courses at the Hochschule was not at all unattractive. I was good in languages and rather looked forward to tackling this latest challenge. It was another way to shut out the bitter realities of our shrinking universe, and retreat into a domain that had not been touched by the Nazis.

The next day a dark, slender young man appeared, with an unruly mass of black hair crowning a high forehead. He bowed formally from the waist.

"My name," he said, "is Abraham Joshua Heschel, and I am here to help you to learn Hebrew."

In this manner began my relationship with the future great philosopher. He was a good teacher, a few years older than I and very patient. I knew even less than I had thought. When a few months later I began taking courses at the Hochschule I was still totally at sea. Lessons which took others an hour to prepare took me a day. But, as with all matters of the mind, I was persistent. I began to acquire the fundamentals, though I had a long way to go.

The school was located in an old building near the centre of town. We arrived there for early morning worship, then had a dry *Brötchen* and a cup of watery cocoa, and were ready to attend our first class at eight a.m. I had chosen to take Baeck's course in homiletics, the art of preaching—although I had no intention of becoming a rabbi. I was there to learn, and the fame of Leo Baeck was such that merely to sit in his class and listen to him was considered a privilege.

I remember little of those days, but I do remember a few of Baeck's instructions.

"The length of sermons, gentlemen. A sermon that is short and good is excellent. A sermon that is long and good is still good. A sermon that is short and bad is also good." It was one of his many quips—and coming from one who was notoriously lengthy in his disquisitions it had an odd emphasis. Or this:

"When you quote the Bible, gentlemen, do not enlarge your quotation with your own encomia. Do not say, 'As Amos said so brilliantly,' or 'As Isaiah said with such insight'. Just quote the Bible. Let it stand by itself; it does not need your praise." This latter instruction has stayed with me all my life.

I studied history and Talmud with Ismar Elbogen, a small man of enormous learning and quick, often devastating wit. After Sabbath morning services some of us would walk for three

quarters of an hour across Berlin to make *Kiddush* at his home.
Up to this point I had ridden on the Sabbath, but once I entered
the Hochschule I followed the rules and did not use a vehicle.

I took a Talmud class with Chanoch Albeck but understood
little. I could relate better to his brother who was the cantor at
the Rykestrasse synagogue. I still remember that handsome man
with his flowing, black beard as he held up the Torah high above
his head when it was being returned to the ark. It was a thrilling
moment and we jumped to our feet when he intoned the *v'zot ha-
torah** with a sonorous voice.

The law graduate was now enrolled as a full-fledged student of
the Hochschule (the name was shortly thereafter changed to
Lehranstalt, "Learning Institution"—a change demanded by the
Nazis who did not want a Jewish school to bear the impressive
name of Hochschule). I was assigned to be a student preacher at
communal youth services and somewhat later at adult services in
the outlying districts. I still have the full texts of some sermons I
preached in those days at the "mature" age of twenty or twenty-
one. After the Nazis came to power I said on Yom Kippur, "We
cannot make others like us, but we can and must come to terms
with ourselves."

A year later I preached on Jacob and Edom. Edom is another
name for Esau and in later Jewish literature came to stand for
the Romans and then other enemies. In using this term I came as
near to attacking Nazis publicly as I dared.

"It is easier to rule men by force than to rule their hearts. It is
easier to succeed by violence than by the spirit. . . . Each generation stands anew against Edom to assert its right. . . . We must
never cease to struggle, never cease to hope." And I quoted the
Torah (Gen. 12:3): "Those who bless you I will bless, and curse
him who curses you."

As the Nazi clamps tightened, Jews began to gather in their
houses of worship. If previously these had been attended in-
differently, now attendances swelled. At the Friedenstempel,
Joachim Prinz attracted crowds in huge numbers, and other
synagogues too were now well filled on the Sabbath. Even when
I, the unlearned young student, conducted services and preached
I was assured of an audience. Amongst the many things I now
wonder at is the naturalness with which I accepted my role and
the nerve that I had to bring it off. Father used to read my drafts

---

* "This is the Torch which Moses placed before Israel. . . ."

and make some suggestions, but the main effort was mine. I learned far more than my listeners. For the first time in my life I gave serious thought to the future of my people.

I began to develop a missionary spirit. Through my tennis activities I had become associated with the Jewish social set at the west end of town. I met young men and women of my own age who represented a world fundamentally different from mine. They drove automobiles, they went abroad on vacations, their parents were well-to-do and their Jewishness had all but evaporated. Now the Nazis brought them face to face with their identity and they were prey for my new-found zeal. I organized classes amongst my tennis friends and twice a week we came together for an evening of study and sociability. I began to date girls from this crowd and was dazzled by the sudden popularity I enjoyed. Nothing in my previous education had prepared me for being sought after by young, attractive women.

My parents were not at all sure that my new associations were for the best. These people were unknown to them. They represented another universe where money and success had an importance which in our circles was discounted.

"Be careful," Father said. "You're not in their league."

In the past I might not have been, but the time had come when all of us were in one league, whether we liked to admit it or not. The Röhm purge had strengthened Hitler's hand;* tyranny now rampaged open and unabashed, the rule of law was crumbling. Still we hoped against hope that it would all end soon.

We were living in ever tighter isolation, separated from the world at large and lulled into a false sense of security because our restrictions were bearable (so we thought) and outright violence was still at a minimum. Strange as it may seem in retrospect, within the limitations of the invisible ghetto my life was quite pleasant. I had branched out into the upper levels of society, functioning as a sort of guru for young Jewish men and women from wealthy homes; I was a well-known athlete, a sometime preacher, a student of Judaica, and a Zionist—an odd combination which apparently attracted this particular layer of society to me.

I became infatuated with a girl whose father was even then one of German's better-known business tycoons, but neither her

---

* Ernst Röhm had organized Hitler's Storm Troops and when he was perceived as too powerful a rival he was shot on Hitler's orders.

family nor mine was fond of the relationship which, however, was at all times little more than platonic. Her family felt moved to forbid her to phone me or receive calls from me. When this did not work they removed her for some months to a foreign country. In time her ardour cooled and it was she who one day unceremoniously broke off the affair. We never saw each other again. I heard later that she had gone to England and married there.

In the spring of 1935 I joined my fellow Jewish athletes on a trip to Palestine to participate in the second Jewish Olympic Games, known as Maccabiah. Athletes from all over the world would participate. Plans to hold a similar festival the previous year in Cernauti, Roumania, had been aborted but competitions in Tel Aviv and Haifa appeared to be well in hand for this year.

There was much talk in our group about staying on in Palestine after—which was of course contrary to the rules of the mandatory power which provided that only a limited number of Jews could legally immigrate. It was contrary also to the promise which we had to make prior to going. As the trip drew closer I tried to analyse where I stood, and discovered that my Zionism was primarily of the intellectual kind. It had not moved me to a will towards settling in the land. I was by that time chairman of the educational committee for the Youth Division of the Zionist Organization and did a very poor job of it. I did not have the faintest notion how one went about creating committees or stimulating other people. I had much to learn—especially in the personal realm. I had disregarded my cousin Leo's warning and, buoyed by success in school and sports, had developed what must have been an insufferable edge of arrogance. Except for Heinz, I had no real friends to speak of—though it was now different with the opposite sex: there I was now as successful as I was unsuccessful with my male peers. I was talented in many ways, yet my self-image was an unhappy concoction of conceit and insecurity. I was socially and emotionally immature and unfortunately did not know it.

Mother went along to Palestine. Her younger sister Ada lived in Rishon le-Zion. She was married to Adolf Rosenberg, a lawyer of total integrity and fine aesthetic impulses. (His sister Anne was married to Rabbi Hugo Hahn of Essen, later New York; she was killed when an El Al airliner was shot down over the Ploiesti oilfields in Bulgaria some fifteen years later.)

If I recollect correctly, we were about two hundred athletes from the German Maccabi (the Jewish sports federation). I was the number two man on the tennis squad and was also registered for the soccer team (although a conflict of schedules prevented my playing on the latter). We took the train from Munich to Trieste where we boarded the *Roma*. The team was in tourist class and had to be satisfied with a fairly spartan routine of exercise and controlled meals, but Mother had a first-class ticket and from time to time I would get by the guards and savour the wonders of first-class travel, which in those days was nothing short of extravagant. On the trip I met one of Germany's best-known sports-figures, Martel Jacob, who in pre-Nazi days had been the German javelin champion. We became good friends and kept up our contact for many years thereafter.

Also among the passengers was Martin Buber. He held some informal teaching sessions on board, and one of his comments has remained with me. As we approached Haifa he pointed to the starry sky and said, "Nowhere else in the world are the heavens as close to earth as here in the Land of Promise." He himself had not yet left Germany permanently; he settled in Jerusalem three years later.

We docked in Haifa late in the afternoon and transferred our considerable gear to a train bound for Tel Aviv, where most of the competitions were to be held. We traversed a landscape that was glaringly empty and the ride seemed very long.

We arrived in Tel Aviv at two o'clock in the morning. We disembarked at a siding and looked for ways of getting to our various destinations. Needless to say, taxis were not in evidence. I was to room with Franz Kehr, the son of one of my mother's friends, and asked one of the station personnel how I might get there. The man looked at me quizzically.

"You have no feet?"

"It is not far then?"

"Not far."

"How far?"

A shrug of the shoulders.

"Ten minutes, twenty minutes?"

Another shrug. "Maybe, it depends."

"But what shall I do with my gear? I can't carry all this stuff."

"Who asked you to carry it?"

"So where would I leave it?"

"What's wrong with the place where it is now? The rains are over. It won't get wet."

"And security?"

"Listen, *habibi*, you are now in Eretz Yisrael. We have no thieves in this country."

Apparently all my friends must have received the same advice from whomever they asked. We left our suitcases and other equipment by the siding and tried to find our quarters. It must have been four o'clock in the morning before I arrived at my friend's address. The door to the apartment house, which in Germany would have been securely locked, was wide open, and when I came to the second floor where Franz lived I found his own door equally unguarded. I was warmly welcomed and installed on the couch where I must have slept for twelve hours. When I awoke I immediately inquired about my valises.

"Don't worry," said Franz as if he had talked to the man at the station. "Who would take anybody else's stuff?"

He calmed my fears and I did not retrieve my belongings until the next day. They were in fine shape and there were still dozens of other valises standing around, mute witnesses to a country of new social and ethical adventures.

The opening of the games was exciting. It was preceded by a march through the streets of Tel Aviv, each national unit decked out in its own specially designed uniforms. Then followed an assembly at the new stadium which was jammed with spectators. Here were Jews from many countries, all competing in the land of their fathers. As we stood at attention under the clear blue skies the wonder of it suddenly overcame me. I had not yet seen the land, and I was anxious to experience its presence.

The results of my athletic efforts were disappointing. I could not adjust to the conditions of the courts. They were a light grey, surrounded by white stucco buildings, and we played with white balls and, of course, were dressed in white—in the glaring light of Tel Aviv I could see nothing. Also, in the heat of the day the balls bounced quite differently from what I was accustomed to. We managed to squeak past the first round against Syria (in those days there was a Syrian Maccabi which sent its representatives!), but thereafter it was a walk-away for the South African team who had been in the country for two weeks and who, I suspect, also had the best players.

After the games Mother and I travelled around the country. It was a poor land. The sand of the desert was always encroaching on the soil that had been reclaimed with so much sweat. But it was a land filled with extraordinary people, idealists, men and women of a new era who worked for each other and for the future; whose labour had goals that reached beyond themselves. I do not know what would have happened had our plans called for another four weeks in the country. I think I might have stayed. I was beginning to understand just what it meant to live on a kibbutz, what it meant to think not primarily of oneself. What would have become of me had I remained there? My schoolmate Georg (Giora) Josephthal joined a kibbutz and later became one of Israel's most prominent political figures, a Cabinet member and, until his untimely death, a potential Prime Minister. Would my career have been similar to that of Giora?

But we made the trip back—that now unbelievable journey from a free Palestine into the prison of Nazi Germany—and voluntarily so! Hindsight is a great distorter of reality. The fact is that we did what then still seemed reasonable, for we still lived under the illusion that Hitler was doomed and his regime temporary. How else can I explain this journey back? Worse, it was not to be my last demonstration of restricted vision.

It was after Passover when we returned to Berlin and I went back to the seminary. On the first day Dr. Baeck called me to his office.

"I have here," he said, "a letter from Cincinnati. You know that is where the American Reform Seminary is located. I have been there, it is a splendid place. President Julian Morgenstern writes that Hebrew Union College has invited five of our students and offered them scholarships to complete their course of study there. I think you would make a good candidate."

I knew at once that I wanted to go. The moment I had come back to Germany I had felt in my bones that I had made a mistake. I informed my parents of the latest development. I had their reluctant agreement but with one understanding: that I would stay no more than two years. That was to be the limit. Walter was now in a Jewish school and finding his own level, but he needed a brother and my parents would want me back. I agreed.

To get a student visa for the United States was easy, and the Nazis too were "cooperative", in their way. They wanted the Jews out of the country and allowed them to take anything with them except jewelry and money. My parents bought me a ticket on the *Aquitania* which was to sail from Le Havre at the beginning of September. Father made sure that it was a return ticket. I think I still remember the price, which included the railroad fare to Le Havre and one night's stay in Paris, plus railroad fare from

New York to Cincinnati and return: just $148.00. I took a few books and became acquainted with my co-travellers: Wolli Kaelter, son of the rabbi in Danzig; Herman Schaalman, son of a high-school mathematics teacher from Munich; Alfred Wolf, who hailed from a small town near Heidelberg; and Leo Lichtenberg, who like me came from Berlin. Four of us knew some English, but Leo, who had a classical education, would arrive in the United States without knowing a single word of its language.

We knew little about Hebrew Union College and expected that the education we had received in Berlin would be more than adequate to meet all requirements. We further assumed that the College would be religiously comparable to the Berlin institution. In both these respects we were in gross error.

I checked with our precinct police, who were Social Democrats and unfailingly helpful and friendly. They handed me my exit permit.

"Come back," they said. "We'd like you back."

I said I would return. They meant it and so did I.

# Chapter 2

# ALICE IN WONDERLAND

THE *AQUITANIA* WAS A BOAT OF the old and well-tested type: spacious, with enough facilities even in tourist class to make a crossing pleasant. For the first time I had an opportunity to reflect on where I was and what I was about to do.

I was now going to be a full-time student at a rabbinical seminary. Did this mean that I would be a rabbi? The question had, of course, occurred to me, but I had avoided facing its implications. I was by nature a doer rather than a thinker. Although I could address myself successfully to specific problems, philosophy, theology and deeper questions of faith had not, up to then, been my strong points. Most certainly I was not "called" to be a spiritual leader. Only a few years before, the rabbinate had been furthest from my mind. Lawyer, judge or career diplomat—these described the content of my professional dreams. But Hitler had changed my course of life. Clearly I was adrift; events—or was it "fate"?—had now brought me to a fresh beginning.

What did I believe? I can no longer clearly reconstruct it. Overlaid with the encrustations of time, my thoughts of that period are no longer accessible. To be sure, I have texts and notes of sermons I preached as a student in Germany, but they are not conclusive because they deal with accepted and expected generalities. I think it is accurate to say that I was committed to being Jewish and to doing something about it. The rest would have to follow. My morning and evening prayers were said silently and, especially in the evening, I abandoned the prayer-

49

book text. Although I was bound for Hebrew Union College, I
made up my mind that I would try to enter law school as well, if
that was feasible. Much would depend on how quickly I could
breeze through my rabbinical courses—as I, with my imagined
European superiority of knowledge, was surely bound to do.
There was a lot I did not know about the New World.

To begin with, my English was in ragged shape. My grammar
was good and my basic vocabulary not bad, and I could read un-
complicated texts with fair comprehension, but my ability to
speak and my understanding of the spoken word were poor. On
the boat we ate in the kosher section and we were seated at a
large, round dining-room table. A man with a yellow sweater
repeatedly rose during the meal, leaning forward in my direction
and appearing to make a German-type bow, and said something
in English. At last I too rose, bowed in return and responded,
"My name is Plaut." There was laughter from his friends. Only
afterwards did I understand its cause: he had been asking me to
pass him the salt and pepper.

My two main recollections from the trip are the seasickness
which both my cabin-mate, Wolli Kaelter, and I sustained, and
meeting Beatrice Rothaus, a law student from Brooklyn. An intense young lady, she took an interest in our group. She had just
come back from a tour of the Soviet Union and held distinctly
leftist views which, however, she did not try to impose on us. She
spent a good deal of time with us introducing us to American
ways and teaching me how to dance. One can learn a great deal
in eight days.

On the fifteenth of September, 1935, the Statue of Liberty came
into view. Whatever sentimentalists may claim about its impact
is but a fraction of what it means to the confused new arrival
who faces a world he does not understand. Somehow the lady
calms one's anxieties, and the unspoken promise—I did not yet
know the words written by Emma Lazarus—was real. She was
shrouded a bit in the morning fog but her hand lifted high was
clearly in view. I suddenly felt that America might mean more to
me than a place for study.

Of all the impressions, overwhelming as they were in their ac-
cumulated assault on me, one stands out. It was on an elevated
train in New York where a man across from me was reading a
newspaper. He then folded it casually, put it aside and prepared
to get off at the next station. As he was walking to the exit it was
clear to me that he had forgotten his paper, and I ran after him to

return it. He looked at me with astonishment. It was obvious to him and the other passengers that I was a greenhorn. He laughed and left the train, while I stood holding the unwanted newspaper. This was my introduction to the world of waste and obsolescence. I had never seen anyone discarding a newspaper in this fashion, for papers in Germany had their uses long after they were read: they served as wrapping material and lining for shoes and windows in cold weather; they were used as toilet paper, and finally they provided added kindling for the stove. Yet here the man had thrown his paper away disdaining its continuing value—and this at a time when America was still in the throes of depression. Though soup-lines were no longer in evidence, poor people were, and lots of unemployed roamed the streets. Beggars were frequently stationed at the subway entrances. Veterans of the last war were sitting on the sidewalk playing harmonicas, with their caps spread next to them, inviting the charitable to share their wealth. How then could anyone throw something away?

We arrived in Cincinnati early in the morning, in the city's old and spacious Union Station. Nelson Glueck, Professor of Bible and future world-famed archaeologist, was there to greet us. So were reporters from the local newspapers. We were the first refugees to arrive in town and we were news. We said little that was worth printing. We could not tell the truth, so we thought, for fear that our families might suffer grievously. We were afraid, and the reporters were disappointed. Thus ended our first meeting with American freedom: in our failure to use it.

It is easy, in retrospect, to hold such fear in contempt. But it was the time of the Nuremberg laws, which brought the Jews of Germany to a new low. They were deprived of their citizenship and designated "subjects of the state", and were forbidden to enter into marriage or engage in sexual relations with Germans; their children were dispersed, and the diminishing remnant was gripped by fear. Were we now, in the safety of America, to add to their woes?

Dr. Glueck spoke perfect German. He had received his Ph.D. at the University of Jena, and such a background, as we were to find out, was common amongst the professors at the college. With one or two exceptions, all had taken their graduate education in Germany, then the centre of modern Jewish studies. In those days you needed two languages to become a Jewish scholar: Hebrew and German. One could not do without either.

We were taken to Dr. Glueck's home, where his wife Helen had prepared a steaming hot breakfast for us. We were famished. Alas, we were served bacon and eggs—and despite our distressed condition I managed to speak for the group.

"Thank you very much, but we are not hungry. We have already eaten."

I must have sounded desperately unconvincing, for the Gluecks got the message. A new batch of eggs was prepared, without the bacon, and this time we managed to do justice to the offering.

## Student Days at H.U.C.

The campus of the college seemed unreal in its splendour and extravagance. Built in the 1920s by the munificence of Adolph Ochs, publisher of the *New York Times*, it was located conveniently across from the University of Cincinnati. Compared with the modest structure which housed the Hochschule in its somewhat squalid surroundings in Berlin, Hebrew Union College appeared as a series of castles set in spacious grounds; it reflected the opulence of America during the days of roaring self-indulgence. Designed in traditional style with heavy features, it also bespoke solidity. In those days the present Administration Building housed all the classrooms; there were also a dormitory, gift of the Sisterhoods of the Reform congregations in America and Canada, a library, a museum and—*mirabile dictu*—a gymnasium and swimming pool and two outdoor tennis courts. The courts have since disappeared, having given way to more intellectual usage, but for me they were the crown of an institution which I was bound to like. As it turned out, I was somewhat disappointed; there were few rabbinical students who had heard of tennis, let alone played the game acceptably. It was then still an upper-class sport and the designers had probably thought it a good idea to include such facilities for the training of gentlemen. After all, Reform rabbis were primarily serving the upper strata of Jewish society.

If the tennis courts did not receive much play, they were the subject of at least one memorable story told about Professor Jacob Zallel Lauterbach, who taught Talmud and Jewish folklore. One day, it was his task to conduct a Christian scholar around the campus, and when they passed the tennis courts the visitor saw the sign which was prominently posted on the fence:

```
┌─────────────────────────────────────┐
│          STUDENTS ONLY              │
│      NO VISITORS ALLOWED            │
└─────────────────────────────────────┘
```

"Where is your religious spirit?" twitted the visitor. "Why would you be so uncharitable as to exclude others and permit the use of the courts only by the students?"

"Ah," quoth Dr. Lauterbach, "you forget that this is an institution at which Talmud is being studied. You see, the text of a Talmud page is printed without any punctuation. The reader has to supply it in accordance with the sense. You did not read the sign properly. It is to be interpreted as follows:

```
┌─────────────────────────────────────┐
│          STUDENTS ONLY?             │
│      NO! VISITORS ALLOWED!          │
└─────────────────────────────────────┘
```

The president (who died in 1976, well into his nineties) was Julian Morgenstern. In his younger years he had been a splendid athlete (he had played football for the University of Cincinnati) and, in fact, my first meeting with him had to do with his athletic habits. Someone showed me the fabulous gymnasium. As we entered the pool area we saw a man ready to perform a head-stand jump. It was customary not to wear bathing suits in the pool, since this was an all-male preserve.

"There," said my companion, pointing to the stocky figure of a bald, middle-aged individual in the upside-down position, "is the president of the college."

That is how I met him a few moments later. Naked and wringing wet, he shook my hand without embarrassment. It was another of those cultural shocks which was to last me for quite a while.

I was assigned a room on the first floor of the dormitory, not far from the common washing facilities. The room had all the requirements then thought necessary for us: an army-type bed, a desk and chair, an easy chair and a bookcase. Best of all, my window overlooked the western reaches of town and brought me spectacular sunsets and a sense of space that I had never known. It would turn out to be a good place to study and to be alone.

But all of that was still in the future on that first day when we inspected the facilities and met the matron, Lilian Waldman.*

---

* Later the wife of Rabbi Morris Lieberman.

She was warm and courteous and immediately gained our confidence and soon our affection. There were no other students present at the time—it was shortly before the High Holy Days—and the dining room was opened just for us. That too was, for us at least, an aspect of unknown luxury: to sit down and be served rich and varied meals. "Service for gentlemen" was obviously the rule that had guided the founders and donors.

We did not have to make up our rooms (daily service was supplied) and we did not have to worry about our laundry. There were no fees to be paid by any students: everything, including tuition, was free in accordance with the ancient custom of taking the burdens of livelihood off the shoulders of aspiring scholars. It had been true in Europe even in the poorest *shtetl*, and the spirit of caring for scholars was transplanted to the New World. Hebrew Union College was set apart from the world, a school for students and gentlemen. If we could not be one, at least we would be the other. In this respect the school was hardly ever a total failure and more often than not it was a resounding success.

If the first day had been overwhelming for us, the next day was to exceed it in impact. We were to be guided to the synagogue for Sabbath morning worship, and were told to be ready at an appropriate hour. Attired in our Sabbath best, which then consisted of suits with broad shoulders and narrow waists and large broad-brimmed hats, we stood at the dormitory doors ready for our first encounter with an American synagogue.

After a while an automobile drove up. From it alighted a shapely blonde with skirts abbreviated in the fashion of the day. She was our age, perhaps a few years older. "I am," she said, "Sally Cohen. My husband is Rabbi Mort Cohen and I am here to drive you to temple."

Ah America, what a great, marvellous and frightening land you are! How many surprises you harbour! I had seen rabbis' wives before, but none of them looked even remotely like Sally. Furthermore, I did not know a single rabbi who owned a car, let alone a rebbitzin who would drive one. Last but not least, this was the Sabbath and none of us rode on the day of rest. Whatever our own background, it was simply not done at the Hochschule.

Sally discerned our embarrassment. "When in Rome do as the Romans do," she quoted—and what was there left for us but to follow her? She drove us to a magnificent structure on Rockdale Avenue, the home of Cincinnati's oldest congregation, founded in

1824 by English immigrants. The synagogue was large though simple, and at first sight not unlike the buildings to which we were used.

An usher took us all the way up to the front and there we sat somewhat inattentive to our surroundings. It was obvious that it was a Liberal synagogue, for men and women were seated together. Also, attendance was sharply different from what it was in Germany, where the houses of worship were jammed with people to whom the synagogue had become the centre of their constricted lives, their place of hope and community, their place of instruction and spiritual security. Not here. The large hall was nearly empty, peopled by only a few—mostly elderly men and women.

The books we were given were unlike any prayer-books we had ever seen. They were mostly in English, quite thin, and opened from left to right. There was a good choir and I judged that one of the two black-robed men seated on the *beema* was a cantor. It turned out, however, that he didn't sing at all—and later I found out he was the assistant rabbi. The senior man in charge was a silver-haired gentleman who, I would learn, was the famous Rabbi David Philipson, a member of the first graduating class of Hebrew Union College in 1888. While I noticed that he did not wear a prayer-shawl I did not see that his head covering too was absent. The service was strange, and with our lack of English and the minimal use of Hebrew by the congregation it was a difficult though not devastating experience. We were simply overcome by the newness of it all, and I remember far more of what came afterwards than of what happened during this first American service.

At its conclusion we went to wish the rabbi a "Good Shabbes", as was our custom. Dr. Philipson glowered at us and unceremoniously lectured us in stentorian tones, well within the hearing of other congregants who stood about.

"So you are the new arrivals from Germany," he said. "The first thing you have to learn is manners. In our temple we have long given up the wearing of hats. If you ever appear here again with those things on your heads I will have you physically removed."

I am reconstructing his speech to the best of my memory. My English was not secure enough to record it precisely, though I understood enough to catch both his tone and his stern warning.

I have no idea why Philipson should have allowed himself this outburst. He was an intelligent man of some learning and could speak flawless German. (In his first pulpit in Baltimore his contract had provided that one Sabbath a month he had to preach in German.) He knew that we were newcomers and refugees, and ordinarily would have inquired after our welfare.* Perhaps his reaction came from some premonition of the changes ahead. The five of us would bring a different spirit to the college and—it can be stated with due immodesty—would have a significant influence on the Reform movement itself. Philipson was then the chief exponent of its classical expression: a movement which attempted to wed American and Jewish ideals, which stressed the prophetic rather than the ritual and embraced assimilation, up to a point, as both desirable and necessary. We five must have appeared to him as the antithesis of his ideals. We all spoke English with a heavy accent, except for Leo who had no accent because he knew no English at all. We represented the Old World from which Philipson's branch of Judaism had tried to escape as far as possible. That we were also refugees from Hitler did not, it appeared at that time, rank high on his list of recognitions.

The other rabbi, Victor Reichert, did not say a word. Apparently it was his custom not to speak in the presence of the master, which was an attitude well familiar to us. But when it was his turn to greet us he was cordial and inquired where we had come from, what our background was, and he expressed the hope that we would come again—"properly attired of course," he said with a bow in Dr. Philipson's direction.

We did not respond. I swore to myself that I would never set foot in Rockdale Temple again as long as Dr. Philipson was the rabbi. It was an oath I had no difficulty keeping.

We had our placement tests to determine how we would fit into the structure of the school. At the time there was a lower and an upper level, each one of four years' duration. Some of the students would come directly from high school and obtain their BA degrees at the University of Cincinnati, while at the same time receiving Bachelor of Hebrew (BHL) degrees at the end of the first four years at HUC. The second half of their studies would then be graduate work leading to their rabbinical degrees. Increasingly,

---

* Wolli Kaelter recollected in 1979 that Philipson ended his warning by saying, "When in Rome do as the Romans do. After all, you would take off your hats in church." Whereupon I responded, "I am sorry, I did not know this was like a church." I have some doubts that I would have had the nerve to say it. But Wolli is certain I had.

however, students would come after receiving their under-graduate training elsewhere. Even so, they would usually spend at least five or six years at Hebrew Union College, depending on their previous Judaic preparation. We had no idea how the professors would evaluate our secular training. What was the equivalent of a German high-school degree?

The teachers were very kind to us. I was asked to translate a portion of Genesis and failed quite badly. The examiners blamed it on my sparse knowledge of English and suggested that I translate the text into German. I was equally incapable of performing—so they put it all down to nervousness and difficulty of adjustment, and determined that I should be entered at once into the graduate department to spend four years getting my rabbinical degree—if I could stay that long. The other four did not fare that well; they were sentenced to five or even six years.

The school opened after the Holy Days and the dormitory came alive with some sixty new and old students—about half of its capacity. Rabbinical jobs were scarce during the Depression; our original invitation to the seminary had expressly indicated that we could get an education there but should not expect any job placement. Congregations which yesterday had flourished were today on the brink of bankruptcy, and many of them were getting along without a permanent rabbi, satisfied to import a student every two weeks.

Bankruptcy was a concept the five of us could well understand. We were without any funds and were each given twenty dollars as a loan to be repaid when we left the college. I guarded this capital sum with the utmost care. When the boys suggested that we go down to the corner to have a Coke (five cents at that time) I would pretend preoccupation with studies. When someone hinted that it was time for me to get a haircut (a twenty-five cent expenditure) I would say that I liked the longer style.

In the Bible the Israelites are warned repeatedly to take care of the stranger: "You know the soul of the stranger for you yourselves were strangers in the land of Egypt." Unfortunately students and teachers—with notable exceptions—did not understand the meaning of this injunction. We were rootless and needed roots. We needed anchors in a strange sea. We relied on each other and retreated into the warmth of our own company where we found shared memories in a language all of us could speak. The teachers who had been educated in Germany—and they were the majority—called me "Dr." Plaut, as was the custom in the old country. For me, it was a small but important measure of the identity which I had brought with me, a recognition that I had a past. My fellow students did not appreciate the title and made fun of it.

I was a greenhorn and not a very likable one. I must have fitted the general stereotype of German Jews: arrogant know-it-alls who were not properly grateful for the marvellous opportunity afforded them in the New World, and who did not fully appreciate that they had been saved from the Nazi scourge. Objectively the judgement was accurate, but it was pronounced in a vacuum. It did not take into consideration the desperate need of a newcomer to find a place on which he could stand. My background, so important in Germany, accounted for nothing over here, my education for little. My reputation as an athlete was worthless. I was a new boy who pretended to know much, but in fact knew little that was of any account in my new environment. I was a greenhorn of greenhorns.

The dormitory lounge was known as the "Bumming Room". It had some couches, a piano and a table on which the *Cincinnati Enquirer* was placed in the morning and the *Post* in the afternoon. Cincinnati was a baseball town then no less than now, and baseball news frequently made front-page headlines. One morning when I came down for breakfast the front page was partially torn away. Only the blaring headline was still visible:

REDS MURDER CARDINALS

"My God!" I exclaimed. "The revolution has come to Italy."

Much later, after I had learned a great deal about the American national sport, the subtle but effective lesson I was given that morning in Cincinnati came back to me, and I have retold the story many times. It was a classic case of information presented without a proper context.

"Suppose," I have said on many a lecture platform, "that this little scrap of newspaper is discovered by archaeologists one thousand years hence, after some great upheaval has wiped out most vestiges of our civilization. Not knowing the context in which the headline was meant to be read, they will rewrite the history of the 1930s."

There was another bonus that this joke produced. In its way it was my cousin Leo speaking to me, and I now made an effort of serious proportions to act on his advice. But it was hard and I never succeeded as much as I wanted to. The scars of displacement were to be with me for many years to come.

## Strangers in Paradise

In later years I would come to see that Hebrew Union College had
saved our lives. But at the time—when we still thought the situation in Germany would soon be remedied—we were less aware
of the college as a saviour than of its strange and, to us, unaccustomed ways.

There was first of all the fact that head coverings were worn
at prayer only by the five of us. We quickly learned that they
were called yarmulkes (rather than *kippot*), a word then
unknown to us.* In time four of us would remove our yarmulkes;
Wolli Kaelter alone persisted and was ordained with it in place.
Today the tables are reversed: the one who is ordained without a
yarmulke has become the exception.

The yarmulke was only one sign of our differentness. Our
religious emotions fitted badly into the context of a highly rational environment where Zionism was officially frowned upon
and ethics—preferably universal ethics, whatever that meant—
reigned undisputed.

Our fellow students were at first somewhat leery of us. We
observed the custom of *benshing* (saying the blessings) after
meals and chanted in unison. The first time we did so many of the
students rose from their tables in disbelief and left the room jeer-
ing. It was a scene which deeply affected me. Why should anyone
be scornful of someone else's religious habits, especially if these
were grounded in many centuries of authentic Jewish tradition?
It would take me some time to understand: the resentment was
not against *benshing*, but against the attempt of five greenhorns
to impose their ways (so it was felt) on the student body. In this
particular case we were to be successful in rather short order:
within a year after our arrival *benshing* became the norm for
everyone and the melodies we introduced at the time are still in
use amongst the students today.

There was a small group of fellow students who were attracted to our fivesome, whose own religious inclinations were
touched by ours. Chief amongst these were Dudley Weinberg and
Lou Silberman. Dudley was one of the most sensitive and
beautiful human beings it has ever been my privilege to know. He
had a poetic soul, was highly musical, had great gifts of learning

* Its etymology was long in doubt. Twenty years later I wrote an article about it deriving it
from the Latin *armucella*; *Hebrew Union College Annual* 26 (1955), pp. 567-570.

and oratory and became a marvellous rabbi. He was, in many ways, like Jacob: one who wrestled with God and whose struggles led him into great agony of soul. He died, alas, long before he had reached the fullness of his years.

Lou was from an old California family, resident in the United States for several generations. He became so closely attached to us that he began to speak English with a German accent—much to the amusement of everyone. Lou was a thinker and scholar and later taught at Vanderbilt University, as one of the most distinguished graduates of HUC. His German accent is long gone but not, I hope, the memory of those days when he was part of a group of strangers in paradise. For in many ways paradise was the proper name for our college. It was an ivory tower religiously as well as socially. No depression was apparent here; looking back I can say objectively that we lived in the lap of luxury—without paying a single cent for the privilege.

We did pay some homage to certain social conditions in the outside world, especially the Spanish Civil War which was a matter of great concern, and one of our fellow students went to fight. We demonstrated and picketed the Dow Chemical plant. I had only the vaguest understanding of the issues which were involved, but at the time my social philosophy was very simple: the capitalists were more likely to be the source of evil and the workers its victims. The rich were seen as evil incarnate, the poor as the purveyors of good. I had previously read and studied Karl Marx's *Das Kapital* and held informal classes with fellow students on the text.

My innocence came to an end after a while. I participated in student activities at the University of Cincinnati and found myself on a committee for the planning of a large-scale demonstration. It was heady wine: until then I had always been a drone, distributing leaflets at street corners in Heidelberg or carrying picket signs. Suddenly I was on the inside and therefore took my responsibility seriously. My English was still very hesitant and faulty, but apparently the timbre of my voice as well as my apparent dedication convinced my fellow students that I should speak at the rally. I was greatly flattered and slightly scared—not of the social implications but of making a public speech in a language which was still largely a closed book to me.

However, this involvement with the activists was of relatively short duration. We had endless committee meetings and finally resolved how to handle the demonstration and the rally. It was then that a slightly older person, obviously past thirty, joined our committee, brushed aside everything we had determined and told us precisely where, when, and how we were to act. I was stunned and began making inquiries about this man to whom everyone else seemed to defer. It took me little time to find out that he was the representative of the Communist Party assigned to control us.

The whole thing became suddenly clear to me: I had been duped and used. I was to be part of a front organization, a pawn moved around by the Party apparatus. I left the activists in short order and never did speak at the rally. But I did not forget the lesson taught me at that early age. Communists were not my cup of tea, their methods were the very antithesis of what I believed. Henceforth, everything and anything that came out of Soviet Russia was suspect. I had many a heated discussion with fellow students but this was one point of view I never abandoned: democracy and communism were incompatible. When Stalin made a pact with Hitler a few years later, I was not surprised.

The number of arrivals from Germany began to increase, and towards the end of the first year of our stay at the college we formed an organization called the Gate Club, for German-Jewish immigrants. Its name betokened its objectives: it was to be a gateway to full integration into the new land. I became its first president. The Jewish Center provided us with facilities and we utilized them to the fullest, sponsoring programs of various kinds and providing the newcomers with an opportunity to meet members of the resident community. It was one enterprise which would reward me with the greatest of prizes: it was through the Gate Club that a few years afterwards I met my wife.

Because of the introductions provided by the Warburg–Hahn families (whose son I had instructed in Berlin) I was taken up by the "best" families in town. Dr. Friedlander, dean of the medical school, Alfred M. Cohen, international president of B'nai B'rith, Murray Seasongood, later the mayor of the community, were among the people who constituted "our crowd", the kind I had known in the old country. They had similar characteristics: they favoured frugality, lack of ostentation, and good manners; their Jewishness was affirmed proudly but not worn on their sleeves. I felt at ease in their company but at the same time I thought that they lacked a measure of unqualified emotional commitment to the Jewish people. This commitment I was to find in later years, in Cincinnati's East European community, after I had joined the

Labour Zionists and moved into a circle of attachment and conviction which was as far removed from the "Avondale crowd" (as the German Jews were referred to) as if they did not live in the same city. Both groups had their values and their shortcomings and both contributed greatly to my growing up in America.

At the end of the first year I had learned a good deal of English—from my courses at the university as well as from my fellow students—and had picked up a modicum of knowledge from my teachers at Hebrew Union College, although not as much as I should have received from these knowledgeable people. In Berlin my Jewish background had been insufficient for me to take full advantage of the seminary; in Cincinnati it was my inability to function fully in English, in addition to my slow adjustment to new circumstances, which was in the way. The bulk of whatever learning I acquired came from my studies long after I finished at Hebrew Union College. The college was my ticket to a new life and that was more than enough to elicit my permanent gratitude. I have frequently been critical of the school, its staff and its programs—but no matter, it is the institution which made it possible for me to begin a new existence in America.

My relationship to the teachers was good, but I was not close to any one of them. Some of them were unusual personalities and scholars of note. Of the latter, Jacob Mann was an authority in his field, Egyptian Jewry in the early Middle Ages. Unfortunately I could not understand his English. On the other hand, while Dr. Abraham Cronbach's pronunciation was utterly precise and easy to follow, his political philosophy escaped my comprehension. He was a total pacifist, he practised sexual abstinence (of which he spoke repeatedly in class) and preached social justice for everyone regardless of station or conviction. He was even said to have collected money for Nazis imprisoned in Austria by Chancellor Engelbert Dollfuss, but that may have been a rumour only.*

Nelson Glueck, that charismatic personality who had greeted us on our first day and would later succeed Morgenstern as president, was an irascible teacher of whom I was slightly afraid. It was said that on one occasion he had thrown the nearest book at a student—and the book had turned out to be a Bible. An apocryphal tale, most likely.

Morgenstern—called Morgy by the students—propounded

---

* Austrian Nazis subsequently murdered Dollfuss.

certain theories of biblical criticism that had no relationship to anything I had read or learned before, and I had grave difficulty with him. I also had problems in another course in biblical criticism, taught by that gentle and justly beloved teacher of teachers, Sheldon Blank. At one point he asked us to bring scissors and paste to rearrange a Hebrew text in accordance with critical theory. I could not get myself into a frame of mind which would permit me to cut up a biblical text; it was a desecration. I tried to explain my point of view to Dr. Blank. He did not try to change my mind but informed me that if I wanted to pass the course I would have to do what was required. I never did pass, yet somehow when I graduated this lacuna was overlooked or omitted on the records.

Jacob Rader Marcus, the great authority on American-Jewish history, taught a field which I liked at once. I got on well with him and his material, and he later employed me to search Russian-Hebrew magazines for certain types of references. It was my first paid job in America—at fifty cents an hour, ten hours a week, a veritable fortune.

Israel Bettan taught Midrash* and Zvi Diesendruck philosophy. Both had acerbic tongues and were impatient with the students. Theology was taught by Samuel ("Shimshi") Cohon, and like Mann he was hard to understand. He had a fund of knowledge but expended enormous amounts of time on pursuing his pet hatred: the teachings of Mordecai M. Kaplan, who had created the school of Reconstructionism and was then publishing his *Judaism as a Civilization*. The book was a target of many a barb by Cohon. The immediate result was that I read Kaplan's book from cover to cover and became a devoted follower of his. His integration of liberal theology, traditional practice and total commitment to the Jewish people had a great attraction for me.

I was forced to take a course with David Philipson who, as Dean of Reform Rabbis, taught the history and philosophy of the movement. Since our first unfortunate encounter I had tried to keep my distance from him, and as a matter of principle disbelieved everything he taught. This attitude had at least one measurable and beneficial result for me.

Philipson informed us that the first confirmation service in the New World had taken place at a certain time in St. Thomas, Virgin Islands, in the 1840s. He said that the first confirmation

---

* A body of ancient homiletical and legal interpretations of the Bible.

certificate had, in fact, been published and he gave us the reference.

That afternoon I was at the library to check on Philipson's instruction. To my delight I found that he might be wrong—the published certificate bore in the upper right-hand corner the number "14" from which I concluded that there might have been thirteen previous confirmations.

Deciding to spend some of my carefully guarded money, I wrote to the Governor of the Virgin Islands requesting him to forward my inquiry to the proper place. Could I have a copy of the earliest confirmation registered if it was still in existence? Some six weeks later I received an answer from the minister of the St. Thomas congregation. Yes, they still had the books. Yes, he had located the proper pages and was enclosing a copy.

My hunch had been right: there had been thirteen previous confirmations. Eventually I published the findings as an article in the *Hebrew Union College Annual*, a highly regarded scholarly magazine which ordinarily was not open to contributions from students. Philipson was quite gracious about the matter when I called the correction to his attention, and later on in his memoirs made note of the incident.

The article was published in 1939 but it was not my first appearance in print in America. Shortly after my arrival in 1935, the *H.U.C. Monthly*, a magazine published by the students, asked me to write about the Hochschule in Berlin and my first impressions of America.

In my summation I compared the student at the seminary in Berlin with what I found in Cincinnati. (The editor let my English stand as submitted.)

The HUC student is not only a Jew, he is also a product of his American milieu. In this respect he is more "worldly" than his Berlin colleague. Moreover, the German student lives today under conditions which make him still more earnest than he used to be. It is probably this special contrast which is most visible to one who compares these two types. The German student sees with his own eyes an important period of Jewish history. He feels himself responsible for the future of German Jewry. This responsibility lies on him and he cannot take things so easy as the American student can.

The difference between the HUC student and those of Berlin, therefore lies not only in their contrasting systems of education, but to a large extent in the present mental attitude of the German Jews.

After encountering the often fanciful theories of biblical criticism I followed this with an article criticizing the critics (who were my teachers at HUC) but did not have the nerve to publish it under my own name. Instead I used my Hebrew cognomen, Moshe, which thirty years later was to reappear on the cover of my first book published in Israel.*

I tried my hand at writing an English poem which the editors proceeded to publish—a tribute, I am sure, not so much to its worth (of which it had little) as to the *chutzpah* of a greenhorn who pretended to know so much that he could write even poetry.

Of greater importance was a request I received later on from Berlin. Its Jewish community, the largest in the country, was publishing a weekly *Gemeindeblatt* which combined the features of a newspaper and magazine. Would I write a series of impressions of America? Many people now contemplating emigration would be interested.

I did not anticipate the enormous response which these articles produced.** Here was a young man who was evidently finding the New World a place in which a German Jew could live. How could one get to the United States? What could I advise? Would I know anyone to sponsor a prospective immigrant? Could I find their relatives? The requests were endless, and came from everywhere. Often they came in envelopes with barely sufficient addresses: one letter was sent to "Dr. Plaut, Hebrew Julian College, Middle America." The missive reached me, as did others which were just as enigmatically inscribed.

My most encouraging literary venture came when I visited my schoolmate, Malcolm Stern, in Philadelphia, at his family's beautiful home at Fox Chase. Malcolm had an *Atlantic Monthly* lying about the house. It announced a competition for writers under thirty who were invited to state their hopes for the future.

"Why don't you enter the contest?" Malcolm encouraged me. "Yours will be a different voice."

I sat down at his typewriter and composed a few sentences— the limit was 650 words. My host suggested several changes in English syntax and we mailed the letter that afternoon. Some months later the magazine carried my contribution.† It was a thrill to have broken into one of America's most important

---

* "Moishe Cries Out," *Hebrew Union College Monthly* 24, 1(1937), p. 15 f.
** They appeared on June 27, July 4, August 1, November 21, 1937, and February 6, 1938.
† *Atlantic Monthly*, November 1938, p. 659 f. I signed the article W.G.P. rather than using my full name. Was I still afraid of repercussions in Germany? I cannot remember.

publications just three years after my arrival. It was a simple article entitled "Testament of Exile", and ended on a hopeful note:

America is not entirely what people abroad believe it to be. Below the seemingly smooth surface there are the same smouldering forces of unrest. America today suffers the birth pangs of social consciousness, much the same as industrial Europe did twenty and thirty years ago. The American youth of my generation begins to take not only an interest, but also an active part in the political, economic, and cultural movements of the day. He shifts from mere discussion to organization and action. The "future" is no longer conceived of in terms of generations and lifetimes. Who knows what the morrow will bring? The "future" at its best extends till the next year or two. This may be historically unfortunate, but it shows that a subconscious unrest and uncertainty have gripped the roots of American civilization. In addition, I see the gospel of Jew-hatred spread also in this country, a fact which does not add to my spiritual tranquillity.

With a changing world before me, with *motion* being at the heart of things, I often wonder whether the present situation is not really the desirable one, whether one ought not to be thankful for the challenge which proves to be the stimulus to a worthwhile and responsible life. And America has, in my mind, added confidence to this outlook. For in her people I detect a keen awareness, a healthy alertness which fortunately has not yet been dulled by economic and moral exhaustion.

Thus I look at America with some bewilderment, with apprehension at times, but with hope nonetheless. And, braced by this hope, I set out to do what little I can towards the further development of this country.

At the end of my first year the president of the college called me into his office. I had already been summoned to his office once and warned about promoting too many "orthodox" customs amongst the students, and told not to press my Zionist views too hard. This time the matter was more serious.

"I have to tell you that we are very disappointed with you, Ginther," Morgenstern said. He always called me "Ginther"—a mutilation of my name which cut me to the quick.

"We had expected a great deal more from you, seeing that you have a university degree and are quite obviously mentally capable of doing your work adequately. But your work is barely

average and in your second year you will have to do very much
better."

I tried to tell him that the first year was extremely difficult for
someone uprooted from his customary environment, that all of us
had great anxieties about the fate of our families and the future
of the country which we still considered our own. He nodded and
told me that he understood—but this was intellectual comprehension only. Neither he nor most of the other teachers ever fully
knew the heart of the stranger.

## From Maine to Oklahoma

My classmate Arthur Lelyveld, who was already married and obviously a man of the world, asked me casually one day what I expected to do during the summer. I was nonplussed.

"Why," I said, "I expect to stay here."

"But the dormitory will be closed."

This was news to me. No one had told the five of us that this
was to be the case. I consulted the matron, who was astounded
that we had not been officially informed.

"What are we supposed to do?"

"That's up to you," she said.

We got together and made our plans. It was best to follow up
some of the contacts which we had made both amongst the
students and in the Cincinnati community. Arthur suggested that
I apply as a tennis counsellor to Camp Indian Acres (located near
Fryeburg, Maine) and he volunteered to make the proper contacts. I had no idea what such a camp was like or what the functions of a tennis counsellor would be, but through Arthur's good
offices I was engaged. At the same time I was asked to persuade
a Cincinnati couple, Elsa and Julius Hahn (whom I did not know)
to send their son to Indian Acres as a camper. It was a fortunate
meeting for me, for later on the Hahns would provide me with an
affidavit for immigration.

The young man consented to come and I began the long trek
eastward to explore a new part of American living.

It turned out that I was to be not only a tennis teacher but also
an assistant cabin counsellor. This meant that all day long I stood
on a court with very poor facilities and tried to instruct children
of various capacities in the art of the game, and then I had to
spend the rest of the day and evening supervising their other ac-

tivities. Night after night I fell into bed exhausted. Half-way
through the season it occurred to me that I had neither the same
time off as other counsellors nor the periods of rest which they
were accorded. I began to suspect that I was being exploited, but
I had nothing by which to measure my suspicion. The ugly surprise came at the end of the camp season when we all went to the
front office to receive our pay cheques. Instead of getting any
money, I was presented with a bill—it appeared that I had
worked for room and board and was now being charged for items
drawn from the tuck shop as well as for laundry. Since I had
come without money, I was quite incapable of paying the bill. I
was shocked.

But worse was yet to come. The day before closing I
demonstrated how to pole vault, something in which I was very
much less than expert. This kind of ego-trip was still part of my
make-up and I was to pay heavily for it. On coming down I injured my knee and tore the cartilage badly. I could not leave
camp when it closed, and had to stay over a few days. The only
consolation was that the accident caused the camp administration to forget about my bill and to worry instead how to move me
to acceptable quarters where I could be cared for. Somehow I
was shipped to New York and provided with some crutches, and
for the next two weeks I was laid up at the home of second
cousins in Long Island to contemplate my misery. Some two
years afterwards, I received three hundred dollars through
Workmen's Compensation. It did not put me on the road to
wealth, but it was in those years enough to spell a modicum of
financial security.

While recuperating I received a letter from Hebrew Union College informing me of my assignment to a High Holy Day position.
This meant taking charge of services for Rosh Hashanah and
Yom Kippur in some small community that could not afford a
resident rabbi and therefore imported a student each year. My
pulpit was to be in Ardmore, Oklahoma.

I had heard neither of the city nor of the state and did not have
the vaguest notion where it might be; I had to look it up in my
cousins' atlas. I wrote my parents informing them of my good fortune. They, of course, were in the same position as I: they had not
heard of either Ardmore or Oklahoma. They went to the family
atlas, which was a magnificent luxury volume with an ex-
haustive index, the very best of German geographic scholarship.
(We still have it, and though it is eighty years out of date, it

continues to serve us splendidly.) The atlas had been published some years before Oklahoma became one of the American states and the area was listed as "Indian Territory". I received an urgent letter from my parents filled with more than their ordinary anxiety.

"Please be careful," they pleaded. "You can never tell about the Indians."

It was not, however, the Indians that I had to deal with, it was primarily my own ignorance and the heat of the late summer. I borrowed money and took the train from New York to Dallas. It was a long journey lasting several nights and days. The heat on the plains was oppressive, and the coaches were not air-conditioned; when we opened the windows we were soon blackened by the engine smoke that drifted into every compartment. I put myself on a meagre diet to conserve my funds, as I still had to pay for my return trip and I had no idea what financial arrangements might be involved in my employment.

This was before the days of the big oil boom. I found Ardmore to be a small town, with Main Street as its artery, typical of the midwestern and south-western landscape. At the station I was met by an elderly gentleman who introduced himself as Mr. Daube, president of the congregation. He spoke with a strong German accent. He had come to the town in his youth as one of the earliest settlers. His general store was the major commercial establishment of the community. He was solicitous about my physical incapacity—I was still walking poorly, and had to use a cane—and I was put up in the hotel. He also offered me the use of an automobile which I was thrilled to accept. Unfortunately my skills in driving, acquired during a brief course in Germany before I left, had totally evaporated; on my first attempt to view the environs I landed the car in a shallow ditch. I was pulled out by a friendly trucker and was wise enough to return the car to my benefactor without abusing it any further. I thanked him but told him that I really had no need for it, that instead I would use my free time to prepare myself adequately for my spiritual tasks.

My efforts at preaching and conducting the service, the first I had attempted in the English language, were received most generously by the members of the community and other Jews who came from surrounding localities. I think the sight of a young man who was struggling with both his injured leg and the English language elicited sufficient sympathy to make them overlook any weaknesses.

When Yom Kippur was over and we had broken the fast, Mr. Daube drove me to the railroad depot where I was to catch the night train. On the way he said, "I believe you have never been in my establishment."

I answered that indeed I had not.

"Let me show it to you," he said, "it's right on the way."

He opened the store and turned on the lights and I looked around his emporium, a one-floor enterprise which sold everything there was to sell, especially in clothing. He took me over to the men's department with its long racks of garments.

"I bet you have never had an American suit in your life."

He was right, of course. If fact, I had never seen ready-made suits. In my sheltered youth I had only known tailor-made suits by Herr Paeschel, my father's trusted expert craftsman.

"Now, let me see," said my host and eyed me critically, with the practised look of an old merchandiser. "I think you are about size 38."

I knew nothing about sizes either, and I stood speechless as he picked a dark grey suit from the rack.

"Mr. Plaut, I want you to have this. We enjoyed your service, and this is a small way in which we can express our gratitude. Oh yes," he continued, "and I have this for you."

He handed me an envelope.

"This represents the fee as agreed with Hebrew Union College, plus your railroad expenses."

I thanked him profusely. On the way out he chose a grey hat and asked me to put it on. It fit perfectly, and I only hoped that the suit which looked so marvellous would also be the right size. Unfortunately that was not to be the case. When I tried it on, back in Cincinnati, it was at least one full size too small. But no matter; I now had an American suit and I forced myself into it. So what if my gait was somewhat restricted, so what if I could not move about without keeping my arms firmly pressed to my sides? I wore it on every festive occasion for as long as I was at Hebrew Union College.

But there was nothing wrong with the fee. It was $150—in 1936!—and it was a lot of money, all of which the students were permitted to keep.

During the winter vacation of that year I accepted an invitation from my classmate Zelig Miller to go home with him to Philadelphia. He came from a well-to-do family, textile manufacturers who maintained a large house with a kind of informality of going and coming which was new to me but very attractive. Christmas day was the twenty-fifth anniversary of my parents' marriage and I made my first transatlantic phone call to them from the Miller home. The conversation was brief and to the point.

"We have only one message," my father said, "and it is urgent. Find a place for Walter in America right away. He is graduating from high school. He must get out."

The three minutes were quickly gone and I was left with a new challenge.

Zelig showed me the city and the environs and proposed a trip to Lancaster, the heart of Amish country and the home of the Pennsylvania Dutch. Naturally we paid a call on the rabbi. He was Daniel Davis, a quiet-spoken man to whom I was at once attracted. He inquired about my family and I told him that somehow I needed to get my brother to the United States. He responded without hesitation.

"I can't imagine that bringing him over should be very difficult. Would you consider having him go to Franklin and Marshall College right here in town? It's a good school with a good reputation and perhaps I can arrange for the Jewish college fraternity to take him in."

Dan Davis was as good as his word. A few months later I received a letter from him that all had been arranged. I wrote the good news to Germany. I reply I received Walter's acceptance: he would be graduating that spring and could commence college in Pennsylvania in the fall of '37. But Walter, so the accompanying letter from my parents said, was very young. Could I visit Germany and take him back with me? After all, I had promised to stay away for only two years and that time was up. Meanwhile my mother would pay a visit to the United States and she would fill me in on all the details.

She arrived in the spring and I met her at the boat in New York. We paid a visit to Lancaster, where she had an opportunity to thank Dan Davis personally, and then she spent some time with me in Cincinnati. To her, travel was second nature. She was and remains a most enterprising spirit and even in those days—despite her otherwise sheltered life—she was quite independent when it came to being abroad. She had shown it on our joint trip to Palestine, and now it was demonstrated again.

We talked at length about the situation in Germany. Mother had no political opinions apart from Father's—that would never have done. She reiterated my father's desire that I should go home during the summer for a visit.

"Would it be safe?" I wondered.

"Quite," I was assured; there was no danger at all. "Life is going on as usual—except that there is no future for our young people. That is why Walter must leave this year."

I discussed the matter with some of my professors, especially with Jacob Marcus whose knowledge of Germany and comprehension of history were superb. He was very dubious about my intended journey.

"Why take the chance?" he commented. "They might never let you leave again."

But I was brash—and half persuaded by my parents' confidence. Besides, I already had a return ticket, and Herman Schaalman was contemplating a visit home too. Wolli had gone the year before and all had gone well.

## Idiot's Journey

In retrospect this must surely be one of the most stupid chances I have ever taken—for Walter would have been quite capable of leaving Germany by himself. He would soon prove that he was self-motivated and had as much independent judgement as I who was seven years his senior. I think my parents knew this too, but Father wanted me home. He needed to see me, and he could not believe that there was any real danger—that was the long and short of it.

The Cunard Line brought me to England. From there I took a small boat to Hamburg, where my uncle Raphael and my cousin Max awaited me at the pier. My arrival was routine, my passport was good and the first stage of dealing with German authorities passed without a flaw. In those days I had blond, wavy hair and was not usually taken for a Jew. My old but still valid passport did not indicate that I was Jewish (later issues had a big J stamped on them). The representative of the Nazi Party asked no questions and there I was back in what I still considered my homeland, feeling that my parents' advice was obviously good.

I fell back into the old routine as though I had never been away. Father looked the same, although he was far less convinced about Hitler's early departure than he had been two years before. He savoured my visit and asked me endless questions about life in the United States. I went back to my old tennis club where I found the membership had dwindled. But there were still tournaments amongst the Jewish players and the results of the matches were published in the Jewish press. I played again, travelled to various communities, and for a while moved in the invisible ghetto as if nothing had happened. It was characteristic of the Jewish community always to carry on as normally as possible in order to counteract the Nazis' aim of dehumanizing their victims. They held together, they strengthened their cultural, social and recreational activities, and continued to do so even in the concentration camps. I preached, and accepted an invitation to speak in Berlin's newest and prettiest synagogue, which was located in Prinzregentenstrasse. It was the "Sabbath of Consolation", which follows Tisha b'Av, the traditional day of mourning for the destruction of the Temple. Both days then had a very special dimension for Jews mourning the destruction of their community and looking for consolation.

The Sabbath of Consolation derives its name from the prophetic lesson read on that day, the fortieth chapter of Isaiah: "Comfort ye, comfort ye My people." What comfort was I to offer? Tell them that life was free in the United States and in Palestine, that they should leave at once? Probably. I knew in my heart that Dad's mixture of pessimism and optimism was not realistic, but I could not go against his convictions in public. Of course, many young people had already left for Palestine and other places— there was obviously no future for Jewish youth at home—but the physical extermination of German Jewry had not yet begun.

I could not be sure whether the customary agent of the Gestapo was in the audience taking notes, but I knew it was likely, and this underlined the idiocy of my public appearance. I was almost daring the authorities by calling attention to myself. Why nothing untoward ensued I shall never know.

As the summer wore on I became restless; something told me that I had better leave, and the earlier the better. Walter and I were able to obtain passage on the Bernstein Line, which featured one-class ships out of Antwerp. These vessels were relatively small (about 14,000 tons) and the crossing took nearly two weeks. The fare was cheap. The whole ticket, if I remember correctly, was $98.

So we set out and this time there were tears, even from Father. We did not know that it would be many years before we saw each other again, seven years for me and eight for Walter. The

chances were—and this all of us knew, regardless of our
political analyses—that the parting might be final.

Both Walter and I had received our student visas without any
difficulty for we had the proper papers from our two colleges.
For others, who desired permanent visas, the lines at the
American Consulate were long, and while it was still possible to
gain admission, seeking the proper affidavits from the United
States was a laborious process often ending with failure. To put
it baldly: aside from all else, there were not enough Jews—among
the many millions in America!—who came forward quickly with
their personal guarantees, to rescue other Jews from the
clutches of Nazism. It was partly that American Jewry was not
organized well enough in those days. Whole communities could
have been energized to provide these affidavits, and many more
people could have been saved from suffering and death.

Eventually Walter and I were on our way. We reached the
Belgian border after eight hours of train travel. Then came the
moment when both of us would leave the country of our birth,
perhaps for good. Two officials entered our compartment; one a
customs and passport inspector, the other an agent of the
Gestapo. The former looked briefly at our papers, which were in
order, inquired whether we were taking more than the allowed
ten marks with us, whether we had any jewelry or other contra-
band, and then he gave the passports to the Gestapo man. The
latter inspected them, looked Walter over, looked me over,
checked all the pages of the passports again, looked at us more
closely. The whole process probably took ten seconds or less. To
me it was an eternity. I was cold all over. At that moment I knew
that if I got safely across the border I would never return as long
as Hitler was in power.

The Nazi opened his mouth to say something that was bound to
be devastating to us—how else did Nazis address Jews? But
somehow he said nothing, gave the passports to the customs man
and walked out. A few minutes later the train was on its way. We
were in Belgium, free. Walter and I both knew the formula for
benshing gomel, the prayer for having passed safely through
danger. The other people in the compartment stared at us, two
young men who suddenly broke forth in a Hebrew litany and
started to cry.

## American Progress

The voyage was pleasant and uneventful. I delivered Walter to Franklin and Marshall College and into the care of Rabbi Davis. He was now on his own.

Being together in America did not help us to be close. The years of separation and the difference in our ages stood against it. We were unlike in nature, emotionally and intellectually, and though Walter would visit me during vacations in years thereafter, the gap between us remained.*

In the winter of 1937-38 there were terrible floods in Cincinnati; the Ohio River overflowed its banks, and much of the downtown area was under water. Classes were cancelled at the college and we worked on eighteen-hour shifts helping people move their belongings and setting them up in emergency shelters. Eventually the college was closed altogether and the students were urged to go home. A classmate, Jacob Polish, asked me to be his guest in Cleveland and I gladly accepted. I met his mother, a generous and hospitable woman of the old school. She introduced me to the secrets of *tsimmes*, a carrot dish which I had never tasted in my life, and Jacob took me to hear Rabbi Abba Hillel Silver, whose oratory was magnificent.

When school started again in the fall I was assigned to a small Orthodox congregation in the heart of Cincinnati, in the enclave of Norwood. Somehow, by strange and impenetrable reasoning, Dr. Morgenstern had determined that the best way to introduce this greenhorn to the marvels and practices of Reform Judaism was to expose him to American-style Orthodoxy. Or perhaps he thought that I would never be an American Reform rabbi because I would eventually return to my native land. Whatever his reason, I served the congregation until my graduation. Every weekend I was their rabbi, instructing the few children and practising my English on the members, many of whom had themselves been born in Europe and had never mastered the language.

From them I picked up my first knowledge of Yiddish, a tongue which had hitherto been an enigma to me. In Berlin, where many

---

* In time, Walter too would go to Hebrew Union College and become a rabbi. He would have a distinguished career and leave a living legacy amongst those whom he served in Fargo, North Dakota; Cedar Rapids, Iowa; and, lastly, Great Neck, New York. See further p. 220.

East European Jews lived, Yiddish was considered a corrupt German, something that was not to be taken seriously. Not until much later, when I was in the Army, did I begin to understand the joys of this unique expression of the Jewish spirit. I not only studied the language but learned to love it and speak it, albeit with a German accent.

My studies went limping along. I took Arabic with Julius Lewy who was a great Assyriologist but proved incapable of inducting me—the only student in the class—into the secrets of the language. It was a mutual failure: I put endless hours into the effort but never grasped the essence of the language—which was a pity. Though for a while I managed to struggle through classical texts, today I can no longer distinguish one letter from another.

I studied biblical commentary with the sweetest of men, Henry Englander. He was a person of great patience, and there too I was the only student. The interest evoked in those sessions became the foundation for my later involvement with biblical studies.

I pursued some athletic activities. I organized a Jewish soccer club which was composed of German immigrants and played in the Southern Ohio Soccer League. I also organized a Maccabiah in the spring of 1938, for Jewish athletes from the area, who participated in a variety of events. Unfortunately the date coincided with the hottest weekend in May: the temperature in Cincinnati soared into the nineties, restricting both our contests and our enthusiasm.

But my major project was still the Gate Club, where those of us who had come from Germany gathered for social and intellectual fare. We invited guest lecturers and artists and organized dances which were usually held at one of the two Reform synagogues, with American hosts and hostesses mixing with the newcomers.

One evening the locale was Rockdale Temple, the same place where, some two and one-half years before, the five of us had been chastised by Dr. Philipson. I had a previous appointment downtown—I think it was a political meeting of some kind—and did not arrive at the dance until quite late. When I came to the door I met one of the hostesses. She was a young lady of striking appearance. Her name was Elizabeth Strauss and she told me that she was a cousin of Betty Abraham whom I had known for some time and with whom I was good friends. We danced and talked, but the hour was already late; the affair was soon over and we said good-bye.

When I returned to the college I realized that I had failed to obtain the lady's telephone number, and so the next day I called her cousin (who, of course, promptly informed the object of the inquiry). But the Passover holidays were coming and I was occupied with studies and preparations for my congregational work; I did not call Elizabeth until two weeks later. We began to date, and soon we were seeing each other daily.

Our backgrounds were compatible. She came from an old Cincinnati family with roots in England and Germany. Her father had died when she was only two years old, and her mother—known to her friends, young and old, as Therese—was a lady of the old school, with handsome features, and a musician of exceptional talent (she had once been offered a contract at the Met). Therese received me warmly in her apartment on Reading Road where the two of them lived. It was a home of quiet elegance, bespeaking cultured tastes which were expressed with uncommon and appealing modesty. Everything was understated.

Elizabeth's education had been wide-ranging. She was a top student, with a BA, an MA in Zoology, and a Bachelor of Science, and was now engaged in getting a degree in Education as well. We often sat on the lawn of the university, in Burnet Woods, to talk. We would go dancing at the "Normandie" or listen to the radio together. She introduced me to concerts, the first I had ever attended. We had met on the sixth of April and by the end of May we were clearly headed for a permanent alliance. But there was as yet nothing official about it. I did not think I was in any position to marry, having no visible means of support; and the promise of a rabbinical job—if any—was well over a year away.

That spring Herman and I made our way to Cuba to become immigrants at last—for we had come in as students, and one had to leave America in order to come back as a permanent immigrant. It was not possible to change one's status while remaining inside the country. (Walter would later immigrate via Canada.) Zelig Miller's family in Philadelphia and the Julius Hahns in Cincinnati vouched for me. We took the train to Miami, stayed with a school-mate overnight and then flew to Cuba. In Havana we had been given the address of a Jewish family who would put us up, but when we arrived at the address—with our nonexistent knowledge of Spanish—the woman who answered the door was nonplussed. She decided, however, that our story, which she may or may not have comprehended fully, was genuine and admitted two absolutely strange young men into her house.

Despite the fact that Jews all over the world were clamouring to get into the United States, our admission through the American Consulate in Havana was astoundingly easy. We had made the arrangements in advance, we were expected, and in a matter of an hour our papers were processed and our applications fully approved. We returned to Miami and went through the immigration port there, and thus Herman and I were on our way to becoming American citizens. In retrospect I realize how lucky we were, for entry into the United States was becoming more and more difficult. I had left Cincinnati on the tenth of June and I was back there a few days later.

It became clear now that we would be seeking pulpits in America. Other students, amongst them Teddy Wiener (later to become Librarian at the Congressional Library in Washington), Ernst Lorge (later a rabbi in Chicago), and Joshua Haberman (later a rabbi in Washington, D.C.) had arrived from Germany. A few graduate rabbis and professors also swelled the number of refugees—chief amongst them Fritz Bamberger (who had been my philosophy teacher in Berlin and who later became professor of intellectual history at the college) and my former Hebrew teacher Abraham Joshua Heschel. Heschel was very unhappy at the college, however—the institution did not fit his religious style—and he later shifted to the Conservative Jewish Theological Seminary in New York, where he became a philosopher-poet of world renown and a potent intellectual force in the country.

## Marriage

Summer was approaching and, despite my gruelling experiences two years before, I went back to Indian Acres as a counsellor. Elizabeth persuaded her mother that they ought to take a vacation nearby. The countryside was well known to her, for she herself had been a camper and counsellor in that area some years before. Walter too became a counsellor at our camp, and this time my experience had neither the uncertainties nor the ill ending of 1936. Elizabeth would call for me by car on my day off and we would go sailing and swimming, and by the beginning of August we were admitting what we had known for some time: we were going to marry each other. I approached her mother with the proper petition and she in return asked the expected question: would I be prepared to support my wife? I remember clearly the answer I gave: "I will work hard and if I am a rabbi in America I will make an adequate living. I will not be wealthy, but there are some rabbis who make as much as $5,000 a year. Maybe I will be amongst them."

While Elizabeth's family background was easily accessible— the family had arrived in Cincinnati in the 1820s, and her brother Billy, a brilliant scholar and merchant, was married to the daughter of a Reform rabbi—my own was not. But Dr. Marcus was going to Germany that summer and it was suggested to him that he might visit my parents and, incidentally, bring back a report. He did so, and apparently the report was satisfactory. In turn, my philosophy instructor in Berlin, Fritz Bamberger, who was then visiting Cincinnati, met Elizabeth and thus was able to reassure my parents about their prospective daughter-in-law.

Purchasing an engagement or wedding ring is always a major event in a couple's lives. In our case that acquisition had about it the touch of fate.

On one of my visits to New York, long before I had met anyone whom I could consider seriously as a future mate, I was attracted to a mini-circus on 42nd Street. It turned out to be a jewelry auction; I stepped closer to see what was going on and became fascinated by the proceedings. Midway through my gawking a man tapped me on the shoulder and said, "Please come to the back." I did not know what he wanted, but I went. I soon found myself seated in a small office facing three characters. One of them addressed me bluntly.

"Mister, you just bought a diamond ring. Have you got the cash with you?"

I said that I had not bought any ring and that I did not have the shadow of any cash, with me or anywhere else.

"That's too bad," said another. "You raised your hand and you bought it, so you'd better come through."

I tried to tell them that I could not remember raising my hand and that I had no intention of buying anything.

"Listen, mister," said the first one, with an unmistakable threat in his voice, "you don't want any trouble, do you? You may be new in this country, but you've got to learn. You come to an

auction, you raise your hand at the wrong time and you've bought
it. Now here's the ring."

I looked at it, a small ring with a few diamonds set modestly in
a not unattractive pattern—but I had no desire to own it and had
obviously no use for it.

"Thirty-five dollars," said the man. "You can pay it on the in-
stalment plan."

I had no way of knowing whether the ring was worth that
much—at that time it was a considerable sum. But I also had the
uneasy feeling that I had better say yes and get out. I paid them
five dollars on the spot, and sent them monthly cheques until the
whole mess was cleared up—although I felt I was throwing my
money away. And what to do with the ring? Leo Lichtenberg told
me that his fiancée's family would be glad to keep it for me in
their safety deposit box. I gave it to them and forgot all about it.
When I became engaged the question naturally arose: what kind
of ring would I buy for Elizabeth? Suddenly it occurred to me that
I owned one already. We took it out of the box and it fit Elizabeth
perfectly; moreover, she was delighted by it. She has never
wanted another one and it is her wedding and engagement ring
to this day. Thus was played out the drama of 42nd Street.

We first planned our wedding for 1939, after graduation, but
then advanced it to the time of the winter vacation and then
again to Thursday, November 10, 1938—the beginning of the
long Armistice Day weekend, as it was then called. We did not
know how fateful a date that would be, not only for us but for
Jews in general.

We also did not know how badly the situation in Germany was
deteriorating. Hitler and his henchmen were determined to abandon the gradualism of the last five years and reduce the Jews to
total degradation at one fell swoop. All they needed was an excuse, and it came in the first days of November.

A young Jewish man, crazed by the hardship inflicted on his
parents by the Nazis, attacked and killed the Third Counsellor of
the German Embassy in Paris. The Nazis organized a popular
"wave of indignation" and in the night of November 9-10 the majority of Germany's synagogues were put to the torch, their windows and the windows of Jewish shops shattered (hence the
name Crystal Night). The leaders of German Jewry were in-
carcerated and a huge fine was imposed on the Jewish community. It now became evident even to the most optimistic that the
Nazis were going to destroy the Jewish community's existence,

and degrade the Jews from second-class subjects to pariahs who could be dispossessed, expelled, jailed or killed at will. Crystal Night with its terror and its flames represented the effective end of the German Jewry and was, in the larger context, the beginning of the destruction of European Jewry as well.

That night my father fled from home. When the Gestapo came to arrest him, my mother said that she did not know where he was. (He was hiding with friends and stayed in hiding until March when he and Mother left for England. Mother would meet him clandestinely so that he, who alone had cheque-signing powers, could help to keep the Auerbach institution alive.) When the tenth of November dawned, German Jewry was in shambles, its leaders in flight and hiding or else in concentration camps. Many were killed that night. Father was amongst the fortunate ones. He survived the day—and it was that very day, November 10, 1938, that his son was married in Cincinnati, Ohio.

We, of course, had no inkling of the events. We had picked the date because it was a convenient weekend and Walter could come down from school. The wedding was small and the ceremony simple. It took place in the Strauss apartment, with my German friends—the "gang of four"—in attendance as friends and choir, plus Elizabeth's small family: her brother and his wife Elsa, her mother's brother Charles and his wife and their two children. Three rabbis attended: Henry Englander, Julian Morgenstern and—somewhat to my chagrin and over my slight opposition—David Philipson. He had been the family's rabbi since the 1880s.

We were married at five o'clock in the afternoon. Elizabeth taught public school until one and I worked at the Bureau of Jewish Education until three. Half-way through the service, the telephone rang—a message from Western Union. The maid who answered assumed that it was a congratulatory wire and asked the operator to call back in a little while. But when the call came again, after the ceremony, it turned out to be someone from New York who informed us of the events of the previous night in Germany. He was speaking on behalf of Herman Schaalman's family: Herman's father had been arrested but would be released from concentration camp if an exit visa could be obtained for him. Dr. Morgenstern promised Herman that he would take the matter in hand at once, but it took several months before Mr. Schaalman was freed. He eventually emigrated to South America with the rest of his family.

While the full impact of what had happened did not become known to us until a few days had passed, a shadow was cast over our honeymoon; besides, Elizabeth had come down with the flu and a high fever, so we didn't go away for the three days we had planned. It was by all odds an inauspicious beginning for a marriage. Fortunately the old saw about beginnings did not hold true: it turned out that I had chosen an ideal partner, a superior human being, loving, straightforward, compassionate and intelligent. Much of what I was to learn in the years to come, I learned from her. From the very beginning our marriage was that of two equals. We shared everything, we made all decisions together, and whoever could best perform a task was the one who assumed it.

I signed up for my rabbinical thesis: a study of eighteenth-century records in German and Hebrew which would cast a light on the social history of German Jewry. Dr. Marcus was my advisor and, as always, his great learning and complete command of the field set the student on the right path. While I prepared my thesis Elizabeth finished her educational program at the university and did student teaching. We had rented a one-room efficiency apartment with a pull-out bed not far from her mother, and I proudly put up our name-plate, "Dr. and Mrs. Plaut". That proved to be an error. Soon after we moved in I was called during the night by the superintendent. A tenant had become sick. Would I come at once? I told him that he had the wrong kind of doctor but thereafter I was more careful with the use of my title.

The news from Germany became worse. My parents were at last trying to leave (leaving was still possible if one had a place to go) but it was now hard to bring them to the United States. However, my cousin Helen (Uncle Levi's child, who was living in England where she had emigrated with her husband) provided the necessary papers and in March my parents went to the hospitable British Isles. They were fortunate and obtained a position in Brighton, guiding a hostel for refugee children. Of course, this was to be temporary—since both Walter and I were in the United States, America was my parents' ultimate destination. I was commissioned to make all necessary preparations to obtain the proper affidavits and I set to work at once. Little did I know what lay ahead and how difficult it would be and how long a time would elapse before I was successful.

# Ordination

As I neared the day of my ordination in the spring of 1939 I was very uneasy about my capacity to perform adequately as rabbi and pastor of a congregation. I had but the vaguest notion about the organization of such an institution, its financing, its staffing, the functioning of trustees and committees. I talked to Dr. Marcus about it and he was blunt.

"Gunther,"* he said, "I don't believe you are ready for an American congregation."

I agreed. He suggested that I apply for a fellowship at the college. I liked the idea, for in the back of my mind was always the thought that I was best suited to be a scholar. I had never been naturally sociable; I did not possess the innate, gregarious drive which makes other people reach out to you and constantly want and enjoy your company. It was not that I felt uncomfortable with others, but neither did I feel entirely at ease with them. Somehow I was suspended in a vacuum between solitude and company, between introversion and extroversion. I am convinced that my scholarly efforts of later years were an aspect of my somewhat introverted nature.

But my application for a fellowship was turned down, and of necessity I was now headed for the congregational rabbinate. A Chicago congregation asked me to come for an interview sometime before ordination. They suggested I take a plane—obviously this was a well-to-do institution. The post offered was that of assistant rabbi. I had never been to the Windy City—I had, in fact, been to very few places in America in the four years that I had been there—and I agreed at once to go and be examined by the selection committee. I was to preach a trial sermon on Shavuot morning, which that year fell on Wednesday, May 23. A few days before, I received a telephone call from the synagogue's vice-president, Philip D. Sang, who himself had been for a brief time a student at Hebrew Union College.

"Have you prepared your sermon already, rabbi?" It was customary to call us by that title even before graduation.

"Yes," I said, "but it is not quite finished."

"May I ask what you will be speaking about?"

"I thought I would speak about Palestine and the problems there and our opportunities and obligations."

* By this time I generally went by that pronunciation, much to my wife's distress. She has always preferred "Günter".

"May I suggest," said Mr. Sang, "that you choose some other
topic? We are a Bohemian-Hungarian congregation and are old-
line Reform. While Zionism is not a prohibited topic, it will most
certainly not help you to obtain the position if you speak on it in
any favourable fashion."

I thought of the story of Stephen S. Wise, intrepid American
Zionist and the country's most widely known rabbi and orator.
He had once been invited to become the spiritual leader of
Temple Emanu-El in New York and had rejected the offer
because his freedom of expression was to have been cir-
cumscribed. The spirit of Wise made me bold.

"Mr. Sang," I said, "I do not believe that I can preach only to
suit your congregation. I always thought that a rabbi should
speak freely and insistently even on things that his people do not
wish to hear. If I come I will speak on Zionism, Palestine, Arabs
and American Jews. Do you think that under the circumstances I
should not come?"

There was a pause.

"No," he said, "you come. Despite what I said before, I think
you'll do all right."

The fact was that Sang himself was a man of conviction who
spoke brilliantly in public and possessed a highly creative mind.
He had called me, I think, to test me; and while we never became
close friends and never discussed the telephone conversation
afterwards, we respected each other. So I went, and found a
huge Byzantine synagogue presided over by Rabbi Samuel
Schwartz. I preached and was then invited by a group of congregational leaders to join them for lunch. Afterwards they said,
"Rabbi, will you please wait outside while the Board meets?"

I left the room wondering what a "Board" was. A piece of
wood? I thought of Dr. Marcus and of his unequivocal judgement
that I did not yet know enough about America to be a congregational rabbi. Not only did I not know what a Board was, I had no
idea what authority was granted the rabbi. I had hardly had an
opportunity to speak to Rabbi Schwartz. He had not told me what
he would expect of me nor had I asked him the questions I should
have asked. I was filled with doubt when my ruminations were
cut short and I was invited back into the room.

"The Board has decided," I was informed, "to invite you to
become our assistant rabbi. The pay will be $2,400 a year. What
do you say?"

Long before I had gone to Chicago for the interview, even

before that invitation had been extended, Elizabeth and I had made a pact: I would accept the first position offered, whatever the terms, whatever the salary. If she and I—for she was as much a part of the team as I was—were serious about serving the Jewish people, then the place made no difference and the salary was of no concern. We would make ends meet somehow. To have a position was more important than what kind of position it was. As long as one could serve, that should be enough. I therefore had no hesitation; I accepted on the spot.

"Well then," I was told, "find yourself an apartment and start on September first. I'm sure you will like it in our midst and we will like you."

We shook hands all around. I was now the assistant rabbi of B'nai Abraham-Zion, more commonly referred to as Washington Boulevard Temple. The congregation was composed primarily of Hungarian and Bohemian Jews, with the latter firmly in control. That was all I knew about the congregation; I knew nothing about its history, its aspirations, its finances, or, most important, its expectations of the new young rabbi and his wife. I would be a rabbi and I would serve them. They were Jews and I was willing to be their partner in the grand enterprise of building Jewish lives.

In June 1939 I was ordained in the chapel of Hebrew Union College, which then still had clear windows (not the stained glass of today), a traditional platform with pulpit, and a choir loft. I do not believe that more than two hundred people could fit into the room and consequently attendance of families was severely restricted. Nowadays the exercises are held at the old Plum Street Temple, a national monument.

I wish I could say now that ordination was a great spiritual moment in my life. It was not. I have no clear recollection of the crucial moment when Dr. Morgenstern laid his hands on me.

Truth be told, I had drifted involuntarily into the rabbinate. To be a member of the elect group had not been a long-standing ambition of mine nor was I committed to God as the sole guiding force in my life. I had still to come to terms with Him and myself. Fortunately I was married, and from that foundation of stability I was more likely to begin a decent and worthwhile career. Certainly Jews were facing difficult and dreadful times—how dreadful we did not know as yet. To them at least I was committed heart and soul. I was a Jew. Not a very learned one, but I was willing to undertake whatever was necessary for my people.

After ordination Elizabeth and I were invited to attend the seventy-fifth anniversary celebration of our new congregation, all expenses paid. We took the overnight Pullman at clergy discount rates and, to save the congregation money, we purchased one single berth only. We were recently married, after all, and the idea seemed highly attractive. But it turned out that these berths did not have space enough for two, not even two newly-weds, and we arrived in Chicago cramped and weary. However, we were received with warmth, and the celebration at one of the city's hotels seemed very elaborate to my unsophisticated eyes. We also met the congregation's most prominent member, the eminent Adolf J. Sabath, senior member of the American Congress in Washington, who had by then already served for thirty uninterrupted years. He and I were to have some important dealings together in the next few years and I was to learn something about the American political system from one of its most astute practitioners, though what I was to learn was devastatingly disillusioning.

Meanwhile, political tensions were heating up. The Russians and Germans had concluded their vicious pact and carved up their spheres of influence, clearly a prelude to dividing up Poland at the first opportunity. Austria had been incorporated into the Reich; Czechoslovakia had fallen victim to Chamberlain's umbrella tactics and Hitler's bullying. Germany was preparing for war. France and England were blind and Americans had other preoccupations, primary amongst them the final glimmering of the Depression's end. Jews were struggling to get out of the Nazi trap, but everywhere the ports were closed and ships could not discharge their human cargo. The Evian Conference had been a farce, convened to assuage the possible stirrings of public conscience. Its conclusions had been drawn in advance: Jews were a commodity that no one desired; everyone would gladly dump them somewhere else.* "Somewhere else" turned out to be such places as Panama and Shanghai, Mauritius and Cyprus—the latter two temporary holding-places for unwanted Jews, pending some future decisions. Names like *Struma*, *Exodus* and *St. Louis* were attached to ships and in time became symbols of the free world's loss of conscience. Palestine was almost

---

* This conference to consider the growing refugee problem had taken place in 1938 in Evian-les-Bains, on Lake Geneva. Twenty-one countries had participated and the results were negligible. Only the U.S.A., which had convened the meeting, enlarged its immigration quotas somewhat.

totally closed; the British mandatory power held off all but a few
who were allowed legal visas, and another few thousand who
made it illegally at night by land or boat. Germany's Jews—
perhaps fifty per cent of them—had fled; many of them at first to
Austria and Czechoslovakia, only to be caught again in the Nazi
vice; others were now in the Low Countries and in France, not
far enough to be securely removed from the rapacious enemy.
What remained of German Jewry was totally delivered over to
Hitler's will.

The old country was now part of my past. None of my close
family was left there. My parents had gone to England. Heinz
Frank and his wife Sabina were in Canada; Bruno Sommerfeld
(now called Bruno Bernard) had gone to Berkeley, California;
some of my old law, tennis and soccer mates were in Palestine.
After a few attempts to keep up with these friends, the contacts
became more and more attenuated. I melted into the American
amalgam. Once I was away from Cincinnati I no longer joined the
groups of exiles or refugees. Not that I wanted to deny them; I did
not. My life had simply taken a different path.

# Chapter 3

# APPRENTICESHIP

I WAS TWENTY-FIVE YEARS OLD when, on the last day of August, 1939, Elizabeth and I boarded the train to take up our first post. We arrived in Chicago on September first. When we alighted from the train the newsboys were shouting, "War in Europe! Germany invades Poland!" It had started. We had been married on Crystal Night, and now my rabbinate was beginning on the day the war broke out.

We put up for a few days at the Graemere Hotel, a staid old place located in a pretty park in West-Side Chicago. We took a look around. What we saw was not encouraging. The neighbourhood was neglected; there were a few signs of former splendour, but if there were Chicago homes of the kind that we had known in Cincinnati, they were not in this area. The West Side was inhabited by first- and second-generation Americans who were trying to earn enough to escape to the better parts of town: the North Side, the suburbs, the South Side. Our temple was located near a business district composed of modest stores and one of the Balaban-Katz movie emporia. The streets were flanked by endless rows of apartment buildings, usually three to five storeys in height. Around the temple they were still in modest repair; as one went towards Independence Boulevard—the centre of Yiddish-speaking Chicago—many of them had already deteriorated into tenements.

We started our search for an apartment we could afford. Several were suggested to us, but they were so dark and dank that we were disheartened. Since I had to start my work at the temple, Elizabeth pounded the pavement, looking at every conceivable place within walking distance of my office. At last she found a third-floor walk-up on Hamlin Avenue which overlooked a park. It had two bedrooms and was relatively spacious. It seemed nice enough, especially after what we had previously seen. The rent was fifty dollars a month, a little more than the quarter of my salary we were advised to spend, but Elizabeth's mother offered to help us in the beginning. An Italian doctor who was a modest art collector was living below us, and our third-floor neighbour was a woman with two daughters who were quite pretty and had, so we thought, rather frequent parties. It took us several years to find out that the woman ran a common house of prostitution. There was much we did not know.

The elevated trains ran close to the apartment and at first the noise was disconcerting—until we managed to shut it out of our minds. The temple was two blocks away, at the end of a street that was a veritable wind tunnel. It was pleasant enough in the fall when we arrived, but later when the winter became bitter it was a long and arduous journey. Perhaps it's not just the temperature and the wind I remember; work conditions were also hard in my first position.

The congregation had suffered badly during the Depression years. There were times when Rabbi Schwartz did not receive his salary but was paid off with cemetery lots which the congregation owned at Waldheim. The rabbi was an utterly decent human being and, in fact, the best part of our stay in Chicago was the relationship we enjoyed with him and his wife, Charlotte. The latter was of superior intelligence, a great analyst of human relations, and had an innate talent for tact and for the right word. She laboured hard for the congregation, and none admired her more than Elizabeth whom she took in hand and taught the complex profession of the rebbitzin, the rabbi's wife. The two women were of the same mould, straightforward, despising doubletalk and gossip, and both had an enormous capacity for work which they put fully at the disposal of the congregation. Whenever I received my salary I knew that Elizabeth had earned a good deal of it—without her help and Charlotte's, our stay in Chicago would have been less productive than it turned out to be.

Sam Schwartz had come to the United States from Hungary. He had attended a seminarians' school in the old country but on his arrival in the New World did not at first choose to pursue a rabbinical career. After a while he went to Cincinnati, armed with the usual array of Old World Jewish knowledge: a good com-

mand of the liturgy and of the basic Hebrew texts, many of which
he knew by heart. But his strength lay in human relationships. He
was not a reader or theorizer; debates in theology and politics
were not his cup of tea, and preaching was his weakest point.
Before coming to Chicago he had been in Cleveland, Jacksonville
and Montreal. At Washington Boulevard Temple, a splendid
structure which he had helped build, he was primarily a father-
figure, not the intellectual leader of his congregation. Consequently some of the temple's leaders took advantage of him and
employed him for tasks which were clearly outside his rabbinical
calling. He had become, for example, the prime dues collector—an unpleasant role which the trustees wanted me to take
over, although I had no inkling of this at the time.

I was assigned a tiny ante-room from which one entered the
beema. It had no daylight to speak of and no room for books;
there was barely enough space to accommodate a small desk and
two chairs. It was not a place for study nor even for counselling—for the depression engendered by this confined and
gloomy space was an obstacle in itself. Since the temple had only
one telephone line there was no way of communicating from my
office with either the senior rabbi or the temple office.
Whenever I had a question or needed anything, it was one steep
flight up to Sam Schwartz and another flight up to the secretary.
Originally there had been an intercom telephone built into the
walls, but it had long been out of commission. Its crystal sets,
however, did from time to time spark into unexpected life, to
bring me unwanted announcements from a nearby radio station.

I had other surprises in store for me. Shortly after I arrived the
rabbi asked me to come to his study for a briefing and a heart-to-
heart talk. He confessed to me that he had not been consulted
about the engagement of an assistant rabbi; that it had not been
his idea and if he had had his say no young man would have been
brought to the congregation, which did not need another rabbi
and, as I had probably found out already, could not afford one.

This was news to me. A congregation that could bring me by
air, and then bring both Elizabeth and me for the seventy-fifth
anniversary celebration, seemed affluent enough to me—and,
after all, they possessed one of the finest edifices in Chicago.

"I wish it were so," said the rabbi, "but it isn't. We had high
hopes when we built the temple in the 1920s, but we lost
everything during the Depression. Our people have no financial
security and most of them just barely make a living—for the last

few years many have really been unable to pay their dues. We are being supported by a few dozen families who have independent businesses and whose generosity I must constantly stimulate. In fact," he said mournfully, "that is where most of my work-load lies."

He looked at his books along the wall of his little study.

"I have no time to read. If I want to live and feed my family, I've got to go and raise the money."

To say that I was appalled is to put it mildly. I felt that I had been badly deceived. I had had no idea that my senior had not wished me to come and that I had been forced upon him. One of the consequences of this misarrangement was that he rarely let me preach—which was probably just as well, for I could prepare my few sermons that much more carefully. But there was more to come.

I had been told at Hebrew Union College that assistant rabbis usually took care of the religious school and of the youth group. However, the religious school turned out to be firmly in the grasp of a lay member of the Board, Jake Beck, and the youth group, so I was informed, was the exclusive and untouchable preserve of Phil Sang and his brother Bernie. The two had, in fact, every right to feel protective about their work, for they were a remarkable team. Bernie was the younger of the two and still a struggling lawyer, while Phil had already made his mark in the world of business.

The two of them held Sunday-morning classes in the little Alumni House which the congregation had purchased next door—a rickety structure which would doubtless have been condemned had a fire inspector ever entered it. The "Alumni", as they were called, were those who had been confirmed at the temple (which was at age thirteen at the time). The younger ones were handled by Bernie on the second floor and the older ones by Phil on the first. For an hour and a half each Sunday morning the two lectured on various subjects of Jewish or wider import—from politics to book reviews to issues of morality or whatever else struck them—and they did a fabulous job. At the height of their success they had as many as 150 students, some of them twenty-five years of age.

What then was there for me to do? I established a Young Marrieds' group. It became so successful that long after Elizabeth and I had left Chicago and long after most of its members had moved to other parts of the city and had left the temple the

members continued to meet, and as late as 1980 it still existed as
an independent group. I also had some unorthodox tasks. During
the winter months, we abandoned the large synagogue and worshipped instead in the much smaller community hall which was
less expensive to heat. One day the janitor was missing and I was
delegated to go to the basement to keep the hall warm while the
service went on upstairs. We had no automatic devices, not even
a coal-feeder for the boiler. So there I was, shovelling coal to
keep the flame of Judaism burning.

Only in the Hebrew School was I permitted full range.
Elizabeth studied hard and learned enough to be a teacher of
Hebrew beginners. I also visited the people at their work and in
the hospital. The latter proved to be somewhat awkward, for
nearly all the hospitals were in other parts of the city. I took
public transportation and usually had to transfer once or twice. I
remember how once, having been advised that a parishioner was
sick, I spent a cold winter day waiting for streetcars, and when I
finally reached the hospital found out that the patient had been
discharged several days before. So back I went on my trek to the
temple, having used most of the day getting intimately acquainted with the public transportation system of Chicago. But
my time was not altogether ill spent. I always had a book with
me. I read while waiting in the street and while riding the streetcar. I devoured as many as five books a week and tackled
everything from Jewish subjects to books on science. In this way I
made up my deficiencies in English literature and covered the
realm from Chaucer to Hemingway. Even my wife once became
the victim of my avid reading habits. I used to help her with the
washing and drying of the dishes, but one day, spurred by an im-
pish spirit, I asked her:

"Would you rather that I helped you with the dishes or that I
made some money?"

"Well of course," she said unhesitatingly, "go and make some
money if you can."

A while later, finished in the kitchen, she came into the livingroom to find me on the couch reading a book.

"Is this how you make money?"

"Of course," I said holding up the book. "It's from the rental
library. The sooner I finish the book, the more money I save." The
ploy worked once and once only.

Come February I received a summons from the Executive
Board of the congregation. They told me in no uncertain terms

that they were very dissatisfied with my work. For one thing, they suggested, I should preach more often.

"But that is the province of the rabbi. He has not invited me more than once a month."

"Well then," they said, "we expected you to get the finances of the congregation into better shape. If you were as assiduous as Rabbi Schwartz and went out and collected the dues, we could meet our obligations."

I told them that while I was prepared to do almost anything for the congregation, including physical labour, I would not collect dues in order to pay my own salary. If they felt that under the circumstances they no longer wished my services, I would leave.

They decided to keep me. Nonetheless, the idea was planted in my mind that my future did not lie with Washington Boulevard Temple. When summer came the president informed me that "due to circumstances"—he lingered on the word "circumstances" while looking at me with eyes that bespoke hidden meanings—the congregation was not able to pay my salary. If, he added, I had difficulty making ends meet until they were able to pay, I should let him know and he could arrange for a loan. We never availed ourselves of this courtesy.

The 1940 convention of the Central Conference of American Rabbis, held in Charlevoix, Michigan, was as memorable as any I have ever attended, quite aside from the fact that this was my first. I forget the contents of the day sessions but I will always remember the night-long debate during which the members shared their anxieties about the future of our people. They put these wartime worries against the background of long-held convictions, chief amongst them a commitment to pacifism which had been characteristic of many Reform rabbis. The discussions became a sharing of agonies and lasted into the small morning hours.

One after another, deeply troubled men got up and renounced their pacifism. The pressing need for the salvation of their people, the threat of Nazism's ever-widening horrors, caused them to look at their most cherished beliefs and revise them in the light of bitter necessity. That night was a cleansing of the spirit; for me it was "a night of watching".

It was a great company I had entered. I was overawed by their ability to express themselves. When I heard men like Jacob Weinstein, James Heller and Philip Bernstein I knew that I was in the presence of men whom I could never hope to approach in

knowledge or depth of insight. At these early conferences I began
to develop a deep respect for my colleagues. Gone were the
cheap prejudices I had formed in Europe—about Americans and
their culture, about the backwardness of their Jewish life. I had
never met men like these in Berlin and I was proud to be amongst
them.

I sought their company in Chicago as well. Since I always had
a strong sense of *Kelal Yisrael*, the totality of our people, I never
restricted myself to associating with Reform rabbis only. We
kept a kosher home so that everyone might eat with us. Soon
some of the leading luminaries came to visit: the incomparable
preacher and imaginative Bible scholar, Solomon Goldman, a
fiery orator of the old school who presided over the Conservative
congregation Anshe Emet; scholarly Felix Levy, rabbi of Temple
Emanuel (later succeeded by my good friend Herman
Schaalman), a lover of books who had a splendid, wide-ranging
library.

We began to spend a great deal of money on books—a great
deal, that is, by our standards at the time. In everything else we
were still counting pennies: we treated ourselves once a month to
a restaurant dinner (seventy-five cents a person downtown) and
a movie (twenty-five cents), and made every attempt to stretch
our meagre income to the limits.

Although money grew very short during the time when my
salary was not being paid, and we had to dip into our wedding
reserves, artists came regularly to our door offering their wares.
Zahava Schatz, daughter of the founder of Palestinian art, Boris
Schatz, paid us a visit and with some of our wedding money we
bought two of her brother Bezalel's watercolours which still
hang in our dining room. Occasionally we even housed an
itinerant artist.

We entered the gentile community as well. One of our best
friends was Charles Hoskinson, minister of a congregational
church in our neighbourhood. I conceived of the formation of a
community structure that would tend to the needs of a rapidly
changing Chicago West Side. Eventually, Austin Community
Council was founded and attracted considerable attention in
other cities. I also became active in the Rabbinical Association,
was elected secretary and as such wrote a regular column for
the *Chicago Sentinel*.

About that time I received a most welcome letter from Rabbi
Isaac Landman, the editor-in-chief of the *Universal Jewish En-*

*cyclopedia,* who invited me to contribute articles to the on-going work. I did this gladly, for it provided a focus for my studies. I wrote sixteen articles and was made a contributing editor of this ten-volume work. Unfortunately the completed encyclopaedia lacked depth and never achieved the status for which it aimed. It neither supplanted the old *Jewish Encyclopedia* nor came anywhere near the ambitious undertaking of the later *Encyclopaedia Judaica.* It did, however, bring much information up to date and, having being written in the early 1940s, can occasionally still serve as a mirror of its time. Beyond that, it had little to recommend it. For me, however, it was a godsend. I worked hard and the reward was, if not the reader's, most certainly mine.

Working on my encyclopaedia articles also gave me an opportunity to visit the library of the Hebrew Theological College on Independence Boulevard. I began to meet the Orthodox and ultra-Orthodox leaders of Chicago and established deep rapport with them. I came to know Rabbi Meyer Waxman, author of an important work on Jewish literature and a comprehensive scholar. I found that though Reform Judaism was generally maligned and often despised, I, nonetheless, was accepted. This became remarkably evident when the senior *darshan* (preacher) of the Orthodox community died. He was Rabbi Isaac Caplan, an Old-World figure with a lovely library, a gentle and deeply learned person who enjoyed the great admiration of the traditional community. It turned out that he had requested that I deliver the eulogy—a startling and, in those days, unheard-of request. Some of the ultra-Orthodox must have deemed it well-nigh obscene to share the platform with a Reform rabbi. I took the task seriously and spoke lovingly of the man whom I had come to respect and admire profoundly. I still remember the gratitude I felt that in the midst of these learned men who belonged to another world I was privileged to praise the departed teacher.

Since I did not preach often I had much occasion to think about the subjects with which I wanted to deal, and how I might present them. I would read the traditional sources and contemporary books, then I would prepare an outline and eventually create the first draft. Now came the time to read it to Elizabeth, who would tell me frankly what she thought and, in addition, would correct the mistakes which I still made. I came to rely on her judgement implicitly—although on occasion it was a bitter pill to swallow. One year, after I had slaved over a Yom Kippur sermon with which I was particularly pleased, I read it to her. When it was finished there was a telling silence. At last she managed to say, "What is it precisely that you want to convey?"

I replied heatedly, explaining my thoughts and ideas and the theme I had tried to develop.

"But why don't you say just that?" she said sweetly.

I looked at her, tore up the sermon and started afresh.

I would also give considerable attention to the titles of my sermons, sometimes spending hours over their exact formulation (which leads me to believe that I might have been a success in the advertising business). Amongst those I still recall were "My Favourite Assassin" (dealing with the repentant murderer of Walther Rathenau*) and "Where Now is God?" (dealing with God's presence in a world of war). I began to give a series of book review lectures. These were free at first, but after a while we started charging a modest entrance fee, the money going to the Sisterhood which sponsored the series. The lectures were a fair success in the beginning but—much to our surprise—the attendance doubled once we began to charge.

Success bred success, and my sermons too were well attended. I started to have some confidence in my ability as a speaker.

In my reading I paid particular attention to the sciences, which caused the Rabbinical Association to invite me to give a lecture on the relationship of religion to the theory of relativity. I was familiar with the outlines of the scientific proposition but I was uncertain about its implications beyond the scientific realm. There were books on the subject, but none of them seemed to come to the heart of the matter. Being young and undaunted I sat down and wrote to Albert Einstein himself, who was then at Princeton. He wrote back setting forth his ideas. His letter became a prized possession and is now in the Public Archives of Canada in Ottawa.** I do not recall how my talk was received. I do know that it left me with the hope that some day I would write more on this subject. I continued the patient process of collecting notes, but it would be another twenty years before my *Judaism and the Scientific Spirit* made its appearance.

While Chicago had much to offer we could not take full advantage of it. Many of the things we wanted to see and hear were beyond our financial means. Books, radio and friends filled what

---

* See above, p. 14.
** Text and translation will be found in Appendix 1.

little time was not taken up with congregational duties. The
neighbourhood was changing for the worse. People were moving
away, and each person who left the congregation was a severe
loss to the already impoverished temple. Often Rabbi Schwartz
and I would visit a family and urge them to remain affiliated with
us. Sometimes we would succeed, more often we would not. It
became harder and harder to attract people, and although I put
endless hours into my work I felt I was having little success. Only
my books and my study seemed to return my affection in full
measure. We visited friends on the North Side, especially the
Van Straaten and Loeb families who had been old friends of
Elizabeth and her mother. We were asked, "Why do you stay
with your congregation? It's not for you. There should be places
that are more responsive to your capacity."

In retrospect, this was both true and untrue. The people at
Washington Boulevard Temple were too much consumed with
their problems of making a living, pulling out of the Depression
and moving to better quarters. They did not have enough of a
Jewish or educational background to make them truly partners in
an intellectual search. On the other hand, the synagogue was
often their sole means of recreation. They were simple people,
frequently of sterling qualities. They were as poor as we were
and just as frugal. No one despised hard work. The synagogue
was important to them—though the nature of this importance
was often on the surface only. It was perhaps not the ideal congregation with which to begin one's career, though now I am glad
to have had the experience. It intensified my capacity for hard
work and I obtained an abiding understanding of the needs of an
important segment of society. I learned that the lower middle
class is in one respect more poverty-stricken than those who earn
less: while the poorest people may have few aspirations, those of
the lower middle class are always struggling to improve their lot,
and therefore they feel their deprivation even more.

## Unwanted

The year of 1941 was a fateful one for us. Walter graduated
from Franklin and Marshall and enrolled at Hebrew Union College. I had completed my three years of waiting and was now
ready to apply for American citizenship. The paperwork and the
examinations took a little while and eventually I was given a date
in mid-December for the swearing in.

Pearl Harbor came on December 7. America was changed radically that night. So was my own life: my citizenship date was cancelled and, being of German birth, I suddenly became an "enemy alien". I now could not leave Chicago without permission of the Attorney General's office downtown. The rule was part of that anomaly which would have been amusing had it not been so sad. But what could I say about the few restrictions which were placed upon me, compared with those forced on my parents in England? After war broke Father was interned in a camp on the Isle of Man. He had had to leave Germany because he was a Jew, and in England he had to leave his home and work because he was considered a German. Moreover, my parents were exposed to all the civilian suffering of the war years, and for a while the subway tunnels served as their refuge from air raids. Eventually they were permitted to return to Brighton, despite its sensitive position on the coast, to continue guiding the youth hostel throughout the war years. My father never complained about the internment and felt that it had been necessary. In fact, he became in time a staunch Anglophile.

But Anglophile or not, my parents wanted to come to America to join their sons. They had never met Elizabeth. In letter after letter they exhorted me to do everything possible to get them to the States.

Fritz Ury, my cousin Helen's husband, had wired me from England when Dad left for the internment camp. "Get him a visa," he had said crisply.

Naive as I was, I did not think it would be too great a problem. After all, I had the famous congressman, Adolf J. Sabath, in my congregation and I contacted him repeatedly to see whether matters could not be expedited. Sabath, of course, was in Washington most of the time and I was rarely able to speak to him. When I did he was unfailingly courteous but always said that his staff were seeing to the application.

The staff too were reassuring and used phrases like "We have been advised that the matter needs additional consideration," or "We are looking for some additional help." Many years afterwards, when I reviewed my futile inquiries and urgings, someone put me wise.

"Those nebulous expressions," he said, "meant that they wanted their usual 'consideration' or 'help', that is to say, their customary under-the-table fee for doing something for you."

Whether the congressman himself was aware of these goings-on I have no way of knowing, and now that he is long dead I would like to give him the benefit of the doubt.

I was also to learn that even had Sabath's staff been diligent about their responsibilities, there might have been other opposition. Sometime after that—I think it was in 1942—my parents' immigration visa had still not been granted despite excellent affiants. I was suddenly summoned to Washington for a "final hearing". By this time I thought my appearance in Washington would be a mere formality. I took the night train, sitting up and trying to imagine what it would be like to be at long last reunited with my parents. It was about four years since I had seen them. I washed up at the Washington railroad depot and was on hand when the appointed hour came. I was ushered into an austere room where, on a slightly elevated platform, five men were seated: one from the Department of Immigration and Naturalization; one from Justice; one from the Secretary of State; and the other two from security organizations.

"Your name?"

I stated it.

"Any questions, gentlemen?" asked the presiding officer.

"You are here," said one of the men, "in the matter of Jonas and Selma Plaut."

"Yes, sir."

"Why do you want to bring these people to the United States?"

I was taken aback, but did the best I could to preserve a polite demeanour.

"Sir, Jonas and Selma Plaut are my parents. They have two sons, their only two children, and both of us are in the United States. They wish to be reunited with us. We have not seen them in four years and that's a long time for parents and children not to see each other."

"Any further questions?" said the presiding inquisitor. There were none.

"Thank you," he said. "You will be informed of the decision."

I had a terrible feeling that something was seriously wrong. Certainly it was not the papers that had been submitted and resubmitted and resubmitted again. I had splendid affidavits and the forms were most certainly in order. Transportation was not the issue; the Liberty Ships went fully loaded with war supplies and troops from America to Great Britain and came back empty. Something else was causing a problem and I did not know what.

Several weeks later I received the answer. It was a

mimeographed note informing me curtly that my parents' application had been rejected. There was a further note: "Do not inquire after the reasons. There will be no information. You may reapply after six months."

I was devastated and did not know what had gone wrong. Today I know. Antisemitism was running deep in the various levels of government. The idea of taking in even two aging and harmless Jews whose remaining goal in life was to see and again be with their children—people who would be fully cared for and would never be a burden—went against that persistent stream of anti-Jewish prejudice. Jews were simply unwelcome, whether they faced extermination like the majority of our people in Europe, or whether they wanted nothing more than to still the yearnings of parental hearts. I would not have believed that to be the reason for the refusal then, but I know it now.*

This is why the Evian Conference had failed—or rather, one should say, why it had been a sham, a "refugee conference" with a predetermined result: that nothing would be done. Refugee ships would be turned back. People would be returned to their prisons and then to slaughter. The Nazis' wildly expanding atrocities were already becoming known; still the Western governments, and most particularly their lower echelons, refused to do anything. The fewer Jews alive the better.

In the beginning of 1942, America was shifting into a new and unaccustomed gear: preparing millions of people for combat; changing a peace economy to serve the interests of war; introducing rationing; and doing all the things that go with full-scale militarization. Rabbis were enlisting in the armed forces as chaplains, and pulpits were served sometimes by women or, more usually, by students. Walter went to Duluth to take the place of a rabbi who had entered naval chaplaincy.

Meanwhile, I was still an enemy alien. My application for citizenship was indefinitely shelved. I could have entered the Army as a private but felt that there my contribution would be negligible. I decided to wait until my citizenship was resolved and I could apply for the Chaplains' Corps.

An important opportunity arose for me in the fall of 1942. Dr. Louis Mann, rabbi of Temple Sinai, then the most influential Reform congregation in Chicago, was stricken with a severe case

---

* As this book goes to press I have discovered, thanks to the American Freedom of Information act, that another black mark on their application was my membership in the Zionist Organization of America.

of laryngitis. He could not get a replacement from Cincinnati so he looked about in Chicago and vicinity. Julius Mark, then rabbi on leave from Nashville, Tennessee, was serving as chaplain at the Great Lakes Naval Station north of the city, and was available for some Holy Day services, and I, as the only assistant rabbi in town, was asked to fill in for the rest. I took the evening services on Rosh Hashanah and Yom Kippur, and Mark (who later became rabbi of Temple Emanu-El in New York) took on the responsibilities of morning worship. It was my first exposure to a large radio audience (the services were broadcast) and to a highly discriminating congregation. Many of the members were university-trained or even teachers at the university; there were numerous professionals, the kind of people who were notably absent from Washington Boulevard Temple. Still, I did not prepare a special sermon for them. I used the same lectures that I had prepared for my own congregation and apparently did well enough. Because of Dr. Mann's illness, I suddenly became known to an important new segment of the Jewish community who had never heard of me, and this was to make a significant difference in my career.

The old auditorium on the South Side which Temple Sinai then used as its main worship hall was cold and uninspiring. This was the place where Rabbi Emil G. Hirsch, a powerful figure in Chicago a generation before, had held forth and, incidentally, had held his own congregation in terror. It was said that people jammed his Sunday-morning lectures because they were afraid of two things: that he might speak about them, or that they might miss his speaking about someone else. For Hirsch was not above attacking people publicly if he felt that a moral wrong needed to be righted. I was aware that, in this vast hall that seated several thousand people, I stood in a place where great ideas had been promulgated and great sermons preached. For the young man three years out of school it was quite a place to occupy.

Many things changed as the war went on. More and more of our friends were leaving. The son of the Italian doctor who lived on the floor below had been drafted and his mother was not slow to question why I was still in civilian clothes.

Meat was difficult to obtain and our kosher butcher began to demand payments under the table, an illegal procedure which could have landed him in serious trouble. We were faced with a dilemma: should we accept his gouging practices or should we begin to eat non-kosher meat? We had not adopted our lifestyle

because we felt it was a divine obligation; rather, we had wanted
to be at one with the majority of our people. Our decision was to
give up buying kosher meat at least for the rest of the war.

There were many other changes in our life. Elizabeth became
pregnant. We had acquired her mother's old Chevrolet and were
now significantly more mobile. Our friends in the Young Marrieds' group were going into the Army one by one. It seemed to
me that the harder I worked at the temple the smaller the return,
at least from those in charge of the Board. Elizabeth did a thousand jobs for the congregation. I suppose that was expected of
the rabbi's wife; an independent career for a rebbitzin would
have been frowned upon in those days. On one occasion, when
we had laboriously prepared a large float for the religious
school's participation in some annual parade, we loaded our
creation on a borrowed truck and Elizabeth drove it downtown.
It turned out that the conveyance had no brakes, and for many
months thereafter we recounted the trials and tribulations of our
profession: from shovelling coal to driving brakeless trucks.

## The Comic Touch

Weddings and funerals supplied us with a good deal of extra contact and frequently with special heartaches, but also with
laughter. I had become quite popular as a "Marrying Sam" and
from time to time I would have to leave a party or a meeting to go
to the office and officiate at a brief ceremony.

When I came to my study on one such occasion the party were
already assembled. Without paying too much attention to
anything else I proceeded with the ceremony. It was only then
that I realized that the groom was very badly dressed. His shirt
was open and hanging out of his pants and he was chewing gum
furiously. He was a thoroughly unattractive fellow, while his
bride was rather nice-looking—and apparently all the members
of the small party belonged to the bride's side. I asked, "Do you
take this woman to be your lawfully wedded wife?"

He glared at me and said nothing, shifting his wad of gum from
one side of his mouth to the other. At Hebrew Union College I had
never learned what one did when faced with a recalcitrant
groom.

"Well," I said, getting somewhat warm under the collar, "do
you take this woman to be your wife?"

He glared at me again, said nothing and put his gum back where it had come from. I was perspiring profusely by this time and was wondering how one called off a ceremony under such circumstances. Did one say, "Ladies and gentlemen, the groom is unable to reply because of gum trouble?" I tried it once more.

"Mr. B., do you or do you not take this woman to be your lawfully wedded wife and do you promise to love, honour and cherish her throughout your life? Do you?"

There was a pregnant pause.

"Yeah," he said at last. "I do."

It was the most unwilling affirmation I have ever heard. Later I found out that it was not only the pause that was pregnant, and therein lay the tale.

On another occasion, a Sunday afternoon, I arrived late at the synagogue. The wedding party were standing outside the door and were very impatient. The janitor was on one of his drunken spells and had not opened up. I apologized and told everyone that we would start at once. But that was more easily said than done, for nothing had been prepared. The *Kiddush* cup and wine were nowhere in sight. The janitor's apartment was locked. (He probably had bottle and cup inside—both empty.) I rushed to the upstairs study where I thought I might find some wine in Rabbi Schwartz' office. No such luck. I then recalled that he had told me some years before that he always kept some wine hidden behind the organ loft for an emergency. I stuck my hand back of the pipes, and lo and behold, came out with a dusty bottle. I cleaned it off quickly, rinsed out a loving-cup which an Alumni basketball team had won as a prize, and was ready for action. Everything went fine until I gave the groom his drink. He took a deep swill, stared at me briefly and collapsed ungracefully. There was, of course, a general commotion and it was assumed that he had fainted from excitement. I, however, had a horrible thought: what if there was some deadly cleaning fluid in that bottle rather than wine? Had I perhaps killed or seriously injured the man? It took quite some time to revive him. He then explained that he had fasted all day and that this was the first liquid he had taken. That, added to the excitement, had apparently been too much for him. To say that I was greatly relieved is to understate the case. For quite some time I had nightmares about headlines: RABBI POISONS UNSUSPECTING BRIDEGROOM.

I never charged any fee and usually received very little, or nothing, for my efforts. We were a poorly organized community and the majority of Chicago's Jews were unaffiliated. They had a free ride: they took advantage of rabbis whenever they could, used them for weddings and funerals, paid them a pittance and were done with their obligations. Still, in those days my answer was always the same: "I charge no set fees. If you would like to show your appreciation it will be welcome, but in any case I will perform the ceremony."

One day I dealt with a particularly meticulous fellow. Prior to his wedding he had his interview with me and made sure that every small detail of the ceremony was clearly fixed in both his mind and mine. Nothing was to be left to chance. He wanted to know how much I charged and was not satisfied with my open-ended answer.

"Well," he said, "will fifteen dollars do?"

I said that whatever he gave me would be fine. Fifteen dollars would be most acceptable.

The wedding-day came, the ceremony went as prepared and on his way out the best man handed me an envelope.

"This," he said, "is from the groom with his thanks."

It was apparent that my young, meticulous friend had overlooked nothing. I went upstairs to change and put the envelope in my pocket; it was my custom not to open it but to give it to my wife for extras that she and I might need. The envelope felt rather fat. Surely the groom would not have provided me with fifteen single dollar bills? Meticulousness had its limits, after all. I opened the envelope and found sixty-five dollars in it. Obviously this was the young man's going-away money. I rushed downstairs. People were just getting into cabs. I spotted the groom.

"Here," I shouted, "you have forgotten something. I think I received the wrong envelope. This does not belong to me."

He paled.

"Oh my God!" he said. "You bet that's not yours! Thank you very much." He jumped into his cab, and that was the last I heard. I am still waiting for my fifteen dollars.

Among funeral mishaps, one stands out above all others. I did not know the family; they were not affiliated with a synagogue, and matters had been, as usual, arranged by the undertaker. The chapel ceremony was to be at eleven o'clock and I was to meet the family of the deceased man some fifteen minutes beforehand. Shortly after these arrangements had been finalized the funeral director called again.

"Could you take another service at ten o'clock? This one is a woman, Mrs. X. I can arrange for both families to meet you before ten o'clock and then you'll have a little time to rest."

I agreed. The next day I met the families early in the morning and then at ten proceeded with my first funeral. I placed the *Rabbi's Manual* on the stand but it slid off and all the papers scattered on the floor. When I picked them up I was suddenly not certain which of the two funerals I was conducting. Was this the man or the woman? I began to recite Psalms and meanwhile studied the mourners. Could I detect a widow or a widower? Were there any signs to let me know which of the two I was burying? No luck. I went through as many Psalms as I knew by heart—bless the seminary in Berlin!—and meanwhile prayed hard for some form of inspiration. I received it. I spoke of immortality and referred to "your deceased" or "your loved one"; I never used "he" or "she". When I was finally finished and the last prayer had been said, one of the family came up to me, shook my hand warmly and said, "Rabbi, thank you for that lovely eulogy. It was as if you had known her all your life."

## Unfulfilled

But officiating at life-cycle ceremonies did not fill my need for meaningful work. I found little intellectual response in the congregation. I prepared conscientiously and worked endless hours, but somehow the temple and I were a mismatch. I began to think that I should leave, yet did not know where to turn. I had no connections and there was in those days no apparatus which would help a rabbi find another pulpit. You had to know someone, or else you went through Dr. Morgenstern in Cincinnati, who arranged most job changes and who might or might not be able or willing to place you; and in that case, you surrendered yourself to his prejudices and whims.

During a vacation in northern Michigan I had met Dr. Abram Sachar, then the national director of the Hillel Foundation, designed to give Jewish college students a foothold in their tradition. I confided my problems to him.

"Sure," he said, "I'll be happy to take you on. I'm sure I can find a place for you."

I knew even less about Hillel than I knew about congregational work, but at that time getting out of Chicago seemed like the necessary thing. A few weeks later Dr. Sachar called. "There is a congregation open in Austin, Texas. It is small; but the rabbi also takes the Hillel job at the university and that is the major opportunity. You can go there at double your salary."

Without any hesitation I accepted his offer.

I was not sure where Austin was. It seemed far away, even farther than Ardmore, Oklahoma. The more I thought about it, the more worried I was that I might be unable to deal with American college students. I had never gone to an American university as an undergraduate student. I did not know the problems of American youth. I was not sure that I was up to the task. Also, if I was isolated in Chicago, what would Austin, Texas, offer me? So, after much discussion with Elizabeth, I told Dr. Sachar that I had changed my mind. He was sorry to hear it.

"Maybe something else will come along. I understand."

Something else did indeed appear to materialize. The congregation in Lexington, Kentucky, invited me to be a candidate for their pulpit. Elizabeth and I went to visit and on our return home were not sure what to think about the prospect. Lexington relieved us of any further indecision: they did not think I was suited to them. Looking back I know they showed good judgement.

On October 7, 1942, our first child was born. We named him Jonathan Victor—the second name to bind him to Elizabeth's family, many of whom had carried the name Victor with distinction. The thrill of parenthood was great. Rabbi Schwartz was Jonathan's godfather. Despite all my unhappiness at the synagogue, our relationship to him and Charlotte always remained good, and it never changed even when in time I became his associate rabbi, and then his successor.

We began to have increasing difficulties with the "madam" in our apartment building. On occasion she stole Elizabeth's linen from the line and at other times took our dog's excrement and threw it in front of another neighbour's door to put us in bad repute. The neighbourhood was going downhill.

I began to publish articles in local and national magazines and was invited to lecture in different places. I was not only coming to terms with the English language, I was beginning to love it.

On March 30, 1943, I was at last sworn in as a citizen of the United States. The next day I applied to the Chaplains' Corps of the Army and was accepted at once. We gave up the apartment, and Elizabeth and Jonathan moved to Cincinnati. I took leave from the congregation and went off to Chaplains' School at Harvard. War was now my business.

# Chapter 4

# ARMY YEARS

THE COURSE AT HARVARD, WHERE the Army had rented space, lasted for six weeks. We were instructed in the order of ranks, how to salute, how to march, what to expect, how we would get paid, and the thousand and one things that go with army routine. We received an inkling of the rigours of the service; we rose early in the morning, marched long hours, bunked with others in small rooms, and were even instructed in how to compute an azimuth. Somehow the whole program appeared to me not to be quite serious. To begin with, we never learned what we should really have studied; namely, why the United States was at war and especially the nature of Nazi and Japanese militarism. Later, when I had become a chaplain, I realized that most people were very uncertain about our reasons for fighting Germany. As for the Japanese, they had attacked us at Pearl Harbor and that appeared to be enough.

Furthermore, although we had the rank of first lieutenant, we were treated like high-school students. While we were taught about the Army's hierarchical structure, we were not made aware of how the system reduced the initiative of the individual and lowered the level of mature reaction in everyone from the rankest private to the advanced-grade officer. The process was one of insidious infantilization, yet there was no discussion of it even amongst otherwise thinking persons.

The people who ran the school—chaplains in the regular service and other support personnel—were men of severely limited views who had become totally integrated into army life. The Army was their father and mother, the womb into which they had crawled. They did what was necessary and no more, and they rather enjoyed moving several hundred formerly independent human beings around like pawns on a chess board. I was anxious to be done with this farce and, eventually, I was.

My first assignment was to Camp McCoy, located in northwestern Wisconsin between the towns of Sparta and Tomah. I arrived there ready to serve America and, if possible, to save the Jewish people.

The camp was built in typical army style: the roads and barracks neatly arrayed, a model of sterility. No frills here. It was obvious that everything was business. The Chief Chaplain, a colonel in the regular service, briefed me about my duties, assigned me an office in one of the chapels—and I was on my own. I slept in the officers' barracks, ate at the officers' mess and soon learned lesson number one: contact with enlisted men was restricted to working hours which were from eight to four. Afterwards one saw them only as servants in the mess hall or on other assignments. Social contact was ruled out by army discipline. I made up my mind that this was one discipline I was not going to observe.

I approached my duties with abandon. I held services and study groups, visited the hospital and tried to come to know the Jewish men on the post as intimately as possible. I helped them draft petitions, corresponded with their families, and spent my off-duty hours in the enlisted men's barracks talking to my charges about the problems which moved them: their future, their Judaism, their beliefs.

Not long after my family arrived—we had found a former roadside restaurant as living-quarters—I was called in to the Chief Chaplain's office. From the way he received me I knew that something was wrong. He did not ask me to sit down.

"Chaplain," he said, "there have been complaints about you."

In my mind I rehearsed the permutations of putative misdeeds I might have committed. Had I failed to salute a superior officer? Had my first monthly report been insufficient? I had learned that the reports of service attendance, hospital visits and other duties of the chaplain were always expected to be duly inflated in order to provide a good picture for the public-relations officer. Had I used too little imagination? I awaited a recital of my transgressions.

"You give all of us a bad name," he said.

"Beg your pardon, sir. I do not understand."

"You have been seen after hours in the enlisted men's barracks," he continued. "Did you not learn in Chaplains' School that socialization with enlisted men is strictly taboo? Their barracks are off limits to you."

"But I was doing chaplain's work, sir," I replied. "Counselling, relieving their loneliness and the like."

"Counselling belongs to the daylight hours in your office. The men can get a pass to see you. You are supposed to sign in at eight o'clock in the morning and sign out at four. By working overtime and being seen with the enlisted men at all hours you put the rest of the Chaplains' Corps on this post in a bad light. You make them look like slackers when in fact they understand the ways of the Army much better than you, a mere rookie."

While I tried to grasp this, he continued.

"You haven't been here long, but I think as far as the Army is concerned you are hopeless. I have requested a transfer for you at the first opportune time. You may go now."

I was shattered. My whole image of what I was supposed to do had come apart. This was an aspect of army life about which I had not been instructed. This man seemed to put whatever might affect his career and his own reputation above the welfare of the soldiers.

So we were going to move again, at an unspecified time. Little Jonathan was getting used to being bundled up and shlepped here and there. Meanwhile, he and we had to make an adjustment to the most bitter winter northern Wisconsin had seen. One day in January the temperature fell to 40°F below zero. Still, the baby seemed to thrive on the clear, crisp air and so did we. On the whole we spent a good few months at McCoy. After the Chief Chaplain's instruction I went home every night and had more time with my family than in some years.

Near the camp was a compound for German and Japanese prisoners, and on one occasion I was called in to interpret during an interrogation. The German was a cocky and self-assured youngster who had served in Rommel's Africa Corps. It was the first time that I had talked in this fashion to a Nazi—for that is what he proudly proclaimed himself to be. I asked him some routine questions and it turned out that he was born in Münster, my own native city.

I found that I was totally incapable of conversing with a man whose very presence shackled my mind. It was as if I had never been liberated, as if it were I who was the prisoner and not he.

The fact that both of us came from the same town emphasized our paradoxical relationship. I was deeply disturbed, and it took me some time to sort out the encounter.

I was not the only one to suffer from such meetings. One night I was awakened by a loud knock at the door. The caller identified himself as a sergeant from the hospital staff.

"The colonel," he said, "requests that you come to the hospital. An emergency operation on one of our men. He is Jewish and he may die."

I dressed quickly and we went out into the cold night. At the hospital the Chief Surgeon explained.

"Corporal S. is Jewish, a native of Germany, and has been assigned as a guard to the prisoners' compound. He has repeatedly requested a transfer but we didn't have anyone else with his qualifications. The man has a good education; I believe he's an architect in civilian life, and his command of English is excellent. We have used him as an interpreter and go-between for our people and the German officers in the camp. You know the Geneva Convention and all that; they get special considera- tion, bastards though they are."

"What happened?" I asked.

"Well, Corporal S. couldn't take it any more. As an enlisted man he was expected to kowtow to German officers, and it simply got to him. He lost his parents to the Nazis, I believe. A few hours ago he tried to commit suicide. Very poor job, I might say. Tried it with a penknife and I think the damage is not ir- reparable, but it's tricky all the same. Anyway, he's conscious, so you go and talk to him. I have to do some preparing. You can stay for the operation if you want to."

I said I would.

The corporal was able to talk. He knew what he had done and why. But he did not care to tell me about it then.

"You must live," I said to him. "You can't give them another victory."

"I know," he said. "It was a stupid thing to do. I do want to live."

It was the first operation I had ever watched. S. survived and we visited often thereafter. A fascinating, sensitive young man, he had been caught in the turmoil of conflicting emotions: being American and Jewish, being of German origin and being forced to defer to unregenerate Nazis. The combination had brought him to death's door.

During that winter I received a call from the camp comman-
dant who asked me whether I would be willing to give lectures to
officers and enlisted men on the nature of Nazism. I agreed
eagerly, and the entire camp population was paraded through
the theatre in shifts, to listen to an hour-long lecture on why
America had to defeat the Nazis. I was asked to go on tour to
other camps and for a while I occupied part of my time in this
way, feeling at last that I had made some contribution to the
Army—my colonel notwithstanding.

I found to my shock, though, that Hitler was admired by many
people, and the questions I received from my audiences revealed
a total incomprehension of the nature of Nazism. By the winter of
1943 the truth about what Hitler was doing to the Jews and many
others had finally come into full light. Many studies have been
made of how the world learned the full extent of the horrors
behind the wall of silence erected by the Nazis. The Allied
leadership knew as early as 1941, and after December 1942,
when an official condemnation of the developing Holocaust was
issued by the Allies, there was little excuse for not grasping the
scope of the terror. Still, it remained largely unknown—and not
only amongst non-Jews.

Explanations have been offered for the insensitivity of the
world to Auschwitz, but none tells the whole story. Perhaps it
was primarily an inability to comprehend that, in the twentieth
century, the "people of poets and thinkers" would deliberately
and methodically set out to destroy millions of human beings. But
there was more: the large and bitter residue of persistent antisemitism in Western countries which rendered the destruction of
the Jews into something acceptable if not actually desirable.

What I cannot understand now, looking back, is how we Jews
preserved our sanity in the face of the knowledge which was
then available. How could my wife and I go dancing on Saturday
night in the Officers' Club and pretend to be at ease? How could
we divorce the Great Reality from the small reality of our lives?
None of us did enough. Even the self-immolation of a desperate
Jewish survivor who killed himself in England to arouse the
world's conscience had contributed little. I sometimes wonder: if
a thousand Jewish leaders in America had gone on a hunger
strike, could they have awakened millions of caring people to the
butchery of the extermination camps? And even if they could not
have roused the whole world, could they not have roused every
last Jew to some act of witness? As for me, I had at least enlisted

in the Army to fight the Nazis; the uniform shielded my conscience. But not entirely. Not then and not now.

I volunteered for shooting practice and came home at night
nearly deaf, my ears pounding from the noise of all-day exercises. But I learned the craft. I had already made up my mind
that, were I to be assigned to a combat unit in Germany, I would
carry a gun, which was, of course, against the Geneva Convention and against army regulations. When the time came I did just
that. I think my superiors knew about it, yet I was never called to
task.

I expected to be sent overseas but instead, in the spring of
1944, was detailed to Camp (now Fort) Campbell on the border of
Tennessee and Kentucky. We found an apartment in Clarksville, located half-way between Nashville, Tennessee, and
Hopkinsville, Kentucky. It was unfurnished but the Army lent us
the necessary beds and furniture. For the first time in my life I
lived in the presence of open racial inequality.

In the north blacks were hidden away in ghettos and the
white conscience was rarely confronted with the realities of
racism. Things were different in Clarksville. Blacks lived ("existed" would be a better term) in shacks erected behind white
apartment buildings and by community consent and pressure
they were "kept in their places". The caretaker of our apartment
building, a wizened man, would do his chores by day and then
retreat to his shack at night. He would also babysit for us. On one
occasion, when we came home late at night, we found him asleep
on the floor. Elizabeth chided him: why was he not sleeping on
the couch?

"Oh no, Ma'm," he said, "I wouldn't dirty your couch."

He, like millions of his fellow blacks, had been brainwashed;
they knew that their use of a white man's couch or, heaven forbid, his toilet facilities, would constitute a serious breach of the
great racial divide.

A chapel was assigned to me, as well as an assistant. He was
Jacob Susanoff, in civilian life an actor with the Second Avenue
Yiddish Theater in New York, a dramatic-looking individual even
in his army uniform. He had a good voice, some knowledge of
Hebrew and the barest minimum of English—just enough to get
him into the Army, an organization which he detested with all his
might. Susanoff and I could not have come from worlds farther
apart: the chaplain with his German academic background and a

fairly rational orientation, and the Russian-born actor-singer with the world of the East European *shtetl* and its emotive qualities permeating his every word. I don't know what Susanoff learned from me, but I learned a great deal of Yiddish from him. The strange combination of the two of us produced a marvellous result: services were packed—but not on account of me. There were lots of boys from New York, and this was their chance to hear and see Susanoff. He was a smash success.

I preached to the boys on loneliness and related subjects of personal import; I tried to teach them Torah; and above all, I attempted to make them feel that they were part of a great cause: to wipe out the Nazis, rescue their people from extinction and save the world from being dominated by Hitler.

## Going Overseas

June 6, 1944, brought the news that D-Day had arrived and the invasion of Europe had begun, in the final phase of the struggle against Nazism. And here I was still at Camp Campbell, preparing for the time when I too would be able to do my share.

That time came in the fall. I received orders to report to Camp Reynolds, Pennsylvania, which was a staging area for overseas transport. Elizabeth and Jonathan came along—it was evident that my stay in the States would be over in a few more days. We received lectures on combat activity from returned officers who had fought in North Africa—I remember how remote it still seemed to me.

We were each given an overseas trunk in which to pack essential gear and, in my case, such books as I thought would be needed. We received a precisely drawn list of "recommended clothing for combat". In due time the trunk went off to somewhere on the Western front—for I was, in fact, going to Europe!—but alas, I never saw this treasure chest again until after V-E Day, when I had returned from Europe to the United States. When I opened it, everything was just the way I had packed it at Camp Reynolds—all the items without which, it was said, I would not be able to fight the war successfully.

In the little rooming-house where we had found temporary accommodation I said good-bye to Elizabeth and the baby. I can still see myself standing at the crib where Jonathan was sleeping. I said a fervent prayer that I might see him again. We kissed good-bye—for how long? Of course I was only one of many millions who underwent the same experience, but that did not make it any easier. It was harder on Elizabeth than on me. I, at least, was going to do something that as a Jew and as an American I needed and wanted to do. She would stay behind, waiting. She was pregnant and would give birth while I was overseas. I left for New York; the family went to Cincinnati.

After a few days I received a note: I would be flown to Europe at once. The rumour was that one of the Jewish chaplains had been killed in battle and they wanted a replacement forthwith. It was not exactly a comforting thought and I did not write my family about it.

My first transatlantic flight was taken with a large group of soldiers in one of the old transports, and turned out to be not entirely a smooth affair. We had to make a detour to avoid Nazi airplanes. Eventually we arrived in Prestwick, Scotland, were loaded onto trains and sent to London. It was the time of the V-1 bombs and the capital was in total darkness. Soon I saw the first of these monsters streaking slowly overhead—an eerie feeling. A few moments later came the dull explosion and the flames on the horizon. I was not as yet at the front but the taste was there. I was quartered at an officers' billet in Grosvenor Square and at once went to search for a telephone book so that I could contact my parents, who were now back in Brighton. It was seven years since I had seen them last.

What I did not realize was that new telephone books had not been printed since the beginning of the war—and for Britain the war was already five years old. What few telephone books were left were in tatters. It took me several hours of cajoling a variety of operators to finally track down the number of my parents. They of course had had no idea that I was coming over—and when I finally made myself understood, there was only one question, "When will you come?"

"I'm on my way," I assured them.

That was more easily said than done. I went to the officer who was in charge of shipments to the continent and asked him whether it would be possible for me to see my parents. He looked at me and he looked at his files and his orders, and in the gentlest way possible suggested that, while he could not give me permission to go—for my name could be listed on army orders that very afternoon—he would like to feel that I had not asked him the question. But please to remember, he added, that I would probably be shipped out no later than forty-eight hours hence. I took the hint, and was on my way to the south coast.

When our tears had dried I had a chance to look at my parents. They appeared to be in remarkably good shape, though older of course, and with the strain of the war showing on their faces. But their spirit was unimpaired and they had useful work to do, which was most important for them. They had a house full of refugee children for whom they cared. Their relationship with the Jewish community in Brighton and Hove was excellent; it was obvious that their remarkable ability and their great experience were widely respected. The house had three storeys. It was cold, and the few fireplaces which were in operation were not nearly enough to create a comfortable environment, though no one seemed to mind; we were all alive and together. We talked through half the night. I slept under a multitude of covers to keep my teeth from chattering, but I knew how fortunate I was to see my parents again in the midst of war. I stayed until the next evening, then I left—another parting, with the same pain as at Camp Reynolds and the same unanswered question: when would I see them again? A few days later I found myself on the way to France.

My destination was a replacement depot (in army lingo, "repple-depple") somewhere near Paris. I saw nothing of the French capital, although it had already been reconquered by the Allies. The camp had been inundated by endless rains and was now a huge mud-hole. Here were ten thousand American soldiers awaiting assignment to some front unit.

I had one immediate need: I had no clothes except my dress uniform, in which I cut a rather incongruous figure. But since the repple-depple was also a staging area for wounded soldiers going home, I discovered several who were more than happy to part with their combat outfits.

My assignment took a while in coming. They had flown me over in a hurry and now had me holed up totally useless—the old "hurry up and wait" game of the Army. At last the orders arrived: I was to be the Jewish chaplain for the 104th Infantry Division, the "Timberwolves" as they were called. They were commanded by Major-General Terry Allen who was famous for his night attacks. This was both good and bad: at night he had the element of surprise in his favour, but at the same time it was hard for his own men to tell who was foe and who was friend Night fighting was a double-edged sword.

# Front Lines

I joined the division at Brandt, a suburb of Aachen (Aix-la-Chapelle). Suddenly it dawned on me: I was back in the country from which I had fled, and was not too far from Münster, where I was born. It was a strange feeling to be returned to my roots, under circumstances which no one could have predicted. Now I was an American, and above all I was a Jew who had come to help in the battle against inhumanity. I felt a strange mixture of emotions: I was elated to be cast in the role of liberator, yet oppressed by the sight of German civilians who by their connivance or their silence had brought the world, and especially my people, to near-ruin.

On December 13, 1944, I reported to headquarters, met the Chief Chaplain of the division—a Catholic padre—and was assigned to the Signal Corps, a mobile unit of the division whence I could easily get in touch with soldiers of the 413th, 414th and 415th regiments who formed the bulk of the division's 12,000 men.

I soon noticed that priorities were different in this war-zone: dress was inconsequential; saluting was a luxury; everyone was biding his time until the next offensive.

From the time I arrived in Europe I wrote daily letters to Elizabeth. She kept them all faithfully and while I could not write everything I saw, the record has the advantage of immediacy.

*December 13*
Went out for a little while and took a look around—the Germans sure caught their due rewards here. It did my heart good to see a German being halted by an MP and made to show his identification papers. How well I recall when the *Herrenvolk* did all the halting. Well, they'll learn different; and very fast I hope.

*December 14*
This afternoon a soldier halted me and said unbelievingly, "A Jewish chaplain?" Answer, "Right." "I can't believe it," he says. "It's wonderful, it's good just to look at you, chaplain." Makes you feel as if the gleam in his eyes was worth the long trip across the ocean. . . .

I was assigned a chaplain's assistant. His name was Kurt Joseph Flamm and in time our military association would bloom into a lifelong bond of affection between us and our families.

Joe—then Private Flamm—was one of the most unusual people I had ever met. Born in Frankfurt to an ultra-Orthodox family, sent to Belgium to study in a *yeshivah*, he spoke his native German with a Yiddish accent. However there was nothing wrong with his Hebrew and Yiddish. His knowledge of traditional sources far exceeded mine and his generous and compassionate nature made him an ideal assistant. The fact that he did not know how to drive our jeep did not faze him; nothing ever did. He was (and is) one of those persons who believe that with will and imagination all problems can be solved, and he had both. Above all, he had a total devotion to his people. No trip was too long, no task too difficult for him if it served to help a soldier. He was also deeply convinced of the necessity of the war—except that he was at war with army bureaucracy as well. Joe despised discipline and regulations. He believed that independent, free people would win the war more quickly and painlessly than those who were regimented. He and the Army never got along. But for me he was literally a godsend: he would accomplish things that nobody else could, he was *chazan*, *shammes*, driver and, to me, a dear friend.

Joe and I had long discussions on Orthodoxy and Reform, and debated the possibility of maintaining a semblance of *kashrut* (kosher diet) at the front. Joe had not eaten any meat for many months, but the supply of substitute foods was getting shorter. Spam would soon be our unit's main staple—an amalgam of ham and other substances. The rabbinical authorities in America had ruled that in special exigencies ham and pork could be eaten but that one should avoid obtaining pleasure from them, such as sucking the bones. We eventually established a simple rule for ourselves: wherever we could avoid Spam we did; we ate it only when no other food was in sight.

*December 15*
Our services today were held in the back room of a German house and in a Catholic church without windows, but with pews still standing. Who would have dared to predict a year ago that Hanukah services would be held in these spots? The wonderful development of things was in everyone's heart and the Hanukah hymn had its special message for us here.

A Roman Catholic priest came to see me. He brought with him fragments of a *Sefer Torah** which had been salvaged after

---

* A hand-written scroll of the Pentateuch, treasured in the synagogue ark.

Crystal Night and which he had buried. Now, with the Americans here and the knowledge that a rabbi was back in the city, he felt that he had to surrender these relics. The man was simple and straightforward; although he did not know the meaning of these torn pieces it was clear to him that they had a holy character. I accepted them gratefully. Eventually we packed them in a bazooka case and sent them home. They have been with me ever since and usually rest in a private ark at the synagogue.

The rumour mill was working: something big was in the offing. A few days later the Battle of the Bulge was on. The Germans were making their final effort to regain the initiative on the Western front. Gerd von Rundstedt had launched a desperate breakthrough attempt in the Ardennes Forest and almost succeeded in his objective of reaching the port of Antwerp. In the process, American units were isolated. Up to this point, the war had been going well; suddenly there was the possibility of drastic reversal. The German attack was helped by bad weather which grounded the American Air Force. We waited and after a while our anxiety receded. People were dying a few miles away but I was still not seeing war.

Strict blackout and security regulations came into effect. The password was changed every day, for apparently some German soldiers dressed in American uniforms had been parachuted behind our front lines.

*December 20*
The morale of the men is pretty high. Much higher than among the perpetual gripers back in the States. In fact you rarely hear the men gripe seriously; when there are hardships they know that they have to put up with them and their only concern is to do the job the fastest and bestest they can.

*December 24*
You see a German airplane shot down and the pilot falling to his flaming death before your eyes. Yet strange what war does to you: you feel no pity—on the contrary, you have a feeling of satisfaction. I guess it's just the plain instinct of self-preservation asserting itself. I had never known before that a group of American planes could present such an absolutely beautiful sight—but they do have to be ours or the beauty of it is gone.

[I had listened to Goebbels before writing this next passage.]

*December 26*
It was, in his own way and for the purposes he had set himself, a very good sermon for Nazis. I'd hate to have him compete for the same pulpit—he'd preach me out of it in no time. In his soft, *schmeichly* voice he presented his arguments very glibly. It reeked of sentimentality. He insisted: "You can be proud of Germany. In the midst of enemies all about, she stands firm. Now we're moving again, this time towards final victory. You can't despair now when all is at stake. You wouldn't want to be untrue to your fate and destiny." *Schicksal* and what-not—all along these intangible lines. He held out a beautiful Germany after the war, but what beauty it would have he did not say. Mystical allusions were rampant. The mothers of the dead, German honour, and of course the Führer played a great role in his oration. I have no doubt that the average German who listened to it was actually uplifted by his promises and pictures, because he has been brought up on sentimental generalities or has become so used to taking mystical abstractions for real things. I wish more Americans could have listened too and understood this. They would have realized that we are fighting an irrational, fanatical enemy who will not give in but must be done in.

*December 28*
You get so used to the sight of dead horses and cows lying around that you wonder how some animals have still managed to stay alive. . . . In one of the villages which was completely reduced to rubble there was not one living thing, or at least it seemed that way—until we turned the corner and discovered some motion in one of the first-floor windows. There was a she-goat, peacefully looking out through what had been the window and was now a gaping hole in the wall. She was chewing on something and on closer inspection was reclining on a davenport which miraculously had survived the war. War brings strange sights.

A Bible-story book for children, published under the Nazis in 1940, came into my possession, well written and quite devotionally conceived. Ingeniously the author managed never to mention the word Israel while retelling the stories of the Bible. I had not thought it possible.

Incoming mail was never censored, only spot-checked; but outgoing mail always was. Officers censored and initialled their own letters, and took turns doing those of the enlisted men. My turn came after a while. It was a disturbing experience to read other people's most intimate outpourings. Somehow I have managed to forget it all, except that this unwanted occupation provided me with my first contact with pornography. I remember one letter: it went into such details that I wondered for a moment whether I should let such stuff get through. But of course I was appointed a military, not a moral, censor; and after my first hesitation it was easy to keep the two apart.

But strangely, I myself ran afoul of the authorities. I had whiled some of my hours away with chess problems and one day I decided to submit a problem to the chess editor of the *Christian Science Monitor*. For some reason my letter was caught by another censor and I received a visit from the G-2 section.* It did not take me long to clear up the mystery but I was warned to forget about chess correspondence until after the war. "Too easy," said my visitor, "to use the chess symbols for coded messages."

It was at this time of the German advance that, in visiting our men in the front lines, my first serious brush with war occurred. We had been shot at from time to time, but somehow managed to pretend it was happening somewhere else. Even potential danger has a dulling sameness about it.

Joe and I found ourselves in a little town which had been left relatively unscathed by the war. We actually located a bed in some house and were ready to go to sleep when the word was passed around to be on the alert: we had been cut off and were surrounded by German troops. Suddenly war took on a personal face. One of the most terrible things that can happen to a person is to be made unable to change his fate, to be left with nothing to do but wait for the sword to fall. Our troops had withdrawn into the houses and were ready to defend themselves. Joe had a rifle, I had my pistol and I was prepared to use it. A thousand thoughts went through our heads: what would the Germans do if they captured two Jewish soldiers from America, especially two who had once been German citizens? We talked about destroying our dog-tags, which had the identification H for Hebrew impressed upon them, but decided against it. If possible, we promised ourselves, we would not be caught alive. The bed was forgotten as we stood all night at the window listening for the sounds of battle to ap-

---

* The Intelligence and Counter-intelligence group.

proach. At last, just before dawn, the tanks came—and, to our immense relief, they were American. They had broken through and liberated us. We looked at each other and then said the traditional prayer of gratitude.

Thereafter, I was no longer afraid. The reality of killing and the possibility of being killed became totally remote to me. We were now in the midst of combat. I functioned in a state of slight detachment—war had become "normal" in every sense.

*January 10*
Snow covers the landscape. The sun is shining brightly in all its mid-winter glory and its rays and reflections are silvering even the dullest object. It is hard to remember that the land is enemy country and that there is a war on. Nature seems to take no notice at all. In war and peace alike the rolling hills and winding roads present a picture of unmarred beauty. The snow lies heavily on the branches of trees that arch the alleys; it is fairytale land. It is all a testimony to the essential silliness of human behaviour, which passes by these things in order to "enjoy" the imagined satisfactions of powerful play and counterplay.

Joe Flamm and I managed to publish a newspaper for our men. We called it *Forward-Kadimah* and it bore the insignia of the division on one side and the tablets of the Ten Commandments on the other.

A syndicated columnist in America, Alfred Segal, wrote about his reaction to seeing the first copy of the paper.

> ... They were speaking with no gloating satisfactions, with no vengeful enjoyment of men who had seen their enemy humbled. In the way of civilized men they were looking at a most dazzling manifestation of justice with becoming humility. Retribution was a cup to taste and savor but not to get drunk on. ... The *Forward* published in Germany looked inward and enquired what God is and what man is and how a Jew may fulfill his manhood. Something constructive came out of Germany.*

The German attack was coming to a standstill and the Battle of the Bulge was now turning. The tension under which we had lived slowly subsided, but never for long. Visiting the forward units sometimes meant dodging between houses and trees, for we were in sight of the enemy. The nearest I got to being killed at

* Published in the *Jewish Criterion*, March 23, 1945.

that time came, however, when one of my friends cleaned his gun in front of me, forgetting that he had not emptied it of bullets. It was a close call but left no scars.

A copy of the *Morning Journal*, New York's largest Yiddish paper, arrived. It carried our article entitled "An Outpost in Germany".

> In a destroyed building which is full of holes from bombs and which used to be a Gestapo headquarters, in the little town of ——, stands a young Jewish chaplain with an ark nailed together from packing boards. With sacred intonation he unrolls the *sefer* and begins to read. At this moment the Gestapo building changes into a synagogue.
>
> The Torah which Lieutenant W. Gunther Plaut, former rabbi of Washington Boulevard Temple in Chicago, unrolls comes from a synagogue which the Nazis burned during the pogroms in '38; a Jewish family brought it to England. Another Jewish chaplain, Emanuel Poliakoff, brought the *sefer* to Germany. Lieutenant Plaut's assistant, Kurt Joseph Flamm, tells me with a sharp German accent that this is the first time that a *Sefer Torah* has been unrolled in Germany behind the American lines and that this is a symbol of the return of religious liberty to Germany.
>
> Twenty-five Jewish soldiers sit on boxes. They wear helmets and with deep devotion they listen to the rabbi's prayers and reading.
>
> From time to time their eyes wander to the walls of the building where Nazi slogans are posted. Most of the men can translate them easily. Behind the chaplain on the wall there stands in large letters, "Only he who fights truly lives."
>
> *Boyd Lewis, UP Correspondent.*

The German offensive had now been turned back and we relaxed. I received permission to visit Brussels and went there to secure a *Sefer Torah* for ourselves. I found one in a Jewish orphanage and it was given to me for safe-keeping until after the war. It came from Kassel, had been rescued in 1938 by a nineteen-year-old boy who took it to Antwerp, and there it was left with a gentile when the Germans came. It was brought to Brussels later and placed in a synagogue, then buried in a cellar when the Jews were being deported. After liberation it was placed in the orphanage. It had beautiful script and I was thrilled.

Later on I discovered that on the rim of the wooden stay the name of the scribe was clearly legible: it was Gruenebaum. When I wrote my father about it I learned that Gruenebaum was a cousin of his and that he had seen him write a *Sefer Torah* many years before. I liked to imagine that this was the one we were carrying into Germany.

The end of February brought the long-awaited push. Our division crossed the Roer at night, in the midst of horrible carnage. The wind was heavy and a lot of boats capsized. Soldiers drowned by the dozens. The fighting was heavy and we lost many men. For the first time I saw how desperately ugly and unromantic it all was. Human beings were torn apart like bits of paper. And I? I closed up like a flower at night; my mind shut itself off from the terrors of killing and maiming. It would be some time before I was once again open to normal sentiment. Sometimes I felt as if my humanity had been drained away, and I hated myself for it.

Columns of German prisoners marched towards the rear, their hands over their heads. I went to the aid station and there were a few of them sitting around slightly wounded. I asked them about their morale and they said there wasn't any hope any more.

In the midst of the excitement came news from England that the hostel in Brighton had closed. My parents had at last received their visas and were about to sail for America. And I would not be there to greet them!

*February 27*
Today is Purim. Haman isn't hanged yet—but one of these days he will be. . . . Please excuse the incoherence of this note. We are a bit unsettled—I hope you'll understand.

The push was on in earnest. We quartered for a while in Düren and settled down in a bombed-out house; at least we had a roof over our heads. Strange, how one gives to the temporary the aspects of the permanent. Even though we would stay in this rubbled town for but a few days, we tried to fix up our quarters. We even obtained a Persian rug. Then the push was on again and now, with increasing frequency, we encountered a new phenomenon: civilians by the thousands on the road, German refugees.

We had seen them in film clips—and decades later television would bring such sights to our homes as regular fare. But then it was new to us—and our natural feelings of human sympathy were aroused even by the enemy. There were still many men in our division who were uncertain why we were fighting the Germans. They had homes with hot and cold running water and

seemed so civilized in their behaviour—quite different from
people in French villages, where dung heaps were found in lit-
tered alleyways and where the people had a "disagreeable"
measure of pride and independence. But not the Germans; they
were obsequious and anxious to please and, circumstances
allowing, very clean. For many American GI's these externals
blurred the view of a war which they did not understand in its
depth. Not until a few weeks later, when we came to our first
concentration camp, did these soldiers begin to grasp the nature
of the struggle.

*March 6*
I feel that in a measure all these people are guilty and bear
part of the burden for the things that have happened to the
world. I remember the things they have done to me, to my
people, to the men who are now in their graves. But who is
guilty in the full measure of the word, who is innocent? There
is much misery amongst them, yet it doesn't touch you. You see
it so often. It leaves you fairly indifferent. But then there is the
individual, and the human conflict starts. How can you check
an oncoming of pity? I at least can't. Maybe I'm all wrong but
that's the way I feel. An old man looking for his wife, a younger
man searching for his sick children whom he has lost. German
or not, there is individual human misery which messes up the
ordinary schedule of values with which you come prepared.
War is no good for anybody, and that's just about the long and
short of it.

But my feelings were to undergo a decided change. Up to this
point we had not seen the truly dispossessed and had not come to
our first experience with evil incarnate, the concentration camp.
At this point I think I was still trying to draw a philosophical line
between individual and collective guilt. That line was soon to
disappear into an overwhelming abhorrence of everything
German.

Cologne fell with relatively little fighting, and I made my way
to Roonstrasse where the great synagogue had stood. It was still
there—the walls, the structure—but the inside was all burnt out.
That was the work of the Nazis in November of '38 and not—as
some local residents were eager to convince me—of American
bombers. We spread the word that a service would be held, and
out came civilians who had somehow survived the war: half-
Jews, and some full Jews who were married to gentiles and had

escaped transportation to the East. Chaplain Robert Marcus of
the Eighth Airborne Division joined us and by the time we began
we had the largest congregation since I had joined my division.*

That evening I wrote home:

> All the women cried—and so did many men; and I myself had
> grave difficulty to keep calm. We didn't have enough seats—
> just a few benches for the infirm. The ark—our ark—stood
> behind us, symbol of Judaism coming back to these people.
> Most of them live in mixed marriages—all of them, perhaps—
> and that is the reason that they were able to survive the de-
> portaiions. But many of the gentile parties have accepted
> Judaism—and there were some who had come in memory of
> their [Jewish] husbands and wives.
>
> Need I tell you that it was an unforgettable scene? Rubble
> all about us, but the air and atmosphere of the temple per-
> vading all—and in front of me people who because of their
> religious affiliation had gone through hell. Of any "firsts" I
> cam claim, this is one I will cherish: the first service for Jews—
> civilian Jews—in Germany in a synagogue since—? Who
> knows, too long. . . .
>
> One woman beyond herself with tears said to me, "Rabbi,
> this was the very place where my son was Bar Mitzvah" (he is
> somewhere in England, they don't know where). As we stood
> conversing at the entrance, people passed between us.
> Automatically, seeing soldiers at the gates, they showed their
> passports bearing a large "J".

Today the synagogue has been rebuilt by the German government and is one of the stateliest in the country—but nothing can
restore the old Jewish community which went back to Roman
times and was a proud adornment of culture and learning. The
building today hides the rubble of yesteryear and somewhere
under the rubble lie the memories of generations of Jews who
worshipped there.

In the rubble we found torn pages of prayer-books and then,
near where the ark would have been on the east side, the broken-
off but well-preserved wooden sculpture of a lion that once had
graced the ark. I mounted it on my portable Torah case and thus
the presence of Cologne went with us to the end of the campaign.

---

* Robert St. John broadcast an account of the service over NBC (March 13) and Marcus
published an account of it in *Congress Weekly*, April 20, 1945.

With the Catholic division-padre, Mussell, and the assistant divisional chaplain, Walker, a Protestant, I paid a visit to the cardinal resident in Cologne. His pleasant home was in good repair and he received us cordially though with obvious reserve. He could not at first comprehend that I was a Jew and a rabbi. He did not realize that the American Army had Jewish chaplains— I think that the years of Hitler had made him forget that there were still countries where Jews were treated as human beings. He refused to say anything about the Nazis—in fact he railed against Americans.

"They don't have any manners," he said. "Some came here and did not wipe their feet. Look at these lovely carpets, they dirtied them without so much as an 'excuse me'."

The three of us looked at each other and left shortly thereafter. Mussell especially was deeply disheartened.

"If they can do this to a cardinal," he said, "a man who has to be a person of intellect, discretion and political savvy, what can we expect of other Germans? The man has been brain-washed pure and simple."

I said, with respect, that cardinals too were human beings and were different from one another. Perhaps the man had found it possible to combine his cross with a swastika. But there had been others in the Church, Faulhaber in Munich and von Galen in Münster, who had stood up courageously and spoken for freedom and for the humanity of Jews. They would not have worried about Americans dirtying their rugs.

Now the roads were filled not only with Germans but also with liberated slave labour: Belgians, French, Poles, others. On the thirteenth of March I wrote from Brauweiler.

Saw a pitiful sight today. Ten men who had just been freed by our troops from a Gestapo dungeon where they had been held. I say "men", but the description hardly fits any more. One fellow shown to be twenty-one looked fifty-one. They were all broken. Two were blind or half-blind. The fact that they had been liberated meant nothing at all to them. They are virtually dead to the world and I wonder whether they will ever be able to return to reality. Right now they are blunted beyond immediate repair, undernourished—terrible sights. . . . Where the Nazis have trodden they have left misery in their wake. . . .

On the seventeenth of March we lay outside Bonn. That was the day my parents arrived in Cincinnati although I did not know it at the time. They had had a difficult time getting there, first being lost in Montreal and then reaching New York and being totally unfamiliar with the American transportation system. But Elizabeth, after endless telegrams and with the help of HIAS* and relatives in New York, finally arranged it all. They arrived and were welcomed by her, her mother, Jonathan and, later, Walter and his wife Hadassah. Their adjustment was to be very difficult, especially in the beginning, and in fact my father never became accustomed to the United States; he did not live very long thereafter. But at least he had made it across the ocean, and it would not be long before we were all together again.

We now had continuing contact with German civilians and, if one believed them, the whole country had never contained a single Nazi in the first place—certainly not. A number of people even claimed to be Jews.

We were quartered in Bonn when Passover arrived and on the university grounds I found a large enough room for Seder. The fact that it was the morgue did not faze us—death was all around. In any case we were seeing things perhaps worse than death, people maimed in the most dreadful fashion—basket cases, men without arms or legs. There was often not enough time to pay visits to the hospitals in the rear, but up front in the field stations there was more to be seen than one cared to record in one's memory. Later I was able to visit a temporary cemetery and watch the burials. The corpses were stacked on trucks like cordwood and were handled not much differently. What did one write home to families? That was the toughest job of being a chaplain—telling the grieving family back home that their dear one was really dead (they had, of course, been informed by the War Department already) or, sometimes worse, that he was alive but. . . .

We began the Seder but did not get past the first few songs. The news spread quickly: "Everyone back to his station! We're on the move!" The Rhine had been crossed at Remagen by the Ninth Armored Division of the First Army. I threw the boxes of matzos into the jeep and off we went towards Remagen. There, at that lovely bridge which afforded the Allied troops their first crossing en masse, I stood with Joe on top of our jeep crying, "Matzos, matzos!" Heads emerged from tanks, troops came by on trucks. "Seder tonight," we yelled. "Pesach, matzos!

* Hebrew Immigrant Aid Society.

Celebrate the liberation!" Within half an hour all our boxes were gone—it was the most exhilarating time I could remember.

Now the big push was on. On the thirtieth of March I wrote:

> Let your imagination go and you still can't fathom the things one sees nowadays. The Germans just can't believe their eyes and the French, Belgians, Russians and assorted former PW's* are hugging us. . . . Nobody knows where he is going—but the French do, they are walking west, waving and shouting at you.

We, of course, were still pushing east and the pace of pursuit was picking up. In Warburg I visited two Polish Jewish officers in a former PW hospital. One had been in captivity for six, the other for four years. Their Jewish interest had never lagged. By and large they had been treated fairly by the Germans, but as Jews they had been segregated. In 1942, when segregation by the Germans was not yet in force in the camps, *their own Polish comrades* had insisted on having them kept separate. No wonder the Germans chose a Polish town, Auschwitz, for their worst horrors!

## The Presence of Evil

April twelfth was a shocking day for me and, as I was to find out the next day, for America. On that day we came on the little city of Nordhausen—important militarily because V-2 bombs were manufactured nearby.

> This afternoon I saw a sight that I won't forget as long as I live. Nearby was a German concentration camp [Dora]—for Russians, Poles, Jews and political unreliables. When our first American troops came, there were about 4,000 dead lying around and 400 scarcely alive—if alive they could be called. Death for the others had come mostly through starvation, a fearful sight indeed. Our troops were out in numbers staring at the incredible scene. There were many who for the first time in their lives were convinced—because they couldn't help seeing what they saw—that what they had heard about the Germans wasn't all propaganda.

I did not know then that Dora-Nordhausen was the first con-

---

* Or POW, prisoner of war.

centration camp to be liberated. In the scale of camps it was a "minor" installation—except for those who perished there. For me, it produced a shock of major proportions, because the reality was far more inhuman and ghastly than I had imagined. Nordhausen breached my protective shell as nothing else had done.

With our arrival at Dora-Nordhausen the entire sentiment of our division changed and I myself went through the last phase of my development. It was one thing to see displaced persons crowding the roads; it was one thing to meet the occasional prisoner of war—but the sight of Nordhausen was something altogether different. There we were confronted by the true nature of Nazism—and that without seeing the ovens of Auschwitz. (They did have three small ovens, but according to the survivors they were used to burn those who had died from starvation or had been executed on some trumped-up charge.)

I was put in charge of the burials and I insisted that the Germans from Nordhausen come for the occasion in their Sunday best. Of course we did not have enough spades to do the work, but in my anger—now turning towards revenge—I told the burghers to use the knives, forks and spoons from their homes. I ordered the women to come out and help wash the bodies. The protest from the town's population was loud, but I paid no attention. "We didn't know what was going on," they said, even though the camp was but a few miles from the city and the stench alone must have told them that something was amiss. Time and again the old excuses: "We could not help ourselves." "We too were prisoners of the regime." "I never was a Nazi." "Some of my best friends were Jews."*

A day or so later General Eisenhower arrived. He looked briefly at the sight, shook his head and said, "I would not have believed it." I do not know whether later on he saw Dachau and Bergen-Belsen, but I do know that Dora-Nordhausen was his first acquaintance with what the Nazis had done.

It quickly became known that the Americans had a Jewish chaplain in their midst. After all, a flag with the Ten Commandments and the Magen David, the Jewish star, flew from our jeep. The survivors constantly surrounded us. Above all they wanted to know where their families were and whether we could get in touch with relatives in the United States. One man had a little

---

* It is worth noting that the Jewish community in the city went back to the year 1290, and that it numbered close to five hundred before the Nazi era.

piece of paper secreted away in his pocket, grimy and tattered;
the script was almost impossible to read, but he had committed
the address to memory. I contacted the Red Cross and told them
to find the family and let them know that their brother was still
among the living. But another was not so fortunate. He had no
slip of paper and his memory had failed him. "Cohen, Cohen," he
said over and over again. "Cohen in Brooklyn or New York or
somewhere in America. You must find him." He wept with
frustration. Now liberation had come and both he and I were
helpless—at least for the moment.

Thirty-five years later I met one of the liberated prisoners.
Lilly Jacob (now married to Eric Meier, a hero of the French
Resistance) was then a teenager. She had survived Auschwitz
and had been assigned to work in the Nordhausen bomb factory.
She fell ill with typhus and upon liberation was put into the
hospital ward formerly occupied by German soldiers. Next to her
bed she found a picture album that had been left behind. It contained photos taken by a Nazi guard of Jewish prisoners as they
alighted from the train and went through the process of selection: one side to the gas ovens, the other for work and temporary
survival. Lilly saw with disbelief pictures of herself—and of her
family, all subsequently gassed. She guarded the album carefully
and eventually brought it to the New World. In 1980 she received
wide publicity when she donated it to the Yad Vashem, the
Memorial Foundation in Jerusalem. Our meeting was one of
mutual joy, of gratitude, and of recalling our vastly different experiences in Nordhausen.

Fifteen wandering Jewish women who had escaped the last
death march came our way. I found them shelter and food in the
next German village. Clad in burlap, without shoes, heads
shaved, they had nothing to protect their modesty. Our men soon
fixed that: they requisitioned the finest clothes in the village. It
was a joy to meet the girls again a few hours later, bathed,
cleaned up and dressed like human beings for the first time in
years.

Some of the women had been in Auschwitz. They told us about
arrival, inspection, selection, the whole dreadful, unbelievable
tale which, since that time, has been told so often. But for us,
then, it had the punch of grim immediacy.

As I came into the mess tent for breakfast on April thirteenth
we heard the news of Roosevelt's death. To all of us he had been

a father-figure. Many of the youngsters could hardly remember
an America without Roosevelt as president. We had not known
how ill he was, nor did I know then the double game he had
played with refugees; at that time he was simply the father of the
nation. Much later I heard that in some American communities,
especially in wealthy suburbs, there had been joyous celebrations throughout the night. To these people (amongst them some
friends who told us about it) Roosevelt was not father but the
devil incarnate and his death was considered a release from the
tyranny of governmental paternalism. But at the front we did not
know about these things, and we cried.

During these days an additional person was added to my staff.
The colonel, a particular antagonist of the unmilitary Joe Flamm,
decided that we had lost too many jeeps and that a more experienced driver was necessary. This judgement of Joe was not
altogether fair. There was simply no repair work being done during the advance. If a vehicle didn't work or had a flat, you left it
by the side, picked up a new one and hoped someone else would
fetch the old one and have it repaired. Still, our list of
replacements showed too many vehicles, and the colonel informed me that despite the fact that the Table of Organizations
did not provide for my obtaining an additional man, he was going
to make an exception.

So I took a trip back to the nearest replacement depot and
picked a name at random from the list which the sergeant shoved
in front of me: "James McDermott". Late that night he joined me.
He could hardly believe that he, a Roman Catholic Irishman from
Brooklyn, was assigned to be an assistant to a rabbi. But he was
delighted and turned out to be a splendid friend.

He had several years of university behind him, had entered the
Air Force and had been on his final lap of training as a pilot
when, in his bravado, he had "buzzed" a girlfriend in Dallas. He
was summarily sacked for this indiscretion. In the reckoning of
the Air Force the $30,000 which had been spent on his training
was wiped out, and in their books any man who would do such a
thing could not be relied upon to follow orders precisely and
function adequately in combat. In the style typical of the military
a bit of additional revenge was wreaked upon him: he was discharged from the Air Force, put in the Army, and listed as a rifle-
battalion man—a very dangerous assignment, especially for a
replacement. (The latecomer to a unit did not know his fellow
soldiers and their ways; they looked out for each other first, and

only then for the newcomer, who was therefore more exposed. Jim was well aware of what had been done to him, but he harboured no resentment. "I have only myself to blame," he said, more than once.) He was, therefore, doubly happy to be assigned to me, because it relieved him of combat duty.

He was 6 ′2 ″, handsome and highly practical in his approach to many things. He knew how to requisition supplies, or find eggs and meat from German civilians, and he was acquainted with the intricacies of the automobile. But he too lost us a jeep or two and it was with him that I had my most serious accident. We were crossing a wooden bridge in the rain when the jeep began to slide. It hit the embankment and we were both thrown clear. Jim fell on his arm and bruised it badly; I was shaken up thoroughly but without visible injury. I only ached for a few days afterwards. In Jim's case it turned out to be more serious, although we did not know it at the time. (After the war he joined the New York Police Force and received a medal as a hero. Then it was found that he had cancer in his wrist. His hand was amputated; too late. He died a young man. I had a terrible time helping prove that the injury was service-related, but with the help of Senator Edward Thye and then-Congressman Eugene McCarthy, a good friend, we were finally successful and Jim's widow received a pension.)

With Jim taking over driving duties, Joe Flamm could devote himself to helping the liberated. His simple and all-embracing love for his people was enormous, and there was an instant rapport between him and the freed prisoners. He not only *would* give but *did* give the shirt off his back.

*April 21*
In my meanderings today met Count Felix von Luckner, the "Sea Wolf" of the German cruiser *Emden* in the First World War. Still firm and straight-looking, the old-type German officer, he said that he had been a staunch anti-Nazi—of course.

*April 26*
Just listened to Mrs. [Clare Boothe] Luce reporting on what she saw at Buchenwald.* Now they all see it: for twelve long years they wouldn't believe it and even the four million dead Jews were not proof enough. [The full extent of the tragedy was still not known.]

* A concentration camp south-east of Nordhausen, near Weimar.

*April 30*
This morning visited a place where I found nine Jewish
Hungarian girls aged fourteen to twenty who had gone through
the most harrowing experiences. They are simple, really nice
kids—Orthodox and religious throughout all their untellable
troubles. Without having access to a calendar they still kept
the Holy Days as best they could. After the liberation the first
thing they did was to fast in gratitude. They wouldn't let me
go—we sang some Palestinian songs together, they danced the
hora for me—I could have wept for their joy. We set them up
beautifully. They now have clothes, good quarters and food.

The war was winding down. There were rumours that the Russians had conquered Berlin and that Hitler had died.

*May 2*
At 10:26 last night I happened to be tuned to a German radio
station—one of the three or four still left—when the announcement of Hitler's death came. And now as I am writing to you,
announcement is made of a surrender of the German armies in
Italy. These are tremendous pieces of news. Last night when
the German radio told of Hitler's "heroic" passing I was just
overawed, with the final hour so close at hand—incredible.
When it happened, three former PW's—Jewish boys from New
York—were in my office and you can imagine the additional
tenseness of the atmosphere created by their presence. We
opened my last bottle of cognac, ate a whole salami and celebrated.

Still, Hitler's death left me with no exultation. Perhaps it is
because we saw the end approaching that it has not moved us
so much. After the first excitement everything went its normal
way. Occasionally you heard someone make a remark. The
Germans seem untouched by the event although they all know
about it. "*Heil Hitler, der Hund ist tot*"* is about all people
have to say—to Americans, of course. But Hitler has ceased to
be an object of personal hate; he long ago became a symbol
rather than remaining an individual personality. His death just
presages the total collapse—and I am certain that by the time
you read this, V-E Day** will already have been celebrated.

* "Hail Hitler, the dog is dead."
** Victory-in-Europe Day.

"Praise the Lord for He is good and His mercy endureth forever."

## May 3
Came upon two camps with 1,100 Jewish Hungarian girls and attempted all day to get them organized and somewhat straightened out. There are medical problems, food and shelter troubles—what a mess these noble Germans have made of millions of lives.

The brief note in my letter could not reveal the stark reality of what we saw: 1,100 human beings trying to return to life. Our GI's wanted to be helpful, showering them with sweets and other delectables—but what the girls really wanted were *mezuzot* and prayer-books. Prayer-books above all. Joe rose to unbelievable heights of helpfulness. He literally spent twenty-four hours of his time begging for supplies and where he was refused he took them anyway; we requisitioned clothing from German homes—we did everything but make the past undone.

Contacting these girls was not as simple as it may now appear. The camp was located behind the Russian lines and I had to get official permission from the Russian liaison officer who was attached to us before I could pass through the lines. After the first joyful meeting, feeling between American and Russian soldiers deteriorated markedly. The Russians wheeled their guns into position facing us, and I think all of us had a hint of things to come in the years afterwards. The liaison officer wrote me a note and confidently I took it to the Russian lines. They read it and at once placed me and Joe under arrest. I waited for an hour in a small room wondering what had gone wrong and what the officer had really written. Eventually a Russian colonel appeared, and fortunately he was a Jew from Odessa who still remembered a few Yiddish words. He apologized and then permitted me to do whatever I wanted for the girls who were in their custody, and to come as often as I pleased.

# V-E Day

We prepared for V-E Day services in anticipation of the official end of the war. We were now in Delitzsch and I had the programs printed in style by a local German printer. The man understood a bit of English and when he saw the celebration we planned he said, "I envy you."

## May 4
Two abject Polish Jews reminded me today that Hitler's death and the collapse of Nazism are only the beginning of untold terrible problems. Here are two men reduced by the Nazis to a level hard to describe, who have nothing, no place to go. They do not want to go back to Poland. All their families have been destroyed. Worst of all, they have hardly any hope left for any real future. The hopelessness of these two is just a miniature of something that is repeated all over Europe a million times. The heritage of evil is evil.

## May 5
We had a lovely service this afternoon. There were also eight of the Hungarian girls and one Polish boy present. When they saw the Torah and heard it read, there were tears in their eyes, and sobbing from their choked throats filled the hall. It was their first service in two years and for the boy, aged twenty-two, it was his first Torah blessing (we called him up of course) in six years—a moving moment.

## May 7
My heart is so full with the news [of Germany's surrender] that I will abstain from any comments. Only a heartfelt prayer of thanks can adequately give expression to my feelings. One could almost quote, "This is the day which the Lord hath made."

And so tomorrow it will finally be V-E Day. We have seen it coming, of course, and the thought that I have been in it, that in a minor fashion (but somehow nonetheless) I have participated, gives me a keen feeling of satisfaction and fills me with humility.

## May 8
V-E Day. What a perfect lovely day. When it dawned upon us it took its cue from our happiness and shone bright and warming upon a world which, here at least, had fought and finally ceased fighting.

## May 10
Another beautiful warm day shone upon our V-E Day religious

services. The men were truly inspired. It felt like a *yontef* [Holy Day] and so it was. When the men left the "synagogue"—a lovely movie-house in town—they shook my hand and said, "Good Yontef." Need I tell you how I felt on this day to which we had looked forward so fervently? We thought much of home, particularly during our silent prayers. The Catholics and Protestants had their services at the same time. There was a holiday mood throughout the division, something that we needed after these arduous months. Thanks be to God that He has kept us alive and brought us to this day.

P.S. The radio just announces that—after the surrender!—the Germans are bombing the hell out of Theresienstadt,* the last remaining Nazi ghetto for Jews—those bastards.

*May 11*
Went out early today following a call that help was needed for some Czech and Roumanian Jewish girls who had been admitted to a camp in our area. I found 250 of them and now will have my hands full with caring for their elemental needs. As we were talking to them one of the girls said, "There, look, look." She was pointing to a civilian walking by. It turned out that this guy happened to be their chief torturer at the camp where they suffered last before they were liberated. I had the supreme satisfaction of apprehending him and turned him over to the proper personnel for further processing. He was shivering like a leaf for he felt retribution at hand. That SOB. When we took him he claimed at once that he had been like a father to the girls—father! The girls spat at him and wished him ill luck aplenty, a wish which no doubt will find its just fulfillment.

*May 13*
After much trouble with the Russians I visited another camp of 125 Czech and Polish girls to look after their needs. There followed the now usual scenes of disbelief, tears and overwhelming joy. Something that always leaves me depressed because I don't deserve their adulation and because there is so little I can do for them.

The time when Elizabeth's baby would be born was now getting closer. Due date was still a month away, but I started

---

* A concentration camp near Prague.

writing home suggesting the quickest ways of letting me know—
via air mail, via V-mail, via the Red Cross and other means.

Occasionally we met some half-Jews who had remained in Germany all the while. Were other Jews still alive anywhere? On
May fifteenth I wrote home:

> I wonder where they are. Maybe Buchenwald had some and I
> hope that Theresienstadt will reveal a goodly number. If
> there is any kind of community—large enough in one locale to
> be able to form a congregation with a rabbi—there will of
> course be a need for spiritual leadership. There are still rab-
> bis in Europe (German ones) who would then go back because
> they have nothing now. Possibly there are one or two of those
> now in America who might consider remigration. Now here is
> one more interesting angle: if the German economy holds out to
> some degree there may be some restitution of property—and
> the process involved may draw additional Jews back here. But
> who wants to live in this hole? I think though that on this ques-
> tion of economic stabilization hang all the answers to the ques-
> tion: will there be Jews in Germany?

From the sixteenth of May on the censors permitted us to identify
the place where we were. I was then in Halle where I visited the
famous Francke Institute with its old but sadly outdated library.
The librarian, who at first probably thought I had come to
burn the place down, was grateful for my interest and much
relieved. He gave me a duplicate copy of Menasseh ben Israel's
*Conciliator*, published in 1636, a collector's prize. I also found Otto Eissfeldt, world-renowned biblical scholar, working quietly in
his study. Old Testament professors were not favourites amongst
the Nazis and he had kept a low profile, but all along had pursued his research which soon afterwards would result in a splendid new *Introduction to the Old Testament*, which has since
become a standard work.

On May eighteenth came a letter from Elizabeth.

> The folks and I are well but—prepare for heartbreak. Our
> new baby was born Wednesday night but had been dead for
> forty-eight hours. The doctor says there is no known reason
> why she should have died—just one of those things that is in-
> explicable. I had feared that all wasn't well as Tuesday and
> Wednesday I felt no life, and when I went into labour Wednes-

day night the doctor couldn't hear a heartbeat, although he told me that wasn't always hearable.

We must be thankful, darling, that I went into labour and had—really—a very easy delivery as such . . . we must figure that it was better for the child to die in utero than to be born and live when obviously something was wrong with her that would have kept her from being normal—although what was wrong—no one knows.

The news reached me on the twenty-third of May and came as a grievous shock. I wrote:

Time will heal the hurt. It is a sad disappointment—but the main thing is that you are well and that it left you unharmed. We have each other and we have Jonny. God has been very good to us and we have little to complain of. I am sad to think of your sorrow but I know of your great resources, inner strength, and I think that you have been and are mainly worried about me—so don't be, sweetheart. We have taken the good things in life and have taken them willingly, we will have to accept the other side too. . . . It is good that we can't look into the future; let's take things as they are, live as well and happily as we can—that has been our philosophy and it has served us well in the past. I am not trying to comfort you—your comfort must come from within and I know you have what it takes.

This concludes a chapter in our life but, God willing, it won't be the last one.

# Willingshausen

I tried to visit Berlin but could not obtain a pass, so I made up my mind to go back to Willingshausen, the little village in Hessen where my father's family had come from. I received permission from the general and went to reconquer my past. I did it for my sake and even more for the sake of my family. After centuries of living there they had been mistreated with the advent of the Nazis, and those who remained had been shipped away. To be on the safe side I requested a half-track with some men to accompany me, and off I went—in search of my roots.

As we came into the hills around the Schwalm we saw at once

that war had not touched these backward areas. In village after village all was in order—but the men were absent, except for a few wounded soldiers. The rest were women, children and old men. It was early afternoon when our small convoy rumbled into Willingshausen. The people had not as yet seen American soldiers, but the news of our coming had preceded us and white bed-sheets were hung from all the windows. A delegation of the village's notables greeted us as we entered. I was unshaven and had disguised my chaplain's insignia. I wanted to be unrecognized and to teach the villagers a small lesson.

The first thing we did was to order the collection of all weaponry including knives of more than ordinary length, hunting knives and, of course, guns of all kinds. I then asked the people to gather around. I cannot now remember how many of the members of the village were on hand—around six hundred, I suppose. What I said, in purposely broken German, was something like this:

"I have here before me [I pulled out a mimeographed sheet of some kind] an order from Washington, the capital of the United States. The records show that on the tenth of November, 1938, the Jews of this village, and especially a certain Levi Plaut,* were seriously beaten and then carted away to concentration camps; that their property was confiscated; and that in general the population of this village behaved illegally, cruelly, immorally and must therefore be considered war criminals. It is my task to obtain the names and the persons of the chief culprits of that day and at the same time to restore all stolen property to its rightful owners."

The crowd was silent. Faust, the same burghermaster whom I remembered from my childhood, spoke up.

"Herr Hauptmann, we do not know to what you might be referring. We are an innocent group. You can see by the look of this village that we did not participate in the war. We are far removed from any action."

There was no other response from the crowd. I ordered a court-martial to be held in the nearest house. Several soldiers from the half-track served as the jury and I as prosecutor. Jim helped me. I chose to try Burghermaster Faust by himself. The people of the village crowded around the windows, which I ordered opened so that they might hear.

* My father's eldest brother, see above, p. 6.

"You are Burghermaster Faust."

"Yes."

"Did you on November tenth have a Levi Plaut in this village?"

"I cannot remember such a name."

I signalled to Jim (who, like our "jury", did not understand a single word of German) and he cocked his submachine gun and poked Faust in the ribs.

"Mr. Faust, you may save your life if you can jog your memory," I said. Jim jabbed him a little harder. Faust's memory began to return.

"Yes, yes," he said, "I do remember such a man."

The fact was that he and Uncle Levi were about the same age, in their seventies, and had grown up together. Their families had known each other for more than a couple of hundred years. Matters went on in this fashion, Jim poking and Faust remembering. Eventually he told me the names of two main culprits. They were men in their sixties and not in service. They were produced forthwith.

At first both men denied their guilt, but with Jim's help they finally admitted it. Yes, Uncle Levi had been beaten, but they had been obeying orders from on high. Yes, he had been innocent, but after all he was a Jew and Jews were considered criminals. Yes, he had been taken away to a concentration camp. No, nobody knew where he was.

I asked Faust what had happened to his house and to the houses of the other Jews. They told me, and in turn I informed them that as of that moment all property was restored to its former owners. If in the future there was the slightest difficulty about reclaiming that property I would hold him personally responsible.

"Washington is watching you," I said. "The arm of our government is long. We have reached out to find you all the way over here in the backwaters of Germany. Do not think we will not know what you are doing."

We took our leave, threw the prisoners into the half-track and delivered them to the rear as war criminals. I do not know what happened to them thereafter; they were doubtless released in due time.

*June 8*

A new experience today. A refugee girl—she was a Hungarian—was here today and she made a pretty good sketch of me. But it is too big to send; you will have to await my own arrival to see it.

To this day the watercolour reminds me of how one soldier at the end of the campaign, victorious though it was, looked years older than he should have.

*June 11, Halle*
Today I got notice that my bedroll and foot-locker, which have been (or rather have not been) following me around for the last seven months, are on the way!—that's a fine time. Even if they came now I wouldn't know what to do with them.

Chaplain Walker informed me that he had put my name in for a decoration. I had been made a captain some time before, now I was the recipient of the Bronze Star. I had not been a hero, far from it. I, like everyone else, had done what needed to be done, and so the decoration was fairly routine. But I still wear it occasionally at special events which call for medals, because the war played a large part in the shaping of my life and my consciousness.

# Return

Our reassignments came through and we headed back towards the States. We reached Paris just as General Eisenhower marched through to a rousing reception from the French population. The streets were jammed—and the prices were sky-high. After living in Germany for six months and spending no money, we found everything outrageously expensive.

From Paris we went to our embarkation camp—appropriately called Camp Lucky Strike. Our thoughts were travelling ahead of us—they were already back home. How much had changed? What would we find?

A little mimeographed sheet made the rounds, a satire on what to expect. It was couched as an army order. Subject: Indoctrination for return to the U.S. The twenty-odd suggestions dealt primarily with the language we had acquired, which was not considered fit for use amongst civilians. We were also reminded that American homes had bathtubs; that it was no longer necessary to use the helmet for a variety of functions; that in fact helmets were not recommended attire in either church or synagogue. American dinners, it said, consisted in most cases of several items, each served in a separate dish; the army practice of mixing foods—such as corned beef and butterscotch pudding, or lima beans and peaches—in order to make them more palatable should be avoided. Beer, we were advised, would sometimes be served in bottles, but bottle openers would also be available and it was not considered good form to pry off the caps with one's teeth.

Behind this satire lay something far more serious—and the sheet did not deal with it. We were returning to a society that had not changed essentially, that was pursuing its normal goals in a normal setting, that had its eyes on social position, advancement, remuneration and all the small conflicts and worries of everyday existence. Life and death were not part of the daily agenda, and concerns which appeared picayune to us would be treated as urgent matters. We would find ourselves sadly out of step—not because it was anyone's fault but because our different experiences had led us apart. It would take some time to bring us together again.

We sailed, towards the end of June, on a very crowded ship. No one seemed to mind. The main feature of the return was the pervasive gambling which affected enlisted men and officers alike. It was said that many men lost all their outstanding pay to professionals in our midst. My own stakes were low—besides, I played bridge as I had done throughout the campaign, and rarely any poker. I spent the two-week crossing mostly daydreaming. At last, New York! Again I was struck by the beauty of the Statue of Liberty, and its message seemed more clearly emblazoned than ever. I cried, and so did many others.

We docked. The question was how to get to a telephone "firstest and quickest". The wait was interminable, and it was not improved by the Army's sense of priorities: with thousands of soldiers waiting to get off and call their families, the general's touring car was slowly and painfully lowered from the side. It was the first item to disembark, and the curses which were hurled at the army "brass" expressed the long resentment of a civilian army against the tyranny of military hierarchies. Of such things are mutinies made.

I forget now how I did reach a telephone. In any case, I did and a few days later I was home on thirty days' furlough. I was in one piece. I had not been hurt and for that I was deeply grateful. What lay ahead was hidden in the dark clouds of the future.

Homecoming was unalloyed exultation—seeing Elizabeth well, the baby grown and my parents now in America. For thirty days I would be a civilian. It didn't work.

To my distress I found that the month we had been granted was not enough; I was an alien on a brief visit to an unfamiliar world of civilians. They would stay in their accustomed places, I would have to go back to the Army to train for the planned invasion of Japan. And I could not help replaying in my mind the scene of our earlier parting, when I had said good-bye to Elizabeth and kissed my sleeping child and asked myself, when shall we see each other again?

Everyone was very nice and solicitous, but my friends did not understand what agitated me nor did I appreciate their sense of what was important. I was the stranger who did not fit.

I remember a party at the home of Dr. Maurice and Diana Levine, good friends and deeply concerned human beings. I joined this group and that and listened to the conversation—but nothing people talked about had anything to do with blood and sweat, with fear and hope, with life and death. After a while I went off into a corner to sit by myself for a while. I deeply resented the whole scene, and to this day I remember the pain I suffered. Of course, there was no one to blame.

My parents too were not happy. They found adjustment to America very difficult, though for different reasons. After Father had worked for a while in the library of Hebrew Union College, he and Mother took jobs at the Child Guidance Center. The accommodations were unsatisfactory, but at least they had work, and for the time being I could do nothing further for them. Elizabeth was trying her best. Walter was in Minnesota and far away. The pressures were great on Elizabeth, though she did not complain. Above all, she too faced the impending separation and she feared it no less than I.

The thirty days were gone and I returned to Camp Atterbury. From there we were to go by troop train to San Luis Obispo in California. The ride was a nightmare. We were given railroad cars that had long ago been taken out of regular service. Nothing worked, neither the toilets nor the water faucets. There was no air conditioning, and it was the middle of summer with the prospect of intense heat in the southern plains we had to cross. The train suffered repeated break-downs. Because of the heat we travelled with the windows open, and because of lack of water we were in a short time indescribably filthy (the trains ran, of course, on coal). Sometimes the train stopped in a fairly inhabited neighbourhood which had to endure the spectacle of several thousand people dismounting and relieving themselves in what was literally the back yard of the community. We presented a view quite different from that portrayed on the posters where bright-eyed helmeted American youngsters were urging their fellow citizens to do their duty, conserve energy, observe the ration regulations and buy war bonds.

Unrest spread amongst the soldiers. Where similar conditions would have been accepted without any question in Europe, they were unacceptable in America. It all came to a head one hot afternoon, somewhere in Kansas, when—as had happened so often—we were put on a siding so that an express train could pass. We, the begrimed, dishevelled and discontented, waited under the boiling sun. The grand express passed by, civilians reclining comfortably in their seats. Then came the sight of sights, the dining car. While we were served lukewarm slop three times a day, there in regal splendour rode the civilians for whom we were fighting the war, sitting at tables, being served by white-clad Pullman waiters, napkins tucked under their arms.

It was too much, and hundreds of our men left the train. Some made their own way to the west coast, others deserted altogether. They were fed up with being treated as cattle, when they were on their way to defend the civilian way of life.

I did not have the courage or the imagination to follow their example; I stayed with the train. I think we travelled for four days and five nights, from Indiana to California. When we arrived, the famed 104th Infantry Division—or at least those of us who had been on the train—was a thoroughly demoralized bunch of guys who were of no conceivable use to the Army.

For once the brass realized what was happening and did not indulge in recriminatory action. Those who later arrived as stragglers were taken back with no questions asked. For a week we had no army routine to rein us in; we were given time off to play and enjoy the California landscape. By and by we fell back into the soldier's mould.

Soon after our arrival America dropped atom bombs over Hiroshima and Nagasaki, and shortly thereafter, on August tenth, Japan sued for peace.

But as late as August twenty-first, more than two weeks after the first bomb fell, the 104th Division was still slated to go. I wrote home:

As matters stand at the present time, if you come out right away we would probably have a few weeks together—I have no exact information on that but a little is better than nothing. Don't you agree?

Elizabeth and Jonathan came at once. But where to put them? No one would rent us space for more than five days, not even a hotel. The prices were, by our standards, exorbitant—five dollars a night. We finally obtained temporary shelter in a ratty fifth-grade hotel where the ants literally crawled out of the woodwork and where DDT powder was our primary line of defence.

We did not, at the time, think about the implications of atomic warfare or the fact that the world had just been changed fundamentally. We did not think about the 75,000 who died in one single raid on Hiroshima and the tens of thousands who were to be maimed or killed by the effects of radiation. We thought about ourselves, about the fact that the war was so suddenly over and that there was a chance that the 104th Infantry Division might not be sent abroad again—that that duty might now be assigned to troops that had not yet been overseas. There was no guarantee, considering the Army's traditional snafu, but we could hope. For once we were right. The news spread: the 104th would be dissolved and the men shipped home by the point system—an intricately devised method whereby the sequence of discharge from the Army was determined. Those who had served the longest were let out first, and overseas combat service counted double. Since I had not joined until August 1943, I would be a bit down the list.

The night that I told Elizabeth the news the dam of her iron will—the will that had held through my absence overseas and through the still-birth, through the arrival of my parents and the difficult and often lonely life of an army wife in the midst of a civilian population—broke down. That night, in the sagging bed of a forgettable hotel, she started shaking uncontrollably from head to foot. The defences she had so valiantly kept up, the strength she had gathered over the years, dissolved, and all the anxiety and repressed tears of the past burst forth. Fortunately she recovered in the morning and took up her next job: finding a place where we could live for the next few months. She knocked on every door and even halted strangers in the street asking the same question, "Do you know of a room we can rent?"

Fate intervened at last. Total strangers we met while walking—they were army people—told us there was some space available in their own place, and the next day we moved in with them. To be sure, our new hosts were strange people—at least the wife was. She had a small child whose pyjamas she insisted on washing every day, and she had a complex about cleanliness that went beyond the reasonable. But that was their problem, not ours, and for the rest of our time in San Luis Obispo we occupied a pleasant place and were relieved of anxiety about our future. We soldiers spent our days in what the Army charitably called "organized athletics": we played baseball and golf and did nothing, except of course that I as a chaplain was confronted with an avalanche of requests for special consideration. Soldiers are known to be inventive, and in these cases the range of imagination was staggering: they found the most extraordinary reasons for needing an earlier release. But I could sympathize with them. We were all longing to return to good old civilian life in the golden land of opportunity.

In due course I was notified that I had been transferred to Fort Knox, Kentucky, not to guard the gold, but to watch over the Jewish soldiers in that permanent army post.

# End and Beginning

In comparison to any other post at which we had been, Fort Knox was utter luxury. The section in which officers were assigned their houses was called Goldville, and rightly so. We were given splendid quarters, and this time our dog came along with Elizabeth, Jonathan and the car. A few weeks later my parents came to visit.

I had véry little to do and contributed some articles to the Indianapolis *Jewish Post* (now called the *National Jewish Post and Opinion*) whose editor, Gabriel Cohen, was an old friend.

I played the prophet—and missed. I urged much closer cooperation between Jewish-faith groups than had existed heretofore. I pleaded for an end to polarities, for greater mutual respect. The servicemen returning from war, I argued, would be disturbed by the divisiveness of Jewish life and would look for a sense of common purpose. I was proven wrong by subsequent events. When the serviceman returned he happily adjusted himself to existing civilian situations. Synagogue membership was booming and he participated in this boom. If his experiences in the war had made him a different person, it was, I am afraid, not visible in his religious outlook. Or so it appeared to me in the years that followed.

At Fort Knox, the working hours during the day were extended leisure activities. My new assistant, a serious eighteen-year-old neophyte from the Bronx, Sol Rothstein,* would call for me just before eight o'clock in the morning and drive me to head-quarters, where I would check in. I would then go to my office, make a few calls and visits and by eleven o'clock saunter over to the officers' mess. There we would play billiards for two hours: in time, I developed a fair capacity for playing the three-cushion variety. I was simply waiting for enough points to accumulate that I might be discharged. Meanwhile I was becoming reac-quainted with my wife and child.

Jonathan was growing up beautifully. At three years of age he was a polite young gentleman and once startled a group of soldiers whose truck we were passing by saying to them, "Nice day, isn't it?" They broke up in unbelieving laughter.

We celebrated Passover at Fort Knox and shortly thereafter I was released. A crucial phase in our lives had ended.

Yet not quite. Throughout my army years, and especially the time of combat and of uncovering the dreadful traces of evil, I had had no time to stand back and reflect on deeper meanings. In a way I had lived on the surface. Yet sooner or later there were questions that had to be asked.

Where, in Nordhausen or Auschwitz, was the God of the cove-nant? It took me some time to frame my answer, and even then I was haunted by uncertainty. Out of the conflicts of my own soul arose the conviction that these very contradictions were part of the world's essence: that its opposites were, so to speak, in need of each other. Twenty years later I made these thoughts part of a book.**

> I beheld the world sustained in the tension of opposites. There is no life without death, no good without evil, no order without disorder. Fear and confidence, joy and sorrow, love and hate, kindness and cruelty dwell inseparably side by side. Creation is the process which makes this spectrum real from the microcosm to macrocosm. And

---

* Sol later became a Conservative rabbi, and at this writing serves in Fort Lee, N.J.
** The Case for the Chosen People (Garden City, New York: Doubleday, 1965), p. 190 ff.

God to me became He who holds this impossible structure in possible balance and who for me provides the opportunity to transcend my own contradictions and consciously avail myself of freedom's choices. I do not know what freedom there is for the rest of His vast creation; but I know that, in however narrow limits, it does exist for me. . . .

Standing at the graves of so many, contemplating the unknown burial places of uncounted millions, I learned less about God than about man. I know now that man is "evil from his youth"—but yet is more than evil. I have seen him at his murderous worst and his heroic best. Man, like the universe, is both cruel and kind; when he is cruel none surpasses him in viciousness, when he is kind none equals him in love. The presence of God assures that love and justice may become real. This is His goodness and this is why we can call Him the Righteous Judge. We say, our Father, our King, because we acknowledge that we have a relation to His being; we speak in personal pronouns because our souls are involved. He is a "personal God" for He relates to me and I to His being. I am a person because there is God. . . .

I have learned to live with partial answers even in the realm of faith. For me belief is not congruous with total knowledge and unquestioned certainties. I do not know how to answer the question of the six million murdered ones although I feel it is forever directed to me who remains to contemplate their fate. How does the presence of God relate to his chosen people at the Hell gates of Auschwitz? I do not know, though I marvel at the possibility of men affirming Him even in the throes of death.

"Yet will I believe"—they said it and I repeat it. Yet will I believe that there is purpose to our striving, that death is overcome by daring faith and deeds of righteousness, that His people still have their tasks and their place.

# Chapter 5

# TAKING UP THE THREADS

MY PARENTS HAD MOVED TO Toledo where they had taken on the position of heading an old folks' home. Walter had gone to St. Paul as assistant rabbi to Harry Margolis, but Margolis had then suffered a fatal heart attack, leaving Walter with the temporary responsibility of the congregation. We moved back to Chicago sometime after Passover—I via Camp Atterbury once again, where I was officially mustered out—and we tried to take up the old threads.

First and foremost on our agenda was of course the question of having another child to replace the one in whom we had put so much hope. We received conflicting opinions about the reason for the still-birth. One doctor held that it had been Rh incompatibility, so we visited an obstetrician who was an authority on that condition. Elizabeth had now had two miscarriages and a still-birth and had given birth to only one live child. I was definitely an Rh-positive and she was a negative. What were our chances for another normal healthy child?

Dr. Goldfine was understanding but cautious. "Taking all circumstances into consideration," he said, "they would be about fifty-fifty. The decision, of course, must be yours."

We talked many hours about it. Were we prepared to face another nine months of worry and again have a child who would not live, or one who was less than normal—not because it was one of those unavoidable accidents, but because we had taken a deliberate risk? Would such a child ever face us with the question, "Why did you decide to bring me into the world?"

We decided to take the chance. In August Elizabeth became pregnant once more.

149

I was elected rabbi of the congregation, to succeed Sam
Schwartz. With no experience to guide us, neither Sam nor I
knew how complete his retirement should be. He took it for
granted that he would continue to officiate at weddings and
funerals; naturally the families would wish the rabbi who had
been with them since 1919, and who had officiated at life-cycle
events throughout their lives, to enhance these moments with his
reassuring presence. But it did not occur to us that this arrangement—or rather the lack of it—would shut me out of all the
milestone events, and impede my integration as the senior rabbi.
The question of co-officiating rarely arose. When I myself retired
from the pulpit thirty years later, I made it known that I could be
asked by a congregant to co-officiate, but that all basic arrangements rested with my successor and were at his invitation.

The congregation was changing noticeably. The return of
millions of soldiers to civilian life created a flood of commercial
demand. Small businesses that had struggled along began to
prosper. The Depression was forgotten; it had given way to post-
war prosperity. Our members became more mobile and started
moving west, towards Austin and Oak Park, where we ourselves
bought and enjoyed our first real home. I constructed a study for
myself in the unfinished attic, and though the stairs went up from
Jonathan's bedroom it was a comfortable and totally secluded
place where my studies prospered.

No sooner had I started to take up the threads of Chicago life
again when I received a call from St. Paul, Minnesota. Would I
consider becoming Margolis' successor? They knew about me
and of course Walter's presence had encouraged them to look in
my direction. I rejected the approach out of hand. I was
obligated, I told St. Paul, to return to and serve my Chicago congregation; they had kept faith with me during the war years and
we had had an unwritten understanding that I would return.
However attractive the offer might be, I could not accept. We put
the matter out of our minds.

Judy was born during the Passover week of 1947. Elizabeth
had had a false alarm two weeks before, but this time the labour
pains were genuine and she arrived at the delivery room none too
early. The child was born with the umbilical cord threatening to
choke her, but Dr. Goldfine was competent and all went well. The
child gave every appearance of being whole and healthy and she
turned out to be just that.

*(Above)* The old teachers' seminary in Münster where I was born. *(Left)* Aged three, in wartime Germany, 1916.

*(Left)* With my younger brother Walter, 1924. *(Below)* My parents, Jonas Plaut and Selma Gumprich, before their wedding in 1911.

*(Top)* High school, 1927-28. Front row, right to left: myself, unknown, Harry Lewinsky, Arno Lachmann, Bruno (Sommerfeld) Bernard. *(Left)* Marching in Tel Aviv before the Maccabiah Games, 1935. *(Above)* Father (right) with cousin Leo, c. 1932.

Elizabeth Strauss in 1938, the year we were married.

(Top) High school, 1927-28. Front row, right to left: myself, unknown, Harry Lewinsky, Arno Lachmann, Bruno (Sommerfeld) Bernard. (Left) Marching in Tel Aviv before the Maccabiah Games, 1935. (Above) Father (right) with cousin Leo, c. 1932.

FOTO ABRAHAM

JARO VON TUCHOLKA

*(Top)* Heinz Frank teaching at the Auerbach orphanage, c. 1935. *(Above)* With my family in Berlin, just before my departure for America, 1935. (Left) With Walter, in Berlin, two years later; when I returned to America he came with me.

My mother, 1937.
My father, 1937.

German students at Hebrew Union College, 1937. Left to right: Theodor Wiener, Ernest Lorge, the "Gang of Five": Wolli Kaelter, Herman Schaalman, Alfred Wolf, myself, Leo Lichtenberg.

JARO VON TUCHOLKA

Elizabeth Strauss in 1938, the year we were married.

Serving as chaplain in the U.S. Army, 1943.

(Below) Joe Flamm, my in-
defatigable assistant in the 104th
Division. (Right) Return from
overseas, Chicago, 1945.

(Left) My first posting, Washington Blvd. Temple, Chicago.
(Right) My predecessor Samuel Schwartz, rabbi at Washington Blvd.
from 1919 to 1946 (photo 1970).

# The American Jewish Conference

For some years it had been borne upon the leaders of American Jewry that the post-war tasks would be enormous and that only a united community could begin to cope with them. Though the full extent of the Holocaust had not then been known, enough of it had filtered through to Western Jews and enough dislocations had already taken place to make it clear that post-war reconstruction would be enormously difficult. And so, in 1943, an unprecedented national election had been called to establish a representative American Jewish Conference* that would be empowered to deal with the desperately urgent issues of the time.

Elections had taken place in 78 communities and 58 regions, covering every state and the District of Columbia; 375 delegates were accredited by 22,500 electors representing 8,486 local groups. This meant that the total number of Jews represented by the electors was approximately one and a half million. There were many candidates running in Chicago, which had been allotted thirty delegates. I had made up my mind that I too wanted to run. I appealed to the Zionists and to the German immigrant sector as well as to the local area on the West Side where I was well known. When the elections were finally held not only was I one of those who made the slate, but I came in seventh out of thirty. This one-time election served for the entire life of the Conference.

Because I had meanwhile entered the Army I could not attend the first meeting, which took place in New York in the fall of 1943, and was overseas for the Pittsburgh session in 1944. I had attended the third meeting in Cleveland. The fourth would be held in Chicago, where I had now returned.

In Cleveland I had appeared in uniform and—probably to lend the meeting a patriotic sheen—had been elected to the influential Interim Committee. One of its meetings stands out in my mind. It was held in May 1947 at the Biltmore Hotel in New York. In attendance were a small band of leaders, people like Louis Lipsky, Maurice N. Eisendrath, Israel Goldstein, Rose Halprin, Irving Miller, Samuel Rothstein, the incomparable Stephen S. Wise, and the founder and chairman of the Conference, Henry Monsky, President of the International B'nai B'rith. In this company I was out of place and I knew it. I had at least enough sense to keep my mouth shut, to listen and to learn.

* See further details in Appendix 2.

Henry Monsky was in the chair that afternoon. The Biltmore is an old hotel and lights were not as bright as one could have wished, but it was obvious that Monsky was not feeling too well. At one point, addressing himself to Stephen S. Wise, he said, "Stephen, will you take over the chair, please."

He then rose and walked over towards the window and sat down with a heavy thump. Moments later he keeled over. He had suffered a massive heart attack and died later that afternoon.

Monsky's death was a terrible shock not only to us who had witnessed his last hours but to the entire North American Jewish community. He had been the first East European to break the German stranglehold on the leadership of the Jewish community; for a long time all major Jewish institutions were headed by members of the old German families, but East European Jews had now become the vast majority and they had begun to assume important places in the economic and political strata of Jewish life. Henry Monsky was the perfect leader of this new power segment. The permanent adjournment of the Conference and its failure to carry out the plan which the fourth Assembly was to approve was due in no small part to the absence of this man.

The fourth Assembly began on Saturday night, November twenty-ninth, and was held at the Civic Opera House in Chicago. By coincidence it was the very day on which the United Nations had voted on the creation of an independent Jewish state in Palestine. Chairman Lipsky rose.

"Ladies and gentlemen, it is my great privilege in opening this session to make an important statement. It was announced today, a few hours ago, that at Flushing Meadows the United Nations Assembly by a vote of thirty-three for, thirteen against, ten abstaining and one absent, gave official recognition to the Jewish state in Palestine."

The audience was electrified. We had known that the vote was being held but we had not known the result. There was an outbreak of wild emotion; we virtually shouted the *Hatikvah*, the Jewish national anthem. Stephen Wise, one of the spiritual and political architects of Jewish independence, wept openly.

When he rose to his feet the audience stood again, recognizing in him the nearest thing to a modern-day prophet that they had known.

"I want to describe to you," he said, "the Jewish state that is to be: Judea—for Judea, I hope, will be its name. It will be free, it will be democratic, it will be Jewish—Jewish with tolerance and amicability for all people. And if the press be here tonight, I wish to say to them as one of the founders of the Hebrew University: there will never be a quota in the Hebrew University. Christian and Moslem will be as welcome as Jew."

Wise was seventy-three at the time and he took that moment to reminisce about a meeting with President Wilson in 1919.

"President Wilson and I were friends. He put his arm around my shoulder and said, 'Rabbi Wise, Palestine will be Jewish.' That was the prophecy of President Wilson, for which he laboured by the side of Balfour."

Then he recalled another incident, this one forty-five years earlier.

"I was the representative of the Zionist Organization of America at the last session of the World Zionist Organization which Theodor Herzl attended—April 1904, three months before he died. After the meeting we walked together and he said, 'Vise—he couldn't say Wise—how old are you?' I said, 'I am just thirty.' 'You are a young man, I'm an old man.' And the old man was forty-four but the Jewish people had broken his heart and he turned to me and said, 'Vise, I shall not live to see the Jewish state but you will live to see the Jewish state.' I have lived to see the Jewish state. I am too small for the greatness of the mercy which God has shown us."

The plan of organization over which our Conference had toiled was adopted. After several days of discussion—all anticlimactic in the face of the great news—the Conference adjourned and appointed an Interim Committee to carry out the main body of the resolutions. I was co-opted again. We only met once or twice; the dream was not to see fruition. Dissension was rife. The American Jewish Conference and its plan for the reorganization of American Jewry was disintegrating. The future was to see us once again divided into a thousand different fragments, each one struggling to be heard. Unity was elusive—and who is to say whether it was possible at all? Perhaps Monsky could have achieved it; no one else was able to unify all the forces. Goldstein, Lipsky, Wise, Silver—they were all spokesmen for Zion, but American Jewry no longer had a leader who could speak to and for all. Monsky had died too early.

# Westward

I had been active in the Zionist Youth Commission and in 1946
became its chairman for the region. I began to speak more widely
about the State of Israel that would soon be created and was now
threatened by the antagonistic actions of an unhappy and uncooperative mandatory power and by unrelenting Arab foes. I
began to write a column for the *Chicago Sentinel*—mostly about
literature. I wrote for the *Reconstructionist* and for the Indianapolis *Jewish Post*.

I came upon a new way of presenting ideas to the congregation: dramatic readings in poetic form interspersed with organ
and choir music. I called them "dramalogues" and thought I had
invented a new word, but later found it listed in the *Webster International Dictionary*, albeit with a slightly different meaning. I
created such a dramalogue for the Sabbath after the UN vote. A
large crowd filled the old synagogue and a great deal of emotion
was in evidence, even amongst the Hungarian-Bohemian Jews,
who had never been too friendly to the Zionist ideal. Afterwards
I shook hands with the congregation, and when I returned to the
pulpit the dramalogue was missing. It was my only copy and of all
the manuscripts I have misplaced or discarded, this one I have
always missed badly. It would have helped me to recreate
something of my own sentiments at that historic time.

Friday night attendances, in fact, rose dramatically as the
months wore on. It was said—though I had no way of verifying
it—that more people came to my lectures than were to be seen on
Sunday mornings at Temple Sholom where Rabbi Louis Binstock
preached, or at Temple Sinai where Dr. Mann was lecturing. The
statement was probably an exaggeration, but we did very well;
even during the summer months our attendance was large. I paid
close attention to the written word and though now, thirty years
later, both my style and my approach have changed considerably, it is still evident that I gave a great deal of care to
these sermons. (Many years later, when I had assistant rabbis
working with me, I would recall my own early experiences and
insist that they write out their sermons in longhand. Alas, some
of the young men were unwilling to do so, believing that they
could speak extemporaneously with conviction, logic and even
good English. Of these three elements, usually only the first was
in evidence. Whatever success I achieved as a public speaker

was entirely due to the rigid discipline I observed during the first
fifteen years of my rabbinate.)

I received a call from Rabbi Irving Miller in New York. Would I
head the midwest region of the American Jewish Congress?* My
acceptance would not entail much time, and would afford me the
possibility of working in the larger community and on the
national scene. I was thirty-four years old at that time.

Being a conscientious servant of my congregation, I requested
their assent, anticipating that it would be forthcoming. I reckoned that my congregational leaders would be glad to have their
rabbi take a role in shaping the Jewish community. I was sadly
mistaken. They turned me down out of hand, and with great
regret I informed Miller that my answer would have to be
negative. I had done the "proper thing"—but this was one instance when the proper thing was wrong.

The refusal left me with a great sense of disappointment. Once
having asked my trustees, I could not go against their wishes. I
knew in my heart that though I would work hard and give the congregation my very best, I would not stay forever.

The population began to shift with ever greater rapidity. If
people did not move to the North Side, they went to the western
suburbs. It was evident to me that the congregation could not
continue unless it changed its base. I began endless talks with my
own leadership about a possible relocation of the synagogue,
only to meet with misunderstanding and anxiety. They were not
willing, not then at any rate, to think of giving up their splendid
structure, isolated though it was in a part of town where fewer
and fewer of our people were now living.

I took a good long look at the suburb of Oak Park. Just at that
time there was a division in the Conservative congregation; a
number of members, amongst them the most influential and well-
to-do, split off from West-Suburban Jewish Congregation and
wanted to establish a more liberal though conservatively
oriented community. I grasped the opportunity and held long
talks with them. I tried to persuade them that they could enter
our congregation as a unit and for the time being preserve their

---

* Established originally by Stephen S. Wise in 1918 to represent American Jewry in its
totality, it never achieved its goal. In 1946 it specialized in political action, especially in
the field of civil liberties and anti-Nazi and pro-Palestinian activities. Miller was then
Chairman of the Executive and later succeeded as President of Congress. He died in
1980.

identity. If the union did not work out they could always leave.
After long and arduous negotiations I received their agreement.
We began by establishing branch classes of our Hebrew school
in Oak Park. In this fashion thirty families of Jewish commitment
and—wonders of wonders—of financial resources became our
members. Eventually it was this group that became the backbone
of our congregation. Later on, after I had left the synagogue, a
new structure was built in Oak Park; it was they who assured the
success of the building-fund drive, and who gave the congregation a good deal of much-needed fresh leadership.

Two of this group were Hazel and Bernie Kantor, with whom
we were bound in a special relationship. They had a son Bruce
and a daughter Joyce. One night I received a telephone call from
them: inexplicably, five-year-old Joyce had died in bed—no warning, no illness. The family were in a state of severe shock, and I
went to their home at once. We sat together through the small
hours of the morning. We hardly spoke; we just shared our grief
and incomprehension. Many years later Hazel said to me, "If you
had tried to console me that night, I would have shown you the
door. But your silent presence meant everything."

## Parting of the Ways

The year of 1948 was to be one of great change for us.

In May Israel declared its independence. Seven Arab states,
their armies amply supplied by the departing British mandatory
soldiers, made war on the tiny state which was calling itself
Israel (and not Judea, as Stephen Wise had hoped). I remember
the controversy about the name and the doubts which were expressed in many quarters about the wisdom of the choice. How
would one continue to say, "Hear, O Israel"—the traditional
watchword of Judaism—without at the same time thinking about
the new state? As it turned out, these fears were groundless and
the identification quickly took root.

In retrospect, however, it is important to remember that the
first impact of Israel on the Jewish people in North America was
not as great as one might think. Except to a relatively small group
of devoted Zionists, the existence of a Jewish state after a hiatus
of 2,000 years made very little difference. No one talked about
visiting it. Of course, we read about the progress of the war, but
there were no demonstrations to try to move the neutral hand of

government into a more openly supportive position. Though the fact that Harry Truman was the first president to recognize the new state was accepted gratefully, there was no follow-up—and on the whole the Jewish community was not as yet ready for any kind of activism. The plain fact was that the new Israel was accepted intellectually but not yet emotionally.

The same was true of the Holocaust. It now seems inconceivable that in those years when the world—including the Jewish world—first became aware of the enormity of that tragedy, the reaction was not one of abhorrence. One might think that everyone in the free world would be in a state of mourning. No such reaction took place. Displaced persons came to America in relatively small numbers because of the archaic immigration laws which were then in operation. While the majority of the displaced persons went to Israel, many went to South America, Mexico and Canada. Perhaps the fact that so few went to the United States explains the subdued reaction at that time to the issues raised by the Holocaust and the existence of Israel.

In my congregation, despite my best efforts, Israel and the Holocaust were at best marginal issues; our people now for the first time saw the opportunity of making a decent middle-class living, of moving from quickly deteriorating inner-city areas to pleasant homes in Oak Park, River Forest or farther north. I introduced the first art show to our congregation and had to persuade our leadership that synagogue and art were quite compatible—but I could not persuade anyone to buy a picture to grace our halls, which were beautified almost exclusively by images recalling former confirmation classes and basketball teams that had won in long-defunct minor leagues.

In the spring my parents gave up their position in Toledo. It had never been satisfactory. At the time the community was not prepared to invest in an adequate home for the aged, and they exploited my parents' willingness to work for little pay and poor accommodation. They now moved in with us, though our house in Oak Park was not quite suitable for our new extended family. Walter had accepted his first permanent pulpit in Fargo, North Dakota, and was to do extraordinarily well.

Sometime between Pesach and Shavuot a letter came from St. Paul—the same congregation to whom I had said no two years before, after leaving the Army. I was busy with preparations for confirmation and let the letter lie, and after a while I forgot about it. My father had always had a rule about mail: "A letter," he would say, "is either so urgent that if you do not answer it at once it will lose its urgency, or it is not so urgent and then a delay won't matter. In either case there is no point worrying about it."

His principle of delay was certainly tested in this case and it turned out that not answering the letter from St. Paul made the matter more urgent. After confirmation I received a call from an Alan (Bud) Ruvelson who identified himself as the chairman of St. Paul's Rabbinic Search Committee. He wanted to know whether I had received their letter; they had not received an answer. I told him truthfully that I had been very busy and had not been able to give the matter any thought—but now that he was calling I had to tell him truthfully that I did not think I was interested in going to St. Paul. Thereupon Ruvelson presented me with the unassailable argument of a first-class salesman.

"Rabbi, from all I've heard you are an intelligent person. How can a person like you turn down something about which he knows very little or nothing? You don't know St. Paul, and all I'm suggesting is that you come and visit us, talk with us—and if afterwards you don't feel that this is for you, that's the time to turn it down, but not in advance."

He spoke at the right time, for I was still not happy in Chicago. While the congregation's projected move to the suburbs was bound to take place within the next few years, I felt that I was working at the periphery of Jewish life. I thought that I had the ability to make an impact on a community, but because of tradition, location and the high mobility of Chicago Jewry, I could have at best only marginal influence.

Ruvelson then asked me whether it would be acceptable for a group from St. Paul to attend a service and afterwards share some ideas. I told him that I would not turn them away; that they were always free to come to our services; and that I would most certainly be hospitable.

Shortly thereafter, on a Friday night during early summer, five St. Paulites were in the congregation. They identified themselves after services and Elizabeth invited them to have a Shabbat lunch with us the next day. It was a pleasant event and at the end they invited us to visit St. Paul, which we agreed to do.*

Our visit to St. Paul was very pleasant. The people were friendly, warm, open, and it was this openness which was par-

---

* They were, in addition to Ruvelson, Roz Shapiro, president of Sisterhood; Samuel Frank, president of Brotherhood; William W. Wolkoff; and Harold Rose.

ticularly attractive. Harold D. Field, whose company controlled a
string of movie theatres in the state, was president of the congregation and when he showed us through the synagogue
building (a Moorish structure, since razed to make way for a
parking lot), Elizabeth asked him how the acoustics were.

"Mrs. Plaut," he responded without hesitation, "if the architect had tried to build a building with worse acoustics he could
not have been successful." The frankness with which this statement was delivered was encouraging.

I visited the rabbi, Saul Appelbaum, who had been the incumbent for only two years and who, because of personal disagreements, was forced to resign.

"Gunther," he said, "it's a marvelous congregation and the
people here are first-rate. I am sorry I didn't make the grade. It's
my fault, not theirs."

That was a persuasive argument, coming as it did from one
who might easily have been embittered and resentful towards
the leadership of the community. That he did not blame them
proved to be one of the important measures by which I judged the
potential of Mount Zion Hebrew Congregation.

I met with a committee of the Board while Elizabeth was entertained by some of the women. I had learned that the congregation
was of the classical Reform stripe in the old-fashioned sense.
Hebrew was almost entirely absent from the service. The rabbi
was attired with morning coat, striped pants and ascot tie—a
very formal setting. There was no cantor, of course, and the
music reflected nineteenth-century romanticism. The first question I was asked by the committee amounted to this: would I be
prepared to maintain the traditions of the congregation?

I answered that I might not. I would maintain the spirit of
Reform, which was wedded to change and adjustment and not to
standing still. "If you insist on always doing what you did yesterday," I responded, "you are merely an Orthodox congregation in
Reform clothing."

Apparently this response made a great impression on the
majority of the committee, though it would not assure me of a
unanimous invitation to accept the pulpit.

That invitation came to me not long after. I informed my president in Chicago, making it clear at the same time that I was not at
all committed and was in fact—despite all the attractions St.
Paul had to offer—very dubious about accepting.

However, the leadership had already heard from other

sources that I had been in St. Paul. I learned that such matters will not be kept secret. The fat was in the fire. The trustees of Washington Boulevard Temple asked me whether I was prepared to stay. Why would I wish to move from the great metropolis to a small town in the boondocks? Was it money?

I now made a fundamental mistake. I did not fully appreciate that the relationship between rabbi and congregation is like a marriage. As long as the two partners live amicably with each other, occasional disagreements can be absorbed; but when it becomes clear that one partner desires a divorce, the whole tone of the argument is changed. The other partner feels rejected, the relationship deteriorates quickly and the arguments turn unpleasant.

Had I simply said that the offer from St. Paul was so lucrative that I could not afford to turn it down, they would have understood. Instead I insisted naively and truthfully that if I were to leave it would be because I wanted to locate myself differently, in a smaller environment where I could bring my capacities to bear on the total community. This argument only made them bitter.

We went to Eagle River, Wisconsin, to vacation with David and Aviva Polish. They had problems of their own. David was associate rabbi at Temple Mizpah, serving with Rabbi Jacob Singer. The latter was apparently incapable of having another man with him—especially a person of the enormous mental capacity of David, a brilliant and incisive writer and thinker who later became a leading theoretician of the Reform Movement. He would be elected president of the Central Conference of American Rabbis and move it significantly in new directions. Aviva was the daughter of A. H. Friedland of Cleveland, noted Hebrew scholar and founder of the Bureau of Jewish Education. We spent a delightful summer together and became the closest of friends. We laughed together, worried together and talked over our various problems with patience and honest concern. Eventually I came to the conclusion that we should go to St. Paul, and I informed that congregation that I would be prepared to consider the matter seriously if they were still interested in having me.

Saul Appelbaum had meanwhile left the city, and when a death occurred in the congregation I was asked whether I would come to officiate and at the same time discuss all other details. I agreed, and flew to St. Paul—not very suitably dressed, I am afraid. I had not taken a decent suit on my vacation, as I had

hardly expected to officiate at a funeral and then face a committee, so I was clad in the cheapest off-the-rack items then
available. How cheap the material was I would find out shortly:
as I left my hotel room on the way to the funeral my jacket caught
on the handle of the door and I ripped the suit down one side. The
hotel was good enough to supply me with needle and thread, and
I patched it as best I could. I conducted the funeral and then met
the leadership of the temple, was elected and accepted their
terms. I had no written contract, just a verbal agreement which
held good for the entire period I was to serve—thirteen years
altogether. My salary would be $10,000 plus a house supplied by
the congregation. This more than doubled my Chicago income,
which alone provided enough reason for the move—quite apart
from the increased scope and influence I hoped to find.

Upon my return to Chicago I received a nasty surprise: the
trustees had taken note of my intention to leave and our relationship was discontinued immediately. No, they did not wish me to
stay past the Holy Days. They would make their own arrangements. I was free to leave that very minute.

I was stunned. Certainly I had mishandled the situation, but
they in turn had had no comprehension of my own needs. After
all these years of labouring for the congregation and of bringing
it from the brink of bankruptcy to a comfortable membership of
six hundred, with the future well assured, there was not as much
as a good-bye. Only the Youth Group presented me with a token
gift—a pen holder. No party, no service, no recognition, nothing.
It was as if I had never been there.

This did not leave everyone in the congregation happy and
many came forward to lend moral support. But the entrenched
leadership were angry and they wanted nothing further to do
with me. Elizabeth and my parents were happy to leave Chicago.
We put our house up for sale, but were at first unsuccessful. No
wonder. Instead of reading "Five-room house and two-room
garage", the advertisement read "Two-room house and five-
room garage". The house was still unsold when we left in late
September, but eventually found a buyer.

Years later, after we were well settled in St. Paul and had
established close relationships with many people, I asked Harold
Field why the committee had decided on me instead of some of
the other highly attractive candidates whom they had inter-
viewed.

"Well," he said, "the final persuasion came the day you ar-

rived from Wisconsin for the funeral and the interview. You
came in an old torn suit and never once apologized for your appearance. All the other candidates had come in sartorial splendour. Obviously you were more interested in intellect and spirit
than in outer appearance. It made a deep impression on all of
us.''

# Chapter 6

# IN THE NORTH STAR STATE

ST. PAUL, THOUGH IT HAD A quarter of a million inhabitants, had a distinctly small-town flavour. The preponderance of private homes, the sparseness of vehicular traffic, the remarkably slower pace of its business and professional life, the frequency of social contacts—all these were in marked contrast not only to the hustle and bustle of a huge metropolis like Chicago but also to the aggressive, big-town aspirations of neighbouring Minneapolis.

The two cities were called twins, while in fact they were anything but. St. Paul was the older of the two, with an organized Jewish community that went back to 1856, the year before Minnesota became a state in the Union. Minneapolis was of more recent origin but had been the centre of the milling industry, and because of a combination of location, population mix and timing, had outstripped St. Paul's business activities after the turn of the century. Though St. Paul remained the capital of the state, Minneapolis became its business centre.

The Jewish populations of the two cities also fared differently. There were about 20,000 Jews in Minneapolis and 10,000 in St. Paul. But in St. Paul the community was integrated and intergroup tensions were at a low level. Jews belonged to the major social and communal institutions (except the golf clubs). In Minneapolis Jews found themselves far more excluded, in part because they arrived when social and group distinctions had already hardened. In 1948 political analyst Carey McWilliams called Minneapolis "the capital of antisemitism in the United States"—an overstatement, but an indication of the scale of the

163

problem. (The difference was not to last. Within ten years, Minneapolis changed radically and acquired a Jewish mayor and Jewish judges.)

When we arrived in 1948 there was no longer a discernible Jewish neighbourhood in St. Paul, though a new residential concentration was just beginning to develop in the south-western section of town, called Highland Park. The old-line German community, which had been the bulwark of the early settlement, had now intermingled with the East European arrivals and their descendants.

I have treated the story of these relationships elsewhere* and will therefore confine myself to two incidents which illustrate the background of the community and explain something of the religious problems and opportunities I was to face.

In 1899, Mount Zion had engaged Isaac Rypins as its rabbi, despite the fact that, *horribile dictu*, he was of Polish origin. Rypins knew what was expected of him, or rather he thought he knew. He took the congregation to a radical Reform position, discontinued almost all Hebrew, discarded the Hebrew books from the library and introduced Sunday services. More, he tried to be a better German than his German congregants. This landed him in trouble. When the First World War broke out his congregation eschewed their Germanic loyalties and followed President Wilson's leadership. Not so Rypins. He, the vicarious German, was loyal to the image of the Kaiser. When America joined the war he found himself out on a limb, not knowing how to get back. It cost him his position as soon as the war was over.

The other incident has to do with the background of old-line Reform in general. In 1880, when there were very few Jews in St. Paul who were of East European origin (although there were enough to found a small Orthodox congregation, Sons of Jacob), modest Reform stirrings were felt at Mount Zion. Two members of the Board proposed that the head covering be removed during worship service. They were solidly outvoted. Shortly thereafter vast numbers of East European settlers began to arrive in America. The members of Mount Zion were ready to do their duty: they fed and cared for the new immigrants, who did not speak English and were in dress and comportment very different from themselves. But the minute books of the congregation reveal that, not long thereafter, the matter of the removal of hats was

* *The Jews in Minnesota* (New York: American Jewish Historical Society, 1959).

brought up again—and this time it was approved unanimously. Evidently socio-psychological pressures had come into play: the congregation wanted to indicate, to itself and to the outside world, that while they were Jews they were not like the Jews who had just arrived!

In tracing the development of so "hallowed" a custom as the nonwearing of the *kippah* to events such as these, I do not mean to debunk the spirit of Reform. All of our customs are connected with beliefs that were vital and important in their day. The breaking of the wine-glass at wedding ceremonies, for example, may be interpreted in an ever new fashion; nonetheless, its origin goes back to the sexual symbolism of defloration.

While there is no question that a good deal of the genesis of Reform is found in a great desire to strip away outmoded rituals and focus on the spiritual content of Judaism, at the same time there were social and psychological circumstances at play which created different motivations. The Jews of the nineteenth century wanted to be accepted by their neighbours and therefore consciously and unconsciously imitated many American ways.

In St. Paul, with rare exceptions, the old scars had healed and the congregation was now perfectly mixed between the old and new, between East and West European. The president, Harold Field, came from an Eastern background, his wife Gladys from an old German family in Minneapolis. Had I not later taken up the study of Minnesota Jewry I would never have known about the divisions of the past. They no longer mattered.

At that time Mount Zion Temple had a membership of about 325 families. The Conservative synagogue, Temple of Aaron, had the same number, and the Orthodox Sons of Jacob, about half. We were all located in the same general area, near the lower part of fashionable Summit Avenue, which had been the "uptown" of an earlier time. Mount Zion's structure had been built during the first years of the century, and while it was adequate for Sabbath services, it had become too small for the High Holiday crowds. In those days it was not customary to hold double services, so the congregation rented a downtown theatre seating about 1,200 people. My first experience with this arrangement was somewhat negative: the auditorium had previously been occupied by a big show featuring Roy Rogers and his horse, and the lingering smell of the latter could in no way be confused with the "pleasant odour" which the Torah says is acceptable to the Almighty.

# Sorrow

After a brief stay in St. Paul my parents had gone to Fargo to visit Walter. Two days before Yom Kippur I received a dreadful call: my father had suddenly died. If there had been previous warnings, he had chosen to disregard them. He had eaten well the evening before and seemed in good spirits; then he had a sudden heart attack during the night and died at once. We determined that he should be buried in St. Paul—for it was likely that I would stay for a longer time in St. Paul than Walter would stay in Fargo.

I have no clear recollection of how we managed to get through the day. Rabbi Albert Minda from Temple Israel, Minneapolis, conducted the service and we buried Father that same afternoon in Mount Zion Cemetery, a beautifully kept park with splendid trees. The inscription on the headstone proclaims him an *Ish Torah*, a man devoted to Jewish learning.

The impact of it all did not hit me until afterwards. Somehow we lived through the Holy Days. People were most helpful and understanding and did not obtrude into our lives.

My father's death was a great blow to me. I had enormous respect and admiration for him. He had helped to mould my intellectual life; he had set me on my path to become a rabbi; his judgement was keen and often unconventional. I loved to talk with him and to share—as we did in Chicago—long hours of playing billiards, an art at which he excelled. I enjoyed his company and never tired of his hearty laugh and marvellous sense of humour. I was especially grieved that he had died now, because he had not as yet made peace with himself in America; the new environment had still not become his own. I had had every hope that in St. Paul, where he and Mother had planned to move once we were settled, both would find a true home. It was the kind of community that he would have liked, and he would have especially enjoyed seeing me in a rabbinical environment that gave me room to do the kinds of things I most wanted to do. Father was always enamoured of politics and I felt that, sooner or later, I too would move in that direction. He could have helped me in a dozen ways. Alas for him, and alas for all of us, this was not to be.

After spending some months in Fargo, Mother moved to St. Paul. Although she had never been fully independent, she had every capacity to meet new circumstances with vigour and innovative intelligence. With all his other libertarian ideas, Father had believed that women should know their place and above all should not mix in politics. "Why do you bother yourself with this?" he would say. It was so unlike him—and so like him, so much a part of the old traditions in which he and his ancestors had grown up.

Yet it had been Mother who, in the crucial days of 1938 when he was in hiding, had managed Auerbach by herself and had arranged for the emigration of many children as well as of herself and Father. She had the capabilities, but it would take her a little while to adjust to her new status.

## Branching Out

I was persuaded to join the Rotary Club. I enjoyed its fellowship, although the requirement of regular attendance became a burden from which the members excused me after a while. During the ensuing McCarthy days the club became superconservative and even reactionary, and the speakers it imported were usually boring in the extreme. But I met pleasant people with whom I established good and in some instances lasting relationships—and after all, that was the original objective of the club. Its social contributions, at least in St. Paul, were very limited at the time. I even became an officer, and my major contribution to the organization was to help open up the Minneapolis club to Jewish membership. No such problem existed in St. Paul.

Not long after my arrival in the city I was appointed by Governor Luther Youngdahl, a Republican, to the state's Human Relations Commission. Unfortunately, the Commission did not live up to its name and did little more than publish a few pamphlets on Indians; otherwise it was an ineffectual body. What it did for me, however, was to give me my first contact with the State House and to introduce me to a variety of political figures.

Hubert Humphrey was then Mayor of Minneapolis and was running for the United States Senate, to which he was elected in November '48. I met him briefly during the campaign, though our long-term association was not to begin until some time thereafter. It was he who broke the Republicans' stranglehold on state politics and it would not take him long to make his influence felt in Washington and in the country at large. He was a liberal not by design but by nature; liberalism was in his very bones. He had a habit of talking at top speed; his mind was like a computer, and his tongue just as quick. I often felt that this capacity for translating razor-sharp thinking into pithy responses made others—slower-witted than he, and that encompassed the great majority of us—highly suspicious. They felt that he was giving mechanical, pre-rehearsed answers when in fact his words were sincere and spontaneous.

Governor Luther Youngdahl was an imposing-looking man who came from a strongly religious Lutheran family. His brother Reuben was the minister of Mount Olivet Church in Minneapolis, the state's largest, a brilliant preacher who attracted thousands of people every Sunday morning to his massive church. Luther was then running for another gubernatorial term and at a party we talked about the campaign. I asked him whether he had formulated his campaign slogan. He said that he had and that the placards were now being made for wide distribution. I asked him what the slogan was and he told me.

"You don't like it," he said. "You're not impressed."

I told him the truth; I was not.

"Well," he said, "it's never too late. Can you do better?"

I said I didn't know, but I would try and would get back to him in a few days. Several days later I called him.

"How about putting into your slogan the one main platform on which you run? How about your signs proclaiming 'Honesty and Integrity in Government'?"

"I like that," he said.

That was the message eventually proclaimed to the people of Minnesota. He won the campaign hands down. His defeated opponent was Orville Freeman, an aspiring lawyer from Minneapolis whom I did not know at the time. He later became a close friend, but I never dared to tell him that I had helped Youngdahl in his campaign. Freeman did however become governor later on, and served for several terms, until John F. Kennedy appointed him Secretary of Agriculture.

My first year in St. Paul also brought me my first serious involvement in my peer group. At the national rabbinical convention held in Montreal I gave a lecture on "The Meaning and Origins of the Magen David", a field of research in which I had become interested some years before. (As I write these lines a thick file of notes still remains to be translated into a book on the subject.) Also, I was appointed to the newly created Commission on Social Action,* and from that time on I gave a significant portion of my life to the Reform movement.

We took a vacation in the beautiful lake district of Northern Minnesota and promptly made our first mistake. Since we were unacquainted with the area, we asked where one might go with the children. We were given very poor advice. Our hotel reservation was accepted, but when we arrived we were treated in such an off-hand manner, were housed so poorly and in the dining room seated so far away from everyone else, that it became clear that we had been badly misled. We checked out the next morning. It was the first time since Germany that I had come across an open expression of antisemitic sentiment, and for Elizabeth it was the first time ever. We learned much during that one day.

# Building

The congregation was ready for change. People desired a closer identification with tradition. I proceeded carefully—not so much out of wisdom but because my intuition told me that radical change would set up a backlash which might undo my reforms. Slowly I introduced more Hebrew; got rid of the nineteenth-century operatic melodies of the High Holiday ritual and abandoned the stiff morning-suit atmosphere for preaching. After some time I introduced a cantorial soloist. He was Sydney Berde, a young business executive who later turned lawyer and who had a sweet tenor voice and at once enraptured the congregation when he sang Janowski's *Avinu Malkenu*. In my second year I was assisted by a stroke of enormous good luck. I received a telephone call from a young man who identified himself as Alan Bennett.

"I'm from New York," he said, "and I've just graduated from the University of Minnesota. I want to pursue my education further but meanwhile I wonder whether I could go full-time into Jewish work."

I asked him and his wife Florence—they were both twenty-one years old at the time—to come and see me. I fell in love with them at once and persuaded a somewhat reluctant Board to engage

---

* A joint commission of the Central Conference of American Rabbis and the Union of American Hebrew Congregations.

Alan as "Director of Activities", a position which after some
time developed into the Directorship of Education. Alan obtained
his MA and gave a great forward thrust to our young people's
program and to the school. In time he became one of the continent's best-known educators, and today he is director of the
Bureau of Jewish Education in Cleveland. More important to
Elizabeth and me: the Bennetts became dear and close friends
for a lifetime. We were godparents to their children and have remained members of one family. A good deal of my success in St.
Paul was due to the steady hand, devotion, foresight and integrity of Alan Bennett.

Plans went forward for the building of a new temple. The congregation was growing rapidly and we could no longer operate
efficiently in the old structure. Then a major ideological battle
developed about the location of the temple. I was too new to have
a commanding voice in the argument, which pitted two radically
different perceptions against each other. One faction, powered
mostly by the old-timers, wanted to build on Summit Avenue, the
city's grand show street where many of the leading churches
were located. This was where Mount Zion belonged, they argued;
this was where the Jews must have their place as part of the
larger community; we must show our face proudly as a strong
and vibrant congregation. The opposing group pointed to the
demographic changes which had taken place in St. Paul: Jews
were now moving into the Highland Park area, and the new
temple ought to be located in the heart of that developing Jewish
community. The Summit Avenue faction won the day, and it was
the Conservative congregation that eventually built in Highland
Park—with the result that Mount Zion enjoyed civic status and
the Conservative Temple of Aaron a vast membership potential.

The question of design now arose, and specifically the choice
of an architect. Again there were two schools of thought. One
wanted to hire Percival Goodman, who had specialized in synagogue architecture and produced contemporary community-
oriented structures. The other school favoured the renowned
Erich Mendelsohn, one of the pioneers of modern architecture,
builder of the Einstein Tower in Potsdam. He too had experience
in synagogue building and had designed Park Synagogue in
Cleveland and B'nai Amoona in St. Louis—both striking
creations, but with a different approach from Goodman's.
Mendelsohn went for sculptural effect; his emphasis was on the
worshipful atmosphere, the sense of awe which one should feel

on entering the sanctuary. The activities of the congregation as a community were less important to him. Mendelsohn's advocates prevailed, and he produced a highly imaginative design.

There were still those who opposed the project. Some felt that the city commission which had to grant the building permit would never allow a structure with a high tower supported only by cantilevers, with no columns at all, because it might not withstand the high winds of Minnesota and the heavy winter snows. But Mendelsohn appeared before the commission and overcame its doubts just as he had overcome similar objections in Cleveland.

Mendelsohn was adamantly opposed to stained-glass windows and insisted that the windows be plain, even though the afternoon sun would shine straight into the reader's eyes. We went along with him, knowing all the while that sooner or later we would have to do something to reduce the glare. Mendelsohn was also opposed to bright colours of any kind; he wanted the structure to speak for itself. A memorable conversation on the subject took place one evening.

"What colour scheme do you have in mind?" one of the committee members asked.

Mendelsohn glared at him. "Have you ever been to Paris?" he asked.

"Of course."

"Then you have been to Notre Dame."

"Of course."

"Tell me, mister, what colour scheme does Notre Dame have?"

Mendelsohn was not destined to see this project completed. About a year and a half after construction commenced he died suddenly. At first we thought that his San Francisco associate might be able to take over but in the end we decided that a local architect, Milton Bergstedt, could finish the job on the basis of Mendelsohn's plans and notes. He did so effectively, aided by a splendid committee headed by Leopold Pistner, a man of unique engineering capacities and a brilliant mind. He had acquired the habit of using polysyllabic words which made him the butt of many jokes—but behind this word game stood a serious person who was liberal with both his time and his money. He knew Mendelsohn's weaknesses and quietly proceeded in his own way. He himself was an expert in the building of power plants, so the questions of stress which were a point of dispute in Mendelsohn's plans were well within his understanding.

At this time the president of the congregation was Benno

Wolff, a lawyer from an old German family, a man of great devotion and impeccable integrity, whose legal reputation and civic status were second to none. Louis Melamed, a soft-spoken, highly successful advertising executive, raised the necessary funds, and eventually the day arrived when our temple was dedicated. It was Hanukah 1954.

It was a dynamic building: very simple and yet inspiring. Mendelsohn had made the most of the location, and when one drove along Summit Avenue the building seemed to unfold itself to the view. It became one of the sights of St. Paul, and architectural classes of the University of Minnesota included a visit and a discussion of its structure as part of their regular curriculum.

Some of the temple's unusual features were introduced in response to my suggestions. Chief amongst them was the eternal light. In most synagogues it is suspended and is powered by an electric bulb—but at Mount Zion we took the injunction of the Torah literally: "An eternal light shall burn upon the altar. . . ." A symbolic altar of wood stands prominently on the *beema* and a gas flame flickers on it, reflecting its light in a globe suspended from the high ceiling above, and thus its light is dispersed to the congregation.

The lighting of this eternal flame was the highlight of the dedicatory exercises and it was a foregone conclusion that Leopold Pistner would be given the honour. The place was packed and the great moment arrived—the trustees marched the Torah scrolls from the old synagogue to the new and Paul (as he was known) proceeded to kindle the flame. But the protective safety shut-off worked overtime for some long moments. Match after match was lit and no flame responded to his coaxing. I stepped to the front and said to the congregation: "Perhaps here is an omen. Spiritual achievements in this synagogue will not be easy. We will have to go through many trials and errors before we light the kind of flame we want to shine in our lives."

I varied the thought another two or three times until at last the flame did catch.

More celebrations were coming up. The congregation, which had been incorporated in 1856, was approaching its centennial year, and I had promised myself that I would write a history of the congregation. This simple resolve resulted in six years of intensive historical studies, for once I began to investigate the origins of Mount Zion I was inevitably led to an investigation of the history of early St. Paul, and then of Minnesota Jewry in general. I would spend at least two mornings a week at the Minnesota Historical Society, where much of the relevant material had been deposited. The congregation was generous and appropriated the, for that time, generous sum of $1,500 for professional research assistance. Thus the histories of Mount Zion and of the Jews in Minnesota went forward apace.* When the former was in its final stages, Louis Melamed, who had now become president of the congregation, sent the manuscript to Lewis Mumford, who was a good friend of his. The famous author sent it back, annotated for the first five or ten pages. Beyond that there was nothing. There was a letter explaining his unwillingness to proceed.

"The man who wrote the history of Mount Zion will never write a decent English sentence in his life," he wrote.

## Arts and Politics

I became increasingly active in the community. In the early fifties I received a surprise visit from three delegates of the St. Paul Gallery and School of Art, then located on Summit Avenue. I had served as a board member of this fairly modest institution, which was the private domain of the upper four hundred. Would I consider becoming the president of the Gallery? One of the three who came to pay me a visit was Lucy Fricke, who was then president of the Junior League and whose husband was a prominent member of the Minnesota Republican Party. The Junior League was serving as the Auxiliary to the Gallery and I realized that if I accepted the presidency it might create an awkward situation. The Junior League openly discriminated against Jews—it had one or two token members, but that was all. I asked Mrs. Fricke, "How will the members of the Junior League carry out their responsibilities towards the Gallery when the head of that institution is not only a Jew but a rabbi?"

She assured me that their cooperation would be unstinting and that this might in fact serve as an opportunity to put an end to the discrimination, for good. Eventually I accepted and Lucy was as

* Mount Zion, 1856-1956 appeared in 1956; The Jews in Minnesota in 1959. Before then, I had written a small booklet, Children's Services for the High Holidays. First published in 1952, it went through a number of editions and is still in print today; in the course of the years it has sold more than 150,000 copies.

good as her word. Subsequently Jewish women not only were able to join the group but even became its presidents.

Because the Gallery focused on the elite and neglected the general public, it was in poor straits. I determined that this above all had to be changed, and in the seven years that I remained as president, the Gallery altered its image considerably. Eventually we acquired joint space with the Science Museum—after many battles which introduced me to the art of patient politicking. By the time my lengthy term finally ended the Gallery had become a community institution.

The anti-communist fever fanned by Sen. Joseph McCarthy severely impaired America's sense of fairness. People were accused for what they had thought twenty years before, for the acquaintances they had made, for the relatives they had. Suspicion was rife; citizen was set against citizen and a profound xenophobia spread its wretched tentacles. A new immigration bill was introduced which gave expression to McCarthyist sentiments. I testified against its adoption at a public hearing and was subsequently denounced for my views. But I persisted, and spoke on the subject in other cities. After a speech in Milwaukee, in 1952, the city's *Sentinel* reported:

> The fight to repeal the McCarran-Walter immigration law will continue "regardless of who is elected Tuesday," Rabbi W. Gunther Plaut, spiritual leader of Mount Zion temple, St. Paul, Minn., said here Friday. Rabbi Plaut represented the Jews of Minnesota recently before the president's commission on immigration and naturalization and urged changes in the law, which was enacted over President Truman's veto and takes effect December 24. He discussed the McCarran law in an interview.
>
> "The McCarran act perpetuates a principle which in my opinion is unjust, irreligious, and therefore un-American," he said. "That principle is shown in making a racial distinction between people. It evaluates what is good for America according to where a person comes from. By setting up larger quotas for England than for southern Europe, for instance, the law promotes the idea that one nationality is more desirable than another," he said.
>
> "The United States should determine its capacity to absorb immigrants, and then choose the number it can absorb on the basis of merit and need, not on the basis of whether their fathers were born in England. That perpetuates the prejudices of the nineteenth century," he said.

The McCarran act's emphasis on national origin is "pure, unadulterated racial discrimination," he said.

"The revolt against the philosophy of the McCarran act is not a minority sentiment. It is a genuine American sentiment, the decencies of the average religious American are aroused."

Much later, after I had moved to Canada, I would again be concerned with immigration issues.*

The McCarthy years did not leave me unscathed. A professor at the University of Minnesota denounced my liberal attitudes as "subversive"—the key term used by the witch-hunters. Having my civic integrity questioned was highly unpleasant, but I stood my ground. Eventually, McCarthy's power crumbled and America recovered its sanity, though some national and personal scars still remain. Since those days, the defence of civil rights and liberties has had an important place on my political agenda.

I was becoming more and more involved with political figures. As a congressman for District Four Eugene McCarthy had invited me to deliver a prayer before Congress. Later he became the Junior Senator from the state and my relationship with both him and Humphrey was one of close ideological and personal association.

The most amusing incident of my political involvement at the time came during the presidential election campaign of 1956. Adlai Stevenson was the Democratic candidate and one of my heroes. He was urbane, civilized, and possessed a dry wit of very special quality—all of which was the very antithesis of what the man in the street wanted from a presidential candidate. It was clear that he could not beat Dwight Eisenhower; still, the try had to be made. The Democrats called me to let me know that Stevenson was coming to the city. Would I, they asked, give an opening prayer and say a few words at the affair? I readily agreed.

Later that week I received another call, this time from Bud Ruvelson who had become the chairman of the Minnesota Republican Party.

"Rabbi," he said, "Richard Nixon is coming for a political rally and we would like you to give the opening prayer."

The Nixon rally came the night before the Stevenson affair. Nixon was then running for Vice-President and was scheduled to

* See p. 224.

speak at Macalester College. I did not see how I could accept the assignment, inasmuch as Richard Nixon and everything he stood for were anathema to me.

I shared my doubts with Ruvelson. I was asked to pray for a man whom I really did not like and whose political philosophy I found objectionable. But Ruvelson was persistent.

"Rabbi," he said, "you go to a prison, don't you, and pray for criminals? Your prayer doesn't mean that you are endorsing the man for whom you pray."

I knew right then and there that Bud had won the argument, and after sitting up all night I composed a prayer in which I asked God's guidance for the people of Minnesota in their choice of President and Vice-President. It all passed without incident, although I was acutely uncomfortable throughout the evening.

Stevenson came to Minneapolis the next night and Humphrey was the master of ceremonies. When Hubert wanted to be light-hearted there was none to equal him. That evening he was in top form. He razzed me for having prayed for Nixon and for confusing the Lord so badly. The audience loved it and so did I. It was the only time that I was nearly incapable of delivering an invocation because I was weak with laughter.

Israel now demanded more and more of my attention. I organized and became the chairman of the Emergency Committee for Israel. The executive director of our Committee was Sam Scheiner, who was also the head of the Minnesota Jewish Council, our community relations agency. Sam was perceptive enough to tell me once: "Rabbi, you are giving your energy to the larger community because your congregation no longer presents you with a challenge. You have a weekly radio program and a weekly TV show and are addressing the general community rather than your own congregation."

I did not know then how true this was. The excitement of dedicating the new temple and the novelty of programs that ensued from it hid the reality from me.

An interesting controversy arose at that time in connection with yet another observance, the centenary of the state of Minnesota (which had been admitted to the Union in 1858). A State commission had produced a centennial seal and when Sam Scheiner examined it he discovered that a church with a cross was part of the seal. The commission maintained that the "church" was not a church, that the "cross" was not a cross but part of the structural design, that the seal was of such small proportions that only when it was enlarged on billboards would anyone notice it, and that even then the religious symbolism would be dubious.

Too late. Once the Jewish community heard about the seal, all hell broke loose; perhaps they had been looking for some issue around which to consolidate. The Minnesota Jewish Council held, and the Rabbinical Association agreed, that the seal had to be changed. I opposed the motion, believing that we ought to fight a battle that we had a chance of winning rather than one in which we were certain to lose (and lose face as well). But I was overruled, and in order to preserve our unified stand I reluctantly joined the fight. Once in it I gave it all I had. I gave a public lecture, subsequently published, on "The Cross on the Centennial Seal" which attracted a great deal of attention in newspapers, but that was as far as the matter went. The centennial commission ruled that the seal should stand in its current design and subsequently the matter died away. After all, centennial celebrations have a habit of belonging very quickly to the past.

Still, the matter was highly instructive. I learned that a community has to test its strength at certain intervals. I learned also that if this coalescence of intent is the real reason for fighting for a cause, it is not all that crucial whether one wins or loses. But, on the other hand, winning still makes a difference, and it is important to pick one's fights—it is sometimes better not to fight than to fight and lose. Our communities are usually small and have limited resources, and all too frequently we squander them on causes which are not essential. The battle over the cross on the centennial seal—which to this day I believe was no cross at all—was a prime example of efforts we should have directed elsewhere.

A word on the Minnesota Rabbinical Association of which in time I became president. When I arrived in 1948 the association had just voted to eliminate all wedding ceremonies in public places and confine them to homes and synagogues. I inherited the whirlwind which followed this resolution, which my congregation interpreted as an unwarranted interference with private privilege. I fully supported the association; in fact, it had been one of my first opportunities to take a strong position vis-à-vis my own congregation. I held that in our people's personal lives the area of religious sancta was constantly contracting and that maintaining the sacredness of milestone events in Jewish life was an essential task of rabbi and synagogue. It did not matter where the social celebration was held as long as the ceremony took place in a sacred environment. The Rabbinical Association, which represented all rabbis in the state from Orthodox to Conservative to Reform, displayed a remarkable cohesion on this matter—no one defected from its ranks under congregational pressure. We had given the community a year's notice and when our resolution took effect in late 1949, everyone accepted it. In time they forgot that they had ever objected; a few years later a congregant came back from New York, where he had gone to attend the wedding of a relative, and related with horror, "Do you know that they had the wedding ceremony in a hotel!"

# Sabbatical

With the temple built and the centennial in the past, I applied for a sabbatical from the congregation. It was slated to last five months, from March 1956 until the Holidays, and a young graduating student from Hebrew Union College, Herbert Morris, was to take my place. He and his wife moved into our home, and in March we went to New York bound for Europe and Israel. Judy was almost nine and Jonny was thirteen; his Bar Mitzvah had taken place the previous October. We had obtained permission to take the children out of school, had received the outline of their curricula until the end of the year and had sent their schoolbooks ahead, along with boxes of cards which constituted the basic information for my book on the Jews in Minnesota which I wanted to finish abroad.

Our plans were relatively simple. We would go by ship to France, then by air to Israel, spend a leisurely six to eight weeks there; then go to Europe and travel through Italy; then to Switzerland where we had rented what promised to be a fine facility at Lake Thun; then travel some more in Europe; and finally return by ship as we had come. It was in all respects a carefully planned vacation and on the whole it worked out exceedingly well.

We arrived in France after a stormy crossing which made all of us quite sea-sick. In Paris we paid a visit to Israeli Ambassador Jacob Tsur. The international situation had heated up and it appeared that some conflagration in the Middle East was imminent. Back in Minnesota we had been advised against going to Israel. "You don't want to expose your children to war, do you?" was a common query at the time. Very few people in town had ever been to Israel and my own visit in 1935 was now buried in memory. I still expected to see the kind of country I had left at that time, a simple, rural land where collective settlements abounded and where the population was suffused by a spirit of Zionist idealism. During the voyage news came of heightened tension, and my question to Ambassador Tsur was straightforward.

"I appreciate that you cannot take responsibility for our decision, but I have to ask you: do you think we ought to go?"

He answered without hesitation. "If I had a chance to go today with my wife and children, I would go," he said.

That was good enough for us.

TWA took us to Lod Airport (as it was then called) and our stay in the country began. The most noticeable feature that even my three first-timers could see at once was the almost total absence of visitors in the country. Apparently war rumours had kept them away and on this, our first family visit to the land, we met only Israelis—new and old. In our Haifa hotel there was only one other American couple and in other places it was not much different. Consequently we were given unusual attention and consideration—something that in subsequent years, when visitors abounded and hotel space was tight, was not the outstanding characteristic of Israeli hostelry.

We explored the land and the people. We became acquainted or reacquainted with our families that had settled there. Judy celebrated her ninth birthday at Caesarea riding a donkey and digging in the sand for antiquities—one could still find good-sized sherds close to the surface—and generally we had a splendid and instructive time.

The land had changed greatly in twenty-one years. No longer did one dare leave one's valises unattended in the street. The saying attributed to Bialik was being realized: "We will not be a normal country until we have our thieves and prostitutes." Not that there were many of them in the country—the crime rate was still very low, especially in violent crimes. But the curve had started its ascent and was to become much steeper in subsequent years.

We came during the sharp increase in North African immigration. There was not enough permanent housing and the newcomers were assigned temporary structures, ma'abarot, which were often eyesores but filled an important need. As soon as permanent quarters were built the tin huts were demolished and today they can be seen only in pictures of that time.

One thing had not changed: the people's deep and immediate concern for fellow Jews abroad. A goodly portion of Israelis had themselves been refugees and now hundreds of thousands from Arab countries, where they had lived for countless generations, flooded every corner of the land. There were no complaints. To be sure, there were stories of how some of the newcomers had never been exposed to the achievements of Western civilization; how at night they slept under the bed and how they were helpless with eating utensils. But with these tales went no contempt, not even a sense of easy superiority. The attitude was simple: these are our brothers; they seem strange to us today but tomorrow they will be indistinguishable from the rest of us.

Unfortunately, that did not prove to be so. The new Sephardim found themselves at a significant disadvantage compared to the older European settlers who had come with all the technical blessings of Western education (however poor it might otherwise have been). The latter formed the upper class in the country. Thus the seeds were laid for a two-class system—Eastern versus Western Jews—which was to plague Israel as a major problem during the next generation. I had brushed up my spoken Hebrew only to find that in some localities other languages were still preferred. The effect of German immigration was most strong in Haifa; in some sections one heard more German than Hebrew.

For our family the visit had a tremendous impact: they acquired a love for the land and its people and were bound together in a new sense of cohesion and purpose. We had made but a small contribution to the land; it in turn had done much for us.

For our children the visit was their first link with the country, and it also proved to be an eye-opener for Elizabeth, whose attachment to the land and the people became a great force in her life. Since that time she has visited some fifteen times, sometimes leading tours, and has become an expert on Israeli topography and tourism.

Meanwhile the political tensions heightened but they would not break out into war until later that fall. We left in April bound for Italy. In Rome we rented a car, explored the countryside and then, in leisurely fashion, drove north. Eventually, at the beginning of May, we reached Switzerland and the little town of Spiez on Lake Thun, a community of about 3,000 perched on the steep hillside looking across to Interlaken and the majestic peaks of

Jungfrau, Mönch and Eiger. We spent two wonderful months there, and I finished the first draft of my *Jews in Minnesota*.

Of the remaining journey through Europe one experience stands out, our visit to Verdun where so many perished in the First World War and where two of my mother's favourite brothers, Max and Walter, were buried. I had seen war cemeteries before, but somehow I was unprepared for that immense sea of grave-markers which bears mute witness to the desperate enterprise in which men have perfected themselves, the art of war.

And war was to be with us again. Shortly after our return to St. Paul fighting broke out in the Mid-East, with Israel quickly advancing towards the Suez Canal and France and England joining in the occupation of Egypt. Under American pressure the fighting was brought to a halt and eventually the results were reversed, strengthening the hands of both the Egyptians and the Russians. If the first objective of the Americans was to stifle the influence of Great Britain and France in the Mediterranean, they were successful. But John Foster Dulles refused to see that this policy resulted also in the inevitable expansion of Soviet influence and the exposure of Israel to future adventurism. David Ben-Gurion bowed to the Dulles/Eisenhower arm-twisting and the scene was set for further wars. The British retreated like the Israelis, and the French, in time, simply shifted sides. The scenario became something altogether different from what America had envisioned.

In Minnesota the conflict left only a few ripples. There was no thought of rallying Jewish public opinion to oppose Eisenhower's policy; such activity had to await the conflagration of 1967. In 1956 Israel was not yet a strong emotional presence in the lives of American Jews. Still, in a congregation that in former years had exhibited strong tendencies towards anti-Zionism, my sermons began to take some effect. In the years thereafter Mount Zion Temple produced a group of splendid leaders who dedicated themselves to the strengthening of Israel.

## New Vistas

During the fifties a number of rabbis began to gather for theological dialogues. A small group of various affiliations met at Oconomowoc, Wisconsin, to explore the foundations of our belief

in the light of the experiences through which we had passed.*
The discussions were lively and there began to emerge something
that approached a consensus: that the covenant between God
and Israel had to be emphasized as the single most important element in our spiritual existence. In the writings of later commentators who analysed the intellectual and spiritual scene of North
America we became known as the "Oconomowoc theologians" or
the "covenant theologians". While our meetings stretched over
only two or three years, the impact made itself felt in many areas
of Jewish life in the decades that followed, for in this group were
current or future professors at universities as well as men whose
writings would in one form or another reach many layers of
Jewish society. I believe it was at one of those meetings that
Eugene Borowitz (who was then the Union of American Hebrew
Congregations' Director of Education) asked me to undertake a
commentary on Proverbs.

"Consider it a trial commentary, for I hope that you will do
some of the Prophets or even the Torah later on," he said.

Neither he nor I anticipated how prophetic a challenge this
would prove to be.

I agreed, and after a summer's study I began to teach Proverbs
during my Shabbat afternoon classes. A year later I produced a
commentary which, fittingly, was dedicated to my fellow
students at the temple who had helped me explore the text and
had added innumerable insights. It was the first book of mine
that the Union published. More were to follow but not all of them
would sail so quickly from the beginning of research to the date
of publication.

My writing increased. I now published regularly in the *Journal
of the Central Conference of American Rabbis* and devoted
myself more and more to articles on passages in the Torah to
which I tried to bring new insights. It was something I enjoyed
enormously. I refurbished my acquaintance with well known and
more abstruse commentators and I began to read the text with a
fresh eye. I did not then envisage that I would write a commen-

---

* The meetings were conceived by Lou Silberman and began in late 1956. Herman
Schaalman made the local arrangements, I issued the invitations. Over the years the
following scholars and rabbis attended: David Polish, Eugene Borowitz, Herman
Schaalman, Maurice Friedman, Arnold Wolf, Steven Schwarzschild, Lou Silberman,
Dudley Weinberg, Jakob Petuchowski, Emil Fackenheim, and Bernard Martin. From the
Conservatives came Max Ticktin, Hershel Matt, Sheldon Gordon, Sam Dresner, and
Morris Adler. One Orthodox colleague participated throughout: Zalman Schachter, a
Lubavitcher rabbi, then from Winnipeg.

tary on the entire Torah, but clearly my interest was kindled—and I loved studying the minutiae of texts that had been gone over a thousand times by those before me. The Torah was like a prism: however one turned it, the light would refract with fresh and ever vibrant colours.

In addition to my congregational duties I continued my involvement in the wider community: I taught a course in the Department of Philosophy at Macalester College; became chairman of the Governor's Committee on Ethics in Government;* and continued my presidency of the Gallery. We certainly had every intention of staying permanently in a community that offered so many opportunities.

## Canadian Whispers

On one of my trips to New York the president of the Union, Rabbi Maurice N. Eisendrath, took me aside.

"You know, Gunther," he said, "the pulpit of my former congregation, Holy Blossom Temple in Toronto, is opening up and I can think of no one who would fit that post better than you."

I was skeptical. Though I had of course heard of Holy Blossom and its colourful rabbi, Abraham L. Feinberg, I knew little of Canada and even less of Toronto. I had been there once for a Union convention and the only memory I had of the city was that it was clean, rather dead and altogether very unimpressive.

"Look," said Eisendrath, "someone will probably contact you. Give him at least a hearing."

Remembering what had once before happened to me with regard to St. Paul, I was not about to say no without at least knowing what it was that I was turning down. There was no question in my mind that my reply would be negative.

In due time a gentleman contacted me who identified himself as Max E. Enkin, and visited me in my office. It was Friday, however, and I informed him that my time was limited because at noon it was my custom to have lunch with my mother, a custom which I was loath to break for any but the most urgent and overriding reasons.

He understood. He was a charming gentleman to whom I was

* The committee eventually issued a report, "Ethics in Government" (St. Paul, 1959),which became the foundation for far-reaching legislation.

at once attracted, a man whose every word bespoke authentic commitment and broad humanity. He tried to tell me something about Toronto and particularly about Holy Blossom.

"There is no other congregation like it. I think it has a very special quality. I do not want you to take my word for it. Do come and visit us. There is no obligation." The year was 1960.

I informed the president of my congregation that I would pay a visit to Toronto but that I did it only out of courtesy to the president of the Union, who himself had been a rabbi of that congregation. In Toronto I at once called on Rabbi Feinberg, who had not been previously apprised of my coming. When I came through the door he looked at me quizzically.

"You appear to be surprised at my being here," I said.

"Frankly, I am," he replied.

"But why?"

"Why would you want to leave St. Paul to become an associate rabbi of mine?" he asked.

This was news to me. I had been led to believe that the pulpit was open and so I told my colleague. That, in turn, was news to him. He and the president of the congregation, D. Lou Harris, had a brief conference from which emerged the obvious conclusion that the matter needed some clarification. Mr. Harris thought that the terms and time of the rabbi's retirement had been agreed upon, but the rabbi had not so interpreted the understanding.

Obviously there was no place for me. I excused myself and, accompanied by profuse apologies from Messrs. Enkin and Harris, took the next plane back to St. Paul and that, I thought, ended the matter.

But a year later, in April of 1961, I received another call from Toronto. The question of rabbinical succession had been clarified and while the congregation had gone through all the steps of selection, in accordance with the new placement procedure, they wanted to ask me whether I would reconsider and be their rabbi.

Our first inclination was to turn them down. Despite occasional disappointments we were happy. We were extraordinarily well established and my rabbinical as well as public service evoked a satisfying response. Jonathan had just started university and Judy was going to junior high school. St. Paul was our home—as much as any city can become a rabbi's home. But when the call came it made us, and especially me, look at our circumstances in a critical light—and I had to admit that there were some cracks in my armour of satisfaction.

To begin with, I had felt for some time that the very success I enjoyed in the congregation had a negative side: things were almost too easy. I noticed that I was beginning to handle matters in a routine fashion. My imagination was not challenged, and I was putting more and more emphasis on civic affairs.

Just then the Minnesota Legislature was being reapportioned, and a new District was being created which included the very area in which much of the Jewish and upper-class gentile population dwelled. While the Legislature did not elect its members on a partisan basis there was an understanding that parties supported certain candidates whom they felt to be representative of their views. The Democrats with whom I had identified publicly all along asked me whether I would stand for the new seat in the Senate of the Legislature. I felt flattered, but the idea of engaging in a campaign, collecting the necessary funds and having billboards splattered around the District did not appeal to me. All this changed when representatives of the Republican party, many of whom I knew through the Gallery and School of Art, also approached me to stand. This meant that I would likely run unopposed. I was basically willing to accept. There was a small fly in the ointment: the congregation would have to agree because for several months a year my prime interest would be devoted to the Legislature.

I discussed the matter with the president of the congregation, whose immediate reaction was precisely that which I had met some fifteen years before in Chicago. I would be too much away from the congregation and, after all, they were paying my salary. I offered to relieve the congregation of any financial obligation during the time of my service in the Legislature, but the president remained adamant. Were I to persist, I would have to engage in an intramural fight for which I had no stomach.

There were other problems. The city of St. Paul was stagnating and many young people were leaving for Minneapolis. While the congregation itself had grown to eight hundred families, we operated with a minimum of staff. I had repeatedly asked for some additional assistance, especially an assistant rabbi, but it appeared that under our current leadership this request too would not find favour. I was now almost fifty, somewhat beyond the age when a man is likely to be called to a new challenge—but precisely the age when a man passes through a critical time of self-evaluation, and when it is said of him that he will prove his manhood in either of two ways: he will buy a convertible or get a mistress. One might add: or change his place of work. I think now that this must have exerted a powerful influence on me, although I did not recognize it at the time. It felt good to be wanted; it felt good to think of meeting new challenges and calling on inner resources, and working once again at full capacity in my chosen profession.

But there were serious doubts. First and foremost, Elizabeth was not enamoured of the move—not because she did not think that Toronto would be attractive, but because she felt thoroughly at home in St. Paul and did not want to leave. Yet she left the final decision to me. If I thought that the move was important for me, and hence for all of us, she would approve.

There was also my mother, who had just celebrated her seventy-first birthday. But when I talked it over with her she said at once, "Let's go!"—quite the opposite of what I had expected. New faces, new towns, new challenges always intrigued her. As for the children, Jonathan could stay at the University of Minnesota and move to the dormitory; in fact, being on his own would probably be good for him. Judy was more of a problem. She was at a critical time in her life, changing into a young woman. Her relocation would not be so easy.

Holy Blossom itself would be entirely different from Mount Zion. It was not merely its size—more than twice as large—it was its position in the community, its national reputation, the succession of great preachers who had graced the pulpit; Barnett Brickner, Ferdinand Isserman, Maurice N. Eisendrath, and Abraham L. Feinberg. To follow them would be a great honour. There was also Eisendrath's repeated urging: "Don't miss this opportunity. You will become the chief rabbi of Canada, and Canada has much to offer. Sometimes I wish I were still there."

Maurice was then one of North America's best-known spiritual leaders. His words had a strong impact on me. There was also the reputation of the Canadian Jewish community, its strong support of Israel, its unquestioned devotion to religious and cultural causes, and the desire amongst Reform Jews for more and more intensive teaching of Jewish subjects. Toronto Jews were far less assimilated than were our people in Minnesota, but apparently this did not prevent the rabbi of the congregation from making his contribution to the larger community.

Both Feinberg and Eisendrath had been important voices in Canadian social and political life.

I consulted with friends in the St. Paul congregation. One, Mack Wolf—then vice-president of the congregation—spoke without hesitation. "As a member of the congregation and as an official, I sincerely hope you won't go," he said, "but as your friend I must tell you: go and don't miss the opportunity." My friend Sid Barrows counselled me similarly.

Just as we were in the midst of intense family discussions I received an urgent call from New York.

"Could you spare us a few days?" the caller, an old associate from Germany, asked me. "We need you to plead a restitution matter before a committee of the German Bundestag. This committee will make its decision within the next week and is holding its final hearings now. There is every reason to believe that what the committee recommends, the Bundestag will approve. You with your German legal background are the ideal person to handle this for us."

I agreed to go, especially since during that quick journey of four days I could set down the various pluses and minuses of a move to Toronto. I told Elizabeth that I would have my personal answer on my return.

Senator Humphrey had seen to it that the American Ambassador was advised of my coming and I was met by a staff car at the Bonn/Cologne airport and treated with the utmost courtesy and respect. I received the same at the Bundestag. The members of the committee were the "new Germans", even though some of them had been old enough to be fully aware of the Hitler years. I think it was the first time some of them had been face to face with a rabbi. I represented the very people whose sufferings they were trying to alleviate, and my appearance could not have come at a psychologically more suitable time. They were courteous, they were solicitous, and it was apparent from the start that my mission would be successful. So it was: the Bundestag passed some special amendments to the Restitution Law which meliorated some of the inequities.

The journey was successful on a more personal front as well. The long hours over the ocean crystallized in my mind the issue of changing pulpits. I came to the conclusion that I needed a new challenge, and Holy Blossom seemed made to order. In many ways I was naive about the move: I knew less about Canada than I thought. I had forgotten that moving away from a community

meant leaving everything behind: one's friends and one's ac-
complishments, one's private and public credits, one's associations. I had forgotten what it meant to start from scratch. But I
felt in my bones that Toronto would become a great and exciting
city. When I had done my sums the result was clear: I wanted to
go more than I wanted to stay.

I went home and told Elizabeth. She was stunned; she had
expected the opposite answer. We went over everything that I
had reasoned out. In the end she reluctantly agreed. I phoned
Toronto and we fixed a date on which I would meet the Board of
Trustees and finalize my acceptance of the offer.

I went alone, met the Board and later, over coffee and cake,
had a final meeting with president D. Lou Harris and Max Enkin.
Within a mere five minutes we settled salary and the time when I
would begin my service. There was no written record, no contract—just an understanding that I would be rabbi of the congregation and that our association would last as long as it was
mutually agreeable. We also agreed that I would bring an assistant rabbi.

I have already indicated the type of leadership represented by
Max Enkin. D. Lou, his closest friend, was another person of extraordinary capacity. To him, service to the Jewish community
was the content of his life. He was indefatigable, was president
of national organizations such as ORT, Friends of Technion* and
Bonds for Israel, travelled constantly, and had the wonderful
capacity of getting along on a minimum of sleep. He was kindness
and generosity rolled into one. He never turned down a request
that was half-way reasonable, and sometimes even this condition
was unnecessary. He also had the strange habit of disregarding
the clock entirely. I would receive calls from him as late as one in
the morning, or as early as six, and without any apology he would
plunge right into the business at hand. The enormous pace at
which he was going finally brought on his early death. Today a
number of buildings at the Technion in Haifa are named after
him, and every time I visit the institution, my heart fills with
gratitude that it was my privilege to work closely with such a
man.

I received an invitation during my brief visit: the leaders of the
Jewish Home for the Aged (later called Baycrest Centre) were

---

* ORT is a Jewish organization devoted to vocational training in many countries; Technion
is Israel's engineering university, located in Haifa.

about to undertake a building-fund drive and asked me to be their guest speaker for the opening affair in August, a full month before the Holy Days when I was to start my job. The meeting was to be held at Beth Tzedec congregation, so in effect my first public appearance in my new home town would be in a Conservative synagogue. I accepted (after having consulted with D. Lou), but did not anticipate that my appearance at Beth Tzedec before I had appeared at Holy Blossom would set an important pattern for my service—I would serve the whole community.

At the time, the rabbi of Canada's largest Conservative congregation was Stuart E. Rosenberg, who had come from Rochester, New York, and who by dint of his imagination, oratorical skill and commitment had become the most powerful influence inside the Jewish community. Holy Blossom's Feinberg, though in every way the former's match in intellect and oratory, had come to place a great deal of emphasis on the general community; in the years ahead he would spearhead Canadian opposition to America's involvement in the Viet Nam war and would always be identified with progressive social causes. It was as if the community had been neatly divided. "Tony" Feinberg was its face and force to the world at large, Stuart Rosenberg the master of the house within. I suspected (though I was not clearly told at the time) that part of the motivation which caused my congregation to choose me—a man ten years Stuart's senior—was to provide some counterweight to him within the Jewish community. If in later years this did indeed take place, it was not accomplished on the basis of competition. There were many capacities of Stuart's which I could not match, and his contribution to Toronto Jewry would prove to be both outstanding and lasting. He organized the Institute of Ethics which attracted some of the outstanding figures in the Jewish and non-Jewish intellectual world, and his influence was decisive in bringing about the establishment of a Department of Judaic Studies at the University of Toronto. In those days, when the marriage between rabbi and congregation was flourishing, Beth Tzedec was a very special institution.

I determined that I would follow the course I had pursued in Minnesota and establish friendly relationships with all my colleagues. That my opening speech in Toronto would be at Beth Tzedec fit my philosophy perfectly, and Stuart was gracious in welcoming me to his congregation.

I was briefed by Sam Ruth, the gifted director of the Home, and prepared carefully, keeping in mind what I understood to be the nature of the Jewish community. I spoke in terms of history and tradition and quoted liberally from the sources to make my point. I wanted to let the community know that I cared about scholarship and tradition.

I have no idea whether my presence helped to raise any additional funds for the Home, but I do know that my talk made an impact in the community. Within the next few weeks, even before I had come to settle in Toronto, the invitations began pouring in from various parts of the Jewish community. I was on my way to entering the life stream of Jewish existence in Toronto and I took it for granted that my congregation would follow suit. That hope was not disappointed.

When the news of my leaving was announced in St. Paul there was a moving display of affection for the Plaut family. A civic farewell party was held at the St. Paul Hotel, and the roster of guests included dignitaries in political and social life from St. Paul and Minneapolis. Amongst those who signed the guest book was Walter (Fritz) Mondale, later to become Senator and then Vice-President of the United States. He and I had been associated in political life for some time, and his wife Joan had served as secretary of the Gallery when I was president. The event was covered by radio, television, and the newspapers.* It was a great evening for our family, though tinged with sadness and a sense of uncertainty. I was going far from home, not only miles away but into another country. We were presented with a ceramic piece fashioned by our good friend, sculptor Peter Lupori, one of Minnesota's best artists. It was the image of a prophet raising a warning finger. I looked at it that night, not sure what the warning portended.

---

* See further in Appendix 3.

Chapter 7

---

# NEW LAND, NEW DREAMS

ON AUGUST 22, 1961, THE FOUR OF us—Mother, Elizabeth, Judith and I—crossed the border at Windsor. Formalities were perfunctory; in those days immigration was very easy. We spent the night in Chatham, and the next day we arrived in Toronto. It was August 23, my late father's birthday.

It was one thing to make a quick visit to Toronto, it was another to look at it with the eyes of new settlers. Before us lay a city—and indeed a country— that we hardly knew. Though I had read a few books in preparation, I did not know Canada's characteristics, its particular heartbeat, its contradictory sense of nationalism, the emerging problem of Quebec, the contrast between East and West and, most important for us, the inner structure of the complex Toronto Jewish community, which then numbered some 80,000. My earlier appearance at Beth Tzedec notwithstanding, I was a stranger in a strange land. I would have to start at the beginning. My credits and reputation from Minnesota availed me nothing; they were unknown in my new environment. My American political connections had no significance in Canada. I wished that my father were still with me, and prayed that his spirit would not forsake me.

Almost the first characteristic which impressed itself on the newcomer was a patent lack of Canadian nationalism. The country had never had a Joe McCarthy, and for anyone who had lived through the American agony that very absence signified something important. McCarthyism was firmly grounded in a

191

mystical sense of American destiny which, so McCarthy proclaimed, was threatened by dark forces from within as well as
from without. "They" tried to dislodge America as the number
one power in the world; "they" tried to thwart its manifest
destiny. To counteract these powers of evil, McCarthy called on
the good and noble (and usually white) "founders and patriots"
and proceeded to sow the land with suspicion and hatred.

All this was outside the Canadian experience. The land lacked
any sense of destiny or national purpose, or even of identity.
There was no "un-Canadian" to rival the "un-American" of the
southern neighbour. There was no all-Canadian girl who lived
next door, no "spirit of Canadianism" dwelling in the breasts of
the citizens. Whatever overt nationalism existed was, so it appeared to me, negatively based—on a fear of the American
presence. For many years Reform Jews defined themselves as *not
being Orthodox*; similarly, Canadians appeared to define their
national existence as *not being American*. Defensive though this
was, it appealed to me enormously. It was a relief from the often
phony and pretentious sentiment which passed for patriotism in
much of America.

As for Toronto itself, it was still a sleepy city. It was obviously
growing—there seemed to be construction everywhere—but the
small-town moralism remained. There were no sports events on
Sunday, for example, nor could liquor be served on that day.

St. Paul was a one-newspaper town, as was Minneapolis, for
both the morning and the evening newspapers in each city were
owned by the same company. That unhappy condition existed in
many of the great American cities. Toronto was different. While
it was not as diversified as Israel, where a small population had
a dozen daily newspapers, Toronto had three separate papers,
one in the morning—the *Globe and Mail*—and two in the afternoon, the *Star* and the *Telegram*. It was fascinating to observe
the differences between the three. The *Globe*, with the smallest
circulation, clearly appealed to the upper middle class, the civil
servants and the professionals. It was a national paper, read
from coast to coast, and especially in Ottawa. The afternoon
papers competed for the mass market, the *Star* hewing generally
to a liberal line, the *Telegram* to a more conservative one.

From time to time Rabbi Feinberg had contributed a column to
the *Globe*, in a series called "Canadians and Their Religion"
which appeared on the religion page. A panel of five clerics
wrote in turn—about holy days, morality, and other subjects. I

was invited to take my predecessor's turn and for some years wrote on Judaism and its beliefs and practices. In time these columns were published in a volume called *Your Neighbour is a Jew.**

A few years later the *Globe* decided to abandon the religion page and to discontinue the special editor assigned to this area. Richard Doyle, the editor-in-chief, phoned me and suggested that perhaps I might like to continue writing for the *Globe*, on matters which need not necessarily confine themselves to what was commonly (and narrowly) called the religious sphere. I agreed, and this gave me a new level of association with the paper; in the following years I must have written some four to five hundred articles on every conceivable subject. A selection of these too was eventually put into a small book, called *Time to Think*.

Some of the things I was learning about Canadian politics seemed very strange to me. I had great difficulty adjusting to the thought that a majority government had quasi-dictatorial powers as long as the members of its caucus went along with Cabinet decisions. There was, I found, a vast difference between the Canadian parliamentary and the American presidential system, the latter with its clear division into Executive, Legislature and Judiciary. In the United States "back benchers" (a term that does not exist there) had a residue of power since they were strongly based and continued to have important connections with their own districts. In Canada they seemed to be rubber stamps and little else. I also had some difficulty understanding the institution of Orders in Council—Cabinet decisions which had the force of law—not all of which became public knowledge. There was in fact a far greater degree of secrecy surrounding the government than in the United States—something which to this day is one of the weakest aspects, and perhaps the most dangerous one, of Canadian public life.

The greatest difference I experienced was in the Jewish community itself. We had never been exposed to a congregation such as Holy Blossom, where the demand was always for more Jewishness and where attachment to Israel was one of the most important factors. There was a commitment to Jewish education the like of which I had not previously experienced. The reason was evident: European roots were still very strong.

---

* McClelland and Stewart, Toronto, 1967. An American paperback edition was published by Pilgrim Press in Philadelphia, in 1968.

But this ambience had another side which I found less attractive: a sense of Jewish inferiority, because of an all too vivid remembrance of antisemitism in the old country. This was reinforced by a rigid exclusion of Jews from the power bases of Canadian life in general.

A few weeks after I arrived Arnold Bruner wrote a feature article for the *Star*.* "Barriers to Jews Crumbling in Canada," the headline proclaimed. Still, Lazarus Phillips (later appointed senator) was the only Jew who sat on the board of a bank; there was no Jew at the Toronto Stock Exchange nor were there Jewish directors in the major insurance companies. The paper pictured nine Jews who had "made it" with the public: Sen. David Croll, Jacob Finkelman, Mr. Justice Samuel Freedman, Louis Applebaum, Toby Robins (of TV and stage), Louis Rasminsky, Nathan Phillips, G. Sydney Halter (Commissioner of the Canadian Football League), and Rabbi Feinberg whose chairmanship of the Disarmament Committee warranted his inclusion.

In Toronto, Jews were not admitted to the Granite Club or to certain golf and city clubs—an indication that there was a minimum of socializing between Jew and non-Jew. In St. Paul, Elizabeth and I had found ready entrance into many non-Jewish homes. For a rabbi in Toronto, this proved to be nearly out of the question. We made some efforts, invited a few people with whom I had come in contact professionally—amongst them some of the best known names in the entertainment and broadcasting world—but the invitations, though accepted, were not reciprocated except in one instance. For quite some time I was puzzled by this, but was too busy to worry about it; there were more than enough opportunities to meet worthwhile people in our own group. However, it was part of that change to which we had to become accustomed.

During the early weeks we went to the Royal Ontario Museum and took out a life membership to indicate that Toronto was to be our permanent home. At the same time I let the people who were involved at the ROM and at the Art Gallery of Ontario know that we had been active in the art world of St. Paul and would be happy to participate in Toronto as well. This too met with silence, not because we were Jewish (the chairmanship of both institutions was eventually filled by Jews) but rather, I think, because, for them, a rabbi just did not fit the image.

* September 14, 1961, p. 7.

# The Congregation

Wherever I went the same question would arise: Holy Blossom—what kind of name is that for a nice Jewish congregation?* Not long after my arrival in Toronto I was, in fact, involved in an unhappy incident concerning the name.

I had been invited to address a meeting of the New England region of the Union of American Hebrew Congregations. It was to be held in Providence, Rhode Island, and I was to speak at the concluding banquet, a formal affair—black tie and all. I thought I had allowed ample time for the trip, but the weather was bad—it was November—and I was on the road for eight long hours. I missed both lunch and dinner and got there barely in time to give my lecture. I was tired and I hadn't even time to clean up. I was rushed into a banquet room filled with some five hundred well fed, happy-looking people dressed to the hilt—and there I was, miserable, fatigued, unshaven and unwashed, in both dress and sentiment an odd figure to face that splendid assembly.

My old friend and much-admired colleague, the eminent scholar William Braude (translator of many important rabbinical texts), was to introduce me. Bill had known me for a long time and he wanted to relieve my tenseness by being funny. Unfortunately he hit the wrong note. His remarks went something like this: "The man who is about to speak is from Toronto. Now we have all wondered what the name of his congregation means—Holy Blossom. It sounds Catholic, it sounds Japanese, but it doesn't sound Jewish [laughter from the audience]. But there is nothing funny about Rabbi Plaut, and we are happy to welcome him. So, ladies and gentlemen, here's the one and only rabbi of . . . H. . .O. . .L. . .Y. . .BLOSSOM TEMPLE! WOW!"

There was a roar from the audience. Bill had struck everyone's funny-bone—everyone's except mine. I was dead-tired, and angry at Bill and the audience for laughing at me and my congregation. I then committed an unforgivable error: I let out my anger on an innocent group of people who had not laughed maliciously but had only responded to an MC's invitation.

"Ladies and gentlemen," I said, "I thank you for your kind, warm-hearted and joyful reception." Then, after briefly describing the problems I had encountered in coming to Providence, I

* See Appendix 4 for a discussion of the origin of the name.

added, "You see, it took me a long time to get here in order to be greeted by your laughter at the name of Holy Blossom."

At this the audience became very quiet, feeling, no doubt, that I was hurt. I continued: "As you were laughing I asked myself: what is it that these good people are laughing at? They're Jews; they represent congregations; they know Jewish life; they are religious people and concerned with the future of Judaism. Above all, they know their own congregations. What are they laughing at? At the word 'blossom'? Hardly. It is such a beautiful word. It speaks of unfolding, of growth, of beauty on which the human eye can feast. There is nothing funny at all about the word 'blossom'. Ah, it became clear to me, ladies and gentlemen, why you laughed. You think it is outrageously funny that a Jewish congregation should aspire to the term 'holy'. That must be it."

There was deafening silence in the audience. I had hurt them and punished them for their good-natured laughter. I was dead wrong, of course, and the unhappy result was that my speech (which was well prepared) fell on unreceptive ears. I learned my lesson that night. They were gracious enough to invite me back in 1970, and this time—it was in Hyannis, Massachusetts—both introduction and address came off without a hitch.

When I became its rabbi, Holy Blossom had been in existence for more than a hundred years and had been served by some of Reform's most distinguished men. Founded by English and German Jews, it had been incorporated in 1856, eleven years before Canada's Confederation. It had been thoroughly Orthodox in its beginning, for British influence was strong and would remain so for many decades. Towards the end of the century liberalizing trends set in, but not until 1920 did the congregation engage its first Reform rabbi, Barnett Brickner. Along with his wife Rebecca, he left a long-lasting impression.* Reform Jews were believed to be snobbish and contemptuous of their European origins, but the Brickners upset this notion. On the second day of Rosh Hashanah Holy Blossom's rabbi would preach in Yiddish at the services of the Poale Zion, Labour Zionists, most of whom were fairly recent immigrants.

Unfortunately Brickner's successor, Ferdinand Isserman, hewed much closer to the popular expectation. He was of the old, radical Reform school which stressed ethical living over religious forms and appreciated very little of traditional practice;

---

* Their son Balfour, who spent his early years in Toronto, is today the rabbi of the Stephen S. Wise Free Synagogue in New York.

moreover, he made sure that everyone knew exactly where he stood. It was said by his critics that on one occasion he ordered ham and eggs in a restaurant frequented by Jews—and placed his order in a stentorian voice so that everyone could hear him. In any case, Isserman did not last long in this essentially conservative community, where even Reform had a distinctly traditional tinge.

In 1929 he was followed by another old-line Reformer, Maurice N. Eisendrath, whose impact on the larger community was enormous. His radio sermons and Sunday morning lectures (which he introduced) were a must for young people and for many of the city's non-Jewish intellectuals. A man of great social vision, he later became, in the States, a powerful advocate of liberal causes. He was the one who, with great foresight, moved the synagogue from Bond Street in the downtown core to the new residential area at the edge of Forest Hill, almost a mile beyond where the streetcar ended in those days. The building was dedicated in 1938, at the tail end of the Depression. Amongst the Orthodox Jews it quickly became known as "The Church on the Hill"—they considered Reform Jews to be quasi-Christians, and Eisendrath a far cry from the image of the traditional rabbi. Like Isserman, he had little use for custom and ceremony, though he had better sense than to parade his personal proclivities in public. But—again like Isserman—he was not a Zionist, and this was to cost the congregation some of its best members. They left for Goel (later Beth) Tzedec congregation when it seemed to them that Eisendrath was exonerating the Arab rioters in the 1929 Hebron massacre. Eisendrath, man that he was, freely admitted in his memoirs that he had erred grievously. Under his leadership the congregation became distinctly and unalterably Reform: hats were removed and Sunday services rather than Sabbath worship were the centre of the religious agenda. But after Eisendrath left for the presidency of the Union of American Hebrew Congregations, the pendulum swung back.*

Joseph S. Kornfeld was briefly the incumbent of the pulpit, and then it was held for eighteen fruitful years by Abraham L. Feinberg who, together with his wife Ruth, gave the congregation vigorous leadership. Feinberg came from a traditional East European home and never forgot his roots. With him as rabbi, the congregation grew enormously in the post-war years. In addition to

* He died unexpectedly in 1973, just as he was about to give his valedictory address to the Union, and was buried in Toronto.

his great capacities as orator he was, like Isserman and Eisendrath, a man of high social ideals and great personal courage. In
pulpit and community he was an irrepressible civic conscience
and he attracted many of the city's best people. In the course of
time his energies were spent more and more on social issues,
especially after America became involved in the Viet Nam
tragedy. Long before it was fashionable to oppose the war he denounced it time and time again, and he even took a trip to see Ho
Chi Minh, America's sworn enemy. Be it said also, to the praise
of the congregation: while most members did not agree with
Feinberg's politics, they never attempted to circumscribe his
freedom of expression. The pulpit was free in practice as well as
in theory.

Feinberg was also able to surround himself with a splendid
staff, amongst whom Heinz Warschauer was easily the most outstanding personality. Brought up in Berlin like myself, he spent a
while at the Hochschule at about the time when I was a student
there; he went into youth work, then into journalism, and was
shipped to Canada as an internee, along with others who later on
became prominent in the country, like Emil Fackenheim, Walter
Homburger and Eric Koch. Eventually he came to teach at Holy
Blossom and became its Director of Education. His genuine care
for young people, his rigorous standards, intellectual honesty
and great knowledge not only made him an outstanding guide for
the congregation's youth, but soon earned him a reputation as
one of the outstanding Jewish educators in North America. Many
of Toronto's finest minds were on his staff of teachers. For the
last few years before my coming he had, in many respects, been
acting as the rabbi of the congregation, as Feinberg's eyesight
had deteriorated badly—the eye problem was the chief reason
for the rabbi's early retirement at the age of sixty-two.*

There were other outstanding members of the staff the rabbi
had assembled: Lester Sugarman, imaginative and artistic (he
later went to CBC); Ben Steinberg, a fine musician and composer;
Ethel Raicus, Hebraist *par excellence*; Margaret B. Davidson, the
Rabbi's indefatigable right-hand executive—a staff which was
not equalled anywhere. I was the lucky heir and I knew that with
such people my ministry would succeed.

I still remember one great highlight of my first year there. On
the morning of the Sukkot holiday—when in St. Paul only a few

* Heinz was desperately ill when I first wrote this; he has since, alas, died.

faithful worshippers would attend—the synagogue was crowded with hundreds of people, young and old. In the back balcony Ben Steinberg was directing a choir of 150 youths. When they began to sing I shed tears of gratitude that I was privileged to serve such a magnificent congregation.

For my first High Holy Day service I changed almost nothing. I wanted the transition to be easy and in stages. I introduced only two musical innovations: I insisted that the *Bar'chu* and *Shema* be chanted in the minor mode of the High Holy Day and I introduced the Janowski antiphonal version of the *Avinu Malkenu*. The latter was an instant success, the former was not. I remember receiving an irate letter from Fred Gans (who became an outstanding lawyer and was later tragically murdered) that the alteration of the melody of the *Shema* had robbed him of his enjoyment of the Holy Day services. What right did I have to do that? In time, I am glad to say, Fred and others like him became vigorous and active supporters of our new directions.

I found that the High Holy Day arrangements provided for a maze of intricate interlocking services upstairs and downstairs, which were then repeated. For the first High Holidays I had one of my sermons broadcast to the downstairs congregation while I was preaching upstairs. The experiment was a resounding failure and was never attempted again.

Immediately after the High Holy Days I began to speak on my perceptions of the nature of Reform Judaism and where we as a congregation might go in the years to come. I titled the series "It's Easy to be Orthodox and Hard to be Reform." The burden of the sermons was simple: Orthodoxy, I held, provided a set system of demands and responses which, once they were accepted, relieved the individual of making value judgements about them. Not so with Reform: it was open-ended. While it established basic goals, it always called for personal decisions. Of course, it was easy to be a neglectful Reform Jew, one who believed that one did not have to observe anything. But this was a serious distortion of our movement. Rather, every action or omission had to be motivated by knowledge and commitment.

The series attracted enormous crowds. It was as if the High Holy Days had not ended; the balconies were totally filled and people were standing in the outer aisles.

Attendance did decrease after a while, to be sure, but it always remained at a high level and on numerous occasions the synagogue was packed as in the early days. It was therefore an

appropriate closing of the circle when, during my last three sermons at the temple in 1977, the original experience was
repeated: the synagogue was filled to overflowing and people
crowded the outside aisles.

The temple service itself was warm and, from my point of
view, far more evocative of Jewish sentiment than the kind of service we had had in Minnesota. More properly I should say that
Toronto Jewry itself was quite different. It was still much more
closely related to its European background than the people I had
left, who were third- or even fourth-generation Americans. At
Holy Blossom, most people were either immigrants themselves or
the children of immigrants. Most of the families came from
Eastern Europe, and the heritage of the *shtetl* remained pervasive. In the first year of my incumbency, the Board of Trustees
still included many men and women who could understand Yiddish. This, of course, has changed. With the passing of generations the old memories and the language have tended to disappear as people moved into the mainstream of North American
life.*

The enormous, in fact fantastic, response that I received
helped at once to secure my future. In this respect I was very fortunate. I had come to a new city and a new country, unknown to
all but a very few, yet within a few months, so it seemed, I was
firmly established. In those days we did not have a Jewish
newspaper that was read by most householders—information
travelled primarily by word of mouth—but that route, I found,
was quick and sure. Invitations came from groups that had not
seen a Reform rabbi, let alone invited him, for many decades, like
the *folksmenshen*** who represented a sizable element of
Toronto's Jewish community; then service clubs and business
associations began to call; and soon the invitations came from

---

* The lay leadership of the temple was equally remarkable. D. Lou was surrounded by
men like Ben Sadowski and Max Enkin, representing the old school of prestige and influence; Norman Borins and Elliot Marrus, leading lawyers; Dr. A. A. (Bucky) Epstein,
prominent in North American welfare fund activities; Morley Pape, pious and learned
interpreter of Yiddish literature; Norman Grant, who in Israel's war of independence
directed undercover shipments of arms from Canada; Sydney Harris, who would later
become national president of the Canadian Jewish Congress; Albert Rose, professor
(later dean) of the School of Social Work at the University of Toronto; and last but not
least, Bora Laskin (later Chief Justice of Canada), who was deeply concerned with
Jewish education. The women were led by Dorothy Hermant, Lucille Lorie, Hortense
Geldzaeler, Beatrice Rosenberg, Marilyn Farber and Henrietta Chesnie, later to
become president of the synagogue and originator of an imaginative outreach program
for temple members.
** A Yiddish term describing the broad masses.

other Canadian communities. There were more than I could accept.

My colleagues too received me warmly and generously. During the first Sukkot week we invited all the rabbis in town to come for an hour of sociability. Most accepted.

"Of course," said one Orthodox colleague to my wife over the telephone, "I will not eat."

My wife was undaunted.

"Of course you will," she said. "What I serve you, you can eat." Orthodox, Conservative and Reform rabbis put in their appearance. For many it was the first time that they had met each other. One consequence of the afternoon was the eventual establishment of a rabbinical fellowship which in the beginning was chaired by Walter Wurzburger of Shaarei Shomayim (later he became a professor at Yeshiva University in New York and president of the Rabbinical Council of America), Stuart Rosenberg and me. Even Rabbi Gedalia Felder, renowned halachic authority, became a participant in the fellowship. The process of religious polarization had not yet hit its full stride in Toronto. That was to come later and would constitute my major disappointment in the Canadian rabbinate.

On the whole, the Reform movement in Canada was weak and its congregations were few. There were two temples in Montreal, but they had not taken advantage of the enormous opportunities which existed in what was then the unquestioned capital of Jewish life in the country. Reform was marginal in the city, even though it included in its ranks some of the finest people. The community itself was largely untouched by progressive ideas.

In Toronto matters were more promising. Since Holy Blossom was the mother congregation in Upper Canada and had gone through the process of changing from Orthodoxy to Conservatism to Reform, it could not be relegated entirely to the sidelines. Also, its membership was large. There were two offshoot congregations: Temple Sinai, founded with the help of members of Holy Blossom by Rabbi Jordan Pearlson, who in time became one of our most articulate spokesmen; and Temple Emanu-El whose first president was Barney Danson, a confirmand of Holy Blossom and later a successful Liberal politician rising to national prominence as Minister of Defence. Temple Sinai began more or less in the pattern of Holy Blossom and turned more traditional in time; Temple Emanu-El was at first more radical but later became fairly traditional and, like its remarkable rabbi,

Arthur Bielfeld, more outward-looking. Beyond these, only two Reform congregations existed in Canada: a new one in Windsor, and the country's oldest Reform Temple, Anshe Sholom in Hamilton, guided by Rabbi Bernard Baskin, a man of many intellectual and artistic gifts.

I resolved at an early stage that I would attempt to spread the ideas of Reform throughout the land. The success I had was far greater than I could have anticipated in 1961. I travelled many times to Ottawa, Montreal, Winnipeg and Vancouver, and in all these cities was able to help create new congregations, even as I did in Toronto itself.*

My installation ceremonies were set for the opening days of Hanukah, December first to third. Rabbis Feinberg and Eisendrath presided over the religious induction on Friday night. Harry Stern, as Dean of the Reform rabbis, came from Montreal and preached on Saturday morning. Saturday evening featured a dinner dance with my brother Walter (who was now rabbi in Great Neck, New York) as the speaker. Sunday afternoon saw the civic installation, with clergy and government figures participating. The events, chaired by Oscar Newman, were a rousing success, and the response from the congregation and the community was overwhelming. There was even some suspense and excitement. Governor Elmer L. Andersen, a close friend of ours, was travelling from Minnesota to take part on Sunday afternoon. The ceremonies were set for three o'clock. At noon we received a telephone call from him. The weather in Chicago where his plane was supposed to have landed was terrible and therefore the flight from St. Paul-Minneapolis had gone on to Baltimore.

"I am phoning from Baltimore," he said, "and I'm not quite sure how I can get to Toronto by three o'clock. But I will try to rent a private plane and perhaps I can still make it on time."

An hour later there was another telephone call.

"I've made arrangements and I will be there. Please have somebody meet me at the airport."

We dispatched a special team to take care of Governor Andersen and we hoped that nothing further would happen to delay his arrival. What we did not know was that when his plane tried to land at Malton it was refused permission, because

* See further in Appendix 5.

Andersen's international flight had not been scheduled properly.

At the synagogue we did not understand the delay; we just waited and waited. Eventually we decided to start the ceremonies, hoping that the Governor would come before we were finished. Everything went well. Ontario Premier John Robarts spoke, as did other dignitaries. Lieutenant-Governor Keiller MacKay, a man of extraordinary intellectual and social sensitivity, gave his expected brilliant address. The time came for Andersen to speak—but there was no Andersen. I decided that I would give my response first, even though it did not quite fit the program. I finished—and still no Andersen. The choir sang its final piece, and I resigned myself to concluding the ceremonies without the Governor's presence. Then, just as the last notes reverberated through the sanctuary, we heard police sirens wailing in the distance. The wail grew excitingly louder and louder, until it ceased abruptly as it reached the temple. The doors flew open and in strode Elmer Andersen in striped pants and swallow-tails—he had changed on the plane, he told us later. The congregation rose and broke out in loud cheers. I found out after that the governor—no newcomer to politics—had overcome the objections of Malton authorities by threatening an international incident!

We recorded some particularly quotable remarks from the installation.

ADVICE TO THE RABBINATE: "In all things that concern you as a person, be humble; in all that concerns mankind, be brave; in all that concerns justice and peace, for which man hungers and thirsts, be strong."—*Rabbi Abraham L. Feinberg.*

ON LEADERSHIP: "A leader must be with his people, and ahead of them."—*Rabbi Walter Plaut.*

ON FREEDOM: "When the maniacal madmen of Moscow turned our skies into a sewer of radioactive garbage, against the protests of every decent human being . . . when the area of freedom seems to be narrowing, the cry of Judas Maccabeus rings out once more—'Let those who are for God follow me.' "—*Rabbi Maurice N. Eisendrath.*

ON THE ROLE OF JEWS: "If there is a Nobel Prize for devotion to the welfare of and progress of mankind, it must go to the Jews. . . . Today's great challenge, for Jews and for all the world's peoples—to be identified with all mankind."—*Governor Elmer L. Andersen.*

ON CANADA: "In this country, men and women of every creed,

country and race come together in dignity of spirit and equality of rights. With its mixture of colours and faiths, Canada can show to the world a pattern of brotherhood and understanding. . . . In these days, when the winds of change are blowing fiercely across the world, and a few regions are still mired in the quicksand of intolerance and misunderstanding, the example of Canada is an outstanding one."—*Premier John Robarts.*

The congregation was large and continued growing. We were nearing a membership of two thousand families.

I had learned in St. Paul that some congregational functions are best undertaken by the members themselves, and with the help of the temple Brotherhood a special "Mitzvah Corps"* was instituted, led by Morris Cooper who assembled a group of volunteers to read the daily services. Soon an anaemic worship routine became a rousing service of participation, especially after we involved lay cantors as well. Members of the group also read services at homes of bereavement, and while at first people wondered why the rabbis did not always officiate, it did not take too long to have these "Mitzvah" congregants fully accepted. The program has now been in place for many years and it is as firmly established as anything that Holy Blossom has ever undertaken.

I instituted Sabbath afternoon study classes which concluded with *Havdalah,*** and soon collected a small group of loyal students. After some years I decided to change the time of these classes—I was simply too tired on a late Sabbath afternoon—to the hour before the beginning of morning services, and the number of students increased considerably. This too is a program which has become a pillar in the educational structure of the synagogue.

The expanded obligations of the cantorate were too much for Sam Stolnitz, who was serving at that time. When he left, the congregation took the big jump and engaged one of the best known cantors in North America, Jacob Barkin, who until then had served Conservative congregations. Jack was of the famous Barkin family of Toronto musicians; his sister Sara sang in our choir, his brother Leo was a well known pianist. For Jack, coming to Holy Blossom proved to be a triumphal return to his native city. He gave our services a great boost. People now came not

---

* Mitzvah, a Hebrew term denoting a religious duty or opportunity.
** "Separation"; a ceremony marking the end of the Sabbath and the beginning of another week.

only because it was the Sabbath or for *Kaddish** or a baby-naming or because they wanted to hear the sermon; now they also came because the music had a new dimension. Unfortunately, friction developed between Barkin and our music director, Ben Steinberg, and we had Barkin for only a few years. He left for Detroit and the congregation again searched for a cantor. This time we took a graduate of the Hebrew Union College School of Music, Sheldon Merel, whom we brought all the way from Oakland, California. He was to be with the congregation for ten years.

But again there were difficulties in the music department. The new cantor and Ben—whose fine Sabbath service I had helped to publish through my discretionary fund—did not see eye to eye. Despite my attempts to pacify the participants in the quarrel, Ben decided to leave after the High Holy Days. It was a great blow to the congregation, and to me personally, for I thought much of Ben and hated to see him leave. He had done great work with our children's choirs and with our Temple Singers. But he felt strongly that unless he was in complete charge of music he could not operate to his full capacity.

With Sheldon Merel as our new cantor and Director of Music, and one of Toronto's best organists, Douglas Bodle, at the organ, our music now took a more experimental direction. Not everyone liked this, but the success of our experiments spoke for itself. We had already had a service with ritual dance—bringing in a team of artists from Boston—and now went boldly into our first folk rock service. It involved percussion and other instruments on the pulpit and a distinctly "with it" musical flavour. There were some who were outraged. One congregant suggested that I would soon be selling drugs from the pulpit. But the majority felt highly rewarded. Best of all, young people were attracted by the thousands. There was standing room only when we first had the rock service, and a few weeks later we repeated it with the same overwhelming attendance. We did it a third time and only then were we satisfied that we had brought Ray Smolover's music the exposure it deserved. A few years later Cantor Merel produced a jazz service which was musically first rate, but unfortunately the congregation failed to appreciate it. It was ahead of its time; not until later did jazz once again become a public favourite. There were evenings of Sephardic and pre-modern music and many

* A prayer spoken by mourners commemorating a close relative's death.

other attempts to explore the religious spirit through the medium of sound.

In many respects the end of the sixties saw the greatest success of our worship enterprise. We had founded a Young Marrieds' group who from time to time had their own services in the Youth Chapel, while the regular service took place in the Sanctuary; in time we instituted a regular alternate service at 5:45 on Friday afternoons; created another alternate service on Saturday mornings for those who did not wish to go into the Sanctuary but wanted a quieter, more personal worship mood; and we introduced what we called the "service in the round". For this last venture we went into the Congregational Hall during what was (religiously speaking) the off-season: the last week or two of the calendar year and the first week of the new year. We placed the pulpit in the centre of the room and had the people sit around it. There was no organ or choir. In this atmosphere—borrowed from the old Sephardic synagogue and, in a more up-to-date fashion, from the Stratford Festival Theatre—we prayed together in an informal setting. Attendances at all these innovations were excellent.

We brought important guests to the pulpit and the community, beginning (in early 1962) with Martin Luther King Jr. The theme of his address was "Nonviolent Resistance", and his nonviolent but determined mood was evident both in his approach to thorny problems and in his voice. I made some notes of his speech:

> Segregation must go, not because this [struggle] is important in our struggle with Communism, but because it is morally wrong; because it substitutes an I/it relationship amongst people for an I/thou relationship.
>
> Time takes no sides. It is neutral and can be used either way, but time is always ripe for doing right.
>
> The long arc of history bends towards justice.

Three years after King appeared with us and talked about nonviolent militancy he was jailed in Alabama. Blacks were hunted with guard dogs. Our Social Action Committee, revivified under the leadership of Milton Cadsby (now a Provincial Judge), sprang into action and established a Martin Luther King Fund in the community. Harry Belafonte came to help us. The idea caught on and soon the campaign became nation-wide, far beyond the

efforts of our own congregation. We were in close touch with the
Southern Leadership Conference— Ralph Abernathy and Coret-
ta King would also speak at the temple. It was at that time that
Alabama's segregationist Governor George Wallace was coming
to town as a speaker for a convention. He was booked for Maple
Leaf Gardens, and with thousands of visitors in town the event
was hailed—in all its controversy—as an important venting of
opinions, however unpopular. Our Social Action Committee
undertook a task to which it had never before addressed itself: it
organized a huge picket action and at the same time a collection
of funds in the vicinity of the Gardens. Many of our members had
never marched in the street; now they carried signs and were
joined by others from the community, black and white. Conven-
tional middle-class congregants overcame their embarrassment
and hesitation, and took their places on the corners of Yonge and
College streets shaking collection boxes and asking the crowds to
make a donation for freedom and equality.* It was an exhilarating experience.

My most successful pulpit innovation was the institution of
public affairs lectures. Once a month or so I would deal with
whatever current affairs were uppermost in people's minds.
Sometimes it was a single event, other times a series of issues,
which I analysed in a lecture which might last as long as forty-
five minutes or an hour. Once these lectures became established,
Jews from inside and outside my congregation, and non-Jews as
well, made sure they attended, and whenever a public affairs
talk was announced I could be certain of a full house.

There was one small change that occurred. On one of my trips
abroad, while seeing the sights of Rome, I fell and injured my
back. After my long period of recuperation the doctor advised me
not to stand for more than fifteen minutes at a time. How could I
give my sermons and lectures? I resolved to take the bull by the
horns. On my return to the pulpit I placed a chair at the front of
the beema, and spoke sitting down. Instead of diminishing the
oratorical effect, the new mode of delivery enhanced the impact
of my lectures. To be sure, I could not rely on waving my arms or
assuming threatening or appealing postures, but neither was I
separated from my listeners by a great wooden bulwark. I found
that people listened more carefully. They were more relaxed,
and so was I. Since that time I have always sat down for talks of

* See further p. 237 ff.

any length. I have often recommended the system to my colleagues, but to my knowledge none of them has followed my
example.

The days were short, too short. Visiting the sick and bereaved,
counselling young and old, spending time with the congregation's
children and youth—all these normal features of rabbinical
responsibility filled my endless schedule. But I was vigorous and
the marvellous response of the community spurred me on.

## The Lost Manuscript

There were also some failures. During the period of our greatest
success with public attendance I thought I had finally convinced
the congregation that Friday night was the time when one came
to the synagogue, regardless of the program. There would be
worship and there would also be something intellectual, artistic
or emotional that would be satisfying to everyone. I therefore
stopped announcing what we would present, and whether my
associate or I would do the preaching. Alas, this was a mistake;
people began to stay away. Reluctantly I concluded that the majority did not come for the sake of the Sabbath but rather
because we presented attractive programs which, as it happened, were held on the traditional Jewish day of assembly. I considered this a major defeat, but it brought me to the realization
that the Sabbath itself had to be fundamentally revived, else its
meaning would slip away from us. Many members never attended at all and had minimal or no home observances on Friday
nights. Moreover, even those who did come to Friday night services considered this the end of their Sabbath observance. They
too were usually oblivious of the fact that the Sabbath was meant
to be a period of twenty-four hours devoted to introspection and
to enriching one's life. It was a wasted potential, a magic key that
most people—except for the truly Orthodox—had lost.

I wrote to my much-admired friend Jacob Weinstein, who was
then vice-president and program chairman of the Central Conference of American Rabbis. I told him of my concerns and
pointed out that not since the beginning of the century, except in
a lecture which Israel Harburg had given to the Conference in
1937, had there been serious consideration of the Sabbath as the
pivotal force of Jewish life. Yet there was not a single member, I
wrote, for whom the Sabbath was not the major focus of rab-

binical and congregational existence. Clearly the Sabbath was in trouble and with it the synagogue and the whole institution of congregational worship. Should we not devote a convention to this one subject?

Jacob agreed, and invited me to give the keynote lecture on the subject, which would be the theme of our very next conference. The lecture I delivered, in June 1965 in Cincinnati, was perhaps the most important I have ever given in my life, for it helped to turn the Reform movement into a new direction. The lecture itself was published separately and eventually appeared in an anthology as well.

Amongst the proposals I made was one which in my own rabbinate I never managed to carry out: I said that the institution of the late Friday night service (begun in 1869 as a convenience for congregants) had run its course and was now a visible failure in most congregations. Fewer than eight per cent of our Reform membership attended with any regularity. It was a bad time to come to services, especially during the severe winters of much of North America. Wage-earners came home tired, often fighting long lines of traffic, and no sooner had they arrived than they had to eat quickly and set out again for the temple. How could one arouse deep feelings of devotion or engage in serious intellectual discussion under such circumstances? The ideal time, confirmed by precedent and long experience, was Saturday morning. Moreover it seemed, at least in Toronto, that Orthodox and Conservative congregations did very well without Friday night services; they were attracting large and enthusiastic congregations for Sabbath morning worship. Would we have the courage to recognize the truth and do away with—or at least phase out—this adaptation which had been around for almost a hundred years? Was it not time to resuscitate Saturday morning services?

Moreover, I said, we had not been honest with ourselves. We had not gone all out encouraging people to observe a full Friday evening at home, because this would have been competition for our Friday night attendance at the temple—which was the measure by which our rabbinical "success" was commonly judged. But with ninety-two per cent of our membership staying away on Friday night, should we not adapt to their needs and help them make Friday night a true Sabbath experience in their own homes?

At the end of my lecture I was given a standing ovation by my colleagues. They then discussed the subject and the paper in separate working groups, and in the end it was agreed that a special Sabbath Committee would be established to work out ways of making Shabbat more meaningful to our membership. I was appointed chairman of the committee and was given a splendid group of colleagues.* After several years of labour we came to the conclusion that Reform Jews needed, to begin with, a handbook, and we submitted a manuscript to the Conference, which finally approved it in Houston, Texas, in 1969.

The book, which at first we wanted to call A Sabbath Guide, was named A Shabbat Manual (Tadrikh le-Shabbat) because "guide" was still too strong a word for the Reform movement. Years before, Morton A. Berman had given a lecture on whether the movement should have an explicit guide. He had made a survey of the rabbis, who had overwhelmingly vetoed any kind of document which would "codify" Reform practices. They were afraid that we would start a new Orthodoxy. The same fears were expressed in Houston, but a new generation had grown up who desired a guide with specific suggestions and were confident that it was a far cry from a code forcing people into a mould. Though the discussion was animated and the opponents vocal, the new idea carried the day and the Reform movement gained its first official guide of observance. To be sure, it was "only" for the Sabbath; still, it was a recognition that Reform did require form, that content without form had proven to be insufficient.

This was the summer of '69. I forwarded the completed manuscript, properly annotated, to the Publications Committee of the Conference, anticipating that the book would be published forthwith as the membership had voted.

What followed appears now as a comedy; however it was a comedy fraught with near-tragedy—at least as far as I was concerned. The tale of the Manual may seem unbelievable to those who think that organizations as staid and proper as a rabbinical group are not subject to the errors of less solemn organizations. Nonetheless, this is what happened.

I enquired from the office of the CCAR** what the progress of the publication was. Sydney Regner was then executive vice-president and wrote that the publication was in the works, but

---

* They were initially Frederick A. Doppelt, Henry E. Kagan and Joseph Narot (all three have since passed away), Herbert M. Baumgard, Robert I. Kahn, Joseph Klein, Herbert H. Rose and Herman E. Schaalman.
** Central Conference of American Rabbis.

that funds were low because of the impending publication of the new prayer-book. A year went by, and a second. The members of my committee were getting impatient, and so was I, but there seemed to be nothing we could do to budge the apparatus. Then Joseph Glaser succeeded Regner as executive vice-president and called me one day from New York.

"Gunther," he said, "we are having an executive meeting and it has been decided to turn the *Shabbat Manual* back to the committee. You can do with it what you want. Publish it privately if you care to. We have decided that we do not wish to proceed and, besides, we have no money."

I could not believe my ears.

"But the Conference accepted the *Manual* at a convention," I finally countered. "You cannot decide to undo the will of the Conference."

Joe was sympathetic but said quite firmly, "No one on the Executive Board seems to know anything about a resolution of the Conference to that effect. So it's yours—do with it whatever you want."

"Wait a minute, Joe," I said, quite desperate now, "I have my year-books here. I will quote you chapter and verse from the resolutions."

I scrambled to find the year-book of the Houston Conference and I read him the resolution. There was silence at the other end of the wire.

"I didn't know that," he said. "The Executive Board will be surprised."

The Board was indeed surprised, and now saw no way of delaying the publication any further. But there was still one snag to come.

Joe called me a few days later.

"I'm afraid we have another problem," he said. "No one seems to know where the manuscript is."

Again, I could not believe what I heard.

"But I sent it to the publications committee a long time ago."

"That may be so," said Joe, "but we simply can't find it. I've no idea what can have happened to it."

I was not too alarmed by this, for of course I had a photocopy. At least I thought I had.

Now began the search for the copy. It took me a while, but I finally located it. Then I discovered, to my horror, that the copying machine had been faulty and that most of the pages had faded beyond recovery. Only the music notations were reasonably legible.

I did not let New York know of my calamity, nor did I write a word to anyone on my committee. I spent the next week sitting up nights redrafting the *Manual* from memory as best I could, and from old correspondence. I completed the manuscript, had it retyped and took it to New York myself.

But the battle was not yet over.

Joe, who wanted the manuscript to be published, was in honest distress. "We just haven't got the money for publication," he said. "I think I have a way out, though. Bernie Scharfstein at Ktav Publishing Company may go in with us and take over the cost of publication."

That is how the book saw the light. While it was not as elegantly produced as other CCAR publications it was at least cheap—two dollars a bound copy. In the first year the Conference and Ktav sold 35,000 copies. It was a rousing success. Whether it had an effect on meaningful Shabbat observance I do not know. But it was a beginning. The Shabbat Committee was now renamed the Reform Practices Committee and I remained as chairman. In time we would publish *Shaarei Mitzvah* (*Gates of Mitzvah*) which appeared in 1979 under the editorship of Simeon Maslin. This book received the fullest attention of the Conference and its staff, and for the first time the movement had a pair of books to guide the Reform family in its day-to-day cycle of observances and in its celebration of Shabbat.

Nonetheless, there was a price to be paid. The drive towards greater observance unleashed a counter-movement within the Conference. Eventually, under the leadership of Eugene Mihaly, the American Association for Progressive Reform Judaism (AAPRJ) was established. The battle moved to conferences and conventions. I debated the new trend in Reform with Alvin Reines* at a convention of the Union in New York, and with Mihaly at the Jerusalem convention of the World Union for Progressive Judaism. The battle-lines hardened. On our side were many of the young people—but not all. On the other side were those who believed that the reforming edge of the movement was being blunted by what they called "rules and regulations reeking of Orthodoxy". Though this was not the declared aim of the Association they also attracted those colleagues who, while they

---

* Both he and Mihaly were graduates of Hebrew Union College, and taught there.

regretted the increase in mixed marriages, saw in them an opportunity for attracting young people, and were willing to officiate at the ceremonies, even with priests or ministers. Our side
gained a narrow victory at the Atlanta convention, and a good
deal of bitterness ensued in both camps.

There was also a personal price to be paid. While I maintained
cordial relations with my colleagues, I now became unacceptable
as a candidate for the presidency of the Conference. It was
feared that my nomination might split the Conference, one
member of the Nominations Committee told me. Though I suffered some disappointment in this regard, I was convinced that,
in the long run, the successful publication of my Torah commentaries, of *Shaarei Mitzvah* and the *Shabbat Manual*—to be
followed by a third volume on the Holy Days and a fourth one on
ethics—would be a greater contribution to the movement than
my presidency could ever provide. But in late 1980 I was most
pleasantly surprised when the nominations committee of the Conference did at last bring my name forward for election as vice-
president in June 1981 in Jerusalem, when Herman Shaalman is
slated to become president. All going well, my election to the
presidency would follow in 1983. Thus two of our original "Gang
of Five" who came to America in 1935 may occupy the top positions in the Reform rabbinate—forty-six years later!

# Writings

For some years I had been struggling with the issue that I had
first submitted to Albert Einstein in the early forties: how religion and science could be seen as compatible rather than as
contesting polarities. I had tried to bring my research in this field
to some conclusion and finally, in 1961, the Union published my
thoughts in a small book entitled *Judaism and the Scientific
Spirit*. The book was later translated into Hebrew and to this day
still enjoys modest sales. We held a special convocation at Holy
Blossom to celebrate the publication of the book, the first of a
number of such occasions. The response of the congregation and
the public was heart-warming. My first major book, *The Jews in
Minnesota*, had been dedicated to my father who loved history.
The second, *A Commentary on the Book of Proverbs*, was
dedicated to the members of Mount Zion Temple whom I had
taught on Shabbat afternoons for many years. The new book was

dedicated to my mother and my mother-in-law, two women who, though their years were advancing, never lost their intellectual curiosity.

In Toronto as in St. Paul, I kept up my literary output. At a London conference of the Governing Board of the World Union for Progressive Judaism I chanced to sit next to Rabbi Solomon Freehof, leader of our movement and soon to succeed Lily Montagu as head of the World Union. During the tea break he said to me, "Gunther, I have been thinking about a book that we need very badly. No one has researched and published the sources of Reform Judaism. You are the one who can and should do it. I'll see to it that it is published."

I said that I would look into the matter and when I considered the idea more seriously I found it appealed to me. In time, *The Rise and Growth of Reform Judaism*, in two volumes, was published by the World Union. (The title was not altogether without problems. I heard of one purchaser who went into a bookstore and asked for *The Rise and Fall of Reform Judaism*.) This became the standard work on the subject, and the first volume especially, republished several times, found a good deal of critical acclaim.

Also, a selection of articles written for our temple Bulletin appeared under the title *Page Two*, and articles from the *Globe and Mail* were published in a volume called *Time to Think*.

But all along I had known that these efforts were only the introduction to what I really wanted to do. I wanted to write a commentary on the Torah—and having tasted the pleasures of writing my book on Proverbs, and having published a whole series of individual studies of Torah subjects in the CCAR *Journal*, I felt I was ready.

I broached the subject to Maurice Eisendrath, who was interested. After a great deal of pushing and pulling we brought together a group of consultants, among them Sol Freehof and the venerable Mordecai M. Kaplan who, though not aligned with our movement, was nonetheless open enough to see the importance of a liberal commentary. No Jew had published such a book in the three hundred years of Jewish life in North America. The accepted commentary was the one edited by Joseph H. Hertz, Chief Rabbi of Great Britain. Though it was written in magnificent English and with great verve and passion, it was hopelessly outdated. It had appeared in the early thirties as a response to growing antisemitism and consequently had a highly apologetic tone. Though it showed some awareness of the progress of scien-

*(Top)* With Chaplain Brasskamp and Congressman (later Senator) Eugene McCarthy, after I gave the invocation in the House of Representatives, 1950. *(Above)* With Franklin D. Roosevelt Jr. (left) and Governor Luther Youngdahl in St. Paul, Minnesota, 1951.

*(Above)* My mother on her sixtieth birthday. *(Right)* Walter at age thirty, as rabbi in Fargo, North Dakota.

Elizabeth's mother, Therese Strauss, at seventy.

(Right) At the gathering of theologians in Oconomowoc, Wisconsin. Left to right: Herman Schaalman, Steven Schwarzschild, Eugene Borowitz, Arnold Wolf; 1951. (Below) Mount Zion Temple, St. Paul, Minnesota, where I served from 1948 to 1961.

*(Left)* With Ontario's Lieutenant-Governor Keiller MacKay, Social Action chairman Milton Cadsby and Harry Belafonte, at a benefit concert in Toronto on behalf of American blacks. *(Below)* Back to the city of my childhood; the Berlin Wall, 1962.

*(Above)* With Milton Cadsby and Martin Luther King Jr., in Toronto, 1962. *(Right)* With Prime Minister Lester B. Pearson, in Cleveland, 1963.

*(Top)* With David Ben-Gurion in Toronto, 1967.   *(Above)* With community leaders D. Lou Harris and Murray Koffler (right), 1969.

Mayor Nathan Phillips taking part in the services at my installation at
Holy Blossom Temple, Toronto, in 1961.

tific inquiry, it nonetheless kept strictly to the traditional line: the Torah was revealed by God Himself to Moses on Sinai; being God's word the Torah was flawless and in every way superior to later insight; all human knowledge was essentially contained in it. This perspective was in accord with strictest Orthodoxy. It would not do for the liberal synagogue, or even for the Conservatives, although it was found in their pews—and, *faute de mieux*, in many of ours as well.

But how to go about a new commentary? Who should write it? How should it be written? I was appointed general editor and asked to prepare a few trial chapters. I now discovered that, however much I thought I knew, I really knew little. While I had been vaguely aware of the immensity of scholarship lavished on the Bible and especially the Torah, I was not conversant with Semitic languages other than Hebrew and Aramaic. My knowledge of Arabic had disappeared and my knowledge of Syriac was badly in need of refurbishing. I knew no Akkadian or Ugaritic, nor could I decipher Egyptian writing.

I began to read widely and found that I had much catching up to do. I also discovered, through trial and error, that writing a book by committee was impossible. Eventually a new method was agreed upon by us and approved by Alex Schindler, who was Eisendrath's vice-president and his eventual successor. He suggested that the five Torah books be the reponsibility of five separate authors. I was to write on Genesis, and the committee would find four others to take on the rest. I was also to have some hand in the final editing process of the total work. I accepted the proposition, although with some reluctance; I had hoped to write the entire commentary myself.

At last we proceeded. I was given three scholars with whom to work and consult on my drafts, Matitiahu Tsevat and Alexander Guttmann, Professors of Bible and Talmud, respectively, of Hebrew Union College-Jewish Institute of Religion, and the orientalist William W. Hallo of Yale.* The latter especially had a major share in the project and wrote the introductions on comparative sources for each of the five books; best of all, he and I established a close relationship based on mutual respect and our love for Torah. My friend Robert I. Kahn served as chairman of the committee that would oversee the progress of the publication.

---

* In 1950 Hebrew Union College had joined with a New York seminary, the Jewish Institute of Religion, under the combined names.

When I had completed my first draft of Genesis and sent it to the committee I found that no one was satisfied. Whenever I had sent out chapters to the committee I had received comments that were contradictory—each member had his own hobby-horse, a particular point of view that he wanted to see expressed. I tried to comply with these suggestions as best I could, with the result that the commentary had no point of view and was neither fish nor fowl. Fortunately, when the committee met, there was a general recognition that the process itself was at fault. Alex encouraged me to do it again and this time I put forth my own conclusions.

Eventually, in 1974—nine years after I had begun the project—Genesis appeared and was published simultaneously in hard cover and paperback. The production turned out to be not only handsome but lavish. Both Hebrew text and English translation and commentary were in attractive large type; the use of white space was generous, and altogether it was a beautiful volume. However, there were a number of disappointments as well. I had hoped that the Hebrew text would be printed with the traditional musical notes (which were also the ancient Masoretes'* signs for punctuation); that the weekly portions would be clearly indicated and the book printed from right to left.

There was a good deal of publicity and the book received wide coverage, from the *New York Times* to the annual year-book of the *World Book Encyclopedia*. The reception was favourable—although the book was still far from what I wanted. I knew that revisions were bound to be made sooner or later. I still had not learned everything I needed to know to write a definitive commentary.

Even though it was now 1974 the other commentaries had not made significant progress, except for Leviticus, which Bernard J. Bamberger had taken over. This great scholar and Bible translator was certain to finish the commentary in good time, and to do a splendid job of it.

Exodus and Deuteronomy were now being worked on but the committee still had not found anyone to write the commentary on Numbers. Some people had been approached but they had not been willing to tackle the matter. And so, with Genesis completed, I was asked to take on Numbers as well.

---

* Scholars in Palestine some thousand years ago who created an authoritative Hebrew text of the Bible, based on the best traditional sources. *Masorah* means "tradition".

I set to work at once, and by 1976 had finished my labours. No sooner had I sent in the manuscript than I was apprised that Exodus also needed an author after all. Would I do it as well? Late in 1977 I finished that commentary, which I thought was my best effort to date. It was exciting material and I could bring my own theology strongly to bear on the subject.

Meanwhile my dear friend Dudley Weinberg, a brilliant and sensitive rabbi in Milwaukee who had begun to write an introduction for Deuteronomy (his assigned book), had tragically died and the writing of that book fell to me as well. In fact, my longtime dream of finishing the commentary would become a significant factor in my decision to leave the active rabbinate. I did not see how I could manage to finish the work in the foreseeable future if I stayed in the pulpit. Thus, by a succession of unpredictable circumstances, I ended up writing four out of the five books. In the summer of '79 I delivered my manuscript on Deuteronomy to the Union, thereby completing the cycle. Bamberger's Leviticus had appeared early that year and Numbers some months later, and Exodus and Deuteronomy were slated as soon as possible thereafter.

During all this time I kept writing on other subjects. I published articles in various magazines, lectured widely in the States as well as in Canada, made a tour of South Africa (of which more later) and of universities in Israel and Germany.

Elizabeth and I undertook leadership of a series of guided tours which were to awaken the consciousness of the congregation with regard to Israel. It turned out to be an eminently successful enterprise—in one year the congregation sponsored five such tours, one guided by our daughter Judy. For us, it meant the chance to know Israel intimately. Elizabeth, with her uncanny sense of direction, unfailing memory, and deep love for land and people, became the heart and soul of these trips.

Again and again colleagues would ask me how I parcelled out my time to do the various things in which I was involved, and especially how I found time to write. They too wanted to write, they told me, but seemed always too busy to do so.

I tried to spend at least two hours every morning writing. By ten o'clock or so I would be in my temple study to put in the normal day of a busy rabbi. I would do my reading and research at night. Also, I would make use of odd moments during the day—before dinner was ready, or in some other "empty" time—to look up references, make corrections on papers or the like. Basically, however, the discipline of a fixed hour was the answer. It was in line with ancient experience: "Create for yourself a fixed hour for study," say the Chapters of the Fathers. To do so was no burden. On the contrary, when I had done some writing or thinking I felt buoyed up; the whole day started off in a splendid fashion and everything went better. And when for some reason I was unable to give that time to writing, I felt as though I had wasted a part of my day—an exaggerated view, of course, but it was the reaction I had. I suppose this amounted to "compulsive creation", but whatever the name, it worked well for me.

I have often asked myself (and have been asked by others) whether this adherence to discipline is in any way connected with my early training in Germany, whether the performance expected from a German student—described by the Yiddish term yekke—is reflected in this meticulous application, punctuality and the like. No doubt there was an educational carry-over from those days and also from the fact that my parents held to a strict time schedule in their work. One does not really have to be born in Germany to be a student, but, as a friend of mine used to say, "it helps."

## Joys and Sorrows

Jonathan had shifted to Macalester College, and graduated in 1964. He opted for the rabbinate. We discussed his decision at great length and, of course, we respected his will. A father is naturally pleased when a son finds his profession attractive enough to make it his own life's calling. That is especially true when it comes to the rabbinate, where the pressures are constant, the hours extraordinarily long and the material rewards fairly modest. There's always a danger, of course, when a son enters a field where he may end up competing with his father, or perhaps with the image of his father. There may be tensions and disappointments. Nonetheless we were happy that our son, like Walter, would go to Hebrew Union College. And this happiness has grown; many years have passed since that day when he first entered, and he has made a splendid name for himself, and my own rabbinate has received an additional dimension because of his.

I remember 1970 as a great year for us. Mutti—as Mother is

affectionately called—celebrated her eightieth birthday, Judy graduated from college, and Jonathan (who in 1965 had married a lovely Torontonian, Carol Fainstein) was ordained. It was a very hot day in June when our families and friends assembled at the Plum Street Temple in Cincinnati. When the moment came and President Nelson Glueck laid his hands on Jonathan he invited me to stand by him. I tried to find Elizabeth in the huge crowd but could not. The emotion of the moment almost overcame me. Parents invest so much of themselves in their children, yet they are rarely aware of the intensity of their involvement. Once in a while all the years—or rather all the days and nights—coalesce and are felt in a single moment. This was one of them. I felt as if my soul was detached from my body. I tried to recollect the sentiments of my own ordination. Then suddenly it was over and Jonathan kissed me. Our son was now a rabbi.

I preached the ordination address which I called "The Rabbi's Role: Divine Ridicule and Human Loneliness." The rabbi, I said, was engaged in a lonely profession.

"If Jews are a lonely people, if they are *perushim* (set apart), then the rabbis and rebbitzins who serve them are even more set apart and often, like their people, expendable. You will have many companions but few friends. People want you to be one of them, yet not entirely so. They want you to be like the God you proclaim, a lonely eminence. It is hard to merit and match this yearning.

"The man who is a rabbi in the true sense will always stand apart. Not because he is the kind of man who believes when few others do, and speaks when silence rules the day. I am rarely worried when people disagree with me, I am worried when they agree too readily—for then I fear that I have lost the vision, have come down from the watchtower and speak words they want to hear, not words that need to be said. The pressure is always on us to be assimilated to the world; to be good guys for the crowd; to be relevant, which mostly means to be practical and up-to-date. But our Hebrew language already knew it: it linked the man who gives the *perush*—the clear explanation of our situation—to the *parush*, the man set apart. Perhaps that is the way it has to be: the true *meforashim* (preachers) must be *perushim*, set apart."

I was speaking of my own life. In the years that have gone by since I preached that sermon little has changed for us. Things are the same, only more so. As we grow older we do not acquire more friends, just more companions—and even this increase is balanced by the Angel of Death.

Things went well in Toronto but there were deaths in our family that exacted their emotional toll. In 1962 we spent some time in Europe, and the day after we returned we received a telephone call from Cincinnati that Therese, Elizabeth's mother, had suddenly passed away. She was eighty-three, in all respects a remarkable woman, cultured, of total integrity, with principles that were distinctly Victorian, yet with an understanding that the world had gone beyond the ideals of her childhood. She had grown up in the protected luxury of an old family, and was the perfect example of genteel understatement. She had a marvellous sense of duty and, being a great musical artist, a sensitivity to all things aesthetic. She had studied singing in Paris and after her debut was offered a contract at the Metropolitan Opera in New York. She turned it down; her family did not consider the stage a proper place for a nice Jewish girl. She sang with the Cincinnati Symphony, gave musicals, and coached aspiring artists—and never accepted a penny. In her latter years she went back to playing the violin; she took up painting and did very well at it. She never ceased giving English lessons to newcomers and in a sense became the godmother to many people who today have found a secure place in their adopted land. Jonathan and Judy loved her and so did I.

Barely a year and a half later Walter died. While Therese had lived out a long and useful life, Walter was cut down in the midst of his labours. Four years before, an operation had revealed a far advanced cancer of the caecum. He underwent some chemotherapy but the surgeon gave us little hope.

"Six months probably, and if a miracle happens, two years," he said.

The miracle did happen. Somehow Walter seemed to recover. He had great will and was developing his full potential. Like my own children, he had been a slow starter, but as he matured he discovered enormous resources. He became a superb rabbi, creating a core of devoted followers who would carry on in his name after he was gone. In Great Neck, New York, he approached his zenith. He built Temple Emanuel and beautified it with the art of Ludwig Wolpert; he took advanced courses in pastoral psychology and discovered the secret of touching others and being touched by them. "I will lick this illness," he said more than once, and to all appearances he did. Six months passed, two years passed, he grew strong, participated in a myriad of communal activities, became one of the Freedom Riders—a group of men and women who went through Virginia, the Carolinas, Georgia and Florida to open interstate bus terminal facilities to mixed racial groups. He told his story to Rabbi William Berkowitz who published this interview along with those of other famous men.*

"Friday after Friday and Saturday after Saturday," said Walter, "I stand in front of my congregation. I have an oversized prayer book in front of me, and as I read certain words out of this prayer book I very often get the feeling that these are merely words; where are the deeds that live up to these words? Do we mean what we say? Do I mean what I say? Do I say what I mean . . .? We Jews who for so long have been crying for an end to persecution and begging for equal rights, we cannot now ignore and must support the same struggle by another minority which is trying to be equal to all other Americans. . . .

"In its final essence the meaning of this Freedom Ride can be grasped if you have the feeling that you were with me, that you were on that bus because all of us together who believe in the great ideas of our faith and of our country, all of us know that in this matter—as in so many others—there is no turning back, there is movement in one direction only and that is forward."

As time stretched on and Walter reached the fifth and crucial year—beyond which one's chances for survival are said to improve greatly—his system broke down. The cancer reappeared again, this time in its most vicious form. He died on January 3, 1964. His death came as a heavy blow to Mother and to all of us. He left a wife and three small boys. He was only forty-four.

His illness and death left me very distraught. Our relationship had not always been of the best; there was the difference in years, in inclinations and outlook and occasionally in philosophy. Our sibling bond became close only at the very end. I was quite unhappy that I was not permitted to speak to him of death.

"No," was the reaction, "this will destroy him."

* *Heritage and Hope* (New York: Thomas Yoseloff, 1965).

I believed that Walter, like everyone else, was entitled to the opportunity of facing his impending death with dignity rather than being involved in what amounts ultimately to a charade: the dying know that they will die soon and that the living are avoiding the truth. To be sure, not everyone is capable of facing the end, and for some the pretence probably ought to be kept up. But others—especially those who have a great deal of insight—should be given the chance to speak frankly and freely about life and death. I believed that Walter belonged to this group.

We were reaching a new level of understanding when death intervened. I have never ceased mourning for lost opportunities, and never more than for the loss that all of us suffered when this rabbi of great power and potential was taken from us.

In his eulogy Maurice Eisendrath called him "a precious prince and great soul, a devoted son, a cherished brother, a beloved husband, a self-sacrificing father, a true Rabbi and Teacher in Israel, a deeply and dearly treasured friend."

Judy was fourteen when we moved to Toronto. She had come from a permissive school environment and now was thrust into the highly competitive, over-stimulated ambience of Forest Hill Collegiate. Parents were pressuring their children to do well and the school prided itself on providing the top scholarship recipients in the province.

Judy did poorly in the pressure-cooker atmosphere of the school. Age fourteen is not a good time to change domicile and friends, and she reacted negatively to her school environment. In time she was sent to the school psychologist, who was adorned with a Ph.D. We were categorically informed that Judy's mentality would permit her to finish only grade nine, or at most grade ten, and we were advised to withdraw her from school and send her to a trade-oriented institution.

That in itself would have been acceptable to us—we had no hangups about a "necessary" academic course or university. But knowing our daughter we suspected that the verdict was wrong. Heinz Warschauer suggested we take her to the Jewish Vocational Service in New York, where an excellent evaluation system had been developed. Elizabeth and Judy went down for several days and the conclusion reached there was startlingly different. We were told that Judy should be able not only to finish high school but to go to university with good results.

In the end she went to the States for her college years, received good grades and in time obtained her Master's degree in Art Education. Gifted, artistic and with a splendid endowment of common sense, she is living testimony to the foolishness of professional prognosticators who arrogantly try to manipulate the lives of others on the basis of shallow tests and analyses.

Mutti has at this writing celebrated her ninetieth birthday. She lives alone in her lovely apartment, sang until recently in the temple's volunteer choir, works at the library and visits the sick. She travels alone on bus, streetcar, subway or airplane, and goes to all parts of the world. Lately she has enrolled at the University of Toronto to study Modern Jewish History and French Literature. In the fall of 1979 she was the subject of a two-page essay written by Kenneth Bagnell.*

She is a slight, strong person with eyes that are bright and curious, the kind of woman you can describe as looking twenty years younger than her age and know you are still telling the truth. When I met her I was anxious to ask her the obvious question: what led her in her ninetieth year to begin study at a university?

"All my life," she said, in a calm and very organized way, "I have liked to learn. But I have gone through stages in my life—as my husband's helpmate, as the rabbi's mother—when though I did many things that were satisfying, learning had to stay in the background. But then when my son retired from his pulpit and began a new career** I thought perhaps I too might begin anew. I did not want a degree as much as a chance to prove to myself that I was still able to learn. . . ."

I said good-bye to Mrs. Plaut on that day in early summer grateful to her not just for her kindness in seeing me but even more for her rare spirit which lightens our path and gives us something beautiful and worth remembering.

* *The Imperial Oil Review*, November 1979; reprinted in *Canadian Jewish News*, March 24, 1980.
** I had made a point of avoiding the term "retirement". Giving myself entirely to writing, lecturing and public service was in fact a new career.

# Chapter 8

---

# INCIDENTS AND ISSUES

NOT ALL MEMORIES CAN BE PRESSED into an orderly time sequence. Some flash without warning and without apparent reason on the screen of your consciousness. Perhaps they are more meaningful to us than we realize, and are therefore pushed forward to be seen with the knowing eye of remembrance.

## The Chief

The fact that I was a recent settler (and an American citizen to boot) did not prevent the press from searching out my opinions. Such an occasion arose not long after my arrival; John George Diefenbaker was Prime Minister at the time, and a matter of immigration policies had arisen. Thousands of people fleeing the People's Republic of China had been refused admission, and Diefenbaker made a mere gesture of concern. He agreed to allow one hundred refugees to enter Canada.

I raised my voice to object to the "modesty" of his effort and said that Canada could do very much better indeed. The *Toronto Star** gave my remarks an unusual double banner headline on its front page: "Ban is Immoral—Rabbi Asks Open Door For Chinese Refugees." The story noted that I was a recent immigrant myself. I do not know how many people were bothered by this reference

---

* May 26. 1962. See also above. p. 175. for an earlier controversy on immigration to the U.S.

to my status but I was not. I have always held that moral questions belong to the spirit and the spirit is not bound by borders and passports.

I met Diefenbaker shortly after, at a private dinner given by one of the groups interested in fostering Canadian-Israeli relations. I found him to be a man of sparkling personality, very warm and forthcoming, the populist whose words and actions provided a unique combination of politics and humanity.

"Ah, so you are our new rabbi," he said, "and you are after me. Don't worry, you are really right, you know. The only difference between you and me is that I'm the Prime Minister who does what he thinks is possible and you are the rabbi who has to hold up the best ideas, even if they are impossible to reach."

Thereafter we continued to have a special relationship. The Jewish community—though they did not often vote for him—held him in affectionate esteem as a true lover of Israel; his love was founded in the Bible, which he knew well indeed. They honoured him at the 1973 Negev Dinner, long after he had ceased being Prime Minister.

For his eightieth birthday, in September '75, I prepared a vignette for the *Globe and Mail*. The newspaper published it with a cartoon that captured Dief's mobile face and twinkling eyes.

"Canadians," I wrote, "admire someone who is homespun yet real; who has opinions and yet integrity; who believes in opportunity without the slag of opportunism; who evokes a sense of nostalgia and yet is not of yesterday alone.

"His very face is like the changing face of Canada; it is nature's gift to the cartoonist, with its splendid lines and crinkles, falling, so it seems, into ever new channels of expression. . . .

"To you, Mr. Diefenbaker, and to your gracious lady, I raise my glass. Long may you wave your flag; and may you for many years lend us your heart and tongue to let us know of our foibles and our possibilities. With millions across the face of Canada I say, in whatever language may be most efficacious: *prosit, skøl, l'chayim, à votre santé*, to life and health, and happy birthday!"

The article appeared on September 17, and Dief (so he told me later) read it at breakfast. At once he dispatched a telegram to me: "Olive and I are deeply touched by your article in this morning's press. Thank you from the bottom of my heart. With warmest regards. John Diefenbaker."

There are a few times when a writer, especially one who

writes for the daily press, has a sense of being truly rewarded. This was surely one of them.

Later that month I presented him with a copy of my commentary on Genesis, and received another warm response after he had read the book.

I have another memory of him, one I hesitate to put on paper—I should hardly recount it myself. I had occasion to be at the Parliament Buildings in Ottawa and had lunch in the parliamentary dining room. On my way out I saw Dief in animated conversation and made my way to his table to say hello. He sprang to his feet, shook my hand warmly and then introduced me to the gentlemen at his table.

"Gentlemen," he said, "I want you to meet Canada's greatest orator."

It was an exaggeration, but coming from the Chief it was something to be remembered. I don't believe he had heard me speak more than once or twice, but apparently I had made a hit with him.

In 1979, when the news of his passing spread across the country, tributes poured in from all over the world. I was pleased that the CBC chose to include a few words from me in its memorial presentation. I hailed him as the champion of the little man. No Canadian politician was more beloved than he, and it will be a long time before another comes along to rival the affection his countrymen had for him.

# Olympic Memorial

The 1976 Games were about to begin, in Montreal. Four years had passed since that dreadful night in Munich when eleven Israeli athletes were slain, when the world stood by in fascination more than horror, when Libya awarded the murderers a prize of millions of dollars, and the Games, after a brief bow in the direction of official sorrow, went on as if nothing had happened. Now there would be an opportunity for the Games to recognize the calamity of Munich, to make some authentic gesture of remembrance. Nothing happened; politics held sway. The Arabs and their Communist allies were strong enough to prevent even a gesture. So it was left to the Jewish community of Montreal to set something in motion that would be meaningful and would preserve Jewish self-respect.

A committee chaired by Tom Hecht tried to enlist support for the kind of observance that would be adequate. They found that there were members of the Jewish "establishment" in various cities, including Montreal and Toronto, who felt a memorial service would be "rocking the boat". Better to do nothing, said these, than to involve Montreal, the Quebec government, and especially the Jewish community in yet another controversy. However, Hecht and his associates were undaunted. They phoned me and asked whether I would come to chair the memorial and deliver the address. I readily agreed, even though I had no idea how extraordinary an event it would be.

Notwithstanding the resistance in some quarters, the plans went forward. Success (if one may apply such a word to this sad occasion) was assured when Prime Minister Trudeau agreed not only to attend but to participate in the service, and when it became definite that the widows of the slain athletes would be there as well, along with the entire Israeli Olympic team.

When we arrived at the venerable Shaar Hashomayim synagogue, the location of the memorial, it was at once evident that something very special was afoot. Security precautions were enormous. Armed sharpshooters had taken up positions on the surrounding roof-tops. A helicopter hovered overhead. The stream of people wanting to attend seemed endless; while the synagogue itself accommodated only a few thousand people, every other room of any size in the vast building was filled and the estimate in the end was that some five thousand people were present to watch the proceedings, directly or via closed-circuit television, or at least to hear it over loud-speakers. Inside and outside, television crews abounded—twenty-two national and international networks were filming the service.

The crowd hushed when the Israeli Olympians marched in, followed by the relatives of the slain. The simple service had a cadence of mounting emotion. Trudeau rose, came to the *beema* and faced the assembly. The cameras were whirring. He had chosen to read the Psalm 86, in French:

> ... O God, arrogant men have risen against me;
> a band of ruthless men seek my life;
> they are not mindful of You. ...

Then I spoke. The atmosphere was highly charged; it did not take much to loose the flood-gates of feeling. The Israelis, hard-bitten sabras as they were supposed to be, began to cry, and then

the audience as well. The Prime Minister, members of his
Cabinet and the Quebec Cabinet were equally moved, and photo-
graphers caught the tears on Trudeau's face (giving them, of
course, top billing in the next day's newspapers). There was a
moment when I thought I could not go on. Somehow I pulled
through. The memorial prayer chanted by the cantor provided a
sombre finale to an hour that none of us would ever forget.

Back in Toronto I tried to interpret the memorial to some of my
friends who had refused to sponsor it for fear of arousing public
controversy. When they heard what had happened they said,
genuinely perplexed, "We got the wrong signals; we misjudged
the feelings in Quebec. We should have been there. Perhaps we
were politically naive." There comes a moment when the authen-
ticity of our emotion must overcome all reservation. That moment
came in Montreal.


# Royal Jubilee

In November 1977 Elizabeth and I were in Ottawa to participate
in the Canadian celebrations of the Queen's twenty-fifth anniversary as monarch of the realm. Since religious representatives
are—like ambassadors—ranked according to their length of service, I had now moved up in the order of precedence and had
become number two.* Only Cardinal Roy had held his post longer
than I had had mine. Protocol required that the Queen and
Prince Philip be escorted to their places at the religious service
by the highest-ranking religious representatives, and so the
Cardinal walked with the Queen and I with the Prince.

The day of the celebration the weather was miserable and
shortly after the beginning of the service, which was held on the
steps of Parliament, it began to rain. The participants, like the
royal couple, were protected by a canopy, but that did not help
the many thousands of others who were asked to develop a spirit
of worshipful devotion while shivering in the rain. The Queen
was most solicitous of the congregation but there was nothing
she could do.

As I walked the Prince from the Parliament to the service he
said to me, "How come you clergymen could not have arranged

---

* This stemmed from my position in the Canadian Jewish Congress: for some years as
chairman of its Religious Affairs Committee, and then as its president.

for better weather?" I replied with an old saw: "Sir, we are in sales, not in management." The Prince gave this old saying wide currency the next day when he addressed a public meeting—and credited me with inventing it. In subsequent months I received clippings from as far away as Australia about my "witticism".

There was a state dinner at Rideau Hall which the Governor-General gave, and after dinner Elizabeth and I had an opportunity to chat informally with Her Majesty. In the conversation my wife said to the Queen, "You know, Your Majesty, your great-great-grandmother and my great-great-grandfather had something in common."

The Queen looked startled, but my Elizabeth relieved the situation quickly.

"My great-great-grandfather was embroiderer to the Court and he made the coronation gown for Queen Victoria."

The Queen was much interested, though she confessed that she had no idea where the gown might be at the present time.

"When I get back to England," she said, "I will have to look into the matter."

# Golda

I have seen our people excited on many occasions, I have seen them cry, I have seen them applaud, yet I have rarely seen them erupt with enthusiasm. But they did once, I remember, in November 1970. Golda Meir was speaking at Beth Tzedec synagogue at a public rally climaxing her Canadian tour. She was Prime Minister of Israel then. Other Israeli leaders had been in Toronto before her and others would follow, but she was special. While Ben-Gurion had always elicited a warm response it was primarily one of admiration and respect, even awe. Golda was different. She was the Mother, and for mothers one has a different dimension of sentiment. She was utterly plain, and deliberately kept herself that way, as if the dressmaker had planned her clothes to fit her mood. The severely brushed back hair emphasized a face that was strong and thoughtful at the same time. I never saw Golda laugh in public. She was not given to jokes. Jewish fate, certainly during her incumbency as Prime Minister, was no joke.

She came to Toronto at a time when the Jewish community had been embroiled in controversies over Israel, when we needed a release, when we craved a clear and present symbol of our people's fate. Golda became the focus of our unchecked emotion.

It was my privilege to introduce her. I spoke of her strength, I spoke of her as the mother of our people. As I approached my last sentence, and even before I was finished, the crowd let go with one tremendous outburst. They jumped to their feet and roared their approval. Golda was the immediate object of their love but Israel was the truly beloved. I never finished the last sentence of my introduction. The applause and cheering were deafening and even Golda, who must have been accustomed to such occasions, was overcome. She came forward, embraced and kissed me. Was it possible that the cheering grew even louder? Perhaps, but it didn't matter and it doesn't now. The memory is loud and clear. We loved Golda because Golda was Israel.

# A Question of Leadership

From time to time studies of the internal structure of the Jewish community are undertaken. Often they are journalistic attempts that exploit the obvious, but some have been serious academic investigations into the inner nature of the community. One such was by Yaacov Glickman, professor at the University of Toronto. It was to be the first of a number of explorations into the dynamics of Jewish life in Canada.

Glickman set himself the task of determining, amongst other matters, who the persons of greatest influence in the community were, and identifying twenty of them by name. He arrived at his conclusions after interviewing a large number of people, from those "in the know" to people in the street. The five top names were Ray Wolfe, Murray Koffler, Donald Carr, Stuart Rosenberg and myself. The most instructive element of this selection was that at the time none of this fivesome held any official status— such as the presidency of an important community group— although of course Stuart and I were the rabbis of the two largest congregations, whose memberships contained some of the leading figures in Canada.

Ray Wolfe, president of Oshawa Wholesale Limited, soft-spoken, perceptive, generous, was an advisor to many leaders in government in Canada as well as in Israel. He attracted the confidence of those who wanted clear, unequivocal and sound advice that was never tainted by self-seeking. Through his persistence and his friendship with other Jewish leaders, he made it possible to establish the *Canadian Jewish News* as the major national Jewish newspaper. He spent large sums of money and enormous amounts of time on it, although he never let this be known publicly, and he took criticism of the paper in his stride. His overriding concern was the fate of the community and to it he gave of his impressive capacity for leadership, with a remarkable degree of selflessness. (In this he was greatly aided by his wife Rose, who became a commanding public figure in her own right.)

Murray Koffler was of different temperament, more outgoing, ready to pursue his goals more openly. President of Koffler Stores, he was distinguished by his generosity with money and time, and had entered the highest circles of the wider non-Jewish environment; indeed he was a good friend of Prince Philip. Though somewhat less politically inclined than Ray Wolfe, Koffler was effective in his own way, well deserving of the accolades which the community gave him.

Donald Carr's record in the community resembled that of Wolfe and Koffler in many ways. A lawyer by profession, intelligent, persuasive and persistent, with a strongly traditional bent, he too usually wielded his influence in an indirect fashion (although he did subsequently assume various community posts).

Stuart was the rabbi of Beth Tzedec, Canada's largest congregation and one of North America's most affluent as well. His wife Hadassah was an old-line Jerusalemite who obtained her Ph.D. at the University of Toronto and went on to teach in the Department of Oriental Studies. At the time Stuart was at the zenith of his powers of oratory and organization. He had made Beth Tzedec a centre of Jewish culture by the establishment of the Institute of Ethics and, after the acquisition of the Cecil Roth art collection, the creation of a Jewish museum. He had been instrumental in introducing Jewish studies as a distinct set of courses into the University of Toronto. Up to that point there had been courses in Hebrew and Bible, but they had been buried in the Department of Near Eastern Studies and not directly identified as "Jewish"—in fact there was widespread suspicion that some of the people in the department did not like Jews.

I did not know then that while Stuart enjoyed wide respect and admiration, his single-handed exercise of power was also attracting the enmity of a growing number of people in his own congregation. In time this led to a disastrous confrontation which resulted in his dismissal, a suit and counter-suit amounting to several millions of dollars, and years of legal and public struggle. The quarrel was injurious to Beth Tzedec, calamitous for the Jewish community, and destructive for Stuart. At the height, or I should say the depth, of the struggle I was one of the few who continued to take his part. My efforts at conciliation were unfortunately unsuccessful; by that time the feelings ran too deep. Families were divided amongst themselves, siblings were not speaking to each other, so I was told. The quarrel spilled over into all congregations and in general weakened the position of the rabbinate. When at last a compromise was reached and the matter was settled out of court, everyone breathed a sigh of relief. But the damage had been done. The "Rosenberg case", as it was called, had been dragged through the newspapers, through endless discussions and debates in a thousand households, and respect for religious leaders in the community had suffered perceptibly.

Meanwhile Stuart had become a non-person in official circles. He was not invited to address any meeting of significance. The community thereby suffered a grievous loss, for he was a person not only of charisma but of large ideas, who had made an incomparable contribution to Canadian Jewry. After the quarrel had been settled he came to me and asked me whether I would chair an event that would, so to speak, reintroduce him to the community. The occasion would be the Jewish Theological Seminary's award to him of the Sabato Morais Honorary Fellowship. I readily agreed.

The affair was held at the Inn on the Park, and some five hundred people were in attendance. Stuart called the evening "one of thanksgiving ... of reaffirmation of friendship," and termed the audience "the congregation of the humane and the steadfast." Participants were Professor Emil Fackenheim, Archbishop Philip Pocock and David Lieber, vice-chancellor of the Jewish Theological Seminary. In my opening remarks I said, "We have not forgotten you nor what you did for us."

There were people in my congregation who became very vocal about my role in this gathering. They criticized me sharply. It did not matter. Stuart had more than paid his penalty, deservedly or not. But though the evening was a success, the community never did reclaim him to a meaningful degree. Of course, as in any divorce—in a family or in a community—there are two sides to the question, and this is not the place to examine them. But I felt strongly, and said so on many occasions, that to keep Stuart in a state of virtual though unofficial ostracism was unfair not only to him but to all of us. There comes a time when the past is over and done with.

Some years later Glickman made another study, similar in nature to the first. This time Stuart's name was conspicuously absent from the list. The more pity—for all of us.

## Two Eulogies

"Mayor of All the People" he called himself, and the self-applied accolade stuck to him. Nathan Phillips—Nate to everyone—was the first Jewish Mayor of Toronto and served for eight years, longer than anyone before or after. He was a most accomplished and astute political figure. He had a sure instinct for the needs, hopes and desires of people; he could insult them and make them love it. And he always "told it the way it was". He and his wife Ett (she had been president of Holy Blossom Sisterhood many years before) were the most familiar figures in the city. They were recognized by everyone and in time they came to be loved as no other political couple had been. It was Nate's vision to make downtown Toronto into a "people place", and to put the world's most fascinating city hall at its heart. He achieved his purpose; within his lifetime a grateful city named the beautiful plaza in front of the new city hall Nathan Phillips Square.

Nate was buried from our temple on January 8, 1976. At the service I quoted the words of William Cullen Bryant: "So live that when thy summons comes to join/the innumerable caravan. . . ." The next day Dick Beddoes wrote in the *Globe and Mail*:

> To many . . . it must have seemed strange to be present in these circumstances. They had known so many years when Nate seemed ageless, wearing his dignity lightly, often the liveliest, keenest, most tireless of them all.
>
> When I speak a few words of affection for a man who bestrode our city for so long, Rabbi Plaut said, I look down at the casket half expecting to see Nate rise up and say, "Look rabbi, I am not sure I appreciate this oily sanctimoniousness you are about to pour over me."

Twelve years before, John F. Kennedy had been assassinated. On that painful day I sat down to make some notes for the eulogy I

was to give, to express my feelings on behalf of the citizens of
Toronto. The civic service was scheduled for Metropolitan
United Church. I wrote:

There is nothing I can add to the eulogies already spoken and
written. A bright light has flickered briefly in the night and has
gone out. But one thing must be said again and again: the President's death involves all of us in a universal guilt—all of us who
in the past have stood silent in the face of violence, who merely
raised our eyebrows when Medgar Evers was killed, when eight
children died in a Birmingham church, when fire-hoses and dogs
were turned on innocent men and women—all of us who said, "It
is not my business." It has turned out to be our business; the bell
has tolled for John F. Kennedy and it has tolled for us. . . . If the
death of President Kennedy can help to jar us loose from our
moral diffidence, perhaps the unwilling sacrifice which he had to
make may not have been in vain.

## Issues of Censorship

On a number of occasions I participated vigorously in the
defence of freedom of information.

In both Minnesota and Canada I fought for the citizen's right to
obtain birth control information. In Minnesota in the 1950s an
inter-religious confrontation had ensued between Roman
Catholics and non-Catholics but the Jewish community backed
me and we stood our ground, although there were voices of anxiety who counselled that the consequences would (as they put it)
tear apart the fabric of tolerance. The result was otherwise:
there was greater respect for those who had the courage of their
convictions. In Toronto I helped found the Planned Parenthood
organization in the early 1960s, and often wrote and spoke in its
behalf.

A more dramatic issue was that of pornography. In Minnesota,
a well financed and widely supported drive had been under way
to hold drugstore owners responsible for exhibiting "obscene"
magazines. A Board of Decency had been established in order to
curb the outpouring of pornographic literature. The proponents
of this campaign were right in one respect: pornography was
spreading, more and more people were reading magazines which
only a few years earlier they would not have touched or even
seen. Much of this stuff was disgusting, and degrading to the

female sex. There was no question that, if this junk could be kept off the market, we would all be better off.

But there was another principle at stake and that was freedom of information. I belong to those who have a deep anxiety about any form of censorship; I utterly reject the idea that adults should be told what they can or cannot read. I also believe that, while legal prohibitions may result in a few convictions, they will never eradicate the demand—or the magazines which fill that demand. All we do is drive them underground. If that is the case, then we might as well let them be accessible, and not introduce a censorship law which may someday be used in a manner we will all regret.

A committee was formed to combat the bill which had been introduced in the Minnesota Senate and hearings were shortly to be held. I was approached and asked whether I would testify. I agreed at once. I suggested, however, that some other clergymen should also be persuaded to testify along with me, and that they should be in ecclesiastical dress if possible, in order to emphasize that one could be a cleric and still find the proposed law abominable. The only trouble was that the committee could not find anyone to come to the Hill with me. At last my friend Glenn Lewis, an Episcopalian priest, agreed.

Wide publicity attended the hearing. Our chances appeared to be dubious, for the majority of the Senators came from rural constituencies where the defence of pornography for any reason would hardly be understood. I gave my testimony, and Glenn Lewis gave his—and acquitted himself admirably. But the leading advocate of the new censorship board was a judge who had apparently gone to great lengths to collect filthy magazines, and he had brought a whole stack of them to the hearing. He rose in rebuttal of our testimony and announced to the committee that he would forthwith convince them of the necessity of passing the law; that what they were about to see would hardly allow any other decision. He then began to take the magazines and leaf through their pages one by one, describing in vivid detail what was being shown. By the time he reached the third or fourth magazine it was obvious that he had become sexually aroused. The members of the committee were acutely embarrassed for him, and the chairman mercifully—before any other consequences ensued—recessed the meeting.

This ended the matter and the bill was dead. I in turn learned a lesson about these so-called "simple" legislators from the upstate regions: they were just as sophisticated in their human perceptions as anyone. They had no use for prurience cloaked in legislative righteousness, and little as they liked the material on exhibit, they recognized that there might be more honesty and even virtue among the anti-censorship forces.

In Toronto I was to be confronted with the issue again. In mid-summer 1966 the Metro police morality squad, under the leader-ship of Inspector William Pilkington, closed down an art show at the Dorothy Cameron Gallery. On view were pictures by Robert Markle which the police considered offensive to public taste— although today such a judgement seems difficult to comprehend. Pilkington, of course, had an impossible job. He was supposed to be the guardian of a moral code on which no one could agree, and therefore whatever he did would be subject to a wide range of criticism. I stood squarely by Miss Cameron but the courts upheld the action of the morality squad and passed sentence on her. As a result, her gallery was thereafter permanently closed—she had simply had enough, and did not want to subject herself to any more of this kind of hassle.

But I was even more offended by what followed. Pilkington made an ill-considered statement saying that Metro's intellectual community had "screamed for civil rights" and was possessed of no sense of responsibility, and that therefore it was the morality officer's duty "to protect the public against itself."

I objected strongly and publicly. Every tyrant, benevolent or otherwise, had piously and self-righteously taken this stand, I wrote. Under the cover of this philosophy had passed some of the most restrictive regulations of autocratic society.

Nine years later another opportunity arose to strike a blow for free access to reading material. Law enforcement agencies had impounded copies of a book called *Show Me*, which the Mac-millan publishing company had tried to import from the United States. The book was created to help parents give sexual instruc-tion to their children. It had a very good text and—here lay the grounds for objection by the customs officials—there were photographs of nude people, including children, exposing their genitals and simulating physical relationships.

The fact that the book had been impounded intrigued me, and I managed to lay hands on a copy. I wrote an article about it for the *Globe and Mail*. I indicated that there were some pictures I could have done without, but that I found the book on the whole interesting and in many cases reverently sensitive, in both its pictures and its captions. Keeping it out of Canada was an unwarranted interference with the rights of parents to educate their children, who were not likely to get hold of the book unless their parents obtained it for them. In other words, this was not so much censorship on behalf of children, as censorship to prevent parents from utilizing the book.

The Attorney-General's department took the Macmillan Company to court. The redoubtable Marshall McLuhan was enlisted in support of the Crown. The publisher approached me to testify for them. I agreed and eventually appeared at the trial.

The Crown attorney held up a picture from the book which showed an older person saying "Disgusting!" to something (presumably of a sexual nature) that he had seen. Then the attorney asked me, "Do you not think that young people will learn disrespect for their elders from such a photograph?"

I boldly asked whether he himself was the father of children. He said he was.

"In that case," I said, "you have not got the faintest notion about the psychology of your own children."

He was taken aback. "Why not?" he said.

I went on to explain to him what I thought were the reaction patterns of small children. The judge was hugely amused at the evident discomfiture of the Crown attorney, who discovered too late that the tables had been turned on him. When he regained his composure he abruptly dismissed me. He had no further questions.

The court ruled in favor of the defendant. Some months later the Crown attorney encountered me in a social setting.

"You killed me at the trial, you know," he said. "But no hard feelings. We win some and we lose some."

## Solidarity with the Black Community

The date was March 16, 1965. The American protest movement against racial discrimination under the leadership of Martin Luther King Jr. was at its height.* Montgomery, Selma, guard dogs—these words punctuated the high emotion flowing into Canada from the south.

A community religious service was organized to take place at Toronto's Metropolitan United Church, and some 2,000 people

* See also above. p. 206.

attended. I addressed them on the subject "Colour-blind and Border-blind."

". . . We are met together in this affirmation of purpose and of faith. We come not to accuse but to support. In our hearts we know that we have reached a new turning. What Little Rock was for the integration of schools—a battle and a beginning—so Selma will be for the franchise of every man. No tear-gas, no horses will drive it away, for the men and women of Selma are joined by millions everywhere who pray and stay until the dawn of day. . . .

". . . There are some in our community, perhaps even many, who view this service and this march of solidarity with apprehension and dismay. 'What place have ministers in political questions?' they say. 'What place have they in the streets, marching and singing?' To them we say, 'Where else ought religion to be if not in the streets, in the factories and in the Houses of Parliament? All too long it has been isolated in churches and synagogues and has become ethereal and utterly irrelevant.' I doff my hat to the students who have put idealism before comfort, and service to men before their own needs. They have shown more true religion than many of us who smirked and smiled with dried wills and comfortable hearts. They have indicted many of us, clergy and laity alike; they have rekindled in many a new confidence in the power of popular will and the strength of the people's voice. . . ."

Afterwards 1,500 of the worshippers formed themselves into a solid phalanx and marched to the American Consulate, there to present a petition. Four hundred clergymen were in the lead, the largest ecumenical effort made up to that date in Canada. Inside, the consul-general received us cordially. Outside, people stood in the cold, chanting slogans of solidarity. Radio, television and newspapers covered the event and made it a national concern.

But not everyone agreed. A letter to the editor in one of the papers wanted to know whether the first four hundred marchers were "real clergymen, or were just bums, beatniks, hoodlums and prostitutes dressed up as clergymen by international Communistick [sic] party together with the NDP. . . ."

A year later, however, the unified support for blacks was weakening. In the wake of bitter upheavals in the U.S.—and especially in metropolitan centres, where Jews sometimes became targets of growing black frustration—a backlash developed among our people. I wrote:

"Among the most perturbing aspects of the current liberal disillusionment with the explosive and vocal black leadership has been a new negativism amongst Jews. It is no secret that Jews, even though living in the South, have in the past openly or covertly supported the Negro drive for full equality. Jews have been amongst the leaders of all major civil rights groups and the NAACP especially has always had a Jewish president.*

"But recently, in the wake of highly emotional events, an always latent antisemitism has come to the fore. In Mount Vernon, New York, a leading member of CORE** said, 'The trouble with Hitler was that he did not kill enough Jews. . . .' On the whole Negro leadership has been regrettably silent on these outbursts. LeRoi Jones is tolerated and even encouraged rather than called to task. This leads me to make two comments: first, Jonesian epithets and even widespread antisemitic feelings amongst Negroes must not deter Jews from continuing their fight for Negro rights. Justice remains immutable and we cannot look for rewards in the struggle. I hear much of liberal 'disengagement'—there must be no Jewish disengagement.

"Second, much of the present frustration of the Negro is now manifesting itself in various forms of hatred. This is understandable even though it is deeply regrettable. At the same time one cannot help but marvel at the fact that the Jewish people, despised, persecuted, beaten, maimed and killed for so many centuries, have never allowed themselves to become a hating people."†

King was murdered on April 4, 1968. I was in Cincinnati to give a lecture at Hebrew Union College and a sermon at the old Rockdale Temple. I cancelled my engagements and flew home. A community memorial service was organized, again at Metropolitan United Church, and once more I spoke from that pulpit. We were stunned and angry—and afraid. The evil genie of violence had at last broken free of its containment. A gentle, beautiful soul was crushed, and all of us would bear the consequences.

* The National Association for the Advancement of Colored People was then headed by my good friend Kivie Kaplan.
** The Congress of Racial Equality.
† In 1979 the disaffection between America's blacks and Jews finally erupted, after the dismissal of Andrew Young as U.S. Ambassador to the United Nations; the rupture has never entirely healed. In Canada, however, the alliance of Jews and other minorities has remained firm. In Toronto, the Urban Alliance for Race Relations was founded with my assistance, and its early meetings always took place at Holy Blossom.

# World Federalists

In the late forties I had become interested in the then fairly new organization called World Federalists of America. Their objective was to create a form of world government, a far broader concept than that of the League of Nations or the United Nations. The world government which was envisaged would command a peacekeeping force; it would be based on regional councils elected directly by the people of various countries, and would feature a House of Representatives which would reflect the national governments of the regions as well as the popular will of their people. I was much taken by the boldness of the idea. I had no illusions about its likely adoption, but I believed that it was the obligation of some to hold up an ideal, however much it exceeded the world's grasp.

At the time I was broadcasting weekly interviews over WMIN in Minnesota, and—though I had never met him—I invited Norman Cousins, who was visiting the city, to be a guest on my program. Cousins was editor of the *Saturday Review of Literature* (now called the *Saturday Review*). He was most obliging, and our meeting turned out to be one of those occasions when two people who have never known each other before establish an immediate rapport.

Norman kindled my interest in the World Federalists—he had been connected with them from the very beginning—and I joined the Minnesota branch. When I came to Toronto I joined the local organization, whose members were professors and idealists of various shades, none of whom represented any part of the power structure. No matter, it was the kind of intellectual environment that appealed to me. In short order I was appointed to the national board and eventually became national president. I began to speak in various communities as well as to attend the national meetings and, once, an international conference in Oslo.

One of the most successful innovations which we brought about was the twinning of cities. Two communities, one here and one abroad, would pass resolutions relating them to each other. On certain occasions they would fly each other's flags, exchange goodwill ambassadors, promote tourism, and children would learn about the other city. Thus Toronto twinned with Amsterdam, and established an Amsterdam Park, and for a time the concept became quite popular.

But not for long. The world went in other directions. Still, the underlying idea was sound: no nation was sovereign any more; no nation could be independent in a world of interlocking interests, obligations and dependencies. The borders of many nations were historical accidents and the fostering of so-called national interests above all others would always be a cause of tension and likely of armed conflict. World Federalists were amongst those groups that constantly spoke of the need for disarmament, limitation of atomic weapons and of nuclear institutions. Perhaps the movement does not have any concrete successes to show, but its larger vision remains right.

From time to time we talked with leaders of government in Canada but I always had the distinct impression that they—even Lester Pearson—looked at me and my colleagues with little more than polite forbearance. While we had some supporters in all parties, the powers did not take us seriously. After all, we were just dreamers, proclaiming that nations could live in a lasting state of peace.

I like to believe that the movement has its influence even now. And my hopes were bolstered, in 1980, by the appointment of Mark MacGuigan as Minister for External Affairs. For many years he had been chairman of the parliamentary faction of the World Federalists and had staunchly advocated their ideals.

Yet there is no gainsaying that the rising disillusionment over the United Nations has affected the aims of the movement. In 1945 no one had anticipated the misuse that would be made of the UN, the distortion of purpose it would undergo through the bald manipulation of its policies by the Soviet and Arab blocs using the organization for narrow political advantages. It became obvious to us that some revision of the United Nations' charter would be necessary and it was in that direction that World Federalists began to work. But in time I became disenchanted with this task, especially when, after 1967, some elements of the organization moved towards a distinctly anti-Israeli stance. More and more, I found my energies were taken up with defending Israel, and Jews in general, against this attitude. Perhaps this seemed parochial to some. But for me there was no point in establishing a World Federalist government to save us in the end, if in the meantime we lost Israel.

In a way my dilemma was like that of the Jewish socialists two generations before. Theirs too was a world-wide ambition: if socialism could be realized in all countries antisemitism would wither away, for antisemitism, they believed, was a creation of the capitalist system. Therefore the most immediate goal of any committed Jew should be the establishment of the socialist Eden. Alas, reality turned out to be very different: such a socialist Heaven was not to be, and hatred of Jews would not disappear; instead it came to be institutionalized in some Communist lands, especially Soviet Russia. Meanwhile, Jews could not wait for the world to be saved; they had to look after their own security. It was a good thing that the Zionists did not wait too long before they helped to bring Israel into existence as a permanent refuge for Jews.*

# The Allan Gardens Riots

It was a mere eighteen years after the end of the Second World War when the Nazis once again raised their heads, and called up the memory of Hitler as a symbol of their "desirable" future. Their Canadian headquarters were in Toronto and it was therefore the Toronto Jewish community which had to face something they had thought buried with the remains of the Führer. Hate literature began to make its appearance again, and at the time there was no legal mechanism to deal with such material (some years later, amendments to the Criminal Code, constituting the so-called Hate Literature Bill, were enacted by Parliament). Anxiety in the Jewish community rose steadily, and in February 1964 an anti-Nazi committee was established under the aegis of the Canadian Jewish Congress.** We monitored the Nazis and, in co-operation with the police, placed an undercover agent in their cell. But since we could not reveal this, and could give no precise figures as to the party's membership, the general impression got about that the Nazis possessed a significant and growing following and that some confrontation with the community was inevitable.

I have written elsewhere about the role which Holocaust survivors played in Canadian Jewish life.† Not only were eighteen years enough to spawn a fledgling neo-fascist movement; that

---

* See also Appendix 6.
** Members with me were Kalman Berger, J. Ciechanowski, H. Gelbard, Julius Hayman, Louis Herman, J. S. Midanik, Harry Simon, and Max Shecter who later became chairman.
† *Movements and Issues in American Judaism*, edited by Bernard Martin (Westport-London: Greenwood Press, 1978), p. 284 ff.

respite had also given the Holocaust survivors enough strength and enough confidence in their new environment that they could speak out, and take action if necessary. I counted myself as one of the survivors and was accepted as such by the group. It was our opinion that the policy of quarantining neo-Nazis, which the Congress officers had advocated and adopted, needed review. They had hoped that if the Nazis received as little public exposure as possible, they would be unable to spread their sickness. It became evident, however, that this policy was failing—the Nazis, led by their self-styled Führer, John Beattie, were managing to gain the attention of the media. In 1965 they launched the Canadian Nazi Party and announced public rallies. Inflammatory speeches were delivered and faithfully reported by the press. This was more than some of the Holocaust survivors could take, and they were driven to physical confrontation. On May 30 there was a free-for-all in Allan Gardens. Many people were there, and emotions ran high. Policemen on horses outnumbered the Nazis, while Jewish activists struggled to break through the police lines to get at their enemies. The result was that a few Nazis were beaten up, the rest fled and the police arrested some of the Jewish assailants.

I thoroughly approved of our activities. I have always felt that, by their advocacy of genocide, Nazis place themselves outside the protection of the law; to combat them with legal niceties is an error. (Much later I criticized the "legal" approach to the projected Nazi march in Skokie, Illinois, for the same reason.) In any case there comes a time when you have to show them, as forcefully as possible, that Jews are no longer easy victims. We were sure that these brave harbingers of the new order would turn heel when they met determined resistance.

However, the leadership of the Congress saw it differently, especially Sydney M. Harris, a member of my congregation, and J. Sydney Midanik, a well known civil libertarian.* Both men had served the Jewish community with great devotion but, lawyers both, they found it difficult to accept actions that transgressed the law. They issued a statement which branded the Jewish activists as "irresponsible vigilantes" and warned against "mob rule and riot which may erase the sympathy of Canadians for victims of the Nazi terror." The letter was written eight days after

---

* Harris (now Judge of the Provincial Court) would later become national president of the Congress and Midanik its national secretary.

the Allan Gardens incident and was addressed to the Jewish community at large. It was released to the papers before the community had received it and had had a chance to study its contents.

The newspapers gave the letter full play. The *Globe and Mail* headlined its report, "Jewish Congress Blames Jews for Fomenting Mob Violence"; the *Telegram* said, "Jews Blame Jews for Nazi Park Riot"; and the *Star* headline read, "Jews Rap Own Rabble Rousers".

This set the already smouldering Jewish community fully ablaze. The voices of protest became so loud, and criticism of Harris and Midanik and the chief Congress establishment so insistent, that the very continuance of Congress, at least in Toronto, was in jeopardy. The leadership were called Uncle Toms (or the Russian equivalent *Shtadlonim*), were accused of "sha-sha"* politics and abject fear unworthy of Jewish leaders. Nothing, it seemed, that the Congress officers or its outstanding director, Ben Kayfetz, could do would still these voices which were calling for a new forum where the voice of the Jewish masses could be heard. It was at this point that I resolved to put myself on the line to preserve the Congress, for I considered it an essential institution of Canadian Jewry.

What we needed badly was a meeting where legitimate hopes and fears as well as criticisms of leaders could be aired. For the community was not what it had been some decades before; the influx of survivors and other newcomers had given our masses a new, more volatile temperament. Submissions, legal considerations, permits, briefs and the like were no longer the way—at least not the only way—to fight the surge of Nazism. My hope was that such a public meeting would be well attended and I invited everyone who had been a delegate to the recent Congress plenary session. We were to meet in the community hall of Holy Blossom.

The response was overwhelming. Long before the appointed hour of eight some eight hundred people, only a portion of them delegates, had crowded into the hall, I started the meeting.

The first question on the agenda was the admission to the meeting of a group of activists who heretofore had had no status at Congress gatherings. They called themselves N-3, a name

---

* The politics of keeping quiet (in Yiddish *sha*) to escape public notice and thereby avoid confrontation.

referring to Newton's Third Law ("For every action there is an equal and opposite reaction"). N-3 had supported the physical assault on the Nazis and had been most vocal in its criticism of Harris and Midanik. Since technically the group had no standing as a registered organization (for it had never made application for membership in the CJC), I had every right to refuse them. But although the motion was made to keep them out, I did not put the matter to a vote. I ruled from the chair that any Jew who was concerned with the welfare of our community was invited to the meeting and had a right to participate. This won overwhelming support and in the course of time it proved most beneficial. For N-3 not only became part of the Canadian Jewish Congress, it was to be a highly disciplined group, and I myself would have many occasions to call on them for help, for guarding meetings and even as personal bodyguards when this was required. Also, because N-3 was composed of our most ardent activists, it preempted the place which elsewhere was taken by the much more aggressive and at times violent Jewish Defence League, which never gained a real foothold in our community. All this went back to that one meeting at Holy Blossom.

My opening statement was simple: "We are here not to fight Jews but to fight Nazis." I called for new methods of battling our enemies, for the use of mass demonstrations and other means of gaining the support of the public. "Let the public know," I said, "that we aim to prevent violence, not to create it." The meeting lasted for five hours and very few of those in attendance left before it was over. But when we concluded, public anger had been vented and the Congress in Toronto was saved. Its leadership had been criticized to its face and the townhall discussion had provided the necessary catharsis. But our community was never the same thereafter. While the Congress itself maintained its structure, the leadership knew that from then on activism had to be part of its program. The leaders of Congress pledged to intensify and enlarge their campaign against the spread of hate propaganda and other forms of defamatory activities.

But the judgement was not unanimous. While the Yiddish Tag-Morgen Journal reported that "Jews in Canada united in their struggle against antisemitism", the Canadian Jewish News had a different version. The then editor-owner M. J. Nurenberger denounced the meeting as a "cabal" and called it thoroughly unrepresentative, a gathering at which the true voice of Jews had not been heard. I replied at length, giving him permission to print my response. Contrary to what Nurenberger had reported, I said, the meeting had been "serious and orderly . . . I felt that the wounds of our people were beginning to heal. Regardless of all attempts to further stir our community to dissatisfaction and dissension, I will continue in my labours to maintain this unity."

As I look back on that evening, I know it is from that time on that my constituency embraced the total community and I became their spokesman.

The Canadian Jewish Congress kept its promise to pursue new avenues of fighting the Nazis and began a campaign to have a hate-literature bill passed by Parliament. It was not the first time that this attempt had been made—in 1953 a deputation of the Congress had advised a special committee of the House that it considered amendments to the Criminal Code essential, to protect the public from statements that incited violence against any group. In 1965, Guy Favreau, then Minister of Justice, had appointed a committee headed by Professor Maxwell Cohen, Dean of McGill Law School. (Pierre Elliott Trudeau was a member of this committee.) With the help of expert assistance from Congress executive vice-president Saul Hayes the main features of the committee's drafts were adopted and became law on May 19, 1970. It is worth noting, however, that the Jewish community was again not totally united. Our civil libertarians insisted that a hate-literature bill would be an infringement of free speech and therefore in the long run injurious to the very community we were trying to protect. But others, like myself, were prepared to settle for less than perfect laws, because we felt that civil liberty never existed in a vacuum, but only when there was a balance between individual rights and the needs of the community—and this demanded some limits to all rights, including free speech.


## Von Thadden Interlude

At the end of 1966, CBC Television let it be known that it had invited the emerging leader of the neo-Nazi party of Germany to come to Canada for an interview. The man—happily forgotten now—was Adolf von Thadden, who was headquartered in Hanover, Germany, and had managed to give the scattered Nazi elements in his country a fresh lease on life. He had founded the NPD (German National Party) and it was gaining worrisome

numbers of adherents in state elections. The phenomenon of
Nazism rising again, albeit in altered form, only twenty years
after the demise of Hitler, caused consternation around the
world, and CBC doubtless felt that bringing the leader of the
movement to Canada would be a great scoop.

The Jewish community here was outraged. We protested
vigorously and obtained wide support throughout the country.
Eventually questions about the matter were raised in Parliament.
CBC thereupon withdrew its invitation to von Thadden and instead sent two of its reporters to Hanover for a taped interview
which would be aired in Canada. The Canadian Jewish Congress,
expressing the overwhelming attitude of its constituency, continued to object: "We would have no complaint about a program
presented in depth and in perspective which examines the
resurgence of political extremism of a neo-Nazi type in West Germany in the light of current and past history. But we do take
serious objection to a program built around the figure and personality of Adolf von Thadden. We say this because we are not
impressed by the previous record of the CBC in 'exposing' the
ideologies of fascists and Nazis. In the cases of its interviews
with Bellefeuille, Arcand, Rockwell and Skorzeny, what emerged
was that the individuals were able to present an apologia for
Nazism and whitewash its blood-stained record. Were von
Thadden to come to Canada on his own, no sizable or responsible
organization would give him a platform. Unfortunately the CBC is
affording him, in the words of its producer, an audience of two
and a half million who would not otherwise be reached." (This
was a reference to the audience of CBC's most popular TV show, a
program called "Sunday".)

The CBC tried to assuage public criticism by sending one of its
ablest reporters to Hanover. Larry Zolf was a Jew from Winnipeg and had become a star performer for the electronic circuit.
With a Jewish interviewer, so it was apparently reasoned, one
could expect the kind of questions that would lead to an exposé
of von Thadden.

The Jewish community resolved to organize a protest march in
front of the CBC on the night the show was to be aired, in mid-
January, 1967. Two days before the airing a representative of
CBC called me and asked whether I would be willing to comment
on the show. The film would be shown, then I would comment,
seated in the "Bear Pit"—so called because rising tiers of spec-

tators surrounded the guest of the evening. The spectators would applaud or hiss and also have a chance to ask questions. The arrangement allowed for a lively interchange and was in part responsible for the popularity of the program.

Despite the solid opposition of the Jewish community to the program, I decided to participate. It would mean missing the march, but I hoped to counter some of the propaganda impact which I felt the show was likely to have, even with a skilled interviewer. I stipulated that I would first have to see the edited interview as it would be presented. The format was to include twenty minutes of the von Thadden interview, and twelve to fifteen minutes of my portion following it.

Since libellous statements can easily slip out under circumstances of great heat and controversy, the show was always taped, usually just before it was aired. I arrived at the hotel across from the CBC for preliminary discussions with Larry Zolf, who was to do my interview as well. To my utter surprise I was confronted by a new development: without informing me, the producers had brought Aryeh Neier, the director of the New York Civil Liberties Union, to Toronto to debate with me "whether Jews should have tried to censor the CBC". Neier's participation had obviously been planned some time before and therefore the failure of the producers of the show to inform me in advance was understandably annoying to me. I refused to debate this new subject but agreed, even under the altered circumstances, to discuss von Thadden's appearance and the issues raised by it. I insisted that the time division be adhered to, so that there would be enough opportunity to comment on the film.

We then went into the "Bear Pit" for the taping. There was an aura of excitement—quite usual for that type of show, especially since the audience consisted primarily of teenagers. They were whipped into a high state of anticipation. The producers had them practise whistling and applause, with flashing lights indicating when to respond. They promised them a popular singer and a go-go dancer if they turned out to be a good audience, as well as a chance to come down from their seats and get on television after the interview concluded. The TV "instructor" said, "Shake it up, kids, but be sure not to face the camera when it's on you; you know this is 'Sunday' and there are some limits to what they will allow." It was in this bizarre atmosphere that Mr. Neier and I sat down to discuss the entertaining and amusing subject of von Thadden, the Nazis, and genocide.

We had already seen the film interview. Zolf was not at his best. He could be sharp and incisive, but on this occasion he let von Thadden present an image which appeared to imply that a man who loved dogs and children could not be all bad. The German came off as rather innocent, as a much-maligned and respectable person living pleasantly in a gracious home. Nothing of the viciousness of his program and the nature of his party came across.

Then came the time for Neier's and my comments on the show. The interviewer tried to put Canadian Jews and especially Congress on the spot, as people who tried to preserve Canada's immaturity by exercising censorship and pressuring people in high places. I indicated strongly that censorship was not the issue; that the Canadian Jewish Congress had never opposed a serious in-depth interview with von Thadden, that on the contrary it would welcome it; but that we all had grave reservations that a show such as "Sunday"—which despite its classification as public affairs was primarily entertainment—should present so disturbing, important and complex a subject in the context of whistling and go-go dancing. I said so and said so strongly, and the more I spoke, the more applause I received from the audience. It was evident that the producer, who was standing in the wings, had not planned on the program taking this turn. In the middle of the show he lost his cool and did the unheard-of: he marched onto the stage and injected himself into the program, arguing and even shouting at me. Unfortunately the public never got to see this display. Contrary to all the agreements we had made, von Thadden's film interview was lengthened and the Neier/Plaut follow-up, with all my cutting arguments, was chopped down to the point where it became fairly innocuous pap.

Meanwhile 3,000 of our people marched silently outside. I later learned that the producer's fury had come in part because he had tried to interview some of the marchers but had been rebuffed by them in a remarkable show of silent discipline.

No sooner was the taping over than Stanley Burke, the popular reader of the CBC National News show at eleven p.m., waylaid me and indicated that he wanted me as part of his newscast a few minutes later. It was a rare come-to-pass: a CBC show barely off the air before it became the subject of a national newscast.

The Jewish community's patience and perseverance in this

matter had been exemplary and we won ourselves wide public support. Douglas Fisher and Harry Crowe, in their popular column in the Toronto *Telegram*,* had written three days before the airing:

"If it is the judgement of sober Jewish leaders that they should march against von Thadden, then in the light of the experience of our generation, it becomes the obligation of sober Christians to march against von Thadden."

# L'Affaire Delorme

In the mid-seventies a radio commentator by the name of Roger Delorme was contesting the riding of Terrebonne, Quebec, as a Progressive Conservative candidate in the federal election. He clearly leaned toward the Arabs, was critical of Israel and was said to have made statements which the Jewish community considered bordering on antisemitism; in any case, Delorme attracted the support of people who were anathema to our community. Although the mayor of Terrebonne was Jewish, there were few Jews in the riding, so that direct communal pressure seemed out of the question. As it turned out, Delorme was defeated in the election, but a Congress delegation was charged with asking the Leader of the Opposition why Delorme had been permitted to carry the Conservative banner. I was on the delegation.

Joe Clark was the new Conservative leader. He and his wife Maureen McTeer received us graciously at "Stornoway", their official residence in Ottawa.

It fell to me to state our concerns. I argued that attitudes which encouraged antisemitism were both loathsome and dangerous. Neither Canada nor the Progressive Conservative Party could afford to identify with a candidate who espoused such dubious views. Clark's predecessor, Robert Stanfield, had read Mayor Jones of Moncton out of the party for failing to support the party's platform on bilingualism. Could Clark do any less with Delorme? And so on.

I thought I had been persuasive, but I was wrong.

"As long as a candidate subscribes to the party platform," said Clark, "we will support him."

* January 19, 1967.

Maureen strongly endorsed her husband's views. "It's a question of freedom of speech," she said. "Delorme is free to say what he wants and his constituents are free to select him as their candidate."

"No one can deny that people are free to choose who is to represent them," I countered. "But can a person like Delorme be said to subscribe to the platform of a party which should find his views unpalatable? And should the party's leader not make the party's position clear? It is not you, Mr. Clark, who reads Delorme out of the Party—it is he himself who places himself out of bounds."

Clark remained unconvinced. He would support Delorme if the latter were to be nominated again. He saw antisemitism as just another controversial point of view. He appeared to understand neither our anxieties nor the special heartache of the Jewish people, the Holocaust.*

We left, much perturbed. Fortunately the Conservatives in Terrebonne were now wise to the issues. They did not nominate Delorme in the next election.

# The French Fact

In 1971, a year after the October crisis in Quebec, the Social Action Committee of the temple organized a three-day conference with the theme "Quebec: A Year Later". The War Measures Act was now a memory, but it was a bitter one; it had left many of us, schooled in libertarian traditions, with an uncomfortable feeling. A whole nation had submitted when the government invoked extraordinary powers, powers exceeding anything I had experienced since the days of tyranny. To this day I believe that the Act confers more powers on the government than are required. Trudeau handled them with restraint, but who can tell what some future Prime Minister might do?

The conference attracted a host of federal and provincial ministers, as well as academics. But, although such luminaries as Secretary of State for External Affairs Mitchell Sharp opened the conference, and a series of controversial figures had a place of the program, there was one star and one star only. He was

---

* This did not prevent both Clark and his wife from developing strong personal sentiments of support for Israel: see p. 275.

René Lévesque, erstwhile newspaperman who later became leader of the Parti Québécois and is at this writing the Premier of Quebec. A chain-smoker, fluently bilingual, small in stature but with a large head and expressive hands, he was a charismatic figure who held everyone's attention.

On Saturday a few of us had lunch and he talked about his hopes. I asked whether his dream of an independent Quebec and the "natural aspirations of the Québécois" included the Jews. Were they, I asked, also reckoned as Québécois?

Lévesque looked at me quizzically across the table. "Come on, rabbi," he said. "You know better. We are Québécois and you are Jews. We will live together amicably and support each other, I hope, but we are not the same." Although he has since broadened his definitions, the conversation stuck in my mind.

In early 1980 we spent some time together at a party. Most of the guests had left, and we sat alone in a corner.

"I remember your article* comparing French aspirations and Jewish ideals as exemplified by Zionism," he said. "There are parallels, but there are also differences. You people are much too clannish."

"Are we now, Mr. Lévesque?" I countered. "Have you not tried to draw a circle tightly around the Québécois, as a separate and identifiable group? How else would you be able to preserve your identity on a continent of 250 million English-speaking people? What you criticize as 'clannishness' amongst Jews you see as an act of self-preservation for the Québécois."

We argued in this vein, partly in French, partly in English. The discussion was inconclusive.

"We must continue this," he said. "When next you come to Quebec or Montreal, let me know; we must speak about this again."

I hope we will.

## The Yom Kippur War—in Toronto

In May 1973 we were in Israel. In Asia the Viet Nam war was winding down, and in the changing context of international forces I suddenly perceived that for Israel, and indeed for Jewry

---

* I had written an article for *Maclean's* which had attracted much comment, including discussion by members of Lévesque's entourage.

in general, the road ahead was filled with obstacles. I had no idea, of course, that less than half a year later there would be the bitter conflict with Egypt and Syria, from which Israel would emerge deeply hurt in spirit despite its victories on the battlefield. But I had a foreboding, and the more I thought about it, the more I knew that I had to share it with my people at home.

So I wrote ahead and said that I wanted to talk to the congregation on a matter of great urgency. I had not made such an announcement in all the years I had been in Toronto. In consequence the synagogue was packed and the news media were on hand as well.

My message took the form of a prophecy. The Viet Nam war, I said, had made it possible for the Third World, for radicals of all kinds, and for the Soviet propaganda apparatus, to focus on America as the ultimate villain. With the end of that war America would at least temporarily leave the chair of the accused—but all these forces would need another ready target. I predicted that Israel would inevitably be cast in the role, that the years ahead would place Israel, and Jews everywhere, on the defensive. They would be held responsible for many ills and would be the subject of unrelenting hatred. I was speaking out now, I said, because we needed to prepare spiritually for the onslaught to come.

I was subsequently attacked by some members of our community as a war and fear monger. I did not reply; I let my warning speak for itself. Alas, I was proven right. The Yom Kippur war set forces in motion that further isolated Israel, and made the industrial powers hostage to the Arab oil producers.

Yom Kippur, 1973, fell on a Shabbat. As usual I had risen early and walked to the synagogue, and as usual I had not turned on my radio because of the day. But others had, and I arrived at the temple to meet rumours of all kinds. The story was that Israel had been attacked, on this holiest of days, by Syria and Egypt; beyond that basic fact, reports were sketchy.

In those years Israel's Consul-General in Toronto was Shmuel Ovnat, who with his wife Berta and his daughter Hana had become close friends of our family. They were open, and fun to be with. Berta was a fine artist and Shmuel a first-rate tennis player and my regular doubles partner. When services began, Shmuel was absent from his seat; he had been called to his office but had promised to report to the congregation in person as soon as possible.

The rumours thickened: Israel was smashing the enemy, it would soon be over; no, matters were more serious than in 1967 and it would be a drawn-out struggle. At last Shmuel appeared. I interrupted the service, and he mounted the pulpit amid silence. He appeared tense but confident. The reports were good, he said; things were going well. We all had a sense of enormous relief.

But Shmuel's information was faulty; he, like everyone in Israel, was being fed propaganda in place of facts. Not until the next day did we learn the bitter truth: Israel was fighting for its life, and the war was going badly—very badly.

The community moved into action. I appeared time and again on radio and television, wrote for the press, preached and spoke at public meetings. Stephen Franklin took on full responsibilities for the congregation, and acquitted himself admirably.

Our local efforts came to a climax with a rousing rally at the Skyline Hotel, near the airport, to raise emergency funds from the top givers in the city. It was Shemini Atzeret, the eighth day of Sukkot, a holy day on which memorial prayers are said and Jews are expected to be in their synagogues. The Orthodox rabbis objected to the rally, declaring that they could not sanction travelling on the Holy Day even for this emergency. I judged differently, and the rally went ahead.

Rabbi Herbert Feder, Conservative leader of Beth Tikvah synagogue, also forsook his pulpit that day and chanted an immensely moving service for the 1,200 men and women who packed the hall. The prayers were offered with a desperate fervour. Our feelings were amplified by the presence of three Israelis who had come to tell us of the country's needs: Pinchas Sapir (Israel's Finance Minister, who was to die suddenly two years later), General Hayyim Laskov (later a member of the War Inquiry Commission) and Leon Dulzin (today chairman of the World Zionist Organization). The outpouring of sentiment expressed itself in our people's marvellous generosity.

In Amsterdam, in the spring of 1980, Dulzin and I reminisced about that rally on Shemini Atzeret. "I have attended services and rallies all over the world," he told me, "but never have I witnessed anything like the spirit of that day."

"We were fired by the heroism of our people," I said.

"Perhaps," Dulzin mused. "Still, it was extraordinary. Your community taught me something about the potential of the Diaspora."

Chapter 9

# THE PUBLIC DOMAIN

ELIE WIESEL HAD HELPED TO awaken the conscience of western Jewry when he reported on the yearnings of Soviet Jews in his book *The Jews of Silence*. But the real awakening came from within Soviet Russia. Slowly the protests, the applications for emigration began to mount. The applicants were harassed as traitors to the Motherland: their children were dismissed from universities, they themselves lost their jobs and were thrust on the charity of relatives and friends. Yet hardly any exit permits were granted. The pressure from around the world became greater, the tales of oppression more alarming, the number of those wanting to leave grew and grew. There were trumped-up trials and the first prisoners of conscience were created by the Soviet system. The term "refusenik" was added to the vocabulary.

Then, in 1971, Soviet Premier Alexei Kosygin paid a state visit to Canada. Suddenly Canada became the focal point of a large-scale effort on behalf of Soviet Jewry. We began to organize the community, and the response, especially from the young, was overwhelming. Kosygin was to visit Toronto, Montreal and the West, and was to spend some time in Ottawa. We decided to concentrate our activity in the capital.

At the time I was chairman of the Religious Affairs Committee of the Congress, and in that capacity I called an emergency conference of all Canadian rabbis. The conference was to precede a march by the Jews of Ottawa and as many from other communities as could make their way to the city.

The date was Monday, October 18. The majority of Canada's

rabbis, of every denominational shading, were on hand. After Rabbi Gedalia Felder had opened the proceedings with a discourse on the freeing of prisoners we left in procession from the Jewish Centre, attended by radio, TV and 250 police-men—four policemen armed with guns for every rabbi armed with a prayer-book. We were guided to an isolated place in Strathcona Park near the Soviet Embassy where we held after-noon prayers and attempted to present a petition to the embassy. It was not accepted. We then left for the eternal flame in front of the Parliament Buildings, for study and a night vigil. During the evening there was a party in the west block of Parliament and Kosygin's official car went almost directly by us. We lined the road as Kosygin passed and shouted our slogans and desires. The RCMP did not interfere. We were sure Kosygin had heard—and we weren't through yet.

We spelled each other through the long foggy night and in the morning we held our *minyan*, again in the glare of television lights.

Cars and buses arrived throughout the day bringing some seven thousand people to town; Ottawa Jewry added another three thousand. Ten thousand men, women and children marched and danced and chanted, "One, two, three, four, open up the iron door! Five, six, seven, eight, open up the iron gate!" Traffic was at a standstill. People came onto their porches, leaned out of win-dows, observed the proceedings from the roof-tops. A plane flew overhead trailing a banner, "Free Soviet Jews!" The sun shone brightly on us; a sense of purpose and joy prevailed. We marched again to the Russian Embassy and, of course, again were not ad-mitted . We threw a petition over the fence as a symbolic act. I spoke to the crowd in the park. Finally we went back through downtown, to a mass assembly in front of the Supreme Court. I spoke again; we sang, then we went home. The Ottawa Jewish community* had performed splendidly. And Kosygin was certain to have taken notice.

The *Globe and Mail* reported:

> The biggest problem created by the march turned out to be a mid-afternoon traffic tie-up caused by the closing of Laurier Avenue, one of Ottawa's major east-west arteries.
>
> ... Most of the demonstrators were young and seemed unaware

* The march was organized by Hy Soloway and Hy Hochberg.

until the march began that more than 300 other officers were looking down at them from the top of the hill.

The first five brief speeches were idealistic and returned constantly to the phrase, "Let my people go".

. . . As key speaker, however, Rabbi W. Gunther Plaut of Toronto addressed his remarks directly to Mr. Kosygin: "I tell Mr. Kosygin that we are not a bomb-throwing group but we are a militant group. We will talk when talking is necessary and we will shout when shouting is necessary.

"Mr. Kosygin, we accuse your government of persecuting Jews. We accuse your government of antisemitism, of looking away from where antisemitism grows in the gardens of your land."

For us the two days had displayed unity and determination. But official government reaction was ambiguous. The government took no exception to Kosygin's remark that the protesters were "riff raff". I objected to what I considered a serious lapse. Only later did I receive a letter from External Affairs Minister Mitchell Sharp, in which he apologized for delaying his response and then went on to give a politically convenient explanation:

> With reference to your concern over remarks made by Premier Kosygin at his Ottawa press conference, I would draw your attention to the Canadian Press story of October 26, a copy of which is attached. You will notice that the Canadian Press reporters present at the news conference interpreted Mr. Kosygin's comment about "riff raff" as directed against a young man who attacked him the previous Monday on Parliament Hill. This interpretation was subsequently confirmed by reporters and officials in discussions with Mr. Kosygin's interpreter.*

The press did not help us either. The *Globe and Mail* (October 21) proclaimed in its lead headline, "Kosygin Denies that Jews have Problems in Russia." The *Toronto Star* reported that Trudeau's aide agreed with the tenor of Kosygin's statement, and columnist Peter Desbarats wrote that Canadians in general resented Jewish interference in the Premier's peaceful visit. But the cool attitude of the Canadian government and the widespread indifference of the public—even the resentment on the part of the Canadian press—did not deter us. A pattern had been set for demonstrations in other cities.

---

* Letter dated October 28.

In Toronto Kosygin stayed at the Inn on the Park, in a top-floor suite reserved for distinguished guests. From there he had a clear view of the park below, and if he looked down he could see ten thousand or more people wending their way along the approaches to the hotel, assembling below, shouting their songs and then gathering in the park to hear a variety of speakers. Elie Wiesel happened to be in town and we asked him to lead us in setting the mood. He stood on top of an automobile and, though his voice did not carry far, he could be seen by everyone.

Half a mile away another demonstration took place, this one by Ukrainian Canadians calling for independence for their native country. A further demonstration occurred at the state dinner for Kosygin. I had declined my invitation, but two of our few local members of the Jewish Defence League obtained admission and during dinner they stood up to shout their demands. They were quickly removed—but again the message had been heard.

Barney Danson, then Parliamentary Assistant to the Prime Minister, told me that Trudeau himself was fully apprised of our plans and aware of the deep feeling that ran through the community. Despite his ambivalence about our demonstrations, he did not waver in his full support of our cause. He and Mitchell Sharp discussed with Kosygin the position of Soviet Jewry and the possibility of emigration.

A few months later the doors of the Soviet Union began to open and the first sizable group of emigrants left. Not long after, more substantial numbers received permission to leave. It was a clear reversal of Soviet policy. I do not know what role Canadian Jewry played in this matter, but I am convinced that here was one case in which we made an important contribution.

In the years that followed, Congress set up a national committee on Soviet Jewry. Telephone calls were made, letter campaigns were undertaken; we kept in touch with dissidents and monitored arrests and harassments. In the winter of 1976 I was invited to participate in a symposium in Moscow on the future of Jewry in Russia. I prepared my paper, but the Soviet government first postponed and then forbade the holding of the conference.*

At this writing over 200,000 Jews have left Soviet Russia. At first most went to Israel but later the number of Israel immigrants dropped and applications elsewhere, particularly to

* My address was subsequently published in *Judaism*, 27, 1 (Winter 1978).

the United States, increased enormously. A wide-ranging discussion took place on whether Jews in the Diaspora should extend full assistance to those who chose not to go to Israel. Were not all Jews part of our people who, if they needed support, should receive it? Should they be punished for their desire to live elsewhere than in Israel? How could Diaspora Jews—that is, Jews who dwelt outside Israel—force others to live where they themselves did not? The position of helping as many as possible has generally prevailed, but not without vigorous opposition, especially from Israeli leaders.

The Israelis claim that were it not for the existence of their state, no appreciable number of Russian Jews would come out at all; they are only able to leave when Israeli visas have been issued to them. But on arrival in Vienna many of them cast these to the wind and go to other countries. While America is their usual goal, Canada has had its significant share of these so-called *noshrim* (dropouts). No one, of course, has argued that emigrants from Russia are not free to choose their habitat. What is questioned is the assistance which international Jewish organizations, primarily HIAS and JIAS,* gives them in Vienna, using funds solicited from the Jewish community in the name of Israel. If the *noshrim* have Israeli visas, it is argued, should Israel not have some benefit of the immigrants? To date the controversy remains unresolved.

I had opposed any limitations unreservedly—freedom is freedom, saving lives is saving lives—but in late 1979 I had second thoughts about it. Not, to be sure, about the saving of lives. Rather, I asked, what do we do with, and for, these immigrants after they leave Soviet Russia? The majority of Jewish emigrants have not the faintest idea of what it means to be a Jew. That is not their fault; they have been brought up under a Communist regime which has systematically suppressed every expression of Jewishness. Those who go to Israel are at least exposed to some Jewish culture. They learn to read and write Hebrew and become acquainted with Jewish parlance and with the signposts of our existence: the Sabbath, the holidays and that whole unseen structure of Jewish references (if not necessarily values) which underlies the existence of the Jewish state and permeates its daily life. And having lived there for a while they may opt to stay or to leave—but at least the decision will be based on experience.

* Hebrew Immigrant Aid Society (U.S.); Jewish Immigrant Aid Society (Canada).

Beyond that, the problem lies with those of us in the Diaspora. Except in the smaller cities we have miserably failed to integrate the newcomers into our communities and to make them truly Jewish. Criticizing is easier than doing, and I bear as much of the blame as anyone in our community. Not until late in my presidency of the Canadian Jewish Congress did I try to rouse my people to the recognition that, unless we match the enormous effort of bringing Jews out of Soviet Russia with an equally concentrated effort to bring them into our culture, the whole exercise has a ring of futility. In Toronto and Montreal, where thousands of new immigrants have gone, the Jewish day schools in each city had (in 1979) but thirty-odd students of Russian parents. While day schools are not the ultimate signs of a family's adherence to Judaism, in this instance they tell a sorry tale, especially since attendance has usually been provided free of charge for the first year. Not only have most children of Russian Jewish immigrants received little or no Jewish education, but often the immigrants have not joined synagogues or made any other expressions of Jewish communality. It is a sad irony that, after suffering years of persecution for their Jewishness, they are unable to enjoy its benefits when they finally reach freedom.

# Barring the P.L.O.

Ever since its beginning, the Palestine Liberation Organization—of which Yasir Arafat's Al Fatah is the main though not the sole component—has been vigorously opposed by the Jewish community. When the PLO indicated in early 1975 that it would send observers to a United Nations conference on law enforcement and terrorism in Toronto, the Jewish reaction was unanimous. The memory of the 1972 Munich slaughter of eleven Olympic athletes was still fresh in our minds; and the idea that an organization whose major means of gaining its point was terrorism against innocent persons would participate in a conference called to fight crime, violence and terror, was both ludicrous and obscene.

The conference was scheduled for early September, and the Canada-Israel Committee began at once to consider the scenario that might develop were the PLO to attend. They struck a small committee to study the possible reactions of our community, and because the conference would be in Toronto, members of the committee were chosen from that city.*

Norman May, Lou Silver and I held some initial meetings and eventually devised a plan that would carry out our purposes to best effect. We adopted a name, "Canadians Against PLO Terror", and it was under the acronym CAPLOT that we set sail for the next few months.**

It was my assigned task to oversee the core of the effort: "To take charge of all political and non-political lobbying and personal contact approaches . . . to be responsible for approaching government on all levels, to dissuade them from participation in the conference . . . to influence the federal government against permitting the PLO entry into Canada . . . to open channels of communication with labour, hoteliers, police organizations, etc. . . . to seek their support and assistance."†

Obtaining the support of national and international groups became an essential focus of our efforts. The group came formally into existence on May 12, but even before then our steering committee had registered some notable successes in involving the larger community. The International Association of Police Chiefs indicated that they would boycott the conference, and the Toronto Police Commission was expected to follow. The Law Society of Upper Canada, which had offered Osgoode Hall as a meeting place for the conference, rescinded its invitation and the paper which one member had agreed to present was withdrawn. Austin Cooper, who had been appointed by the Law Society to oversee the event, resigned. The Canadian Airline Pilots' Association and the Hoteliers' Association also supported our cause. A brief was prepared on the legal aspects of the participation of delegates who supported or were members of a terrorist organization.‡ Eventually even the Conservative govern-

---

* The Canada-Israel Committee (CIC) appointed Lou Silver, a lawyer and president of the Zionist-Revisionist Organization of Canada, chairman: David Sadowski, Ben Kayfetz and Ruth Resnick, staff persons of Congress, were to assist in the work. Since I was then vice-chairman of the CIC I represented the Administrative Committee. Norman May, a Montreal lawyer who had moved to Toronto, also came on board.

** The three of us met on a regular basis, sometimes as often as three times a week, with David Sadowski as our chief staff person; once a week we met with a larger committee including Rabbis Jordan Pearlson and Erwin Schild, Donald Carr, Joe Pomerant, and Myer Bick (national executive director of the CIC) ex officio. Philip Givens, then a member of the Ontario Legislature, also became active on this sub-committee.

† Memorandum of the committee, dated May 8.

‡ Joe Pomerant chaired the legal committee, which included Arthur Maloney, later Ontario's first Ombudsman.

ment of Ontario's Premier William Davis became involved and told Trudeau that it could not act as host for such a conference.

CAPLOT was meant to be "an amalgam formed by concerned Canadians of diverse political and religious interests." It was designed to achieve a Canadian and not merely a Jewish objective. But while we made significant efforts in this regard, and in fact attracted wide groups of sympathizers across the country, including the media, the perception that this was essentially a Jewish lobbying effort persisted to the very end.

One problem was that the conference was not sponsored by Canada as such, but by the UN. Canada, we were told time and again, had invited the United Nations to hold the meeting and offered to be the host, which meant that it had no responsibility for program and participants. Not relevant to the issue but ironic nonetheless was that a Jew, Alan Grossman, then a member of the provincial government, had been the one to invite the UN conference in the first place. (Of course, no PLO participation was contemplated at that time.) Despite Ontario's opposition, the federal government said the conference would proceed.

Nonetheless we persisted. CAPLOT, we said, would "launch the necessary legal proceedings to prevent the Canadian government from granting, or if necessary to require it to revoke, visas for PLO delegates if our representations failed."* If all our efforts failed and the PLO was admitted to the country, we would (said our document) "mount peaceful—yet massive—demonstrations by the public to express their disgust and horror that representatives of a terrorist organization would be allowed to participate in a process in which the United Nations should be seeking ways and means to end terrorism rather than legitimizing it."

Of course, we knew very well that in early September, because of the Labour Day weekend and also the imminence of the Jewish High Holy Days, such "massive" demonstrations would be difficult to arrange. We could, however, recall to the Canadian public the Kosygin demonstrations of 1971: "We are determined that, if public protests are indeed required, they should overshadow the 1971 events."

May, Silver, Sadowski and I took on the job of organizing contact with all members of the federal government. Beginning in

---

* We had not then counted on another manoeuvre—which was later adopted by the PLO. though it turned out to be too late for them—namely, to be represented at the conference by Canadian citizens who were sympathizers of the organization.

June we got in touch with every single Cabinet Minister. We found that the Cabinet was divided on the issue. Trudeau did not reveal his own stance at the time, but there was widespread feeling that, building on the efforts of Lester Pearson, Canada had made support for the UN an important part of its foreign policy and that this policy should be maintained. There was further concern that a conference on housing ("Habitat") which was to be held later that year in Vancouver, also under UN auspices, might be endangered; some 1,500 to 2,000 delegates were expected at that conference, which was highly important to Canada and especially to Vancouver. If the Government took drastic action to bar the PLO the UN in turn might cancel "Habitat", which could produce a backlash and create a feeling that the federal government had caved in to the lobbying efforts of a minority, to the detriment of wider Canadian interests.

Even so, the decision by the Ontario government to withdraw its part of the invitation had had a profound impact on Ottawa. There were political implications that could not be overlooked. Ontario, and especially its metropolitan and south-eastern region, held the key to any future federal elections. Moreover,this same region was vital to the provincial Conservatives' hold on power.

On June 13 I received a telephone call from Prime Minister Trudeau. We had met often but we had never talked policy privately—our contacts had been either social or during official meetings. It was my first opportunity to explore the issue with him personally. He suggested a number of options.

One was to move the conference from Toronto to Montreal. I commented that this would be too obvious a ducking of the issues and would not solve the problem in any case, because Montreal's Jewish community would be just as vocal as Toronto's. It would mean jumping from the frying pan into the fire.

The second option was not to admit the PLO and its representatives. This, Trudeau said, would probably result in the conference being withdrawn from Canada or perhaps even postponed. But he felt it would jeopardize the Habitat conference.

The third was to let the conference take place as planned, with PLO attendance, but to make an official government statement against terrorism.

I countered that there was a fourth option which I would like him to consider; to say to the UN that if the PLO did not withdraw, Canada would find itself unable to accommodate the conference

altogether. I phoned May and Silver and shared with them the
contents of the conversation. I asked them not to let anyone know
that the telephone call had taken place; if it got around, there
might be no further discussions. We agreed that I should stress
Option Four and that my main argument would have to be a
moral one.

When I next spoke with the Prime Minister, I told him that I
had thought about the options and felt that Cabinet ought to concern itself seriously with the suggestion I had made.

That would be difficult, Trudeau intimated.

"But isn't it precisely the Prime Minister's duty to set a tone of
moral leadership to the Cabinet and to the country at large? Isn't
this an opportunity to make Canada's voice heard for the right
thing rather than for the opportune and expedient?"

We spoke further along these lines, but for the moment the
matter remained unresolved.

The immediate result was two meetings, called by Mitchell
Sharp and Allan MacEachen, two of Trudeau's most important
ministers. They were to explore the matter of the PLO conference
with leaders of the Jewish community. The first meeting took
place on June 24 with Sharp. Unfortunately I could not attend.*
Sharp stated that the Cabinet had not as yet made a decision, but
that it was greatly concerned with the international repercussions if the PLO were admitted.

I did attend the second meeting, held two weeks later, with
MacEachen.** He stressed that there were two obvious options
open to the Canadian government: one, to let in certain individuals associated with the PLO but not terrorists; two, to tell
the UN that no members of the PLO would be admitted. The latter
option, he said, might render Canada ineffective in UN circles, at
least for a period of time. Clearly MacEachen himself was hoping
to persuade us that admitting the PLO not only would be the
proper thing to do but could somehow be utilized to the advantage of Israel. It was my feeling that he was suggesting a trade-
off at this point: Canada would let the PLO in and in exchange
would launch a diplomatic offensive on behalf of Israel.

---

* In addition to Sharp the following attended: Alain Dudoit from External Affairs; C. V.
  Svobod, Deputy Director of the UN Political and Institutional Affairs Division; Aaron
  Pollack and Myer Bick for CIC; Alan Rose for Congress; Norman May and David
  Sadowski for CAPLOT; and Hy Soloway for the Ottawa community.
** Present were Myer Bick, Irwin Cotler, Phil Givens, Milton Harris, Fred Lepkin, Herbert
  Levy, Norman May, David Sadowski, Ray Wolfe, Joe Zatsman. Barney Danson, then
  Minister of State for Urban Affairs, was also in attendance.

MacEachen then outlined five risks for Canada, if it voted against admitting the PLO:

1. The crime conference would be moved;
2. The human settlements ("Habitat") conference in B.C. might be cancelled;
3. There might be some adverse effect on the planned location of the International Civil Aviation Organization headquarters in Montreal;
4. Canada's effectiveness in the UN would be undermined;
5. Canada's objectivity in the Middle East would be put in question.

We countered by saying that it was not Canada but the PLO that had delegitimized the UN meetings; that it had done everything in its power to upset any move towards a peaceful solution of Middle-East problems; and that it remained adamantly committed to the destruction of Israel. We reiterated that the subject was not specifically a Jewish one but concerned all Canadians.

As we came closer to the deadline of the Cabinet's decision—which was constantly rumoured to be imminent and to be "sure" to go in one direction, or another—the most difficult problem we faced was what kind of public reaction we should initiate.* We felt that any large-scale Jewish demonstration of intent would at this point be counter-productive. We had done our best to move the matter into the larger realm, and consequently stressing the Jewish side of it would, if anything, be harmful to our cause.

The Arabs on their part did their share of lobbying but their efforts were not effective. Khaled Mouammar, president of the Canadian Arab Federation, and Louis Azzaria, a former president, together with James Peters, a professor at Ryerson, were leaders of the Arab effort.

The break came on July 18, although we did not know it at the time. We learned later that on that day External Affairs Minister Allan MacEachen flew secretly to New York and informed the Secretary-General of the United Nations that Canada requested him to postpone the conference, because political conditions made it inadvisable to hold it at that time.

---

* By this time, our committee had been enlarged and included Herbert Levy, Milton Harris, and Max Shecter.

The government's decision was announced publicly several days later. We were elated and called for a press conference, at which Silver, May and myself answered a multitude of questions. The meeting made newspapers across Canada as well as radio and television that night. But coverage did not mean approval; the reaction was mixed.

Most vehement in its denunciation of the government decision was the *Toronto Star*, which called it "a shameful surrender on the PLO issue." It said that the government was using "weasel words" by "abandoning principle, giving in to threats and copping out of its responsibility to the world community." Richard Gwyn, Ottawa correspondent of the *Star*, was even more direct. "What mattered," he wrote, "were the Ontario election and the search for Jewish votes. For shabby domestic reasons Canada has committed one of its most shabby international acts."

The reaction of the *Star* was not unanticipated. Ben Kayfetz later characterized it as "self-styled even-handedness which inevitably winds up against Israel."

The *Globe and Mail* was also somewhat negative, although it had originally agitated against the PLO's admission to the country in a vigorous editorial. The *Toronto Sun* came down on our side. From the beginning it had been unequivocally against admitting the PLO. The *Sun*, a conservative paper, had berated Trudeau for his indecision, yet when the policy statement came, the *Sun* did not shout "cop-out" as some of Trudeau's political opponents did, but gave it unqualified applause. "Trudeau showed common sense in this one."*

Also in the *Toronto Sun*, Roy McMurtry, a Toronto lawyer who would later become provincial Attorney-General, commented on a charge by the Canadian Arab Federation which the *Star* had featured, that "Fifteen Toronto Rabbis Are Running Canada's Foreign Policy".

"The true and simple fact is that most non-Jewish Canadians are appalled not only by terrorism as a political weapon but by

---

* Rabbi Reuben Slonim was the only rabbinical voice to criticize the decision. A headline quoted his letter to the *Star*: "Canada Sullied Image at the United Nations, Rabbi Claims." In his article Slonim said that pressure from Holocaust survivors had influenced the Canadian Jewish Congress to take the position it did and added disingenuously: "Jewish tradition commands Jews to promote the well-being of the country in which they live." That Holocaust survivors had been the major force was inaccurate, for in this case there had been a near universal consensus in the Jewish community. And the Rabbi's statement about placing the Jewish interest above Canada's was especially grating—such sentiments are usually expressed by our detractors.

the apparent lack of any morality in international politics. Furthermore, an equally large number of Canadian citizens share a strong moral commitment to the survival of Israel. . . . Surely it is about time that Canada be prepared to adopt a strong moral stand. As a country we either denounce terrorism as a legitimate political weapon or cease our pious utterances about international morality."

Meanwhile, the UN switched the conference to a European location but, contrary to Canadian fears, left the Habitat conference in Vancouver. This time we decided not to launch any objection should there be PLO participation, because the aim of that conference was to improve the human condition; it did not present the intrinsic contradiction of terrorists pretending to work against crime. What we resolved to do was to make sure that the PLO did not turn the conference into a forum for their own propaganda. We were assured by chairman Barney Danson that he would make every effort to see that this did not happen. "If it does," he said, "I will resign as chairman." The conference did take place. There were anti-PLO mass meetings in Vancouver, and the small Jewish community there gave us great support. PLO demonstrations were ineffective and, despite some attempts to turn it into an anti-Israel circus, the conference went on with its proper business.

The CAPLOT experience taught us a number of lessons. It was clear that a small group such as we had organized, which had the complete support of the community, was best qualified to undertake decisive political action, especially when the climate and conditions were changing rapidly.

On the other hand our media committee was less successful than it might have been. It did not keep the Jewish community fully informed on our progress, and thus allowed public frustration to build up. Fortunately the success of our efforts erased this feeling; it would have been more serious had we failed.

CAPLOT operated without any budget whatsoever and therefore was unable to utilize the print media for the kind of large-scale advertisements that would have been helpful. Further, we did not succeed in "Canadianizing" the issue sufficiently; important groups such as the Benchers* and the Police Chiefs and the Ontario government supported us, but the image

---

* The directors of the Law Society of Upper Canada.

of the "Elders of Zion" engineering the whole matter for Jewish
purposes was never fully overcome. Headquartering CAPLOT at
Canadian Jewish Congress offices did not help matters either.
And finally, we were not really prepared for the action which the
government took. While I myself had suggested this course we
had not seriously considered the chance that the Prime Minister
might accept the suggestion and had not considered all its consequences.

Some time later, Sharif al-Hout, representative of the PLO at
the UN, was allowed entrance into Canada and announced public
lectures on the PLO position. This sparked a large-scale
demonstration at the university where he was giving his address.
Although Arab listeners were in the majority, the enthusiasm of
Jewish students who had gained admission to the hall actually
drowned out the speaker. This was wrong-headed and it
backfired badly on us, because the whole idea of freedom of
speech seemed to be under attack by the Jewish community.
Disavowals could not undo the damage—our opposition to the
PLO was too well known, and the public was quick to believe that
we would go to any lengths to prevent unwanted opponents from
speaking.

The simple facts of our campaign fail to convey the high excitement and the deep involvement of the community. My own hopes
and fears too are not a part of the official record. For me it was a
time of high tension; I was propelled into negotiations and activities which involved the country in important national and international decisions. For the Jewish community it was a time of
unprecedented unity; we stood together, and it was this sense of
common cause which communicated itself to the government. We
were to be reckoned with because we had a sense of oneness and
purpose. We were in no way conspirators: our policy was clear
and open from the beginning, and we utilized the processes of
democracy to the fullest. Our greatest defence was the climate of
freedom, and to this the Jewish community of Canada was and
continues to be passionately devoted.

## Battles for Jerusalem — Canadian Style

For many years Canadian Jewry was famous for the cohesive-
ness of its community. But this unity came apart in the beginning
of 1979 under circumstances which were never fully disclosed.

The reason is obvious. The political sensitivity of our people forbade it at the time, and indeed at the height of the crisis such disclosure might have led to permanent divisions in the community. Now that some time has passed and the tempers have cooled, many of the facts can be related as an example of how the leadership of Canadian Jewry works and how the community perceives its place in the country as a whole. It is a story which reveals both our strengths and our weaknesses.

For some time Canadian Jews had been unhappy with the extension of the Arab boycott of Israeli commerce into the Canadian sphere. Canadian manufacturers and suppliers were asked to certify that their goods had no Israeli components and, further, were asked to state whether they did any business at all with Israel. Finally, companies with Jews on their boards of directors were in danger of being placed on the Arab blacklist.

In 1976 the possibility of anti-boycott legislation had first been raised. Such legislation would prevent Arabs from interfering with legitimate Canadian business activities and from asking questions which—in a Canadian context—would be illegal. As it was an internal Canadian concern, it seemed to belong either to the Congress or to the Joint Community Relations Committee (JCRC, which the Congress had operated for many years conjointly with B'nai B'rith). However, the proper personnel to handle the political campaign did not seem available, while the Canada-Israel Committee (CIC) had professionals who during a political lull could expend their energies on this issue.

The CIC was the unchallenged voice of Canadian Jews in matters concerning Israel. Norman May and I were then its co-chairmen; May acceded to the sole occupancy of the chair after I resigned in 1977 on my election to the presidency of the Canadian Jewish Congress. The considerable experience which he had garnered during our successful CAPLOT operation stood him in good stead in the years that followed. Howard Stanislowski, a bright young man who was the CIC's Ottawa representative, was given the main responsibility of getting the enterprise under way and he began to lobby for its recognition as an issue in the halls of power. Irwin Cotler, a young, innovative Montreal law professor, was instrumental in forming a national committee which included such non-Jewish luminaries as Justice Emmett Hall and Professor Harry Crowe. Their non-partisan, non-denominational group, fuelled by Cotler's expertise, brought out a brilliant report in January 1977: it set forth the discrimination which was present or threatened in various parts of the Canadian business world. The media picked up the issue and since it was properly portrayed as a question of Canadian civil and human rights, we were able to gain the sympathy and support of wide segments of the public. The object was first to raise the issue, and then to ask government to take action to protect the rights of Canadians.

The government responded, but rather weakly. The Department of Industry, Trade and Commerce was uncooperative—it feared that anti-boycott legislation might stand in the way of lucrative contracts in the Arab world. The Prime Minister—though he made a statement in the House that discrimination of this type was "repugnant to Canadians"—was not keen to translate his disapproval into action.

At first the Jewish public remained unmoved. The issues surrounding the boycott were complex and did not evoke a ready emotional response. But persistent work by the professionals of the CIC began to bear fruit and slowly but steadily—without any restraint from the CIC's administrative committee—the Jewish community found itself in a posture of confrontation with the Trudeau administration. I had hoped that the issue would not be identified as a specifically Jewish matter, but it soon developed its own dynamics. It became less a question of the protection of Canadian civil rights, and more a matter of Israeli and Jewish interests. It was now solidly on the Jewish agenda and as president of the Congress I had to deal with it.

Matters heated up as the Trudeau administration entered the last year of its term. When would the Prime Minister call an election? Trudeau bided his time. Meanwhile his popularity was slipping constantly and the Liberal Party was obviously losing ground. Inflation was increasing, unemployment was high and the economy was fragile. Many people felt that the influence of the Jewish community in a forthcoming election would be considerable. The pundits reasoned that the election would be won or lost in southern Ontario, in areas where Jewish voters had a significant voice.

At this time Trudeau indicated that he would like to address a Jewish gathering. The United Jewish Appeal arranged a dinner for this purpose, in June 1978, and I was asked to introduce the Prime Minister. I praised him for the things he had done for the Jewish community and for which he would be remembered. I mentioned three: the first, his advocacy of Soviet Jewry and the representations he had made to Premier Kosygin; the second, his

decision to bar the PLO from the UN Conference on Law Enforcement and Terrorism; the third, his compassion at the memorial
service for the eleven Israeli athletes slain in Munich, when he
read a psalm and wept with the rest of us.*

"Because of these I make bold to hope that there will be a
fourth occasion of which we shall speak with satisfaction in the
days ahead; that, when I have a chance to introduce you again, I
will be able to add another accolade because you will have taken
notice of the acute distress of our community—and believe me, it
is acute. I refer to the current practices relative to the Arab
boycott, practices which you yourself in righteous indignation
called repugnant to the people of Canada. I hope that in the next
introduction I will be able to say: our Prime Minister seized the
moral initiative, as he did with Soviet Jewry and with the PLO,
and introduced regulations that had teeth and finally decided for
legislation that rendered these practices, which discriminate
against Canadians and set citizen against citizen, once and for
all inoperative and illegal in this country."

I remember the thunderous applause that greeted this introduction and the clear annoyance which spread across the
face of Mr. Trudeau. Of course he could not reply posi-
tively—any change in policy would have to be agreed upon first
in Cabinet and then announced to the House. So in his prepared
speech he stuck to the text, but afterwards let me know with
some vehemence what his opinion was. "We will never introduce
legislation in this matter. There isn't a chance."

"Mr. Trudeau," I said, "never is a large word. Perhaps circumstances will change, or perhaps you will change your mind."

We let it go at that, and a few months later he did change his
mind. He dispatched Defence Minister Barney Danson (the only
Jew in the Cabinet) and John Roberts, Secretary of State (who
had been elected in a heavily Jewish riding) to persuade our
leadership that the government would give us, if not everything,
then at least a portion of what we asked for. We in turn would
publicly agree that a step had been taken in the right direction.
Trudeau (quite properly, from his side) perceived this manoeuvre
as a means of calling off the vocal criticism of the Jewish community, which had now taken up the issue as its own. (I must admit, in fairness to the government, that some of the critics did not
understand how very complex the matter was.)

* See above. pp. 227-28.

Danson and Roberts met with a small group of CIC leaders in a Toronto hotel. The media had been alerted that a statement would be forthcoming that afternoon.

At least three of us, Milton Harris, Phil Givens and I, were unhappy with the venue and with the compromise that was asked of us. But it was clear that, having allowed the issue to be perceived as a purely Jewish one, we had gotten both ourselves and the government into a box. A further confrontation was not desirable because there were more important matters for which we needed the government's co-operation; in fact this issue had demonstrably lower priority even in Israel. The perceptive and capable executive vice-president of Congress, Alan Rose, and I had visited the Ministry for Foreign Affairs in Jerusalem earlier that year. We had been impressed by the fact that anti-boycott legislation was relegated to some third or fourth rank of importance. To make it a do-or-die issue for Canadian Jews made no sense when other matters were of much higher political and economic urgency.

So we agreed to the compromise. The government would introduce certain regulatory prescriptions which it was willing to encase in law and we in turn would stop pushing the matter and await the result of these changes. Legislation in the strict sense was neither promised nor contemplated by the administration and we knew it. Anything approaching the type of law which had been passed in the U.S. was, realistically speaking, out of the question.*

The other two political parties had now begun to understand that here was a Liberal weak point. It was further weakened by the appointment of a former Tory, the new Minister of Industry, Trade and Commerce, Jack Horner, who was frankly opposed to anti-boycott legislation and who said the things Trudeau was probably thinking. The federal Conservatives announced that they would favour meaningful legislation and the provincial Conservatives in Ontario—led by Larry Grossman—introduced a strong bill which would place Ontario clearly on the side of the angels. Extensive hearings were held and some opposition arose over details of the bill, especially in the New Democratic Party. From our side, Irwin Cotler, Norman May, Howard Stanislowski and I were among those who made representations. In time the

* In the fall of 1978 the government's Bill C-32 was in fact introduced; it by and large carried out the limited provisions of our compromise. The bill died on the Order Paper when Parliament was dissolved the following spring.

bill became law, providing a thorn in the side of the federal government and a help, so it appeared, to two Conservative candidates—Rob Parker and Ron Atkey—who would be running in "Jewish" ridings in the forthcoming election.

In October, word came that Trudeau wanted to get six or eight Jewish leaders together for a heart-to-heart talk. He hosted a pleasant and informal dinner,* and afterward the exchange was more frank than usual. Trudeau told us what was on his mind and we reciprocated. Beyond that, however, no new elements came into the situation.

That was to occur weeks later when Israeli Prime Minister Menachem Begin paid his first state visit to Canada. He had been here often when he was a member of the opposition. A good speaker, he had the capacity of holding crowds spellbound by retelling his dreams. He was slated to visit Montreal and Ottawa and to wind up his tour with meetings in Toronto. It was a poor time for him to be away from home, for the peace talks with Egypt had stalled; the U.S. was putting great pressure on the Israeli government and their relationship had become so delicate that during Begin's week-long stay in Canada, Moshe Dayan came from Jerusalem to bring him up to date and obtain his instructions on certain problems.

Begin therefore had numerous worries during his visit which did not relate to Canada at all. Besides, his health was shaky. In May of that year, in Jerusalem, I had been struck by his vague responses to questions which ordinarily he would have handled in a crisp and forthright fashion. He had not looked well then and he looked worse now.

Some fifteen or twenty of us were present when he met with the leadership of the CIC. Begin delivered a monologue; there was no time for give-and-take.

There were two things, he said, which Canadian Jewry ought to be undertaking. First, we had to pay some attention to Soviet Jewry.

There was an embarrassed silence in the room. Ambassador Mordecai Shalev whispered the obvious in the Premier's ear: that if any Jewry in the world had given itself heart and soul to securing the release of Soviet Jews, it was the Canadian community. But Begin charged on undaunted.

---

* Present were Barney Danson, Charles Bronfman, Ray Wolfe, Milton Harris and David Satok (both officers of Congress), and Sol Kanee (a former president).

If we had been doing something already, good, good. But there was another issue. We must see that our government finally moved its embassy from Tel Aviv to Jerusalem.*

The very mention of Jerusalem was also sure to strike a warm chord in Jewish (and not only Jewish) hearts. Jews have always considered Jerusalem as their spiritual centre and, since 1948, as Israel's rightful capital. The unwillingness of most nations to recognize it as such was seen as a symbolic rejection of Israel's legitimacy. Moving the embassy would, so Israel believed, significantly strengthen it and therewith the peace process.

Begin had already mentioned the matter to Trudeau and had met with a negative response. He spoke of it again at a state dinner which Trudeau gave. Though the latter made a very warm speech stressing the friendship which bound the two countries together, he did not respond to the Jerusalem challenge.

In my invocation I kept the matter in low key. In the French portion of my prayer I quoted from the Bible: "Pray for the peace of Jerusalem. May peace dwell within your walls, tranquillity within your palaces. For my brethren's and companions' sake I will now say: Make peace dwell in your midst."

Although I (along with all other Jewish leaders) believed that moving the embassy was morally right and beneficial to the peace process, I purposefully soft-pedalled the matter, for I found Begin's request impractical at that time. I was afraid that in so highly-charged an issue all caution would be forgotten, and Jerusalem—along with our own community—would become a political football in the election.**

Congress leadership agreed with me on this matter and instructed its delegates to the CIC to keep the issue in low gear. Joe Clark, leader of the Opposition, who had a good chance of becoming the next Prime Minister, was on his first tour to Israel. He and his wife were greatly impressed with the country; still, he told the Israelis that he himself saw no chance of moving the embassy in the immediate future, even if he was elected.

Meanwhile, the debates at the CIC became increasingly rancorous and even personal. B'nai B'rith and the Canadian Zionist

---

* Fifteen nations then had their embassies in Jerusalem, amongst them the Netherlands and South and Central American countries. The rest, including Canada and the U.S., had their embassies in Tel Aviv and its environs because, in their view, the status of Jerusalem was not yet settled.

** Howard Adelman, in the most extensive study of the embassy issue so far (*Middle East Focus*, March 1980), appears to imply that I wanted to fan the fires at this point. The opposite is true.

Federation were arrayed on the "Begin" side and the Congress representatives on the other. The "Jerusalem activists" wanted to take advantage of the forthcoming election campaign to pin candidates down to the issue. They were willing to persuade Jewish voters in accordance with the answers which the candidates gave.

The discussions became so bitter and the accusations of "disloyalty to Jerusalem Eternal" so vehement that the CIC was in danger of breaking up. Rumours of our disagreement began to leak to the public, who were wondering what the noise was all about. In hindsight, some of our people now maintain that we should have explained the truth as we saw it: that it was highly divisive to introduce the Jerusalem issue as a major election test.

In the end we struck a compromise which proved to be no compromise at all. Congress approved a "low-key campaign of information", it being understood that the three political parties would not be asked to declare themselves on the question.

There are two interpretations of the events which now ensued. One is that someone convinced Joe Clark that Rob Parker and Ron Atkey could win their ridings if he came out with a strong endorsement of moving the embassy, and that Clark believed he could do so because the peace process between Israel and Egypt, which had earlier broken down, had now been taken up again. Another view is that Clark and his policy-makers honestly believed that the move was historically and morally right and that his promise was thus unrelated to any real or imagined Jewish pressure.

At any rate, Clark made an unsolicited statement at a meeting with CIC leaders. I was not present, but it would have made no difference: the fat was in the fire.

I was convinced that were Joe Clark to become Prime Minister he could not possibly make good on this promise; it was fraught with so many difficulties and would rouse such violent objections that he would have to back down on it sooner or later.

The elections were held in the spring. Atkey won his riding while Parker lost his, despite the general Conservative sweep in Metro Toronto. It is my firm conviction that Atkey attracted few votes because of Joe Clark's Jerusalem promise.

The rest is public knowledge. Clark was victorious and became Prime Minister. Immediately he announced that one of the first promises he would keep was to move the embassy from Tel Aviv. The reaction was overwhelming: Arab ambassadors besieged

Ottawa; Arab countries threatened to cut off trade relations; contracts were said to be cancelled; and some businessmen reported that they found their Arab contacts suddenly unavailable. Representatives of the largest industrial and banking firms in the country descended on Joe Clark, urging him to take back his promise.

The issue hit the headlines in a big way. Editorials condemned Clark as inept, though a few (like the *Globe and Mail*) suggested that, now that the decision had been made, Canada should not give in to Arab blackmail. Finally Clark beat a retreat and appointed former Progressive Conservative leader Robert Stanfield as a special emissary to the Middle East—obviously to take the heat off the issue and allow him to change his mind gracefully.

The unhappy result of the controversy was that the Jewish community was deeply split. There were a few who felt that Clark should be held to his promise, but the majority reasoned that Clark should be let off the hook as quickly and painlessly as possible. He had made a mistake in not foreseeing what his promise would involve; it was now necessary that he disengage himself and the sooner he could do it the better. Meanwhile, the newspapers had isolated the issue as a purely Jewish one. While it had been, in the beginning, Canada's integrity and sovereignty were now at stake. But Jews were said to be threatening Canadian business with financial losses and thereby increasing unemployment in the country. What was said behind closed doors was even worse. Two prominent Jewish businessmen told me that they had attended a function of top industrial and banking leaders and that, when they entered the room, it had suddenly fallen silent. They had had an eerie feeling of being strangers in a strange land.

The loss for Canada was large: its credibility was impaired and its traditional role as a neutral intermediary had suffered grievously. The Jewish community had been injured and anti-semitism had once more become acceptable, even fashionable, in certain circles.

The battle for Jerusalem in 1948 was won by the Jews. The battle in 1979 was lost by us in Canada. For a Zionist like me the matter was painful, to say the least. I saw no point in embarrassing the government further and holding up to its face the fact that the Jewish community felt betrayed. In fact, when Stanfield's interim report was published, and the Prime Minister postponed the issue indefinitely, many Jews were not only not surprised but relieved as well—not because they had less love for Jerusalem but because they saw it becoming a Canadian campaign football and recognized the disastrous consequences for their small community.*

Shortly thereafter Trudeau was quoted in an interview as making some remarks that were highly critical of the Jewish community. He was said to believe that Jews were best advised to go easy on political matters lest they arouse feelings of antisemitism. We contacted his office to ascertain whether the remarks were really his and to give him a chance to amend or correct the report. Did he really mean that Jews should not avail themselves of the democratic process like everyone else, lest they arouse antisemitism? However, Trudeau's office remained silent. We had little choice; our pride and dignity demanded that we make some response. The question was: with the Conservative government now arrayed against us and the New Democratic Party's leader too having come out strongly against our point of view, how far could we go in our reply to Trudeau without being left totally alone?

We put together our response. A few days later in the House Trudeau distanced himself from the interview and said that he had been quoted out of context; privately, he expressed his disappointment with the Jewish community's distrust of his motives. The matter brought home once again the fragility of the Jewish position in the Diaspora—even in a country where Jews had felt so secure. The battle for Jerusalem was—and perhaps it always is—a paradigm of our existence.

---

* But the final Stanfield report, issued at the very end of the Conservative incumbency, continued to exert a baleful effect. It embraced various points of view favoured by the Arabs.

Chapter 10

# OUR QUARREL WITH
# THE UNITED CHURCH

FEW ISSUES PROVIDED ME WITH
more cause for both agony and resolve than did the community's
quarrel with the United Church of Canada.

Jews generally make the same mistake about Christian
religions that the Christians make about us: we believe that the
other side is monolithic and of one mind, at least on certain
matters. Of all the churches in Canada this is doubtless the least
true for the United Church. It began as an amalgam of several
denominations and from time to time has sought a further merger
with the Anglican Church. In its membership and clergy it ranges
from what may be considered the left (which accepts the results
of biblical criticism and lays much emphasis on the pursuit of
social justice) to the right (which remains fundamentalist, highly
traditional and staunchly middle-class in its outlook). It was the
liberal element of the church which provided the first meaningful dialogue between Christians and Jews in Toronto, back in
the 1920s, when Ferdinand Isserman and Maurice N. Eisendrath, rabbis of Holy Blossom Temple, engaged in pulpit ex-
changes and other expressions of mutual religious recognition
which were then a novelty. When I arrived in Canada in 1961 the
relationship of the United Church with the Jewish community
was perhaps as good as any that could be found.

In order to understand the deteriorated relationship and even
open animosity which ensued in the late sixties and early seventies, it is important to note that during those years the Jewish
community began to identify itself with the state of Israel and its
fate to an extraordinary degree. Travellers from abroad, in

278

cluding Israeli diplomats, have averred that, perhaps with the exception of South Africa, there was no Diaspora community more fervently committed to Israel than the Jews of Canada. This is not the place to enter into an elaborate examination of why this should have been so, but the fact was unassailable: we were a mix of oldtimers and newcomers, with a heavy sprinkling of Holocaust survivors, who saw Israel as the emotional centre of Jewish existence. This was especially true for those who had abandoned Judaism as a religious discipline and whose national identity had filled the spiritual vacuum left by the disappearance of faith. (This should not be misinterpreted: those to whom the synagogue was important were as deeply committed to Israel and its survival as any others, but the commitment was more frequently integrated into a theological framework and therefore had another dimension.) Canadian Jews were ready to defend Israel against any and all attackers—and indeed a remarkable number of people volunteered for service with the Israeli forces in the various wars, either as soldiers or as support personnel. In addition, Canadian Jews gave liberally to Israeli causes and their liberality achieved worldwide fame. It was a true reflection of a deep and unremitting love.

But love is, as the proverb says, blind. Our beloved had no faults and was altogether beautiful. In the early and middle sixties Canadian Jews were emotionally unprepared to let anyone cast shadows of doubt across the glow of Zion restored.

The first to do this was a Jew, and a prominent one at that. He was Rabbi Reuben Slonim, a former rabbi of Beth Tzedec congregation. He had become an associate editor of the Toronto Telegram which, until its demise in 1971, was staunchly conservative in political outlook and pro-Israel in its editorial policies. In 1961 Slonim had contributed a moving series on the Eichmann trial in Jerusalem; he was the paper's "Israeli and Jewish expert" and wrote extremely well. His readership was wide, his popularity deservedly large. He had a daughter living in Israel, whom he visited frequently. His credentials were impeccable.

Suddenly, at Passover time, 1963, he published a series of articles which the Telegram featured and which were highly critical of certain internal policies of Israel: the authoritarian reign of the Orthodox establishment, the treatment of Arab citizens in its midst, and other social matters.

The Jewish community reacted as if it had had an electric shock. It is fair to say that we over-reacted—and I include myself in this judgement. I delivered a Friday-night lecture which I titled "The Telegram and the Truth." Before a standing-room-only congregation, I was bitterly critical.

Now, many years later, it has become clear that much of what Slonim wrote was quite true; in today's changed climate the substance of his reportage would hardly cause a stir. But it did then, and despite my overstated lecture title, truth was only part of the issue. What we reacted to was the author's tone. The Jewish community was totally unready to hear so unabashed a critique from one of its own leaders. It was, if I may draw a not quite fitting analogy, like the use of certain words before a Victorian theatre audience. The hearers would have been speechless with shock; today the same words would hardly cause a ripple.

The result was unfortunate in many ways. It exiled one of our ablest people to the periphery of the community—our organizations began to shun him and the book which he later wrote (*Both Sides Now*), which in many ways was an intelligent, restrained and basically loving critique of Israel, found few readers amongst our people. Another sad consequence was that for a while the controversy made Slonim so bitter that everything he wrote had a sour taste, and often contained stinging attacks on the Jewish leadership who appeared to him to be overfed, narrow-minded and power-hungry (my terms, not his). On one occasion he illustrated his point by quoting the precise salaries of Stuart Rosenberg and myself—salaries which, in comparison with what Christian ministers were getting at the time, must have appeared astronomical. The matter caused me some embarrassment, especially when I visited Israel, for the newspapers there promptly reprinted Slonim's comments in this respect and I became the object of numerous barbs. However, though Slonim and I had no communication for some years, I never attacked him personally again, and I, for one, would like to think that the matter now belongs to the past.

I have written about this in some detail because it throws some light on the highly charged feelings of our community and thereby forms part of the background of our quarrel with the United Church. At the head of it stood a man of considerable substance with whom I had frequent and close relations until the controversy erupted.

Dr. A. C. Forrest was the editor of the *United Church Observer* which was (and is) a *de facto* publication of the church, even though technically speaking it is an independent magazine. It is an organ of and for the church, which provides a Board responsible for its publication. Beyond that, however, the editor is free to determine its policy, and Forrest did so with intelligence, a fine touch and a capacity for readable journalism. He once claimed that the *Observer* was one of the few church magazines that managed to stay in the black, with no subsidies. At the time of our falling out the magazine reached about 300,000 homes across Canada and was undoubtedly an important shaper of public opinion.

Forrest was a man of charm and social vision. His concern for the underprivileged in Canada was deep and genuine and he had a vision of ecumenism which went beyond the normal Christian view. He thought that all religious faiths ought to speak to each other with frankness and mutual respect. He broached the idea to me that we should found a magazine devoted to just such an exchange of views. The United Church would publish and fund the enterprise if I would be willing to serve as chairman of the editorial board. I readily agreed, and in 1967 a magazine called *Ferment* made its appearance. We attracted a true cross-section of organized religious life in the country—from the revivalists, fundamentalists, and main-line Protestants to Roman Catholics, and all the way across the board to Buddhists. Our editorial meetings took place in Forrest's office. Unfortunately, before the magazine could fully establish itself we had to discontinue its publication, because the church was no longer able to fund it— and independent funding soon became out of the question, in part because of the events which followed.

The 1967 Six-Day War was the watershed. Forrest had written approvingly about Israel in the past, but that summer he became highly critical of it. At first his criticism was muted and did not attract much attention. However, Ernest Marshall Howse, a former Moderator of the Church, was far more outspoken and revealed an undercurrent that worried me deeply. It was in *Ferment*, of all places, that in the fall of '67, Howse published an article on the subject, "Who Should Control Jerusalem?" That Christians were ambivalent about Jewish control (when they had not been at all ambivalent about Arab control in the past) was no revelation to me; it merely showed that many Christians still had not made peace with a Jewish people who had moved from the shadows of history into the sunlight and tasted the fruits of victory. But I objected vigorously to another dimension of Howse's argument, and I wrote:

> I have neither understanding nor respect for an argument which hits below the belt. It was bad enough for Dr. Howse to say the Jewish "next year Jerusalem" was insincere. This merely shows that Dr. Howse does not know Jewish sentiment nor the implications of this hallowed phrase and the long centuries of exile. When he goes on to imply that for Israel a major enticement of Jerusalem is its high economic revenue, he descends to the level of old-time Jew baiting which identifies Mammon as a Jewish God and money as an all-consuming goal of our people. I am saddened that a former Moderator of the United Church should believe this and shocked that he would consent to give it currency in print.

The controversy heated up. Forrest now emerged as Israel's chief critic—and considering Toronto's long history of anti-semitism, the suspicion grew that there was more to his criticism than the anti-Zionism which he began to profess. On December 15, 1968, the *Observer* gave its pre-Christmas issue over to eliciting sympathy for Arab refugees. Forrest's reportage was as moving as it was one-sided in pointing the finger at Israel as the sole party responsible for the refugees' plight. Not a word was said about Arabs heartlessly refusing to integrate their own brethren into their economies. Not a word was said about keeping them as pawns in a political power game. There was, so Forrest led his readers to believe, something fundamentally wrong not only with Israel but also with the Jewish character—and this is what hit home. It revived memories of years gone by.

After describing the pitiful condition of the Arabs he had visited, Forrest went on to tell us:

> I made my way from that crowded Bethlehem home up to Jerusalem where I met a man in the King David Hotel. We had dinner and ate, I suppose, about a half a kilo of steak between us.
>
> And he told me that this was a great country and that he was in the hotel business and intended to interest some people back in L.A. in building a string of hotels along the Israeli coast so he can get those "fat friends of ours who go down to Florida and sit on their fannies for six months every year to come here and spend some money and build up the country."

Then he remembered his wife who was up in the hotel room resting after an afternoon's shopping, "We were out buying jewelry for three hours," he said.

The implication of the contrast between the poor, persecuted, pitiful Arab children and the rich Jews in Florida was too obvious to be missed. Forrest had ceased to be a critic and had, in the eyes of our community, become an enemy. He appeared frequently on radio and TV and was very good at it. I remember only one time when he was taken off guard. He was debating with Dr. Franklin Littell, Professor of Religion in Philadelphia's Temple University and president of Christians Concerned for Israel. Littell asked him, "You put out a special issue on Arab refugees?"

*Forrest:* Our compassion arises because the Christian churches for whose publications I was writing asked me to make that survey—they are concerned with humanity generally.
*Littell:* And what was the date of the special issue you did on Jewish refugees?
*Forrest:* I have never done a number on the Jewish refugees.
*Littell:* Really?

But Forrest's defeats were relatively few and his victories many. He became the darling of the church circuit. American syndicated publications took him up and he spent considerable time in the Mid-East, headquartering himself in Beirut. Even Slonim (in his book *Family Quarrel* which dealt with the controversy between the United Church and the Jews) was forced to comment: "From 1967 to 1969 the *United Church Observer* lost its sense of proportion on the Middle East. In the eight years since 1969 . . . the perspective has not yet been recaptured."*

Matters escalated further in 1969, though the Jewish community leaders had agreed as a general policy that, if possible, the controversy was not to be exacerbated. Public debate should not be encouraged; we would respond when necessary but would

---

* Slonim's book is an extensive treatment of the subject to which this chapter is devoted. It has some severe lacunae: he does not describe the encounter of Dr. McClure with the Jewish community (see below, p. 284) or Bruce McLeod's appearance at Holy Blossom or my own at the Moderator's church (see below, p. 291). Most important, in 1977 when Slonim's book was published, the quarrel had subsided. Yet he wrote as if it continued as a live issue.

not ourselves give an opening to Forrest and his friends.*

Through some organizational slip-up the Toronto Zionist Council went counter to this policy, and its well-meaning president, Manny Rotman, issued an invitation to Dr. Robert McClure, then Moderator of the United Church, to give a public address at the Toronto Zionist Centre. McClure was the first layman to be elected Moderator. He had been born in China, had spent years as a doctor in the Mid-East, and was known as a fine humanitarian. His appointment to the moderatorship was widely hailed. What we did not know was that he was politically very naive, and he was not discerning enough to abandon the baggage of certain stereotypical Christian views of Jews. The meeting attracted enormous attention from the media as well as from the Jewish community and there was every indication that it would be a memorable evening. I was asked to chair the gathering and prevent it from getting out of hand; I could only hope that our own people would not be so emotionally aroused that they forgot the ordinary courtesies due to a guest.

Ten years after the event, McClure told his biographer that on that evening he was afraid for his life. His memory betrayed him badly. I had dinner with him before the meeting, I was next to him throughout the affair, and my own recollections—put into print within a week or two of the meeting—were these:

> The meeting was attended by some four to five hundred people with many standing along the walls throughout the two hours. Expectations were high, emotions were charged.
>
> Contrary to what bold headlines may have led you to believe, it was a good meeting. While there were some groans and sighs from the audience and even a heated objection was thrown up occasionally, there was no booing, in any sense of that word, as two of the papers reported. Quite the contrary, the audience was polite; on a few occasions it hushed would-be interrupters, and if there were as little private conversation at religious services as there was at the meeting with Dr. McClure, I would be very happy indeed. It is too bad that certain of the media can see the news value of a gathering such as this only in terms of tension, conflict and cat-calling, but not in that

---

* Also that year Forrest published *The Unholy Land* in which his views were set forth. The book had very modest sales and eventually Coles Bookstores took it off the shelves. This gave Forrest the opportunity to accuse Coles (owned by Jews) of instigating a boycott against him, something promptly denied by the owners, who claimed that they always removed books that were not selling. But Forrest now recouped some of his losses; the controversy spurred sales and his volume had a brief popularity.

larger view in which it deserves to be evaluated.

That larger view, to state it simply, was that Dr. McClure's meeting with the Jewish community (in the presence of a good many Christian clergy and laity) was the beginning of a new kind of dialogue. [I was wrong there, that time had not yet come.] Some people, of course, feel very uncomfortable about the public being present at frank interchanges. I do not belong to them. On the contrary, I want to hear and I want others to hear what men like Dr. McClure think—and I am grateful to him that he accepted the invitation in the spirit in which it was extended, and did not in any wise hesitate to be forthright in his expression.

To be sure, most of his audience (myself included) found what he said to be highly unpalatable. He stated, for instance, that in his opinion the *United Church Observer* presented the Middle East picture fairly. I need hardly tell you that I thoroughly disagree with his astonishing view, but it was important for us to hear that a man like Dr. McClure honestly believes in the objectivity of Dr. A. C. Forrest's writing. . . .

It was also highly disturbing to learn that in Dr. McClure's view there are 'Canadian gentiles' on the one hand and 'Canadian Jews' on the other whose relationship is, as he said, protected only by a thin veneer of courtesy and understanding. He felt that Jews viewed Israel in a light quite un-understandable to Christians and I think he was rather taken aback to hear a Christian minister (Roland de Corneille*) oppose him on this score. . . . I know that he came away from the meeting encouraged that he had contributed to mutual understanding. We may not have convinced him nor did he manage to convince his audience, but the meeting was fruitful, good, courteous and altogether worthwhile. We thank him for coming.**

McClure was left with a different impression. He thought that, though motivated by goodwill, he had contributed to greater misunderstanding rather than greater understanding. He was wrong. The subsequent increase in hostility he referred to grew out of later events. For instance, in 1970, after he had made a

---

* His rejoinder to Dr. McClure was movingly expressed. De Corneille later became a chief proponent of Christian-Jewish dialogue and director of the B'nai-B'rith-sponsored League for Human Rights, and thereafter a (Liberal) Member of Parliament.

** *Holy Blossom Temple Bulletin*, January 27, 1969; reprinted in *Page Two* (Toronto, 1971), p. 103.

tour of the Middle East, he said in a talk in Montreal, "The Jew in
North America wants action in the Mid-East so he can collect
money for Israel Bond drives. . . ."

In response I wrote:

Translated into everyday and understandable English, Dr. Mc-
Clure says that we here want Jews and Arabs to be at war so
that we can go out and raise money (from our own pockets,
mind you) for Israel. What a contorted view of reality! It ac-
cords with a new line of thinking currently heard in Arab
circles that the real culprits of the Nazi era were the Zionists
who conspired with Hitler (and urged him on) in his drive to ex-
terminate Jews. . . . Now the matter has been transposed into
our environment; we are said to fan the wars so that the bond
organization can stay in business.

I've always thought of Dr. McClure as a reasonable man,
even though I have disagreed vigorously with him on his view
of Jewish and Israeli realities; but now, to put it inelegantly, he
serves us a piece of baloney shot through with ptomaine
poisoning. I wonder from where he got it!

At the end of 1969 a group of Jewish leaders, alarmed by the
quickly deteriorating relationship between the Church and the
Jewish community, had gone to meet with lay and executive
heads of the United Church. Nothing demonstrates the depths of
Jewish feeling at that time more clearly than that this delegation
(of which I was not part because I was out of the city) was considered a "Judenrat"*—collaborators with the enemy. I defended the group and called the comparison outrageous.**

I believe there is not only room but great need for speaking
calmly yet forcefully with leaders of the United Church and
with other Christian churches on the matter of Israel and the
Jewish community. . . . There is a time to shout and there is a
time to speak. Let us be sure what the time is.†

The visit accomplished nothing at the time. Forrest was on a
one-way mission and no one would deter him. The more we
argued with him, the more determined he became, and in time he

---

  * The name given to the heads of Jewish communities in Europe during the Nazi era. The
    term became derogatory, implying co-operation with the Nazis.
 ** Rabbi Rosenberg and John A. Geller, a prominent Congress leader, were part of the
    delegation.
  † Holy Blossom Temple Bulletin, October 1, 1969; reprinted in Page Two, p. 117.

developed symptoms of a "martyr's complex". He was no longer satisfied to espouse the Arab cause and denigrate "the Zionists" (a term he soon applied to all Jews), but portrayed himself as a man who suffered greatly for his faith and was being crucified for it.

While the dispute had become part of the public domain, it was assuming a highly personal dimension as well. I was unhappy that a clash between two different groups had become focused on two men, as if we were gladiators in an arena fighting on behalf of our constituencies. W. Clarke MacDonald described the situation as the "Plaut-Forrest syndrome" and added that, while we ourselves might accept each other as individuals, "they are symbolic to many people in both the Jewish and United Church communities of two antithetical elements. I doubt if in some minds in the Jewish community anything which Forrest may say is acceptable, as is also true within the United Church community in some places with regard to things which are said by Plaut."

Forrest's sweeping indictments now included the growing number of Christians who found that his speeches and articles exposed some embarrassing layers of deep-seated gentile attitudes towards Jews. In early 1970 he wrote that he could not "respect the arguments being produced by the so-called Christian/Jewish Dialogue people," and thereby implied that those engaged in dialogue were, ipso facto, suspect. I responded:

If one takes Dr. Forrest's argument for what it is, the only way to deal with Jews is to fight them either with a gun or with a pen. Christians are trustworthy only if they oppose Jews. Once they speak peaceably with them their argument, however worthy, is suspected and dismissed.

Forrest now struck an even more anti-Jewish tone, which made it necessary to deal harshly with him. He began to oppose Russian-Jewish emigration because it would strengthen Israel. Another representative of the church, Rev. Donald V. Sterling, contributed some offensive remarks.* Forrest's support came from various quarters including the student press which

---

* Sterling was then chairman of the Committee on Church and International Affairs of the Toronto Conference of the United Church. In a letter to the editor of the Globe and Mail (April 7, 1971) he wrote about an article I had published in the paper: "If the Jewish agency is going to advertise under Gunther Plaut's by-line, the material should bear the word advertisement and your advertising department should charge the head office in Tel Aviv."

headlined (in the *Chevron\**) a highly sympathetic assessment of
Forrest: "Editor Fights Pro-Jewish Liberal Canada." It described
Forrest as a humanitarian journalist cynical about a pro-Jewish
Western press. Israel was now held up as "racist"—
foreshadowing the iniquitous UN resolution of later years. The
final straw was an editorial in the November 1971 issue of the
*Observer*. Forrest had been at a meeting of church editors in
Philadelphia and had criticized one speaker for saying that "no
one did anything" about the Holocaust. Forrest then went on to
write: "We hear this slander repeatedly, especially from Christian Zionists who emphasize that the church did so badly by the
Jewish people in times past it must now throw all its support
behind Israel. . . . Just for the record it should be remembered
that in order to stop Hitler a good many hundreds of thousands of
Western soldiers, sailors and airmen died."

The implication was clear: the war against Hitler had been
fought in order to save the Jews. All the dead of that war could be
laid at the Jewish doorstep. The West owed nothing to us; we
owed everything to them, for coming so magnanimously to our
defence.

Rev. Donald Keating, an ordained United Church clergyman
and then a community worker in Toronto, wrote: "Is Forrest not
lighting candles that stoke the fires that turned to smoke and
ashes the bodies of six million Jews in the Holocaust? . . . what
does it say of the United Church when a man can write such
editorials and still be employed by the *Observer*?"

Keating thereupon resigned his membership in the United
Church, in protest against the anti-Israel stance not only of Forrest and the *Observer* but of the Church itself, which by its
silence condoned and supported Forrest's position.

"I find myself aghast at the United Church's inability to feel
for Jews," he wrote. "The United Church doesn't care about
Jews."

At the beginning of 1972 the war of words hit its full stride.
There was no retreat and no prospect of reconciliation for the
time being. Yet, though I found myself time and again in conflict
with Forrest and fought him publicly, I also knew that he himself
was not the simple antisemite that so many said he was. He was
a liberal who identified the Arab cause with universalism—an ir-

---

\* Published at the University of Waterloo.

rational approach which made him impervious to reason. The activist and vocal consul-general of Israel, Aba Gefen,* always hoped that he might "convert" Forrest and met with him from time to time. In vain—Forrest had closed his mind on the subject.

Keating's resignation proved to be a brief spark only; he was not "important" enough, so it appeared, to make the Church reconsider. But others were. Professor Emil Fackenheim, a German-born rabbi whose writings on philosophy, theology and the Holocaust and its implications for contemporary living had made him internationally famous, was chosen by St. Andrews College, a United Church institution in Saskatoon, to receive an honorary doctorate. Obviously the award to Fackenheim, a highly vocal and effective defender of the Jewish cause, had political implications which could not be overlooked. Clearly, Forrest did not speak for the whole Church.

Amongst the Jews there was some disagreement. Should Fackenheim accept the degree? He counselled with me and I strongly urged him to go to Saskatoon, accept and make the kind of strong statement of which he was eminently capable. He did this and did it splendidly. The *Globe and Mail* reprinted a substantial part of his address on its op-ed page. Fackenheim exposed the deeper levels of the conflict: the long history of anti-Jewish theologizing and practice carried on by the Christian Church and now, under different guise, revived. He made a deep impression. So did Archbishop George Appleton, Anglican Primate of Jerusalem, who visited Canada at that time and managed to bring some measure of balance to this false image of Israel which threatened to become an established "Christian" view.

The worst point of the dispute was reached when the *Observer* published its March 1972 issue. Forrest reprinted an article by John Nicholls Booth, a Canadian by background and minister of a Unitarian congregation in Gainesville, Florida. Originally published in the *American Mercury*, the article accused Zionists of manipulating the news and singled out B'nai B'rith as a Zionist apparatus which had penetrated deeply into the American government, the communications media and educational institutions. The *Observer* reprinted the article under the headline "How Zionists Manipulate Your News." The Canadian B'nai

---

* Later ambassador of Israel to Roumania.

B'rith forthwith called Forrest an antisemite and sued him, and in turn Forrest sued B'nai B'rith for having called him an antisemite.*

The two sides now lined up for battle. Some of the United Church's Regional Councils came out squarely for Forrest, but a few vocal members of Christian churches stood with us.**

In a signed editorial in the *Canadian Jewish News*, I urged the Church to disavow the Booth article at its forthcoming national meeting and to do something about the *Observer*:

> ... all too frequently anti-Zionism (as distinguished from ordinary criticism of Israel's policies) has become the cover for antisemitism, and the *Observer's* tendency to depict Zionism as an historical evil has strengthened the heritage of latent and overt antisemitism in many readers. Surely, given the bitter facts of history, any material which evokes such sentiments ought to be firmly out of bounds in a Christian publication.

But rather than follow the path of reconciliation, the twenty-fifth General Council of the United Church, meeting in Saskatoon in the summer of '72, came down heavily on the side of Forrest and when he appeared in the assembly gave him a standing ovation. It also resolved to initiate an official visit to the Prime Minister (with the help of other denominations, if possible) and plead with him not to extend any further loans to Israel. Despite all disavowals, it was apparent that Forrest did at that point represent the Church.

But the Church itself was changing. It had elected a new Moderator, Bruce McLeod, son of a prominent family and the youngest man ever to be elevated to this distinguished post. At the Saskatoon meeting he was found at the side of those who supported Forrest, a fact which earned him the deep suspicion of many Jews. However, he soon stated—repeatedly—that he

---

* Eventually, a year later, the *Observer* printed an apology and in May 1973 the United Church and B'nai B'rith issued a joint statement on the need for resuming dialogue and settling past controversies. But this agreement was, in the heat of 1972, very much in the future.

** Prominent amongst them were three Toronto academicians, David Demson, Alan Davies, and especially Gregory Baum who in April delivered a trenchant sermon on the subject. Mrs. R. G. Nicholls of Lucknow, Ontario, wife of a United Church minister, became a thorn in the side of the church establishment and there were other voices of moderation within the church: Rev. John Short of Toronto, Gordon Ross of North Bay, and Prof. Martin Rumscheidt of the University of Windsor. Rev. Kenneth Bagnell, once a co-worker with Forrest on the *Observer*, distanced himself from his former mentor and counselled a more balanced view.

wanted reconciliation with the Jewish community. Also, the church had a new Secretary of the General Council, Dr. George M. Morrison, a former senior IBM executive and a warm, gentle, outgoing person whose experience and compassion made it impossible for him to endorse the policy on which the Church and the *Observer* had embarked.

George and I quickly became friends and we discussed how the rift might be healed. McLeod was willing to help and so was a former Moderator of the Church, Dr. Angus McQueen, in whose pulpit I had preached and who had since become chairman of the Editorial Advisory Committee of the *Observer*. With this triad in the lead things began to change. Through Morrison, an invitation was issued to Alan Rose of the Canadian Jewish Congress to spend a day at a retreat of the leaders of the Church. This was a step in the right direction and Alan performed splendidly.

It was high time. The kooks were coming out of the woodwork. I received regular threats over the telephone and by anonymous letters; my mail was now carefully scrutinized for letter bombs and on several occasions the police bomb squad was called in to analyse a parcel; we had plainclothes police at the temple, especially on the Holy Days.

Then, at the Olympic games in Munich, eleven Israeli athletes were murdered. A pall fell over our community. Even our opponents recognized that there was no way of telling what consequences a vigorous anti-Zionism might have, and that the quarrel in Canada had gone too far. McLeod was quoted by the *Toronto Star** as saying, "Our hands must reach out instinctively to Jewish brothers . . . as we with them condemn the strategy of terror that threatens them still, and somehow communicate our oneness with them whom in this land and in this city we have so often hurt."

I invited McLeod to come to my temple and speak his mind. He did so before some of our leaders, the first time the dialogue had been taken up with any hope of success. Subsequently McLeod returned the invitation and asked me to preach in his pulpit, the much-respected Bloor Street United Church, in November.

My appearance at the church was marked by a good deal of hoopla and an abundance of media attention. While I knew that the police would be in attendance, I took no chances; I called on my friends of the N-3 to supply me with the bodyguards who had

* September 11, 1972.

become a regular feature of my public lectures (when I came home from a meeting they would even go into my house to check it over, before letting me enter). So on a bright Sunday morning several carloads of men, some of them quite beefy, accompanied me to the church. When I arrived in McLeod's office he had a worried look on his face.

"I see some awfully strange-looking men out there," he said.

I assured him that this at least was no cause for concern. But my wife too was nervous. Several rows behind her a man sat fingering a little box, and throughout the service she was deeply worried what he might do. In fact he too was one of ours, and was carrying a two-way radio.

The church was packed, but I could pick out the police officers in the balcony and on the ground floor. I preached my sermon sitting down, as was my habit, although this deprived me of the protective cover of the pulpit. I was frank without being harsh. I summed up all the arguments I could muster to show that a good deal of what the *Observer* wrote, and others condoned by their silence, reflected the traditionally inimical attitude of the Christian Church. I asked: do Christians, in their hearts of hearts, still desire the destruction of the Jews? Is this why they cannot make peace with us or acknowledge Jerusalem as our capital? I spoke for about half an hour, long enough to feel exhausted. I spoke with a good deal of passion, sharing with them my sorrow and anxiety. When I was finished, the congregation rose as one and broke into prolonged applause.*

I was deeply moved and knew right then that we had turned the corner. McLeod told me afterwards that he could hardly believe his eyes when he saw the congregation jump to their feet—it had never happened before at a worship service.

A few days later he wrote me: "Just a line to thank you personally for giving of yourself to us. ... We all appreciated your special combination of graciousness and frankness—and the applause reflected that. I have received many letters from both Jews and Christians who would like to meet informally. I hope that begins to happen ... for in human encounter, insensitivity and prejudice will be warmed into mutual listening and respect in a way that 'arm's length' letter-writing and resolution-making can never match."

Soon thereafter Forrest's articles on Israel began to taper off

---

* An excerpt of the address will be found in Appendix 7.

both in frequency and in tone. I know that leading clergymen like George Morrison and Angus McQueen had made it clear to him that there needed to be some change in direction, that Forrest's policies had become a burden to the Church. The Jewish community in turn imposed a rigorous discipline on itself in public speeches and in writings. The name Forrest disappeared from our discussions and the United Church was simply not mentioned. In this way we managed to create an environment in which a new dialogue could begin. Roland de Corneille and Peter Gilbert were guiding special interfaith groups that involved a variety of church and synagogue members, and though this particular effort never reached wide proportions it became symptomatic of a new trend. A group of church leaders in Toronto also met at regular intervals.*

There were occasional flare-ups. In 1974 I gave a progress report on interfaith relations to the triennial convention of the Canadian Jewish Congress. I was quoted (falsely) as having said that we had managed to "stifle" Forrest. This brought about another flurry of anger, but it was short-lived.

However, the genie of antisemitism had been loosed and would do its work for a while longer, even though it was not connected to our relations with the United Church. We had the police out in force once more on a Friday evening in 1975. Just before I left the house, the synagogue received a call that I would be killed that night. I phoned my associate, Rabbi Stephen Franklin, and asked him to carry on with the service. I would come later. (It did not occur to me that I thereby placed him in a very uncomfortable position. Half jokingly he said after the service, "All the time I was standing in the pulpit I was wondering, how does the would-be killer know that I am not Rabbi Plaut?") I made arrangements with the police to dispatch some plainclothes-men to watch me during services, and then proceeded to the synagogue; I did not want anyone to keep me from my duties and from the service. All went well, and afterwards the police took me back and checked out the house. I was glad to be home. The threat, like all the others before, had been anonymous; we never found out who had made it.

In the course of time our quarrel was, if not totally resolved, then at least set aside. The leadership of our community still do not have the kind of warm contact with the United Church that

* This group was led by Professor William Dunphy and Reverend de Corneille.

they have with the Roman Catholics or the Anglicans, but friendliness and civility, both private and public, prevail. When Forrest died suddenly in 1978, his passing created no stir in the Jewish community. I regret that we were never able to resolve our personal differences. We once met on the street in Ottawa and I greeted him, but he countered, with a heavy coating of sarcasm, "I am surprised you still speak to me."

"So am I," I responded and that was the unhappy end of an unhappy relationship that had begun so promisingly a decade before.

I have often wondered what would have happened had we not opposed Forrest as vigorously as we did. Perhaps, had we refused to respond to him right from the beginning, the malady might have been contained. But then again, perhaps it was good that it was aired, for with it were aired many feelings that ran below the surface; it was a time for catharsis for all of us. Who can say whether silence would have been better? History goes its own way.

# Chapter 11

# JOURNEYS

## Israel: Agony and Ecstasy

A JEW JOURNEYS TO ISRAEL EVEN when he stays at home, wherever that may be. For if he has Jewish consciousness, if he is alive to the hopes and realities of his people, then a part of him is always in Israel. What happens there happens to him, what happens to him is also acted out on the stage of Jerusalem. But I have had the good fortune to travel there many times; writing of my visits could fill a whole book. So much of my life has been absorbed with concern for the land and its people that it is impossible to detach my Israel memories and compress them into a single chapter in these pages.*

Here then are but a few random observations, memories and highlights of days past.

### Crisis and Disappointment

It was May, 1967. The Gulf of Aqaba had been blocked; the armies of the Arab world were poised at Israel's border; the iron ring was closing. In every Jewish heart there arose the knowledge that "it" might happen again. They had read in the papers and heard on television that General Shukheiry, leader of the Palestine Liberation Army, was urging his people on to Tel Aviv. "When we get there," he was reported to have said in a radio address beamed to both Arabs and Jews, "we will slaughter not only the men but also the women and children as well. Not one shall be left alive when we finish this holy war. We

---

* For more details, see for instance *Israel Since the Six Day War: Selected Articles, Sermons and Diary Notes* (Toronto: Holy Blossom Temple, 1968).

shall have no mercy." Canadian and American newscasts reported similar threats—and went on to baseball scores and hockey trades.

But the crisis had triggered something in Jewish minds and hearts. Deep down we felt that here was a repetition of what had happened twenty-five years ago, when the world did not believe the threats of annihilation aimed at the Jewish people; when even at the height of the slaughter the Allies refused to bomb the railroad yards at Auschwitz; when all the pleas made to leaders of free nations were to no avail; when the world's disbelief and indifference left a graveyard of bones and ashes and monuments.

Now, looking back on the triumphs of the Israeli army, the fears seem unreal—but when the news of the war broke on June 5 people did not know what would happen. They only knew their fears and their vulnerability and their total involvement. I saw many tough men cry on that day.

Of course we were not alone. There were many individuals who immediately came to our aid, some with magnificent gifts, others with expressions of support and sympathy. But official Christian support was slow, couched in carefully phrased resolutions which started with "whereas" and finished by trying to offend no one and therefore said little.

On that day, with the guns screaming and the fate of the little nation hanging in the balance, I received a telephone call from a respected clergyman. He asked me about an obscure scriptural problem. My laconic and absent-minded reply startled him.

"What's the matter?" he said.

"I am sick," I responded.

"With the flu?"

"No," I said, "I am sick at heart."

There was a blank silence at the other end and then, finally, "I am sorry, I hope you will feel better soon." That was all.

Was he alone in his total lack of comprehension? Somehow I think he was not. That weekend I studied the announced sermon topics of 150 Metro churches. After three weeks of tension in the Middle East and one week of fighting, what were the clergy speaking about to their congregations? With one or two exceptions, the announced sermons were all on the usual topics. They had nothing to say about the war.

Yet the hostilities were not confined to the Middle East. Personal threats on me mounted; callers interrupted our sleep every night. Synagogues were defaced with paint. Someone threw a stone through one of the temple's stained glass windows; we replaced the gap with clear glass and affixed a plaque to remind us that while the stone was thrown at Israel, Israel was us.

There was a terrible feeling of aloneness in those days. Jews felt as if they were talking mostly to themselves, yet they needed their fellow citizens, they needed to talk with them. For peace is built not only in the Middle East but also in Canada and wherever else people of different backgrounds and beliefs live together.

## Hopes Dashed

Independence Day 1973 was to be the country's greatest celebration to date. Israel was still riding the crest of military success, or at least so it believed. A huge military parade was laid on in Jerusalem and self-confidence ruled the day. We were travelling with a temple group and had been in Haifa, so we boarded a bus at three a.m. to make it to Jerusalem in time for the parade. It was an impressive sight, and the picture books published in honour of the event still testify to its splendour. Long rows of young men and women smartly dressed and marching to match their outfits passed by, to the cheers of the multitudes who sat on tiered platforms.

We were caught up in the euphoria of the day, unaware that less than half a year later many of these marvellous young people would be dead. Israel has celebrated other Independence Days since then, but not with military parades to show its might.

In fact, there were many changes after 1973. Where confidence and inner security and even arrogance had ruled before, there was now doubt, self-flagellation and pessimism. It was as if the whole course of Jewish history had been reversed by the '73 war which, though it ended in victory, revealed deep weaknesses in Israel's social and military structure. If the army was not exempt from lassitude, misjudgement and corruption, who could be trusted? With social gaps ever widening, with inflation rising to unprecedented heights, a sense of disillusionment fell over the people. The integration of the Russian *aliyah* (immigration) became a mounting failure, which was reflected in an increasing unwillingness of Jews to settle in Israel.

The ascension of Menachem Begin to the premiership and the newly formed relationship with Egypt buoyed up the people for a while, but the positive spirit of '35, '48 and '67 is gone or has, like the Almighty Himself during the Holocaust, gone into hiding. The

Jewishness of Israel is itself in question. The idea that the "true" religion is the ultra-Orthodox version is an historic perversion, and the secularism of the overwhelming majority of Israelis has put the spiritual future of the land in doubt. Many young people have left the country, and this emigration—called in a judgemental fashion *yeridah*, descent*—has become a national worry.

To be sure, Israel is in most regards still better than other nations, and the fact that after three decades of siege it still maintains not only its democracy but also its sense of humour is a remarkable achievement. Also its intellectual institutions are second to none. But the internal rifts and tensions are mounting and, once the external pressures are eased, may reach a point of serious confrontation. There is no question that when that happens a *kulturkampf* of major proportions will break out—and perhaps it must. Israel will have to cleanse its soul; it cannot go on forever fighting the enemy without and shying away from its mounting problems within. What makes it even more difficult is that a Jew always expects more from Jews; and Diaspora Jews have a habit of expecting the best, if not the impossible, from Israel. After all, the land and its people incorporate our own unrealized dreams. I am now too old to settle there, but were I younger I would probably feel it my duty to throw in my lot with Israel's. Nothing less would do.

## The Battlefield

In November 1973 I participated in a special mission led by then UJA chairman Murray Koffler. We visited the battlefields of Sinai. The cease-fire had just been negotiated and the desert still showed scars of the struggle. Here and there the dead still lay unburied in the sand; one stumbled on them suddenly and looked away. It was *déjà vu* for me. I suddenly experienced the same detachment, the same coldness of heart that had become part of my protective armour at the battle-front in Europe a generation before. As I viewed a dead soldier it was as if my soul was drained from my body. I was an onlooker from far away, not a participant—my companions shuddered and cried, but I was unmoved, transported into another being. Was I fortunate to be able to distance myself in this fashion to prevent my feelings from coming to the fore? Perhaps. Or perhaps it also prevented me from experiencing once again the horror of war, from becom-

---

* In contrast to *aliyah* which means going up (to Israel).

ing a more passionate advocate of peace at all costs. I do not know.

We stood looking across the Suez Canel. There, not far away, at "Kilometre 101", was the tent where the cease-fire had been negotiated. Could anyone have guessed that from there Sadat would one day find his way to Jerusalem?

## The Death of Ben-Gurion

That month David Ben-Gurion, Israel's first Prime Minister, died. People had generally believed that he would go on living forever in his retreat at S'de Boker. While we were visiting, the state funeral was being planned. I was delegated to represent Canadian Jewry and was given a place of honour at the service in front of the Knesset.

We arrived early and stood in the area assigned to us, each of us wearing a mourner's badge. There were no seats, not even for President Ephraim Katzir or for Prime Minister Golda Meir—it was no occasion for personal comfort. At eleven o'clock the sirens wailed. For a brief time we stood in silence, then the service began: prayers, readings, the memorial chant. It had been a special request of Ben-Gurion's that there be no eulogy and his wish was observed—except that the impressive dimensions of the Knesset forecourt and its assembly, the whirring cameras, the nation watching on television, all spoke their tribute with eloquence enough.

It was a slow procession: ten men carrying his coffin on their shoulders, girls in uniform bearing wreaths, the family, the President, the Cabinet and the small cortège. I was amongst those privileged to follow to S'de Boker. We went in five helicopters, leaving directly from the Knesset. Lovely Jerusalem lay below us in all its age-old splendour, the Dome of the Rock sending its golden rays upwards. The wall of the Old City encased its treasures like a proud mother. A few more minutes and we were over the desert, its utter nakedness briefly interrupted by a few cities and settlements. How had this man dared to envision here the seeds of new life? Looking down from above, it seemed almost impossible.

S'de Boker is two places, a kibbutz and a college campus. The library dominates the latter, for Ben-Gurion was a man of books, an important author himself, a keen student of Greek and Eastern philosophy. Beside it, on the promontory which looks out over the awesome, stark, and yet strangely beautiful scenery of

the desert, he had buried his wife Paula. There he himself was
now carried. Soon the earth was filled in over his casket. A
wooden sign marked his name and the day of his death. A final
prayer, the army cantor's chant and it was over. A few months
earlier he had confided to a friend that he hoped to reach ninety.
It was not granted him, even as he never saw his nation enjoy
that peace of which the founding document had spoken with fervour.

On the way back I looked once more on the stretch of desert
which had played so large a role in his vision. Moshe Dayan stood
next to me peering out in pensive silence. He had been protégé
and friend of the old man, and his thoughts were not hard to
read.

## Nine Christians, One Jew

In May 1976 I organized a visit to Israel with a group of
clergymen. We were the guests of El Al airline and the Israeli
government for this one-week effort. Participants were Bishop
Lewis Garnsworthy (now Archbishop of Toronto); David Hay
(Moderator of the Presbyterian Church); George Morrison
(Minister of Timothy Eaton Memorial Church); James Hayes (R.C.
Archbishop of Halifax); Maurice Badoux (R.C. Bishop of St.
Boniface); Reginald Hollis (Bishop of the Anglican Church,
Montreal); Robert Bater (Principal of the United Church
Seminary at Queens); Robert Argue (Executive Director of the
Pentacostal Assemblies of Canada); and Earl Treusch (General
Secretary of the Lutheran Church). None of the nine had visited
Israel before. A political dimension was added to the venture
when Al Forrest criticized it as a cheap junket, but no one was
scared off and the trip was a huge success.

We saw the land and its people; we stood in prayer at Yad
Vashem;* we visited Bethlehem and Nazareth, Capernaum and
the Church of the Sepulchre. The Holy Land of the Scriptures
became a modern reality.

There were three important consequences: the Pentecostal
churches organized regular tours, bringing many hundreds of
Christians to Israel; George Morrison took members of his congregation for a visit; and in 1979 (under the leadership of Rev.
Stanford Lucyk of Timothy Eaton Memorial Church, who succeeded Morrison, and Rabbi Harvey Fields, who succeeded me) a

* The memorial to the victims of the Holocaust.

joint congregational tour to Israel and Egypt took place.

## From the Heights of Carmel

Haifa is a city of dramatic geography. The hills and the sea, the terraced gardens and buildings, and now the University of Haifa perched on the hills of Ahuza, topped by a tower that reaches like a finger into the sky—no rerun, one hopes, of the ancient Babel, for this is a tower built to enquire of but not to displace the Creator.

It is here that I come from time to time to lecture in the Department of Modern Jewish Thought and establish, as it were, an intellectual base in the land. In the last few years the institution's president has been Gershon Avner, a man of unusual intellectual capacity, gifted with an orator's tongue and a large dose of political pessimism. He is a realist and few can match him in acumen of perception and analysis. He belongs to that line of distinguished Israelis who served as ambassadors to Ottawa.

I also had a special relationship with another ambassador, Yaacov Herzog. He was ordained as an Orthodox rabbi and once briefly accepted the Chief Rabbinate of Great Britain. Yet despite his highly traditional leanings he was a man of large spirit and from the first moment we met in 1961 we established a bond of acceptance and respect. He was marvellously sensitive and always looked at the events of the day in the context of the long vision of Israel's existence in history. To him, politics was part of philosophy and philosophy was tinged by politics. We shared our vision of God's purpose for Israel, and perhaps this is why we never failed to relate to each other. When Yaacov died a relatively young man his death tore a hole in the fabric of Israel's spiritual and intellectual elite—and in mine.

## Presidents

Elizabeth and I had called on President Yitzchak ben-Zvi in 1956, and not long after Zalman Shazar was elected President of Israel, we had occasion to call on him as well. In those days the President still resided on Al Harizi Street in a modest house which had great charm, unlike the present stately but unexciting official residence. We presented Shazar with a book, for after all he was an old *littérateur* from his days in Berlin (he was then still known as Zalman Rubashow). The statesman had done his homework. After I had made my presentation he said: "Of course I am acquainted with your work on the Jews of Minnesota. I

learned a great deal from it, especially about the difference between St. Paul and Minneapolis, the way in which Jews took root
in two communities which were so close to each other and yet so
far apart."

To say that I was impressed is to put it mildly. Here was the
President of Israel who was interested enough to read a chapter
in a book on what, from the vantage point of Jerusalem, must certainly have seemed a very distant, even obscure, part of the
world. Where else would one find a nation's president like that?

I called on President Yitzchak Navon in February 1980. It was
my first meeting with him. The Egyptian Ambassador had just
presented his credentials, under the glare of television lights,
and Navon had entertained eight Egyptian journalists, speaking
to them in Arabic. He had charmed them utterly and he was in
high spirits.

The President's office is a combination of book-lined study and
gracious livingroom. On his father's side Navon is an old-line
Jerusalemite, on his mother's he is of Moroccan origin—whence
his thorough knowledge of Arab language and custom.

We talked of many things. It is encouraging to think that Israel
elects such men to its highest office: urbane, civilized,
knowledgeable, and interested in the political scene not as an
end in itself but as part of a nation's life. Not that politics had
been far from him—he came from a political milieu and he may
return there after his term is over. On more than one occasion I
heard people speak of him as a possible future prime minister.
What stayed with me more than anything else was our parting
conversation. We drank a toast to a strong and healthy future for
Israel and for a conclusion of the peace process.

"While we are at it," I added, "let us also drink to a strong and
healthy Diaspora."

But Navon was not enthusiastic.

"The Diaspora belongs here," he said. "Jews will have a
future only if their major strength is here."

"Mr. President," I said, "I must respectfully but strongly
disagree. The Diaspora needs a strong Israel and Israel needs a
healthy and vigorous Diaspora."

"We will disagree then," he concluded, "but let's talk about it
again the next time we see each other." He sounded like Ben-
Gurion, who had always spoken in similar terms—it was and remains the ultimate stance of the pure Israeli Zionist. A man who

had come from the Diaspora and was to return there could not help but disagree.

## Egypt and Israel — The Old and the New

We entered Egypt for the first time the day after I had seen President Navon. We still had to take the long journey via Athens—lightened by a visit to its magnificent old relics. We arrived at last in Cairo, exhausted. It was a while before we began to notice the strange dual face of this old/new country: a nation of forty million built on the ruins of an ancient civilization, but without any surviving link between the two.

In many ways our visit to Egypt was a visit to the past. One cannot see pyramids and ancient tombs and particularly the fabulous remnants of the Temple of Karnak without being struck by the vastness of the vision that built these structures. Someone has said that the Greeks built to human scale and the Egyptians to divine proportions. It almost looked that way—except that the beneficiaries of these vast efforts in magnificent artistry and monumental building were a few dozen royal megalomaniacs who wanted these structures to be their entrance tickets to the future world.

And who could help but think of the millions of human beings who toiled to create these structures and of the unknown artists who lent their genius to fashion them! There was a time when it was believed that Jews helped to build the pyramids; but that was not the case. They did no doubt help to build cities—the Bible attests that they laboured to erect the storehouses of Raamses and Pithom—but these were not the famed pyramidal structures.

Out in the countryside antiquity still seemed to hold sway. Water buffalos turned the water-wheels in the same manner as five thousand years ago. Only the metropolis spoke of today. Cairo has ten million people, and is now one of the largest and most overcrowded cities in the world, with slums and social problems that defy solution.

Two synagogues remain in this city, which not so long ago had 40,000 Jews who formed a strong, proud, productive community. Now some 160 Jewish souls are left in the capital, and perhaps another 100 in Alexandria, pitiful remnants of what used to be. But all of this tiny remnant was there on Purim and crowded into the stately Lotfy Street synagogue, together with several hundred Canadians and Americans, including many rabbis coming from the convention of the World Union for Progressive Judaism held the week before in Jerusalem. Egyptian and Israeli security forces guarded the worshippers, while television cameras were whirring away under glaring lights.

The few children of the Cairo community had home-made noisemakers: boxes filled with chick peas which rattled as loudly as the best commercial product. The chanting of the Megillah resounded to both Sephardic and Ashkenazic traditions; there were welcoming speeches in French, English and Hebrew; there was great excitement.

I have heard the Megillah read a multitude of times but never with a greater mixture of joy and sadness. The very presence of large numbers of visitors underscored the smallness of the resident community. There was a sense of hoping against hope which was put into words by one of the leaders.

"Perhaps the new relationship will bring some Jews here," he said. "We are an endangered species facing early extinction. But we must hope, mustn't we?" He pointed to Ambassador Eliahu Ben-Elissar and his beautiful wife Nitza. "There above all is our hope."

Two nights later we were at the Cairo airport to welcome the first direct flight from Tel Aviv. My heart jumped when the El Al aircraft came into sight and pulled to a halt in view of the terminal. Once again the kleig lights came on in force as the Israeli Ambassador mounted the ramp and greeted the incoming passengers, many of whom were Israeli newsmen.

In the reception hall we drank a She-hecheyanu to the occasion and then it was time to get on board. I had looked forward to this opportunity and now it was on hand. From Tel Aviv to Cairo had taken us a whole day, going back was less than an hour—and on an Israeli aircraft to boot. It was a champagne flight in every way, and when we landed at Ben-Gurion airport the forty years of Moses' travel had been cut down to forty minutes. More important: we arrived not in a land to be conquered but in one that said Shalom, welcome home.

## Germany: Visit to Past and Future

Shortly after we moved to Toronto I was contacted by both the German Ambassador in Ottawa and the German Consul-General in Toronto. The latter, a cultured gentleman with a partly Jewish and politically impeccable background, was Gottfried von Waldheim. He extended to me an invitation from the German government to visit the country and make my own assessment as to whether it was living up to its promises to the world: to eradicate the roots and outcroppings of Nazism and to establish a democratic nation.

I hesitated to accept the invitation, for I did not want to be accused of letting the German government's hospitality soften my view of Germany; I would be speaking and writing after my return, and if any shadow of suspicion were cast on the integrity of my report the trip and the sponsorship would not be worthwhile. I discussed this matter openly with Waldheim and he assured me that the German government was fully prepared to accept any judgement that I might make, and that there was no reciprocity involved. In the end I agreed. But I still had doubts, for I remembered the unhappy experience that we had had on our brief visit to Germany in 1956, during our sabbatical. At that time, since we were travelling as a family and found ourselves in Holland, it occurred to me that a brief visit to Münster, the city where I was born, would be appropriate. We set off in that direction, but the moment we crossed the border I knew that the trip was a mistake. It was too soon. I could hardly speak to anyone. Compulsively I kept looking at people's hands to see if there was any blood on them. Of course my feelings communicated themselves to my family. We stayed one night in Münster—one night too many—and left as quickly as we could. I had not been ready for Germany then. Would I be ready now?

When the plane set down my doubts grew even stronger. The visit suddenly seemed like a betrayal of the victims of that ghastly orgy of destruction. Yet, I reasoned with myself, if there was a new Germany then we needed to know about it—and if it was democratic we needed to encourage it.*

## Berlin

As we reached the terminal I had a surprise. A woman whom I did not recognize came forward with a bouquet of flowers.

She turned out to be Martha Schumacher, who in the old days had been our long-time maid and whose loyalty had never

* What follows is in part taken from my pamphlet Germany Today, a condensation of articles I wrote at the time for the Globe and Mail. The pamphlet has long been out of print.

wavered. At the hotel we reminisced about the past. She asked about my parents, my brother. She was my first contact with that other, now almost forgotten world. Meeting her was somehow unreal; we knew each other, yet we did not. Perhaps it was a portent of what I was to experience during the next few weeks.

The Berlin in which I had grown up was gone forever. Only here and there did the streets seem familiar. Ku-Damm looked more or less the same. At its head the Gedächtniskirche, once an imposing church, now half in ruins, straddled past and present.

That night I preached at a synagogue in the city—exactly twenty-five years had passed since I had last done so. Once Berlin had counted 160,000 Jews, a magnificent community of great social commitment and potential. Now some 6,000, many of them newcomers from other countries, were trying to make a new start. I looked about the congregation. The careworn faces before me seemed to belong to people I had known, people dead long ago. In the corner a woman was weeping uncontrollably; I later learned that she had come from Australia for her first visit back to Berlin, that this was the synagogue where she had worshipped with her parents.

It was not easy to formulate my German sentences. But I spoke of persistence, of faith, and West Berliners—especially Jewish ones—understood what these words meant.

When the war was over about 300,000 Jews were left in German concentration camps, but few of them were German. In the following years most left for permanent homes in Israel, North America and elsewhere. A few thousand stayed behind, because they were either too old or too ill to emigrate or because in the period of waiting they had found some sort of place in the emerging German economy. In time, a few thousand more drifted back from other parts of the world—from Shanghai perhaps, which had housed a large refugee colony during the war, or even from Israel.

The return of Jews to Germany was a source of never-ending questions. Why would anyone wish to come back to this land? Why would anyone come from Israel, particularly? We learned that there was no single answer. Some found the climate of Israel too rigorous; others could not find decent jobs; still others did not feel suited to the demands of a young pioneering land. Some came to recover expropriated goods, to seek restitution for losses, or were attracted by Germany's offer of a cash bonus to every Jewish refugee who resettled in his former home. For a few the answer was even simpler: Germany was still home, the land where their ancestors lay buried, whose language they could speak and whose culture was essentially theirs. And then there were Jewish soldiers with the Allied Armies who stayed on; there were communal workers, teachers, and a few rabbis who felt they could be of service.

We had discussions with many of them and we got as many different answers. Everyone agreed that the German government was outdoing itself to make them comfortable. They emphasized that antisemitism was outlawed and that overt expressions of anti-Jewish feeling were punished quickly and sometimes severely. Officially they were indeed welcome in Germany. Yet many were not sure whether they *should* feel welcome: there were so many memories, so many nameless graves that stood in the way, so many feelings of guilt.

This guilt was especially obvious with returnees from Israel. Not one of them admitted to me that he or she had come to stay. They had come, they said, for a short while to recoup some financial property, to pursue a restitution case in court, or the like. They were all, as the expression went, "sitting on their suitcases".

## Memorials

We visited Wiesbaden, where I found Grandmother's grave in good condition, and went on to Willingshausen and Merzhausen where my father's family had lived for several hundred years. As we approached the villages we seemed to be going back in time. There was no visible change. The villages were still the same, the roads hardly more generous than they had been in the old days, and the streets (or rather alleys) that wended their way through these villages were redolent with the fragrance of the past. Our old house was still standing, bearing the legend "Built in 1783". The neighbours remembered my family more readily than Mayor Faust had done when I had "conquered" the village in 1945.* But for me the most moving part of Willingshausen-Merzhausen was the cemetery, almost entirely given over to two families, the Plauts and the Spiers—my ancestors.

On a bright summer's afternoon we went to Dachau. The ride from Munich was short. There were many visitors from abroad, including U.S. soldiers (an army encampment was in the neigh-

* See above, p. 139.

bourhood). But there was also a steady stream of Germans. Quite a few had brought their children, even little ones. A self-appointed guide who hailed from Yugoslavia spoke to us in a furtive manner. He looked around to make sure that no one was listening. Then he told us, "You know, of course, that all of this was built after the war by the British with American money, in order to discredit Germany."

At the time we thought that the man was indulging in a rare and peculiar—though perhaps understandable—delusion. Later we found that he was not alone; there were others trying to propagate the idea that all the evils of Nazism were a story dreamed up by the Jews and their allies. Fortunately these have remained a small if fanatical minority. But they are still around, and their tentacles have spread abroad, even to certain American campuses.

I had occasion to examine textbooks for German middle and high schools which were then in use. They were at the time still quite sketchy on the subject of Germany's Nazi past and a good deal was left to the teacher. One Stuttgart newspaper which dealt with the subject at the time wrote: "The textbooks are quite adequate in describing Nazi tyranny and terror but they are quiet on the question, 'How was this possible?' The books are in many respects better than their reputation but worse than morality has a right to expect." Things have improved since then.

Everyone admitted that former Nazis occupied official positions right into the higher echelons. Occasionally they were discovered even in top positions. Though a few ultra-nationalist newspapers still published their weary tirades, on the whole the country gave promise of a democratic future.

## People

We met with Bishop Otto Dibelius, one of Protestantism's best known clerics. I was disappointed. He spoke with an old voice rather than that of the new Germany and his use of such terms as "non-Aryan" jarred me no end. His major target, however, was understandable: the rise of German materialism. Wherever I went I heard the problem reiterated by church people. "Religious institutions," they said, "are fighting a rearguard battle until Germans learn to live with their new-found wealth."

In Munich I met a man of different character, Roman Catholic Bishop Neuhäusler, who had defied the Nazis and had served time in Dachau and Sachsenhausen. He was one of those who gave to Germany its brightest hopes in its darkest hours. He presented me with a copy of his book *Cross and Swastika* and inscribed it to me. I mailed it home but it never arrived. If it was stolen I hope the culprit was an admirer of the Bishop, and not a Nazi book-burner.

On August 13, the first anniversary of the building of the Berlin Wall, we looked across that ungainly and miserable structure—a monument of Communist suspicion and weakness. Yet, in the long run, there was no doubt that the Wall would achieve its major purpose: to isolate West Berlin. In 1962 some 5,000 people left the city every month. Berlin with all its glorious, glittering and ghastly past appeared to be a dying city. Eighteen years later the trend was reversed. The city of my youth remains a lively outpost of the West in a sea of Communist, enforced conformity.

We went through "Checkpoint Charlie" to the East side. Where the Auerbach orphanage had once stood there was now a gaping hole. Even the old Kaiser's monument that had graced the courtyard had disappeared. Only the cemetery across the street was still there and in good condition—unfortunately it was locked and we could not visit. Max Liebermann was buried there, along with many of the city's great.

The major Jewish cemetery in Berlin was in Weissensee, also in the eastern sector. We drove there out of respect for the past and also to visit the man who was then functioning as the only rabbi in the East Zone. The gates were closed. After we rapped several times a woman appeared in an upper window and asked our business. We identified ourselves and with some reluctance she let us in. We found the rabbi on the second floor of the cemetery's administration building, apparently studying a folio which lay open on the table. He rose when we came in and then returned to his seat and his book. When I glanced across to see the nature of the book I was appalled to find that it lay upside-down before him. I glanced at the cabinet. It contained two or three Hebrew books and nothing else.

Was this a rabbi? All I could see was that he was wearing the Order of Stalin on his chest. He explained proudly that it had been awarded to him because he had encouraged the workers with speeches and cigarettes when they were building the Wall. I tried to talk to him about the Jewish community. His answers were evasive. He never asked about my work, about Jews in Canada, about the rabbinate or anything else that would show the slightest interest. It became clear to me that the man was no rabbi. Later I learned that he had been the assistant gatekeeper and grave-digger at the cemetery and had been elevated to "rabbi" by the Communist government to give the world the impression that the spiritual affairs of the Jewish community were in good shape. Alas, nothing was in good shape. There were perhaps still a thousand Jews left in the East Zone, most of them in Berlin. It was easy to imagine what kind of guidance they would obtain from "His Eminence".

We had been depressed over the present condition of German Jewry in general, but in comparison to what we saw in the East Zone, matters in the West at least showed promise. They did have functioning communities, they had synagogues that were attended and genuine rabbis to serve them. Whatever the long-range outlook might be, they tried to give it hope, and the government provided them with realistic support.

## Past and Present

My overriding impression of Germany was and still is the amazing physical reconstruction of the land. When I was there during the closing months of the war, the country was a shambles. Its industry was almost totally destroyed, people lived in ruins; anyone who did not see Germany in her state of defeat cannot imagine the degree of destruction.

Yet in 1962, but fifteen years later, the scars of war had been largely erased. Some communities had been entirely rebuilt and in most areas Germany had progressed far beyond its former peak of economic advance. Unemployment was at an all-time low—less than one per cent—and everywhere were signs of a burgeoning economy, the *Wirtschaftswunder*, as they called it. Prices were relatively stable; only Switzerland had a better record. Progress was written on the landscape and on the faces of the people. Super-highways were the favourite playground of the young, for owning a car—which for most had been a dream only a few years before—was now within reach of almost everyone.

At the same time preoccupation with material things was the predominant symbol of success, just as it was west of the Atlantic. Where formerly family connections and cultural traditions had been held in highest esteem, now the desire for acquisition had become overpowering. Where formerly the *nouveaux riches* had had no status, they were now among the leaders of society. People admitted that they had never had it so good. They had still

The rabbis of Holy Blossom: my predecessors Abraham L. Feinberg (left) and Maurice N. Eisendrath join me in celebrating the congregation's anniversary, 1969.

The mission to Biafra, with Hugh McCullum and Eoin Mackay, 1969. Starvation and politics.

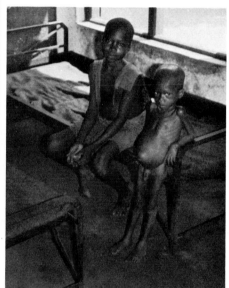

Prime Minister Golda Meir visits Toronto, 1970.

(Above) Speaking out during Premier Kosygin's visit to Ottawa, 1971. (Left) My son Jonathan and I with Prime Minister Pierre Trudeau, 1974.

*(Top)* Conducting noon-hour Bible classes for the staff of Toronto's Mount Sinai Hospital, 1975. *(Above)* With Israeli statesman Abba Eban (seated), Ray and Rose Wolfe, 1975.

*(Left)* Heinz Warschauer leads the fun at my farewell party at Holy Blossom, 1977.

*(Above)* With The Queen, Prince Philip and Cardinal Roy at a Silver Jubilee thanksgiving service in Ottawa, 1977.

*(Above)* Jonathan receives his doctorate from Hebrew Union College-Jewish Institute of Religion; from left, Dr. Gottschalk (President of the College) and Canada's Chief Justice Bora Laskin. *(Right)* Elizabeth and I with our daughter Judy, 1978.

*(Top)* Elizabeth and I with author Elie Wiesel, 1979.    *(Above)* Purim service in Cairo, 1980, with Israeli ambassador Eliahu Ben-Elissar (right).

not attained the Canadian standard of living, but it was clear
that they would soon reach and even exceed it. Germany in 1962
was once again the heart of Europe; the great question was
whether this heart would continue to beat to the rhythm of
freedom.

We returned there three more times, in 1967, 1972 and 1980,
to see, to listen, and to lecture. On my third visit I preached in
Cologne. In March of 1945 our division had taken the city and I
had held a service in the burnt-out synagogue at Roonstrasse.*
Now I was back for another service, this time held by the re-
constituted Jewish community. But what a shadow of its former
self! The synagogue was as imposing as ever—perhaps even
more so, for the government had contributed some four million
dollars, and the new edifice in glass and stone was most impressive. In earlier days such a synagogue would have been
deemed one of the important structures of the country. Yet, when
I came to preach there, it was more a monument than a living
reality.

I tried to reconstruct the days when I had stood there amidst
the ruins. Then there had been tears, immense relief and great
hope. Now none of this was present. The windows created by Ber
Warzager were a remembrance of things past, and so were the
faces of the elderly who formed the congregation. Here, as in
Düsseldorf and Berlin, I preached to survivors of yesterday
rather than builders of tomorrow. I was very pessimistic.

But then, who knows the turns of fate, who knows whether
there may yet be a real future for German Jewry engendered by
some event no one can foresee? Once, centuries ago, the
flourishing community of Regensburg was destroyed, its
members exiled or killed. Not a Jew remained. Ten years later,
however, the Jews were back and in the course of the next century Regensburg again became an important Jewish community
in southern Germany. Predict the future? I could not then and
neither can I now—except that I know that, while the expected
may come to pass for others, it rarely does for us. In 1980 there is
renewed immigration to Germany—from Russia and, again, from
Israel. We are a wandering people.

In 1967, after the Six-Day War, the outpouring of sympathy for
Israel was astounding. Germans stood at street corners and
made public collections for the Jewish state. That has changed

* See above, p. 124.

today. While Germany is still amongst Israel's few allies, the need for Arab oil, the fear of a superpower confrontation, and a worrisome rise of anti-Zionism have made strong headway. The slaughter of the eleven Olympic athletes in 1972 briefly aroused new sympathy for Israel, and in 1979 Chancellor Helmut Schmidt spoke movingly of the lasting responsibility that Germans had for their past. But increasing numbers of young people find this argument irrelevant—it was their parents' problem, it is not theirs.

From time to time I have been attacked in the ultra-nationalist German press, especially when I was identified as one who continued to press for the conviction of Nazi and other fascist war criminals, of whom a number reside in Canada today. I have always considered these attacks a badge of honour. I still will not drive a German car in Toronto. I know that many Jews have no hesitation about driving a Mercedes or a Volkswagen. But I respect the feelings of the survivors, even though I believe that a prosperous and democratic Germany is the linchpin of European freedom. My abstinence is symbolic, yet symbols do play a role. I visit Germany for official purposes, but cannot feel fully at ease. The past casts a dark shadow. There has never been anything simple about the relationship between Germans and Jews, not in my youth, not in 1962, and not today. It appears that another generation will have to pass before we can feel confident about Germany's commitment to democracy and freedom.

# South Africa

October 1968. The journey from London was long, with one false start when the aircraft took off only to land again. After nearly thirty hours we arrived to a warm reception at the airport in Johannesburg. I was to lecture to Reform congregations across the country and to visit my cousins Max and Ralph in the Transvaal.*

It was a fascinating and utterly depressing journey—though certainly we enjoyed the magnificent hospitality of which South African Jews are capable. In a way I became part of the country's tensions. While I wanted and needed to express myself on the race problem, I could not expose the South African Jewish

* They were children of my Uncle Levi; see above, p. 6. Ralph has since died.

community to danger nor could I make them feel so uncomfortable that they would be incapable of listening to me. So I frequently lectured on race relations in the United States, which were then in a state of dynamic, even revolutionary development. In describing how things were progressing in the States and how blacks were obtaining civil rights I was on safe ground, as I was when I described the role of the Jewish community and its alliance with the blacks. In this fashion I was able to allude to the ethical responsibilities of Jews in South Africa. I did not have to draw the parallel between the American and the South African situations. My audiences drew it themselves.

Cape Town and the Cape, nature at its most resplendent. In the city, we participated in the silver anniversary of the Reform congregation, coeval with Rabbi David Sherman's service to the community.

I remember Cape Town for one other reason. We had been quartered in a delightful hotel and were taken aback to find that the room door had no key. But we were assured that there was nothing to be worried about. In the morning—about seven a.m.—there was a perfunctory knock at the door and a waiter appeared with the morning tea. He was black, of course, and seemed quite impervious to our state of undress. It was a humiliating scene, not for us but for him. Apparently this procedure was perfectly acceptable to the South Africans. To them the black man was a non-person and hence that which would have been forbidden to a white waiter—to march into a bedroom unannounced—was permissible for him. I felt dreadful for him and left word at the desk that we did not wish morning tea unless we specifically asked for it.

To visitors like us the race problem was never out of sight. It cast a pall over everything we did, despite many lovely encounters and the ever-present hospitality. I often felt that people wanted to break out of the vice of apartheid but did not know how. Things have become somewhat better, but the essential problem has not been tackled. For me it is symbolized by the little shacks which stand in the rear of the splendid homes. It looks so simple: the black men dwell in the back, the palatial residences are reserved for the whites. Up front they eat lavish meals; in the back cheap rations are consumed. "They don't like our westernized food," I was told over and over again. "They like it the way it is." Intelligent, concerned people spoke that way and the worst was that they believed it.

But not everyone does; chief amongst the dissenters are Alan Paton and Helen Suzman, with both of whom I had long conversations. They are two very different persons, in temperament and tactics. One is primarily a writer and a Christian, the other a Jew, an economist turned social reformer and politician. What unites them is their sense of urgency about the human equation. Paton* lived then in Kloof, a few miles from Durban (he has since remarried and moved). To reach his place we turned off the main road, travelled down a long narrow lane overhung with lovely branches and garnished with splendid hedges. Located in a park-like setting, his home consisted of a series of buildings dominated by an old and rambling house. It was rustic, very quiet and withdrawn.

He showed us around the grounds. The quarters he had built for his help were the first we had seen that came up to "white" standards. They included ample sleeping quarters, with a dining room and modern bathrooms.

"When I built this place," he told us, "the white workmen asked me for whom I was building it. When I told them it was for my black help one of them walked off the job in protest."

Paton appeared vigorous, his jaw set as though in defence against the outside world. When he spoke there was a mixture of shyness and certitude in his voice, and his words were direct, informal, without flourish. We talked about literature, world peace, the student movement, religion and, of course, apartheid.

"I am very encouraged by the rather formless and shapeless rebellion of young people all over the world," he said, "because I think they are saying to us, 'This kind of society isn't worth living in, it isn't worth dying for.' "

Paton was encouraged also by the growing protest of the churches. He felt that, next to economic necessity, religion would prove to be South Africa's best hope for reform.

"I myself take religion seriously, even though I may not be as good as I ought to be. I believe that my life should be guided by obedience to some power higher and greater than I am. There is a real stirring in the South African churches at the moment, a heart-searching over the fact that we have elevated certain ideas above the teachings of the Bible. This whole theory of separate development has become for many people a gospel, and if you don't believe that, then they think you are guilty of the

* Best known for his novels *Cry, the Beloved Country* and *Too Late the Phalarope*.

gravest disloyalty to your church, your people and ultimately to God."

We spoke for nearly two hours. The lonely figure that waved good-bye seemed to highlight the tragic fact that the society in which he lived had drifted far from the ideals that its best minds had set out. Perhaps too far for any possibility of return.

Helen Suzman, South Africa's lone Progressive Party Member of Parliament, was living in Johannesburg. Her home was grander than Paton's, very spacious with a touch of elegance. Where Paton had spoken quietly but deliberately, Mrs. Suzman fairly bubbled over with eagerness to convey her convictions. An unusual editorial of the Johannesburg *Rand Daily Mail* had recently called her South Africa's voice of conscience. After five minutes we knew why her fame had spread around the world. Her dynamism had a prophetic touch in the tradition of her Jewish forbears and she spoke when others did not dare.

We talked on many subjects and to every one of her comments she brought a plethora of facts which she presented with authority, her expressive eyes shining brightly as she spoke. Our conversation covered many subjects. I brought up the question of the little congested quarters behind the private homes and the explanation I had been given: "These people are accustomed to living in small quarters."

"You know," Mrs. Suzman said, "it is just like nineteenth-century Britain, when people said that if the workers had bathtubs they would just store coal in them. People learn to adapt to new conditions, and as conditions improve people improve their lives as well. But whites have a lot of ready-made justifications which they trot out, one of them being that absurd story about the Ph.D."

She was referring to the story, probably apocryphal, of an African who studied in the United States, obtained his Ph.D. at Harvard and came back to South Africa to teach. Then the first time he became ill he ripped off his western suit and rushed to the witch-doctor. The story was widely told in South Africa, so widely that it was obviously being used as an excuse.

"You might ask the next time you hear the story," she said, "if they have ever heard of white people going to fortune-tellers, of graduates of universities who decide they are going to have their tea-leaves or their palms read. I know many highly educated men who wear copper bands for their arthritis—it's just another piece of folklore. So what?

"I see no change around the corner, yet change will come. Those of us who have done political work believe that there are thousands of moderate non-whites who are only yearning for some reasonable concessions, who won't demand to take over this country if these concessions are made now. But if you leave it until the hostility passes a certain level, there can only be violence, guerrilla tactics, all those things that one hopes to avoid."

Was she not afraid to speak? She answered quietly but with great determination.

"If one is in a position to say the things that must be said, one must go on saying them incessantly. Even if it doesn't bring immediate results it is very important to keep those hopes alive."

South Africa is a rich country with an exciting past and a potentially splendid future. If this future is realized, it will be, to a great extent, because people like Helen Suzman and Alan Paton still live, speak and write there.

## Nigeria/Biafra, 1969

Today the name Biafra calls up only vague memories, except amongst those who had some particular involvement in the area. But in the late sixties the word meant hunger, genocide and fratricidal war.

In Canada the press was publishing pictures of children crying for food, too weak to move; their mothers stared blankly from the page at our own well-fed faces. Yet, with all the misery in the world, Nigeria and Biafra seemed a long way from my own life. It was to be otherwise.

Biafra, which had been Nigeria's most prosperous province, had broken away and in 1967 had launched a war of independence. The province was inhabited primarily by Ibos, by all accounts the most industrious and intellectual of the many tribes that made up the country. Most of the Ibos were Christians—as in fact were most people in Southern Nigeria; the north, where the Housas predominated, was Moslem. The Biafrans had some initial successes but by 1969 they were losing their secessionist war, although there was no telling how long the struggle would last, or whether a compromise might be reached which would give them an acceptable degree of independence. But while the war itself was an internal matter, the outside world was growing

alarmed at the deteriorating physical condition of the
beleaguered Biafrans. Their food supplies were steadily
diminishing and they faced the lot of all besieged populations:
starvation. It was all they could do to stay alive. By the fall of
1969, the desperate state had badly shrunk: it had lost access to
the sea, its ports captured by the Nigerians. Its only airfield was
at Ule, since Owerri, the capital, was no longer secure.

On the whole I was ignorant of the country's internal conditions and its military prospects. My sympathies, like those of
many people, lay with the starving people of Biafra—especially
the children. I knew the name of Nigeria's leader, General
Yakubu Gowon, and of Biafra's Chukwuemeka Odumegwu
Ojukwu, but little else.

In October of that year I was approached to assume the chairmanship of the United Jewish Appeal. It was already late—
usually these appointments are made at the beginning of the summer, so that the new chairman can assemble his team and make
preparations for the winter campaign—but someone else had
delayed his answer and had finally declined. I was hesitant to
take on the job, especially starting so late, and besides, I
wondered how I could manage to discharge this onerous task and
at the same time carry out my duties as a congregational rabbi.
When I discussed these matters with my officers and board, they
urged me to accept. They felt that the community—in the throes
of recession, both material and spiritual—needed a boost, and
they flattered me by suggesting that I might be able to help.

Almost coincidentally I was approached by Stanley Burke,
reader of the National News on CBC and a well-known figure in
Canada. He had become greatly involved in organizing relief to
Biafra. He and others associated with him asked me to visit
Biafra and see for myself what the situation was, so that I might
come back and persuade the Canadian government and public
that much more aid had to be provided. It was to be a
humanitarian, not a political mission, I was told.

I was intrigued. If I was to give the better part of a year to the
Jewish community—attending endless meetings, cajoling people,
visiting them, writing letters, preparing news releases and doing
all the other chores that make up the unglamorous job of a UJA
chairman—I wanted to feel that I was still part of the larger
world.

I called Elie Wiesel in New York. I wanted to have a friend's
dispassionate advice.

"Elie," I said, "I have agreed to take on the UJA chairmanship for Metropolitan Toronto. Somehow I feel that I need to concern myself with larger issues, if only briefly, before I bury myself in the nitty-gritty of the campaign."

I told him about going to Biafra. Should I go? Elie understood my question.

"By all means, go. If I were in your shoes, that's what I would do."

I agreed to go, and threw myself into preparations. I was so preoccupied that I did not see the uneasiness of those who cared for me. I did not realize that they were worried—not about the time I would spend but about my safety. They saw what I refused to see: I was not merely going to comfort some starving people and bring back their tale, I was going into the midst of a civil war.

Of course I would not be the first to visit. Stanley Burke reassured me, "It is a mission like any other. You'll go and you'll come back and then you'll tell what you have seen."

Eoin Mackay, Presbyterian minister in Rosedale, and Hugh McCullum, editor of *Canadian Churchman* (Anglican),* would be my travelling companions. There were to have been some others, but they bowed out at the last minute. We would go first to Nigeria to assess the situation from there and then proceed to Biafra. How the latter would be accomplished I did not know. Rarely have I been as unprepared, as trusting and, I may even say, as careless as I was then. My heart had taken over; I wanted to help. I knew this was what I had to do, and no arguments could dissuade me.

I took a camera and a tape recorder and used the latter for interviews and for my daily record. A few excerpts from this diary follow.

## Nigeria

We were received courteously at the airport, but External Affairs had not yet come through with our visas and so we were held in a crowded room. It was my first experience in a country where being white put me so much in the minority. Soldiers with guns were all around us and we were objects of much curiosity. After a while we were given permission to stay for four days. Then came a long drive through the city, immense crowds milling

---

* Presently editor of the *United Church Observer*. Mackay is today minister in Leaskdale, Ontario.

about making a lively picture utterly different from my previous experiences. This is African country and it is black, no question about it.

Our initial contact was with the family of Reverend Earl Roberts, a Presbyterian missionary in charge of the Church Council's relief program for the Federal Republic of Nigeria. For the first time we obtained a view of the war quite unlike anything we had heard before. According to Roberts, a concerned and dedicated person,* the story of Federal Nigeria was totally misrepresented. Biafra had gained the support of most of the world, but without real justification. Genocide? No, indeed. More Ibos were living outside the secessionist enclave than inside.

What should people like ourselves say at home or advise others to do? He hesitated and then proposed what he termed a religiously unpopular and perhaps even impossible solution: "If all relief were cut off to the secessionists the war would come to an end. In the long run, more lives would be saved."

"But how can one let people starve?"

He did not know; one could not really cease relief work and yet it was relief work which prolonged the war and killed more people in the end. He was complimentary about Gowon and the opposite about Ojukwu who, he said, was using starvation as a political ploy to gain sympathy and advantageous peace terms.

I knew then that I was a babe in the woods. My preparation had been very inadequate, to say the least.

It was Shabbat and the second night of Hanukah; I said my prayers in the hotel room and thought of home.

The next day I met Dr. Wolfgang Bulle, the medical officer for the Church Mission Service, who had just come back from one of the border areas. He told us of 10,000 people who had crossed into Federal Nigeria from secessionist Biafran territory.

Starvation? He had seen little of it. He had found only nine cases of kwashiorkor (a serious protein deficiency which after some time is irreversible) and not a single case of marasmus (total starvation of the concentration camp kind). I began to wonder whether perhaps some of the stories we had been told in Canada were not true—but of course, neither Roberts nor Bulle had been in Biafra proper and perhaps things there were indeed as bad as we had heard.

Should relief work cease, we asked? Not entirely, said Bulle.

---

* His family was later involved in a dreadful automobile accident and then moved back to Canada. He serves presently with the Presbyterian Board of World Missions.

Some help had to be given, at least to those who were suffering most. Otherwise he agreed with Roberts.

"In the long run," he said, "the only way to settle this problem is to leave it to the Africans. We whites are finished here anyway. The Biafrans are helped by the French, South Africans, Rhodesians and Portuguese, the Nigerians by the Russians and the British. All of these are strange bedfellows but it is a proxy fight, not a truly African struggle. Nigeria has oil—that is the source of much of the problem."

And the churches?

"They have fallen into the trap of entering political alignments."

I asked whether this was not the case with Palestinian refugees (the parallel was too obvious not to be made). Was it not true that, because the churches and the United Nations maintained the Palestine refugees in an untenable position for political ends, they gave them hope of someday returning to their own homes—even though this hope could no longer be realized? Was it not true that by sustaining them in their tents, these agencies prevented their absorption into Arab countries and their resettlement in part of Israel? He agreed, the parallel was very clear. I was wondering whether my sympathies were already shifting.

My hotel room had a little balcony. I went out there at nightfall, and looked across the street. I could see that even the poorest of the poor have a class structure of sorts. At the bottom is the man who has nothing at all; he sleeps under the open sky with no shelter above and not even a blanket below. Next is the man who has a blanket, and perhaps a pitcher for performing his ablutions. And then there is the one who has the right to sleep beneath a protruding balcony; he occupies the top level in this hierarchy of the deprived. And I—I munched a late snack, retreated into my air-conditioned room, showered and took to my comfortable bed. What would I know of poverty and starvation even if I saw them?

The next few days were spent in meeting as large a cross-section of Nigerians as we could. We spent an hour and a half with Dr. Okoi Arikpo, the country's Foreign Minister. He was open and straightforward, and assured us repeatedly that the federal government had no genocidal intentions. On the contrary, the front-line troops were carrying food for those Ibos who came across the border.

Yes, there was some hunger, and it was this on which the Biafrans based their enormously successful propaganda campaign. They were helped, of course, by the media's appetite for disaster and sensationalism.

"Incidentally," he said, "the first hunger pictures were taken on our side, in areas which have since come under federal control. The pictures are still being shown, though the children portrayed have long since been fed and grown into normal people."

Where did the Biafrans get their money?

"From France mostly, and from other honest but misguided humanitarian contributors."

We told him that we intended to go to Biafra.

"I know," he said, "but see that, however you go, you don't get mixed up with arms shipments. The French planes that fly out of Gabon mix relief and arms. Some nights we see twenty-eight blips on the radar screen; we know that not all are relief planes but we've been letting them go anyway. But if you see Ojukwu, tell him to have his relief flights come in during the day. We promise not to bomb Ule airport during daylight hours, from nine to five. Tell him it is an undertaking by our government and the whole world will be watching. And when you get back to Canada tell your people that there are more Ibos in Federal Nigeria than over there amongst the secessionists."

During the next few days we saw a great many people, from the Canadian Ambassador to the head of the United Nations' mission. Our visit stretched out, for we had still not found a way to arrange a flight into Biafra. I had a vague feeling that perhaps we would not make it at all. I was not feeling well; the heat was getting to me. An attempt to fly to Libreville* failed, though we spent hours in a small airport lounge where the temperature must have been over 120°. But on Friday, a week after we had come, we finally made it. We were met in Libreville by Father Myles Kenny of St. Mary's Mission of the Holy Ghost Fathers, who were to play a very important role for me a few days hence.

## Libreville

Here the story was different from what we had heard in Nigeria, and the sentiment was clearly running in favour of the Ibos. But the Fathers too denied that genocide was involved. For them the most important point was that the Ibos themselves were con-

---

* Capital of Gabon.

vinced that they would be wiped out as a people, or at least
driven underground in an endless guerrilla war.

"If Biafra really becomes independent it will be the first successful African nation," Father Kenny said.

The Fathers repeated what we had heard on occasion in
Nigeria: that the Ibos were much like the Jews. The conversation
drifted to stereotypes. They avoided making outright statements
about Jews, but the implications were clear: Ibos know how to
make money, Ibos are ruthless, Ibos exploit others, Ibos are so
education-minded that the Housas in the north were forced to institute a *numerus clausus* so that no more than thirty per cent of
the university enrollment could be Ibo.

What about starvation? Of course Ojukwu was using starvation as a means of propaganda, but that starvation was real all
the same.

Religion? It had not helped to pacify the people. The colo-
nialism of yesterday was finished here. Look at Gabon: formerly
it had been the German, British and French Cameroons. Was
there anyone who still remembered those names? (I did, from my
father's atlas and from collecting stamps, though it struck me too
as ancient history.)

At lunch, at the Tropicana restaurant by the seashore, I felt
like a beachcomber. The setting was more like that of a film than
of the real business at hand. I began to feel that the distinction
between fact and fiction was becoming fuzzier by the day. We
met the mercenaries who ran the Nigerian blockade: Captain
Alain Noël, whose credentials I have forgotten; Captain Joseph
Deppe, a former RAF pilot; and José Maguin, a Belgian who was
considered daring but also very good. Daring? It occurred to me
that these three men with whom we were to fly at night possessed qualifications beyond what was required by commercial
airlines. The pilots were working for Belgian International Air
Services, a commercial outfit that was making big money from
these illegal relief flights. Going into Biafra took two hours
because the cargo was heavy, and usually the plane had to circle
until given the go-ahead for landing. The air strip, fifty feet wide
and about eight thousand feet long, was lit for a maximum of fifty
seconds.

"Why only fifty seconds?" I asked.

"Give them more and the MIG's which the Federal troops fly
come in to bomb. Fortunately the pilots aren't too good at it."

I must say I felt anxious.

I picked up a few things at the mission and said my prayers with more than the usual devotion. I looked into the sky and wondered what lay ahead. We went to the airport and Maguin waved us onto one of the two planes sitting there; he was tonight's pilot. The plane was full of salt sacks well secured with nets. There were only four seats—evidently passengers were no more than incidental cargo.

## Biafra

Soon we were off. It seemed like any other flight, heading quietly into the night over the sea towards Federal Nigeria. I tried to recollect what my state of mind had been during the last war, under similar circumstances. But either it was too far in the past or it simply could not be compared. I rather think it was the latter.

It occurred to me that the flares below were anti-aircraft fire aimed at us. Never having served in the Air Force, I found this a new experience. But the plane came through safely—suddenly we were descending, and lights flared out of the darkness to mark the air strip. We roared in, the plane turned off the runway, parked, and it was dark again.

"Get off the plane as soon as you can," said the pilot. "Run fifty yards off, and lay down flat. If the MIG's don't come in five minutes get up and you will be all right."

There was a roar overhead but no bombs, no strafing. At once we were surrounded by scores of people whose job it was to unload the plane.

"Welcome to Biafra," they shouted into the pitch-black night.

In the darkness a car came and took us to the "State House" about five miles away, over roads that had been hit and were incredibly bad. Certainly no one could quickly approach the airport overland, using this route. Every hundred yards or so, soldiers challenged the car.

The State House was an experience. It looked like an old farmhouse, but the stable had been converted into a beehive of activity. Candles shone dimly in small rooms and a babble of voices greeted us. There were all the regular formalities: we filled out papers, declared our money. I realized that these people needed formalities to persuade themselves that they had indeed a state, with all its dignity and requirements.

We were on "African time". We waited from eleven that night until three a.m. for the Chief of Protocol. He finally arrived, a splendid-looking fellow sporting an Ojukwu beard. He loaded us into a car that had a diesel engine and needed to be pushed. It stalled, was pushed again and finally we lumbered off. Forty miles through the dark of the night to the provisional capital, Owerri. I hated to think what squalid quarters we would be given for the night. Yet, incredibly, they gave us individual rooms with bath and toilet! VIP guest headquarters, probably the only ones around. I remember pulling down the mosquito netting and falling asleep totally exhausted. The sickness I had felt in Nigeria was getting worse.

The next day, I was sick and I knew that I would have to see whatever I could in the shortest possible time. I did not want to fall seriously ill in this environment—kind as the people were. I had things to do—I had to see hospitals, children, the general state of health. This was what I had come to look at, not the military possibilities or evidences of political opportunities.

At Ogwa, F. G. Ihenacho, formerly president of the Nigerian Red Cross, now president of Biafra Red Cross, gave me a hand. He took us to the hospital. Moses Iloh, who was in charge, told me that a thousand adults and two thousand children died every week from marasmus. Tuberculosis was becoming rampant in adults, but in his hospital we did not see many cases.

"Most of them are out west," he said.

Still, what we saw was bad enough. In the sick bay I took pictures and felt I was trespassing in the worst possible way. The starving looked at me, they could not smile. It seemed as if time had run out.

"They are always in pain," said Iloh.

We left, shaken, feeling helpless. And then—of course!—we went to a splendid lunch at Bishop Okoye's residence. The contrast was shattering. I ate and felt worse than before.

Ted Johnson, a Methodist minister I had seen only a few days before in Toronto, was suddenly there. He moved about with the assurance of one recognized by everyone as the person most responsible for helping the Ibos. And we saw others, Ibos and foreigners, amongst them Dr. Anne Jackson who had been there for a dozen years working at the hospital. I could only admire people like her who with such unselfishness gave their whole lives to serve others.

I was feeling very ill. Fatigue and a sense of deep anxiety possessed me, and it was almost impossible for me to follow the conversations. I became detached—later I heard that in the tropics this was the surest sign that one was coming down with something: total lack of interest, no desire to do anything except crawl away and sleep. But sleep was precisely what I wasn't getting; I had taken sleeping pills every night, but they didn't help. I imagined myself lying in a hospital down here, not a cheering prospect. I told my friends that I had to leave. I felt like a traitor, but I knew I wouldn't be any good to anybody if I stayed.

I had not seen Ojukwu—the others would meet him the next day—but I had heard the whole panoply of arguments and I had seen what I had come to see: the starving and the well. Above all I had experienced something of the utter complexity of a war in which I was an outsider. I had come because of an inner sense of moral urgency, but now I was not sure what I should be doing. Here they felt one way, on the other side they felt differently. And I, was I being helpful? Or being used? Was I involved in *tsedakah*—an act of charity—or was I just prolonging a war? Either way, with people starving and dying, could I look away?

Back to the airport, in the company of soldiers who told me how much they admired Israel because it had withstood a siege of many nations for so many years. I realized that I still had a small ration of bread in my bag and apologized that it was so very little. Would they like it? The eagerness with which each one took a tiny sliver of bread and devoured it was a most vivid sign of what starvation really meant. These boys were working, they were employed by the government, yet they were always hungry; a little piece of bread was something to be savoured and valued. I passed out some candy, something they had not had for ages. At every post the guards challenged us, and I had to produce my pass. The road seemed bumpier than before, the levelled machine-guns more threatening. Finally we were at the air strip. I was suddenly dismayed at the thought of being abandoned out there, but the soldiers were kind.

"We'll wait till you're on the plane, don't worry," they said.

The plane roared in with Maguin again at the controls. Somehow, seeing him, I felt happy. An hour of loading and unloading, then I clambered up the ladder and in no time we were off. I said good-bye with a sense of guilt at leaving the others behind—my visit had been so short. But I persuaded myself that I had made a gesture. I had had to come, and I had come. Next thing I knew, the plane had landed in Libreville; I must have fallen into a deep sleep, the first I had had for a long time.

## Return

A car from the Biafran mission was at the airport and took me back to the Holy Fathers. It was pitch dark, but I had a flashlight and managed to find my room again. It was in the same messy condition in which I had left it. I did not undress, just pulled down the mosquito netting and tried to sleep. Tomorrow, if all went well and I could manage it, I would be on my way to Paris.

It was not to be so easy. I was unceremoniously bumped from the flight and had to stay over. Libreville seemed to me like a place the world had forgotten; it was an isolated outpost in a vast continent. But the Fathers were there and they were very kind to me. We spoke of things material and spiritual. The days passed, the nights were long. Slowly I was getting better. Finally I was successful in catching a flight to Fort Lamy in Chad, then to Marseilles and Paris, and from there to London. It was one-thirty in the morning when I arrived at the home of my cousins, the Urys. They received me with great joy and I was happier than I had been for quite some time. I called Toronto and spoke to Elizabeth.

The next morning I called the people active in the Biafra campaign. They were very disappointed that I was alone, and unhappy that the three of us had not returned the day before as originally planned. The media had been briefed and assembled and waiting and we had not shown up. (With all our delays and my own illness I had forgotten about it.) I tried to convey how difficult it had been for us to get into Biafra, but the gentleman with whom I talked was more interested in his problems than ours.

A week or so later, after McCullum and Mackay had returned to Canada, we went together to Ottawa to see Mitchell Sharp, then Minister of Foreign Affairs. Ted Johnson came with us. We presented our case, with all its complexities. Sharp was prepared with his answer. The federal government would make two million dollars available for aid, one million dollars to each side. To us, it was a great victory, even though I could not help thinking about the warning I had heard when we first arrived: that relief would prolong the war.

That doubt came to an end at Christmas time. Biafra fell and the war was over. I had seen it just a few days before its capitulation. Ojukwu fled, and in the months and years to follow the Nigerians were, on the whole, proven right: there was no genocide and in time the Ibos were reintegrated into the general economy. They did not, of course, at once regain their former prominent positions, but certainly the dire consequences which they had predicted did not occur.

For me it had been a journey into the unknown. I had little reason to be proud of my intellectual preparation and of my physical stamina. Still, my instincts had been right, and now I was ready to give all my time and effort to the United Jewish Appeal and the salvation of my own people.*

## Russian Encounters

In the summer of 1966 the Central Conference of American Rabbis sponsored a visit to the Iron Curtain countries.

Our group was led by Jacob Weinstein, himself of East European birth, and we had one Russian-speaking colleague amongst us, George Lieberman of Long Island, who came with his wife and two children.

The main purpose of our mission was to look at Jews under the Hammer and Sickle. How did they live, how did they feel, how were they treated, what was their future, if any? Was it true, as we had heard with increasing insistence over the past decade, that Russian Jews were exposed to a sometimes subtle and sometimes open system of discrimination? It turned out that we did not visit enough of Russia, did not have enough of the proper contacts and consequently did not see clearly into the future. Still, our journey was unique and memorable.

Estimates were that some three million Jews still lived in the Soviet Union, with three to five hundred thousand in Moscow, a city of six million. Jews were an oddity amongst the Soviet nationalities. By Russian standards Jews were a distinct nationality and their passports identified them as such. However, Jews were the only major group that lacked a territorial governmental structure to advance their own cultural affairs. The Russians had attempted to create a Jewish national enclave of sorts in

---

* Almost exactly ten years later, Ronald Atkey, then Minister of Employment and Immigration, invited me to visit Thailand and Kampuchea (formerly Cambodia). I would see the refugee camps and then bring back recommendations to government and, of course, a plane full of immigrants. The offer, which he and I had discussed some months before, came in the middle of the Minister's election campaign of 1979/80. I had some qualms about the possible political implications, but felt I wanted to go. My only condition was that four of the top leaders of Canada's churches, who were also to be invited, would agree to come along. However, the majority declined, for various reasons, and I had to ask the Minister that the matter be put over until later. I was sorry; my family were not.

Siberia, north of Manchuria—it was called Biro-Bidjan—but it was an utter failure: few Jews were willing to participate in this experiment. They remained where they were, in their particular Soviet republic, *oblast* or *okrug*. A minority everywhere, with no territorial identity to call their own, with no central religious authority to guide them, and few public institutions to encourage their cultural development, our people found their Jewish life steadily eroding. Only half a million Jews still listed Yiddish as their mother tongue and this number was dwindling. As in Western lands, the new generation was adopting the language of the majority.

What then was left of Jewish identity? An official stamp in a passport, a memory, and the word Jew—with its essentially negative connotation. With religion classed as superstition, identification with Judaism as a religion was discouraged. Further, religious education for the young was prohibited. Classes of more than two children were forbidden, which meant that unless a father taught his own child—and this in the face of all social and political pressures—the lifeline of tradition was severed. In the synagogue, much as in the churches, one found predominantly the old, the retired who had nothing to lose. Other religions were suppressed as well, but the Jew had a double problem. That portion of his being which derived from his religious heritage was being destroyed by the anti-religous campaign. That portion of his identity which was national and cultural was weakened by his dispersion amongst the Russians. And for reasons which no one was then able to fathom, there was an official reluctance to grant the Jews proper encouragement in areas in which other nationalities and ethnic groups were given their due: the preservation of their language, the publication of books and magazines. Since then we have learned the reason: Russia was embarking on a period of semi-official and in many instances quite open antisemitism, especially when it came to university admissions and job advancement.

Obviously, the Soviets considered antisemitism to be beneficial to the regime and the advancement of Communism. Did the authorities believe that as long as Jews were really Jewish they would be overly individualistic, unassimilable to the totalitarian stream of life? Perhaps. In this respect, ironically, the Communist regime simply continued the policy of its czarist predecessors.

We started in Poland and the impressions we received were

dismal. The Jewish community leaders, speaking to us in the presence of police informers, were eager to feed us Communist slogans. Warsaw had been rebuilt but the ghetto, where hundreds of thousands had valiantly rebelled against and been crushed by the German war-machine, was no more.

Then we flew to Cracow to visit Auschwitz. There too the Jewish identification was missing. (A Jewish pavilion has since been created, after much international pressure.) Of course, for rabbis who had read about the Holocaust, signs and identifications were unnecessary. For me it brought back all the ghosts of Nordhausen and of the streams of released prisoners in striped garments marching along the road towards freedom. I stood as in a daze at the sight of the ovens. The agony of death hung all about us whispering its unspoken cries.

Ah, dear God, where were You in the hour when the screams of millions rose from this place? My theology says, "You were in hiding." The Psalmist suggests it and Buber and others assert it—yet somehow all explanations faded away in that moment. My colleagues asked me to speak a few words in that dank and dismal spot. I said that instead of speech we should pray—pray that we would be able to continue to pray and lead our congregations in faith. My colleagues wept, but my tears had ceased long ago.

What was there to see afterwards in the city of Cracow? Churches? Monuments? It was all meaningless.

Moscow was next. We had the typical reactions of visitors who for the first time come face to face with Soviet realities. We wondered whether our rooms were bugged and our telephones tapped. For frank conversations we went into the park—though even there we were not safe from the eyes of the ever-watchful police. Two of us were walking away from the hotel—it was at night, and the air was mild with a late summer's breeze—when suddenly out of nowhere a man confronted us.

"You have been walking on the grass," he said. "That is strictly forbidden." Though he spoke in broken English, and though he was not in police uniform, the threat in his voice made his meaning very clear.

On the flight to Vilnius (known to Jews of olden times as Vilna, the "Jerusalem of the Diaspora") we met a Jewish stewardess who was much interested in meeting American rabbis. She suggested that we come to visit her in her apartment.

We did, in one of the few personal contacts we had. She lived simply but by Russian standards, she gave us to understand, rather well. She was interested in jazz and we promised to send her records. Could we see her again? Yes, she said, she would meet us at the plane when we departed from Vilnius. As we left her apartment and walked through the courtyard the suspicious curiosity of the neighbours was unmistakable. We began to realize that foreigners were rarely seen in these environs. Private visits were officially frowned upon by the government, and still are. We visited a synagogue, found a *genizah*\* of old books, but the building was deserted. When we reached the airport to catch the plane to Leningrad we were told that the stewardess would not meet us—and please not to send her anything, no records, nothing. That was all there was to the message. We felt helpless and angry.

Leningrad was beautiful, historic; the sun was still bright enough at eleven p.m. to read by. The Hermitage Museum was a marvellous interlude. But we had not come merely to see pictures and monuments.

Only when we went to Kiev did communion with fellow Jews emerge in earnest. It was the eve of Tisha b'Av, the day traditionally set aside for mourning the destruction of the Temple in Jerusalem.

We went to worship in the synagogue, where elderly people sat on the floor reciting the Book of Lamentations, as is the custom. The next day we went to Babi Yar, the site where the Germans slaughtered Kiev's Jewish population. It had been filled in, made partly into a dump and partly into a soccer field, with new apartments lining the road. We stood there conducting a service appropriate to the day. No identifying plaque or monument had been erected at the time. We hardly knew whether to think the ground on which we stood holy because of memories transfigured, or eternally damned because of human savagery.

My colleague Ely Pilchik\*\* had been growing increasingly depressed. Born in Eastern Europe, a man of unusual sensitivity and inwardness, he suffered the memories of the past more acutely than most. After Kiev he could bear it no longer and told us that he would not continue on the journey—he had to go home. I understood. If we had not been leaving Soviet Russia at that point, I might have joined him. Fortunately our Russian *séjour*

---

\* A storage room for old books. Texts containing God's name were either buried or stored, never destroyed.

\*\* He later became president of the Central Conference of American Rabbis.

was over and we were now bound for the "free" countries, Hungary and Czechoslovakia. As we left, Kiev Jews stood about and watched us load the bus. They waved good-bye and one of them came up to the bus and said, "Do not forget us."

How could we? Would our fleeting visit be enough to sustain them? What was it that was required of us? We did not fully understand then.

In Budapest, on the Sabbath after Tisha b'Av, in the beautiful three-tiered Dohany Street synagogue, I chanted the *Haftarah* to a few dozen people—in a place that could seat three thousand. We visited with Professor Alexander Scheiber, head of the seminary, whom I had met in Cincinnati. We went to Prague to visit the dead. Nazis and Communists have one thing in common: they love dead Jews. The cemeteries were in respectable condition and the collection of Jewish memorabilia saved from destroyed synagogues was staggering; there were inscriptions of dead names, tens of thousands of them, on the walls of one synagogue. We visited the Alt-Neu Shul—another place filled with memories, not with people. We met the communities but there too we came away with little hope.

In an article for the *Globe and Mail* a few weeks later I wrote:

What of the future? If Jewish history can teach us anything, it is that prophecy is a hazardous business. The Jewish people have survived grave difficulties in many eras. If the Soviet Union would allow contact between its Jewish community and those of the outside world, who knows what the result might be, what secret flame of sentiment and affection might be rekindled from the ashes of isolation?*

Not much later Soviet Jews began to discover their own resources that had been repressed for two generations, and more and more boldly raised their voices, at the peril of their freedom and even their lives. The Six-Day War brought the protest movement into the open, causing hundreds of thousands of Jews to identify themselves proudly with the people and the land of Israel. It was not through our contact that Russian Jews would be revived. It was *their* spirit that kindled *ours*. It was they who drew on their secret strength to make the first move, while we in the West helped and encouraged them, and the people of Israel added their voice and their presence. That is how it began.

* Six articles on this journey were published later as a pamphlet under the title *Russia is Different* (Toronto: Holy Blossom Temple, 1966).

# Epilogue

I COULD HAVE STAYED AT HOLY Blossom as long as I desired. We had instituted many exciting programs, the latest being Project Isaiah* which was spearheaded, conceived and to no small degree executed by Henrietta Chesnie, who in the late seventies was president of the congregation, and brought many new ideas to that demanding position. She and her husband Josh were and are among our closest friends.

But for some years I had known that the rigorous schedule I was following could not be kept up indefinitely. As far back as 1969 I had given serious thought to the matter but had come to the conclusion that, however attractive changing careers might be, I could not afford it. But I talked to my friends in the temple administration and we began to plan how my retirement from the congregation might eventually be effected. I knew that I would always have more than enough to keep me active—I would not lack for tasks and opportunities for public service—but, most of all, I wanted to complete the commentary on the Torah, which had run into a hundred snags in New York. After all, it was a project to which I had given many years of hard work, and I was afraid that the treadmill of my daily obligations would stand in the way of its completion.

I had no clear conception of what the professional change I contemplated would actually involve. When I finally announced my decision to retire from the pulpit I met with a good deal of

_____

* An outreach program, designed to help our own members lead more intensive Jewish lives.

332

disbelief from large parts of the community. They were accustomed to seeing me in a thousand places, in so many roles: pastor, preacher, counsellor and public servant, writer and lecturer, community spokesman. They did not see that I was also tired and needed not only a long vacation but a total change, a new career.

Heinz Warschauer had already retired, and I would follow him shortly after I reached my sixty-fifth birthday at the end of 1977. That November I gave three Friday night lectures in which I reminisced about my life. On the first night the congregation crowded the temple; on the following two Fridays there was standing room only. A farewell party filled with nostalgia as well as laughter and merriment was my last official event. And then suddenly it was over and there was a new rabbi, Harvey J. Fields. The congregation was generous and the new facilities provided for me at the temple were handsome. But what would the future bring? I could only hope for the best.

## President of Congress

In November 1976 the province of Quebec faced a crucial election. There was a possibility that the separatist Parti Québécois might come to power. Charles Bronfman, the Canadian head of Seagram's, was then the heir apparent to the presidency of the Canadian Jewish Congress—the organized community of Canadian Jewry. He indicated that were the PQ to gain office he would contemplate moving himself and his company out of the province. When the separatists were indeed elected that month, Bronfman felt that his political stand had compromised his position, at least temporarily, and that he could not at that time head the organization which his father had guided for some thirty years. He withdrew his candidacy. This left the field wide open. A number of people from across the country phoned me and urged me to take Charles' place. I was not fully aware of what the presidency might entail, but the idea seemed attractive, and my impending retirement was an added reason for saying yes. I liked the idea of being able to continue in public life.

However, matters did not go smoothly. Irwin Cotler also indicated that he would stand for the office. He was thirty-eight, a professor of law at McGill University, learned in Jewish matters, deeply committed to his people and a bright star amongst our leaders. We had been friends and co-workers for many years and both of us were uncomfortable at the thought of running against each other. We finally convinced the constitutional committee of Congress that the matter could be solved to everyone's advantage if we had a co-presidency. Irwin would be the field commander in Quebec and the East, and I in Ontario and the West. We would spell each other during our frequent absences from the country and would complement each other in our approach to public policy. In every respect it would be a good match, we thought.

But when the proposition was laid before the convention in May 1977, in Montreal, the delegates were divided. Many thought that our idea was practical, but there were some who felt that a co-presidency would simply not work, and others who hoped that defeating the constitutional change might mean the election of their preferred candidate.

I had criss-crossed the country in search of delegates' support, had spoken in Calgary and in years past had been in Vancouver, had visited Halifax and was known to most communities in Ontario. I attended a meeting of Zionist delegates in Montreal* and though I did not obtain their unanimous support it was a good meeting and I felt that I had gained some delegates. I had the support of past presidents Sol Kanee and Monroe Abbey, and of Milton Harris, the Central Region's chairman. The pundits figured it would be a close race.

On the second day of the convention, Donald Carr, constitutional chairman, guided the delegates to the all-important vote. It was a moment of high drama. The hall was jammed with eight hundred delegates and alternates who had come from every corner of the land. Speeches were impassioned, pro and con. Then came the vote. The proposition to change the constitution and allow for a co-presidency was overwhelmingly defeated. It seemed that Irwin and I would have to face each other as rivals.

But as soon as the vote was announced, Irwin rose and announced that he would not run against me, an old friend and colleague in many battles and councils. With that announcement my election was automatic. The delegates jumped to their feet and cheered for many minutes. I sat holding Elizabeth's hand; I was totally exhausted and very grateful.

I knew little about the responsibilities of the office. I only knew

---

* It was called on my behalf by the president of the Eastern Region, Leon Teitelbaum.

that I wanted to strengthen the fabric of Canadian Jewry, to give our people a sense of cohesion and purpose. I would be, I prayed, a good defender of their just causes.

It turned out that fulfilling this dream was difficult and at times nearly impossible. I spent endless hours travelling to and sitting in meetings. I was often reminded of the Talmudic story about Jerusalem falling to the Romans because the squabbles of two families, Kamza and Bar Kamza, diverted the attention of the defenders while the Romans slipped into the city. No such dramatic event occurred in my incumbency, but I often felt that we faced the same danger—especially during the controversy over moving the embassy to Jerusalem, when tempers ran high.*

Meanwhile, Congress itself gained new strength. Federations were now joining it. Our organization had been tightened and after years of quiescence we were becoming an active force in our communities. Especially in Ottawa was our voice heard. When I spoke to ministers they listened, because they knew that the Congress was the voice of our people.

The office was tiring and the involvement more tedious at times than I would have wished, but it was all worthwhile. The culmination came at the triennial convention in May 1980, when over a thousand delegates assembled from all parts of the country, by far the largest convention we had ever held. No doubt a good deal of the interest displayed came from a hotly fought contest for succession between David Satok and Irwin Cotler—David, who had given himself fully to the organization and had been a great support to me; and Irwin, who had stood aside in 1977 and whose brilliant advocacy of freedom for Shcharansky —one of the Russian "Prisoners of Conscience"—and of anti-boycott legislation had made him known from coast to coast. In the end, with strong support from academics and youth, Cotler won out and became my successor, but not without the convention giving a moving display of recognition and admiration for the defeated candidate.

In my farewell address I set forth my hopes for the years ahead. For instance, I suggested that in the future all Jews should have a direct voice in voting for national officers, with a single election day across Canada. National conventions, instead of taking place every three years, might be spaced farther apart, thereby giving regional conventions far greater importance.

* See above, p. 274.

I paid tribute to Saul Hayes, who had died a few months before the convention:

> He was one of those rare human beings who combined intelligence with compassion, a sense of urgency with a sense of timing, a love for Jews with a love for all human beings, a dedication to Israel's future with a dedication to Canada's welfare. He was a pragmatic idealist and a man of total integrity. Because of him, Canadian Jewish Congress was an instrument of high calibre. He had a sense for history and was himself a maker of history. Honouring him, we honour ourselves.

I dwelt to some extent on my failures, especially on failing to achieve that sense of Jewish unity in the country that I had hoped might lie within our grasp. I then turned to an intensely personal matter.

> There has also been a personal failure on my part, and I speak of it with some hesitancy. In the years past I used to speak clearly and rather frequently on the fate of Canadian Jewry and was able to do so without restraint. I think this was perhaps one of the reasons that you elected me as your President. However, after assuming the office I found that now I was boxed in by structural and organizational restraints. I had to make sure that when I spoke as President I spoke indeed for Congress. Therefore, I had to clear everything. I was now part not only of my Officers and Executive Committees, I was part also of joint commissions, and my ability to speak clearly and boldly was severely circumscribed. Contradictory and strange as it may seem to you, I found that as President of Congress I had less liberty to speak on behalf of Canadian Jewry and less opportunity to do so freely than I had before, when I was unencumbered by office. I will promise you, however, that now after I relinquish my office you will hear me again as you have not heard me clearly for three years.

With the ending of my term came also a deepened admiration for my co-worker Alan Rose, the executive vice-president of the organization. His knowledge, his balanced views, his analytical mind and his humanity made him a dear and close friend and colleague. Canadian Jewry is very fortunate to command this kind of leadership.

With retirement from the pulpit came many pleasant honours.

I had previously received the Negev Dinner Award,* I was now honoured by the University of Toronto with a Doctorate of Law and given the opportunity to be the commencement speaker; the National Conference of Christians and Jews gave me the National Humanitarian Award; the Toronto community awarded me the Sadowski Medal of Merit; and the federal government announced in the Queen's Christmas List of 1978 that I had been named an Officer of the Order of Canada. The Cleveland College of Jewish Studies followed, granting me a Doctorate of Humane Letters.

In January 1978 we had gone on a Caribbean cruise organized by the Union of American Hebrew Congregations during which I served as one of the scholars-in-residence. I preached to the congregation in Kingston, Jamaica, and paid my first visit in thirty years to Cuba. It was a drab-looking place with none of the glamour and glitter I remembered from my short stay in 1939** —but then as now I had had no opportunity to look behind the façade of ordinary life. Castro's soldiers were not in evidence; still, the bureaucracy was everywhere and the oppressive greyness of everyday life all too apparent. It was not a pleasant visit, especially since our meeting with the heads of the local congregations showed us yet another community in a state of desperation and decay. One could only hope that some unforeseen event might turn the tide.

## Human Rights

Afterwards we went to vacation in Arizona. Almost immediately upon our arrival I received a telephone call from Eddie Goodman, prominent Progressive Conservative leader and adviser to Premier William Davis. He asked whether I might be interested in accepting an appointment to the Ontario Human Rights Commission. I told him I was interested—and before I knew it both the *Globe and Mail* and the *Star* were calling me for comments on my appointment. Here too I did not really know what the job might involve, and here too I would undergo a process of slow but enjoyable education.

I would find that there were important areas of life in our province with which I was utterly unacquainted. Intellectually I knew about the many ethnic groups, yet I had no clear concep-

* Sponsored by the Jewish National Fund, the Negev dinner is the community's premier event. Some 1,200 people celebrated with me at the Royal York Hotel.

** See above, p. 77.

tion of their social composition and especially the problems they were meeting, like discrimination in housing and in jobs. Though I knew about women's liberation I did not appreciate the full extent of prejudice against women in employment practices, nor did I know about the many instances of sexual harassment that were part of the workplace. I was acquainted with the problem of unemployment but now learned what it meant to an individual who had lost his or her job because discrimination had been at play. I began to refurbish my legal background and studied the Human Rights Code.

There were those, especially among the so-called neo-Conservatives, who believed that human rights were unenforceable and that the fight against discrimination should not be entrusted to a government agency armed with legal powers. There were people like Barbara Amiel and husband George Jonas (whose marriage I had performed some years before) who were bitterly critical of the Commission*—but then, so were others who believed that it ought to be much more aggressive. We lacked a proper image and I found it was not easy to create one.

The Commission does have serious shortcomings. It is independent, yet part of the Labour Ministry. It operates with a law that should have primacy over all other laws, yet does not. It does not give full range to the need for public education on human rights. It does not allow for class action suits nor for sexual orientation as one of the protected categories. I have never believed homosexuality to be an acceptable alternate life style, but at the same time I have been utterly convinced that gay people are entitled to protection in their civil status as human beings and I had no hesitation about working for the inclusion of a relevant

---

* Just for the record I want to relate my recollections of our meeting, which Barbara set down in her book *Confessions*. The Trans-Canada Alliance of German Canadians had lodged a complaint with the Commission over the use of the word "Hun" in an article Barbara had written. At its meeting in May 1978 the Commission determined that the complaint was unfounded. Meanwhile, however, in a public address in Ottawa, Barbara had attacked the Commission in a manner which puzzled the Commissioners. I volunteered to meet with her to explain the work and philosophy of the Commission. We got together for a most pleasant lunch on which I reported at the next Commission meeting. The minutes state that I met Ms. Amiel and that, " . . . she was most willing to consider the significance of anti-discrimination legislation, but that she held the principle that individual rights of employers should not be interfered with, even when employers' conduct might be prejudicial towards others."

However, in her book Barbara presents her luncheon with me as a meeting with "thought police". She is of course entitled to her impressions, but what the Commission (and I) had in mind was a simple, courteous, informational discussion with a well-known publicist who had been very critical of us.

clause. To no effect: the public mind was quite irrational about this. In its view homosexuals were potential criminals who could not be trusted and who deserved all the ignominy that was laid upon them. That perception too will change in time.

The new chairman of the Commission, Dorothea Crittenden, asked me whether I would be willing to serve as vice-chairman, and I agreed. The work was much and the days were short, for if we were to avoid increasing tensions, the areas of opportunity had to be enlarged significantly. At this writing, new legislation has been planned to bring this about.

Now I also have frequent opportunities to worship in many Canadian and American synagogues, in cities large and small, where my lecture engagements take me. Orthodox *shuls* show the fewest variations; the setting matters relatively little. Conservative and Reform services run the gamut from exciting and worshipful to utterly sterile. In some, the deep yearning for an experience of the Holy is evident in mood and music; in others I wonder why people come at all, for they will surely not find the Almighty in their synagogue.

Aside from the wide range of quality in cantorial and congregational music which I now hear, I have come to observe the varieties of "conducting" the service. In principle, Jewish services do not need rabbis—prayer-books do not call for them. When there is a rabbi his or her function should be preaching and teaching and reading the occasional prayer. But for many rabbis that will not do. They direct the congregation constantly, in their rising up and in their sitting down. "Please rise!" "The congregation will sit." "We continue on page 150" (although, having just finished page 149, perhaps even the dullest worshipper might have worked that out!) Cantors get into the act; if rabbis can be MC's, they will not be far behind. This may be proper for school exercises, but it isn't appropriate for Jewish communal prayer, one of whose outstanding features has always been the self-starting, participating worshipper.

I grew up with a liberal service. By North American standards it was somewhat Conservative, except that the rabbi sat where he could neither readily be seen nor scan the congregation with a watchful eye. We, the people, carried on, singing and *davvening*;* the text of the book led us while the cantor chanted his lines. The rabbi emerged only when he read a prayer, or preach-

---

* Silently reciting the liturgy.

ed. He was our teacher, he did not project himself; it was *our* service.

When the cantor lifted the scroll of the Torah high above his head, who would have dared to remain seated? An announcement, "Will the congregation please rise while the scroll is lifted," would have spoiled the high drama of the moment. That's how I remember it; that's how I perceived the ideal service in my years in the pulpit, and that's how, as a congregant in many cities, I perceive it today. Which is another way of stating (to paraphrase Wilhelm Busch) that quitting the pulpit is one thing, learning to be a congregant is another.

As I had hoped, I used my retirement from the pulpit as an opportunity to write a great deal and concentrated furiously on my commentary. I finally finished the manuscript in the fall of 1979. There would still be proof-reading and the like, but after sixteen years the labour was essentially completed, although the creation of a single volume (comprising all five books, for use in the pews) would still take me another year.*

## Looking Ahead

At Jonathan's urging, I began planning these memoirs.

As I conclude them—rather arbitrarily, at the end of 1980, in my sixty-eighth year—I wonder whether I have told too much or too little. On the whole, I have not elaborated on intimate relationships, my family life, my friendships. I also ask myself how frank I have been, or whether I have occasionally been too frank.

I have tried to be fair and, if possible, to err on the side of forbearance. There have been incidents too painful to set down on paper, in part because I would have to depict certain people in the light of my own highly negative judgement; on the whole I have passed by those events and persons and said little or nothing about them. At best we are all footnotes to history, and one footnote more or less will not matter.

Of course, I have asked myself more than once where I am today and in a sense *who* I am. Am I the same person who in 1965 presented his credo and spoke about his relationship with the Ineffable?** Have I made peace with the inevitability of getting

---

* To my deep sorrow, Bernard J. Bamberger, the great scholar who had contributed an introduction and the commentary on Leviticus, died in early 1980 before the total work was completed. The one volume edition is to be published in 1981.
** In the chapter "Personal Postscript", in *The Case for the Chosen People*.

older and with the fact that I am no longer the head of a great congregation or the titular leader of Canadian Jewry?

Yes and no. Yes, I have now become reasonably (though not entirely) used to sitting in the pew, both in the synagogue and, to a different degree, in public life. Although my new weekly column in the *Canadian Jewish News* and my continuing articles in the *Globe and Mail* are platforms from which to speak, I no longer have a pulpit from which to preach. But I have sought and accepted frequent engagements in other communities, from California to Israel and Europe, lecturing primarily on Bible and Reform Judaism and occasionally on the problems of aging, of which I am now more than an outside observer. I have expanded my commitment to the Human Rights Commission and become editor of *Affirmation*, its official publication. I have more time for thinking and writing, for tennis and for fixing things around the house. My "fourth career" is full, varied and exciting, without the professional pressures which I knew so well.

And my faith? I think its theological foundations have not changed perceptibly. What I wrote fifteen years ago I would still write.*

> My wonder and my doubt are never ended. I behold suffering and torture, the mangled bodies of innocent victims of nature's heedlessness and man's carelessness or homicidal tendencies. I do not know why one dies and another survives, why one is born to idiocy and another to genius. I do not know whether God's hiddenness is necessary so that man may turn freely to Him. This is what Franz Rosenzweig believed, that God makes it difficult or even impossible for man to believe in Him, so that man may have the opportunity to believe truly, that is, to trust out of his own will and freedom.

Still, there has been one change. The moments of illumination which once I was privileged to experience have ceased. Why? Is there a flattening of spiritual awareness even as there is a flattening of the emotions as the years go by? Perhaps. Since I cannot force such moments I am more capable of analysing what I now find altered in my own religious make-up.

Nothing that concerns me is quite as urgent as it used to be. I am far more relaxed, my friends tell me. Yet my level of emotional intensity has also decreased, and with this wind-down I

---

* This and the excerpt on p. 342 are taken from *The Case for the Chosen People*, pp. 194, 196.

may have lost something of the edge of spiritual accessibility.
Religious services are nowadays primarily a *mitzvah*, a duty,
rather than a moving experience. Where on occasion I knew (or
thought I knew) what God wanted of me, I am now never sure.
But if I am no longer the same, neither is the world around me
and neither—dare I say it?—is He. For even as I am involved in
Him, so, in whatever minute way, is He with me.

Human history is in many ways the story of God's disappointments. The biblical record speaks of them in unambiguous terms.
They reach from Adam to Cain to Noah to that recalcitrant
people of whom I am a part, who were chosen in order to help the
Almighty set the world right. Just as we need Him so He needs us.
I help Him and thereby enlarge His reach, or I fail and thereby
diminish Him. With every passing year my debit side seems to
grow even as the intensity of my emotions decreases.

Yet, my commitments have not lessened in the human realm,
and especially regarding my Jewish people. The old sentiments
still prevail. I still stand by my perceptions of fifteen years ago:

> I am a Jew. In the uncertain mission of my people I find my
> own. Judaism is my pathway of truth, "the track of God in the
> wilderness of oblivion," as Heschel called it. Jews are its
> chosen watchmen, now and forever. I speak to them and
> thereby to the world. I care for them and therefore care for
> man. They form the base of my existence, and because of them
> all men have a claim on me.

Who then am I? Where do I fit the scale of commonly accepted
descriptions? Nationality will not describe me: Jew, German,
American, Canadian? All of these, in varying proportions, have a
share in my make-up. Optimist or pessimist? I am both:
desperately worried about the present and yet bound to an
abiding if contradictory hope in the long haul. Lover and critic of
my people—we are a great, marvellous, and most difficult lot. I
am less forgiving in many ways and more forgiving in others than
I used to be. On the whole, I have more fun than I had in the past,
and I am more relaxed about the foibles of others, finding them
more and more often to resemble my own. My physical health has
matched my intellectual aliveness, and every day I thank God for
this double gift. I share more hours with my wife—sitting in my
study at home, reading or writing, and knowing that she is working upstairs on her genealogical studies, gives me a sense of pro-

found well-being. I have, as I said at the beginning of this book, been fortunate, more fortunate than many.

Getting older means, alas, that the circle of one's family and friends becomes diminished by death. We suffered our share during these last years.* Fortunately there is still my mother, who continues to defy the odds.

And I? At the present time, thank God, I function as I have always done—even though my golf score is much poorer than it used to be. My mind is clear, my pen ready, and I lecture, if anything, more persuasively than I did in the past. I don't particularly like to look into the mirror because what I see is an aging man, too aged for my taste. The fact that others also seem to get visibly older is not all that comforting. But our grandchildren afford us a special kind of renewal.

My public activities will continue for a while, God willing. There is, I hope, the presidency of the CCAR to look forward to. There are still books I want to write, fiction especially. In 1977 I published a book of short stories;** another collection lies in my drawer; and I am collecting material for a historical novel.

Beyond that, everything is uncertain. I sometimes wonder how I would face the future were I forty years younger. Would I have the same worries overlaid with a growing sense of pessimism? Or, being young, would I tackle the future with abandon? After all, when I first came into the rabbinate, Hitler was at the zenith of his power and there was every possibility not only that my own people might suffer extinction but that democracy and freedom all over the world would perish as well. Still, I do not remember feeling down-hearted at the time. Optimism is a function of youth—and if the young could be optimistic then, surely they can be so today. Certainly my children look to the future with a reasonable degree of assurance and our grandchildren will probably do the same. In their hope lies a good deal of mine. Added to this is my belief that God plays His role in history. I continue to trust that He may have good reasons for finding our survival palatable. This is my starting point as I look towards my seventieth birthday.

---

\* First Marion, the mother of Jonathan's wife, died after a long illness, as did her husband Sol, a great and concerned physician. Also, in the summer of 1980, Elizabeth's brother Bill Strauss died in Cincinnati, a man of superb intellectual powers and tastes. With him and my brother Walter gone, Elizabeth and I are the only ones left in our generation.

\*\* *Hanging Threads* (Toronto: Lester and Orpen, 1977); republished as *The Man in the Blue Vest and Other Stories* (New York: Taplinger, 1980).

# Appendix 1

## LETTER FROM ALBERT EINSTEIN

den 8. Januar 1940

Sehr geehrter Herr Plaut:

Ich glaube nicht, dass die Grundgedanken der Relativitäts-Theorie in anderer Weise Beziehungen zur religiösen Sphäre beanspruchen können als die wissenschaftliche Erkenntnis überhaupt. Diese Beziehung sehe ich darin, dass tiefe Zusammenhänge in der objektiven Welt durch logisch einfache Gedanken erfasst werden können. Dies ist allerdings in der Relativitäts-Theorie in besonders vollkommenem Masse der Fall.

Das religiöse Gefühl, welches durch das Erlebnis der logischen Fassbarkeit tiefliegender Zusammenhänge ausgelöst wird, ist von etwas anderer Art als dasjenige Gefühl, welches man gewöhnlich als religiös bezeichnet. Es ist mehr ein Gefühl der Ehrfurcht, für die in den Dingen sich manifestierende Vernunft als solcher, welches nicht zu dem Schritte führt, eine göttliche Person nach unserem Ebenbild zu formen—eine Person, die an uns Forderungen stellt und an unserem individuellen Sein Interesse nimmt. Es gibt darin weder einen Willen noch ein Ziel noch ein Soll, sondern nur ein Sein.

Deshalb sieht unsereiner in dem Moralischen eine rein menschliche Angelegenheit—aber allerdings die Wichtigste in der menschlichen Sphäre.

Mit freundlichen Grüssen und Wünschen

Ihr

A. Einstein

# Translation

January 8, 1940

Dear Mr. Plaut:

I do not believe that the fundamental thoughts of the theory of relativity could claim any relationship to the religious sphere except that which is claimed by scientific cognition in general. I see this relationship in the possibility to comprehend underlying connections of the objective world through simple logical thoughts. To be sure, this is the case in a very particular measure in the theory of relativity.

The sense of the religious, which is released through the experience of potentially nearing a logical grasp of these deep-lying world relations, is of a somewhat different kind than the kind of sense usually described as religious. It is more a feeling of awe and reverence for the manifest Reason which appears in reality; which does not lead to the assumption of a divine personality—a person who makes demands of us and takes an interest in our individual being. In this there is no Will, nor Aim, nor an Ought, but only Being.

Therefore, one like myself considers morality to be a purely human matter—albeit the most important one in the human sphere.

With cordial regards and good wishes,

yours

A. Einstein

# Appendix 2

---

# THE AMERICAN JEWISH CONFERENCE

The agenda of the Conference as stated in 1943 had been:

1. To consider and recommend action on problems relating to the rights and status of Jews in the post-war world.
2. To consider and recommend action upon all matters looking for the implementation of the rights of the Jewish people with respect to Palestine.
3. To elect a delegation to carry out the program of the American Jewish Conference in co-operation with the duly accredited representatives of Jews throughout the world.

In each city across the U.S., Jewish organizations elected their share of delegates to the Conference. In Chicago, 528 organizations nominated 46 candidates and from this slate elected 30. Since I could not serve at the first Conference (because of army service), Dr. Felix A. Levy, rabbi of Temple Emanu-El and a former president of the Central Conference of American Rabbis, replaced me as my alternate.

I was abroad during the second session of the Conference, but attended the third, which was held in February 1946 in Cleveland; I was listed officially as "Chaplain W. Gunther Plaut", a co-opted member of the Interim Committee. At the time Stephen Wise was honorary chairman, and Henry Monsky chairman of the committee which included such luminaries as Dr. Moses Barron (of Minneapolis, later on to become a dear friend), Rabbi Philip S. Bernstein, Mrs. David DeSola Pool, Rabbi Maurice Eisendrath, Frank Goldman, Rabbi Israel Goldstein, Rabbi Robert Gordis, Rose Halprin, Sydney Kusworm, Rabbi Irving Miller, Dr. Emanuel Neumann, Adolph Rosenberg (president of the Union of American Hebrew Congregations and an uncle to Elsa Strauss, our sister-in-law), Samuel Rothstein, Ezra Shapiro, Rabbi Abba Hillel Silver and, last but not least, Stephen Wise's famous wife Louise. It was an illustrious and heady company in whose presence I kept silent—except for the last minutes of the Conference when I was called upon to deliver the final benediction.

# Appendix 3

# FAREWELL TO MINNESOTA

The farewell dinner, organized by our close friend Sylvan Mack, took place on August 1, 1961 at the St. Paul Hotel. Next day, the *St. Paul Pioneer Press* covered the event on its front page. Under a picture of Mayor Vavoulis, Governor Andersen and me the headline read:

CITY, STATE LEADERS LAUD RABBI W. GUNTHER PLAUT

All segments of civic leadership in St. Paul and the larger Minnesota community joined Tuesday evening in honoring Rabbi W. Gunther Plaut and members of his family as they prepared to leave for Toronto.

Hundreds of persons crowded the Continental room of Hotel St. Paul to hear the governor, mayors of the Twin Cities, and representatives of religious, civic, and cultural groups pay tribute to the rabbi's impact upon the state-wide community since he came to St. Paul in 1948 to become the spiritual leader of Mount Zion Temple.

In response, after the long succession of eulogies, Rabbi Plaut said that his own personal choice would have been to remain in St. Paul and Minnesota, but that a clergyman often "answers a call, aware that in a peculiar sense he is not master of his own destiny."

He praised St. Paul for shaking itself during the past 10 years from an attitude of lethargy.

"Persons in places of leadership can sense a new pride in our community—in new activities and in new buildings—but particularly in a new attitude toward the potential of the city," he said.

He also pointed out strides taken in Minneapolis in human relations, noting that a nationally known writer said in the late 40s that Minneapolis was "the national capital of anti-Semitism."

Under the heading of unfinished business, Rabbi Plaut called upon both St. Paul and Minneapolis to bring about an extension of human concerns in the immediate future.

He said, "Too many of our fine business and industrial

concerns still refuse to avail themselves of the vast human resource—people of color and minority religion."

In the realm of housing, he said, "Legislation is not enough unless people awaken to the moral imperative their religion would demand of them." He noted that "too many live in ghettos forced upon them by an unheeding and unwilling community."

The rabbi also challenged Minnesota citizens for limiting the social opportunities of minority groups.

"The community goes into its air-tight sections at 5 p.m. daily, so much of our prejudice retreating to places of social intercourse," he said.

Rabbi Plaut will leave St. Paul with his family at the end of August to become the spiritual leader of the Holy Blossom Temple in Toronto, a congregation of 1,600 families.*

---

* The report listed the participants: Edward L. Bronstien Sr., president of Mount Zion Temple congregation, spoke on behalf of the synagogue. Rabbi Albert J. Minda of Minneapolis extended the best wishes of Rabbi Plaut's ministerial colleagues. Gerhard J. Bundlie presented the rabbi with a citation on behalf of the St. Paul Laymen's Group. Arnold Niemeyer represented the St. Paul Council of Arts and Sciences. Dean Errett W. McDiarmid of the University of Minnesota's College of Science, Literature and the Arts praised Rabbi Plaut both as a teacher and as a learner. Attorney-General Mondale spoke for the Governor's Council on Human Relations, and Richard P. Hoffman for the local unit of the United World Federalists. The invocation was given by Msgr. Francis J. Gilligan, and the benediction was spoken by the Rev. Denzil A. Carty. Harold E. Wood was master of ceremonies.

# Appendix 4

## ORIGIN OF THE NAME "HOLY BLOSSOM"

Holy Blossom's Hebrew name is *pirchei kodesh*, literally "blossoms of holiness". No such expression occurs in the ancient writings. The prevailing theory is that it was derived from the Mishnaic expression *pirchei kehunah*, "blossoms of the priesthood". In the 1850s, so it has been argued, members of the new congregation were considered emissaries of the Jewish community in Montreal, and were compared to young priests striking fresh roots in the burgeoning city on the shores of Lake Ontario. From *pirchei kehunah* to *pirchei kodesh* was but one short step.

I have never held with this line of reasoning. First of all, *pirchei kehunah* does not mean "blossoms of priesthood", but is an idiomatic expression for young priests. What then would *pirchei kodesh* mean—"young holiness"? But an even more cogent reason for rejecting the explanation lies elsewhere.

It has to do with the nature of Jewish congregations in North America and with the names which were generally given them by their founders. The names were almost universally biblical. The members were rarely scholars who could quote expressions from Mishnah or Talmud; their Jewish knowledge was centred on the Torah, on prophetic readings (Haftarot) and on the prayer-book. Hence, congregational Hebrew names in North America were of the simplest kind: Beth Israel, Beth El, Shaarei Shamayim. There are exceptions, such as "Congregation Men of the West" (K.A.M. in Chicago), but the usual nomenclature was such as could be understood even by those of minimal learning. I therefore conclude that *pirchei kodesh*, found in neither prayer-book, Bible nor Mishnah and Talmud, was not the original name of the congregation, but that it was the result of a traceable and understandable development.

It is my belief that the congregation's first name was *zera kodesh*—an expression found in the sixth chapter of Isaiah which serves as the prophetic reading for the weekly portion *Yitro*. Perhaps the first meeting of the founders took place during the week when this Haftarah was read; in any case it was certainly something with which everyone was familiar in those days. *Zera kodesh* means "holy seed". Congregation

349

Zera Kodesh would be a perfectly acceptable and attractive name for a synagogue in the new spiritual soil of Toronto.

I can picture the scenario: the Hebrew name was discussed and accepted and now the problem arose of translating it into English. "Holy Seed" somehow sounded wrong; it lacked grace. How about calling it blossoms or flowers of holiness? Then, of course, the Hebrew would have to be altered slightly: substitute *perach* or, better, its plural form *pirchei* for *zera* and you were close to the original name and purpose: the new congregation would be a seed for the development of Jewish life in Toronto. Thus *pirchei kodesh* was adapted from *zera kodesh*—to allow a more acceptable English name for the congregation. In fact, we were at first called "Holy Blossoms" (with the plural 's') and only later was the final letter shed, probably because of newspaper usage.

I cannot prove my theory, but at least it takes cognizance of real people and the limits of their knowledge.

But when people ask me, casually, to explain the name, I don't attempt to launch into this long response. I usually give them a briefer, simpler answer: "We don't really know for sure and there are many theories, but it is a beautiful name isn't it? Once you have heard it you will never forget it."

# Appendix 5

# SPREADING REFORM IN CANADA

Some of my travels across Canada* were devoted to seeking out men and women who might be interested in a Liberal congregation, or at least, as in Saskatoon, in a Liberal rabbi.

Generally, I found the members of the establishment strongly opposed to the arrival of Reform. This was particularly true in Winnipeg; even today, many years after its founding, Temple Sholom has not rooted itself firmly. In Ottawa too there was resistance. Lawrence Freiman, dean of the city's merchants, had me for lunch and tried to talk me out of my enterprise. "What do we need it for in our city?" he said, a question repeated in all the other communities where Reform tried to buck the highly conservative trend. Lawrence (who later on became a good friend and ally) was however contradicted by his relative, young David Alexandor, and it was with the latter's help that the ice was eventually broken in Ottawa.

It took two visits to Vancouver before a Reform nucleus could be formed; today the congregation is firmly established.

In Montreal I was invited to address a meeting in Dollard des Ormeaux and to speak of the nature of Reform Judaism. During the discussion a young man stood up and asked a searching, though not provocative, question. He later introduced himself as David Hartman, rabbi of the local Orthodox congregation. His very presence bespoke an unusual human being. He was the only Orthodox rabbi in Canada who could have or would have attended this kind of gathering and in later years, after he had moved to Israel and made his influence felt there, he would continue to be a good friend.

Sometimes the establishment of a new congregation is a matter of luck or of being on the spot at the right moment. One afternoon I received a telephone call from a young lady in Mississauga who wondered whether she could borrow some prayer-books for the Holy Days. On inquiry I found out that a new group of ten or fifteen families was being formed there, but that they had no direction and in fact did not know which

---

* On some of them I was accompanied by Sydney Harris (now a judge), a past president of the Canadian Council of Liberal Congregations. Few others gave as much time to the community as he.

way to turn, what kind of services to hold or what philosophy to follow. They had apparently called the headquarters of the Conservative synagogues, but for some reason had not received any assistance. I invited a group of them to meet with me. They did, and I suggested to them that forming a congregation and obtaining a rabbinical student for the Holy Days and for a bi-weekly job thereafter was the best way to meet their needs. They had a great potential but it was necessary for them to take a small financial risk on their own future. It so happened that a student from Hebrew Union College, Lawrence Englander, was then visiting the city (he was a confirmand of Temple Sinai) and I asked him whether he would be interested if this possibility arose. He agreed at once. The second time I met with the group I managed to persuade them that they should engage a student rabbi, and said that I had a young man right at hand with whom they might wish to speak. They did, and Larry saw and conquered. Today he is the rabbi of a highly successful Mississauga congregation.

The establishment of Har Zion on the north side of Toronto went a different route. I had caused some demographic studies to be made, and saw that the population of the Jewish community was moving north and east and that our own temple membership, among the younger people, was affected. I met with some of those who lived in the new north-east sector, and they expressed a strong desire to participate in an experiment that would give them a measure of autonomy and at the same time have them remain affiliated with the main congregation. Two or three of the leaders were, in fact, young Board members of Holy Blossom. Eventually the temple Board became interested in this plan and we even looked at some property. However, at the last moment our Board felt that if there was to be a new group it should be fully autonomous, that a "branch" congregation (known in South Africa and some other communities) was not for us.

I considered this decision to be a serious mistake but I lost the battle and did so with reasonable grace, and then helped the new group, which called itself Har Zion, to come formally into existence. My associate, Michael Stroh, was ready to leave our temple after five years with us, so he became rabbi of the new group. Holy Blossom, which had continuously advanced monies to Reform congregations from Vancouver to Ottawa, did not fail its responsibility; it paid the rabbi's salary for one year. Today Har Zion is a splendid addition to the roster of Liberal congregations in Canada.

In April of 1978 a Board meeting of the Union of American Hebrew Congregations in New York approved the formation of a new affiliate that would be the political arm of the Reform movement in the Zionist world. Its name would be Arza, "Toward the Land", the acronym spelling Association of Reform Zionists of America. I informed the Board that this would not do for Canada; we would have to form our own group.

The Canadian rabbis agreed to my suggestion and announced a new—as yet unnamed—Canadian Reform Zionist Organization. In my Yom Kippur talk I urged my members to join "Kadima" (Forward), as I called it, and the name stuck. Over the holy days 1,500 memberships from Holy Blossom were obtained, and we were off the ground. After some months I asked Michael Stroh to relieve me of the leadership, and he is Kadima's president to this date.

# Appendix 6

# WORLD FEDERALISTS

According to Hanna Newcombe, the Canadian organization goes back to 1948, but it was not until November 1965 that it was placed on a national basis. I was amongst the nine applicants for the charter and part of its first Board of Directors, with Charles Burchill, Geoff Edge, Eric Inch, E. G. Brownell, Duncan Graham, William B. Mowle, E. H. Nickel and J. W. Patterson. The purposes of the new body were defined as follows:

a. To secure support for the establishment of a competent world Federal Government elected by and responsible to the people under its jurisdiction with limited functions but real powers adequate for the maintenance of peace;
b. While giving complete support to the endeavours of the United Nations, to bring about a world community favourable to peace, to strive toward the creation of a World Federal Government with authority to enact, interpret and enforce world law.

My predecessors in the presidency were Bill Sheehan (1960-62), Geoff Edge (1962-63), Charles Burchill (1963-66); my term was from 1966-68; Ross Smyth served twice, from 1968-70 and from 1975-77, Harry Weihs from 1970-72, Bert Barnes from 1972-73, and Alan C. Newcombe from 1973-75. Recent presidents have been John E. Robbins and J. Francis Leddy.

During my incumbency, Andrew Clarke, a former air force officer, was the executive director of the organization. He left later to become the director of the World Association of World Federalists.

# Appendix 7

# AT BLOOR STREET UNITED CHURCH

*Excerpts from text of sermon preached on October 22, 1972.
The sermon was printed by B'nai B'rith and published under
the title, "Your Neighbour is a Jew—Reflections on the
Possibilities of Dialogue."*

"Many Christians are aware that their vigorous anti-Israel
stand has rekindled a kind of antisemitism that could not
recently be pursued in public but that now under the guise of
anti-Zionism has once again become possible and in some
circles even fashionable. Calling Jews Zionists and
"aggressive", "scheming for power", "a world-wide
conspiracy", has revived old antisemitic stereotypes and has
made them once again "respectable". For us it revives terrible
memories and renders us highly sensitive. But that there is a
deep and serious moral danger in this also for Christians must
be apparent.

"I do not for one moment deny that Christians have every
right to support the claims of justice for any people including
Arabs. But members of the United Church must ask themselves
why it is that of all the causes in the world today they have
focused with such intensity on this one cause; and why does
the *Observer* never take up the case of 800,000 Jewish
refugees from Arab countries? And you must further ask a
question of priorities: what is it we want to do first and
foremost? Should we first and foremost guard against a
recrudescence of antisemitism at home even at the danger of
not pursuing the quest for Arab justice with the same vigour?
Or should we throw all caution to the wind, press the cause of
the Arabs with all our might even at the danger of revitalizing
antisemitism at home? This you are doing now. But whether
you want to pursue this course, that is the question—and it is
yours to answer.

". . . In our generation which has gone through the
Holocaust and its bitter trauma—in the midst of world silence
and, largely, church silence as well—Jews will not listen to
any kind of Christian moralizing. I will say it more clearly: in
our time the church has forfeited any possibility of instructing

Jews how to be moral and how to be religious and how to act in a godly fashion. . . .

"You may hold with what the editor of the *Observer* is reported to have said in Saskatoon: "Let's not pay too much attention to the Jews!" But if you take this attitude don't look for dialogue, you cannot have it both ways.

". . . I have talked to you today as a Jew. I am not given to bitterness but I am on occasion given to moments of discouragement. Your invitation to me, issued in frankness and fairness, is however a bright spot in what has been in many ways a most frustrating relationship. What divides us presently is—for the Jew—a matter of his fundamental existence. Only if this is clear can we speak to each other. But speak we should, for we need each other. We have much to do in this world that requires our common devotion and our common counsel."

# Index